THE EMOTIONAL POLITICS
OF RACISM

Stanford Studies in
COMPARATIVE RACE AND ETHNICITY

THE EMOTIONAL POLITICS OF RACISM

How Feelings Trump Facts

in an Era of Color Blindness

Paula Ioanide

Stanford University Press
Stanford, California

Stanford University Press
Stanford, California

Printed in the United States of America on acid-free, archival-quality paper

Library of Congress Cataloging-in-Publication Data

Ioanide, Paula, author.
  The emotional politics of racism: how feelings trump facts in an era of
colorblindness / Paula Ioanide.
    pages cm—(Stanford studies in comparative race and ethnicity)
  Includes bibliographical references and index.
  ISBN 978-0-8047-9359-9 (cloth : alk. paper)—
  ISBN 978-0-8047-9547-0 (pbk. : alk. paper)
  1. Racism—United States—Psychological aspects. 2. Social psychology—United
States. 3. United States—Social policy. 4. United States—Social conditions—1980-
I. Title. II. Series: Stanford studies in comparative race and ethnicity.
  E184.A1L623 2015
  305.800973—dc23

                                    2014041547

ISBN 978-08047-9548-7 (electronic)

Typeset by Bruce Lundquist in 10.5/15 Adobe Garamond

To my father, Cristian Ioanide,
who endowed me with the responsibility
to continue the spiritual legacy

CONTENTS

Acknowledgments   ix

Introduction:
Facts and Evidence Don't Work Here   1

PART I   CRIMINALS AND TERRORISTS:
         THE EMOTIONAL ECONOMIES
         OF MILITARY-CARCERAL EXPANSION   27

   1.   New York, New York:
         The Raging Emotions of White Police Brutality   55

   2.   Abu Ghraib, Iraq:
         The Evasive Emotions of U.S. Exceptionalism   81

PART II WELFARE DEPENDENTS AND ILLEGAL ALIENS:
         THE EMOTIONAL ECONOMIES
         OF SOCIAL WAGE RETRENCHMENT   113

   3.   New Orleans, Louisiana:
         The Demolishing Emotions of Neoliberal Removal   139

   4.   Escondido, California:
         The Exclusionary Emotions of Nativist Movements   175

         Epilogue:
         The Other Side of Social Death   207

Notes   223

Index   263

ACKNOWLEDGMENTS

Looking back to the time when this book was in its germination phase, I find it inconceivable that the constellation of people who irrevocably transformed my understanding of the world should all be present in the same geography. The only thing that might account for this is an unwavering and unprovable belief that the universe sends wise guides to those who are desperately seeking answers and purpose. I am forever indebted to the remarkable guidance I received in the History of Consciousness program at the University of California, Santa Cruz, and as a feminist studies fellow at the University of California, Santa Barbara. Tricia Rose, Neferti Tadiar, Angela Y. Davis, Herman Gray, Rosa Linda Fregoso, Jonathan Beller, Saidiya Hartman, Clyde Woods, Cedric Robinson—please always know that your knowledge ignites unlimited desires for growth and justice and transfigures others to bend toward the arc of love, growth, and the beloved community. I am also thankful for beautiful memories of shared struggle, survival, and laughter with Roya Rastegar, Kalindi Vora, Rashad Shabazz, and Tim Koths, who have offered sustaining friendships.

The unwavering support I have received from George Lipsitz over the years is something that can hardly be represented through language. A galaxy of new constellations in the sky, a new genre of music, or a series of collective spoken poetry performances would probably offer more effective modes of symbolizing the gratitude I feel for his guidance, scholarship, ethics, pedagogy, and commitment to do what is right. As you always say, George, we are looking for people who are looking for us, and I feel infinitely blessed that I found you. Your constant willingness to help me and countless other students, activists, and organizers across the world has surely come at a huge cost to you. But please know that your mentorship will continue to produce immeasurable reverberations toward making justice irresistible and white supremacy intolerable.

Ruth Wilson Gilmore and Craig Gilmore, you taught me that it is possible to remain committed to my political principles, to live my ethics through relationships and radical community organizing, and to continue being a scholar. You seamlessly modeled the connectivity between these worlds in your own lives and created invaluable sites of pedagogy and praxis as a result! I thank you for embodying the beautiful struggle and inspiring so many to continue aspiring.

There were many times in the past ten years when I looked around and wondered how it was possible that I was sitting with the very scholars whose work had been formative in shaping my understanding of institutional gendered racism, nativism, and imperialism. They were generous, rigorous, and engaging in ways that combusted old neural tracks of thinking and expanded my brain. Most important, they used their work and institutional power to further antiracist feminist political projects. My core ideas on the emotional dimensions of color-blind gendered racism were first presented to scholars who participated in the Colorblindness Seminar at Stanford University's Center for Advanced Studies in Behavioral Science. So much grew out of that superfun and rigorous week! Kimberlé Crenshaw, Luke Harris, George Lipsitz, Felice Blake, Charles W. Mills, Glenn Adams, Devon Carbado, Cheryl Harris, Claire Jean Kim, Daniel HoSang, and Barbara Tomlinson generously engaged early versions of this book's arguments and continued to help me clarify them through subsequent encounters. Research grants awarded by the American Association of University Women (2010–2011) and Ithaca College gave me crucial financial support toward finalizing the book. Paula Moya, Hazel Markus, and my editor at Stanford, Kate Wahl, offered critical insights that greatly improved the book and facilitated a smooth process toward publication.

The seeds that were planted at the Colorblindness Seminar grew into the amazing Antiracism Inc. collective, organized by Dr. Felice Blake through the American Cultures and Global Contexts Center at the University of California, Santa Barbara. We managed to create the alternative university time and again as we thought through some of the most pressing political issues of our time. Thank you to Nick Mitchell, Chandan Reddy, Swati Rana, Barbara Tomlinson, Glenn Adams, Shana Redmond, Sarah Haley, George Lipsitz, Aisha Finch,

Sunaina Maira, Kevin Fellezs, and Alison Reed for some of the most stimulating, funny, and captivating conversations the world has witnessed!

Throughout the long journey of writing this book, I received incredible lessons, joy, and inspiration from a remarkable group of co-conspirators, artists, and activists who never seem to grow tired of struggling to transform the ills of this world. Their music, art, poetry, organizing, courage, and commitment made me feel like I had finally found a place to belong in this world after an exhausting journey; they always renew my purpose and commitment to dignity during difficult and discouraging times. I felt secure in the fact that we always had each other's back—an incredible thing to achieve in a world plagued by social alienation. Gregory Mitchell, Daniel Silber-Baker, Chris Wilson, David Scott, Edward McWilliams, Eda Levenson, Matt Jones, Chelsea Johnson-Long, Eden Connelly, Colin Ehara, Ebony Donnley, Noelle de la Paz, Josh Fisher, Jeremy Karafin, Pamela Chavez, Dahlak Brathwaite, Dubian Ade, Sophia Terazawa, and Sunni Patterson—please keep creating and building freedom dreams!

A new place of belonging through creativity, activism, writing, and teaching was co-created in Ithaca, New York. The formation of the Shawn Greenwood Working Group (SGWG) gave me a place to live my politics locally. I am so proud of the work we accomplished in the community and on ourselves. I am forever thankful for my relationships with SGWG members Nydia Williams, Phillip Price, James Ricks, Clare Grady, Gino Bush, Aislyn Colgan, Mario Martone, Shawnae Milton, Kayla Young, and baby E. J. Colgan. You offered me a family and a deep sense of interpersonal love and meaning. Ithaca is a crossroads for an incredible array of community folks who pushed me to grow in unexpected ways, including Dr. James Turner, Alan Gomez, Omar Figueredo, Nancy Morales, Linda Robi Majani, Jen Majka, Mary Anne Grady Flores, Candace Katungi, Jen Chicon, Andrea Levine, and Daniel Carrion. My beautiful friendships with Joanne Oport, Krissy Samms, and Shyama Kuver sustained me spiritually, mentally, and intellectually.

It is no small feat to find an academic department that allows you to be your crazy self, encourages politicized interdisciplinary classes, and offers steadfast support for community activism and creative endeavors. My colleagues Sean Eversley Bradwell, Gustavo Licòn, Phuong Nguyen, and our fearless director, Asma Barlas, made my transition to the Center for the Study of Culture, Race, and Ethnicity (CSCRE) seamless. Together, we foregrounded a shared political vision and always kept it real. I am incredibly proud of the ethnic studies program we built and the impact our center has had on students' lives. Naeem Inayatullah, Belisa Gonzalez, Chris House, Peyi Soyinka-Airewele, Beth Harris, and the staff and students of the Martin Luther King Jr. Scholars Program continue to foster a pedagogical and intellectual community at Ithaca College that produces growth and transformation.

My CSCRE students—you all know who you are!—offered me the most incredible life lessons. You have made my life and my work meaningful, beautifully growth producing, and renewing. You challenged me emotionally and intellectually and at the same time offered me unwavering sustenance and love. This book would not be possible without the things you taught me—you are the audience I always imagine when I write. Thank you in particular to Madeline Jarvis for her wonderful research assistance on chapter 2.

My family taught me how to love and always created room for independent thought. I am so thankful for their emotional, spiritual, and material sustenance as I struggled to define myself. I am particularly indebted to my mama, Varvara Ioanide, who has been the cornerstone of our family. She taught us to be generous and to resist calculating our lives according to this world's mainstream formulas of value. She taught us to forgive, to let go, and to stay open to the signs of the cosmos. My brother, Alex Ioanide, regularly amazes me with his insights about how the world works; he taught me to laugh, to enjoy life, and to continue to fight, even when it seemed that it wasn't making any difference. My beautiful sister, Beate Ioanide-Culi, has always been my counterpart in personality and temperament. She has understood me intuitively and reserved judgment as I engaged in zigzagged experiments to find my purpose. I am deeply thankful for her unwavering love and support. Beate's husband, Ray Culi, and my nephews and niece, Andre, Evan, and Cristina, have brought countless giggles and profound joy to my life. Ellen, Byron, Kiora, and Jalen Ridgeway, the Culis, and the Ioanides have created a family of Romanian–Filipino–African-American–Canadian people who have some of the most delicious and unquestionably multiethnic holiday meals! Thank you for being the best multiracial, multilingual, multiethnic, multicultural loving family anyone could ask for. My family in Romania—my grandfather Nicolae Sosnovschi, my aunts and uncle Anica Sosnovschi and Nina and Nicu Sosnovschi, my cousins Violeta, Teo, Ema, and their families—remind me to always keep my sights beyond the United States. They remind me to stay grounded in spiritual cosmologies that are mostly illegible here in the United States and to keep our transnational flows connected.

My intellectual partner in crime and most loving friend has made this journey unforgettable, profound, and deeply growth producing in ways that cannot be measured. Felice Blake, you were with me from the beginning, through countless trials, tribulations, and joys, and are still with me now. Your friendship has transformed the way I relate, feel, and operate in the world. Your unwavering work toward antiracist feminist justice fuels my motivation and commitment. As I always tell you, you are the smartest person I know! Your intellectual insights push me to remember the intricate connections between racism and sexism but to simultaneously consider methods of healing and recovery. You are the only friend I have who can move between academic conferences, girl talk, mind-blowing intellectual conversations, and the dance floor with a flow only Pisces can emulate. I love you and thank you for all the blessings you, Malena, and the Blake family have bestowed on my life.

A year before this book was finished, an assemblage of forces led me to New Orleans, where an inexplicable brew of magic, mist, and music brought me face to face with the man whose soul is connected to mine in ways I still cannot describe. Taili Mugambee, it is with deep humility that I receive the beautiful love you regularly offer me. As we embark on our unchartered path of creativity, struggle, and transformation, I feel the most profound level of gratitude to have experienced our love. Thank you for all the support you offer me, for your critical engagement, and most of all, for giving me the possibility to be an undiminished version of myself.

This book is dedicated to my father, Cristian Ioanide, who crossed into another realm just as I finished my research. Using Socratic methods, he taught me to think for myself and construct propositions at an early age. He endowed me with a sense of intellectual confidence uncommon between fathers and daughters. He came to accept the intellectual and spiritual legacy begun by my grandfather, the poet Costache Ioanide, late in his life. Both of them endowed me with an intergenerational legacy that comes with great responsibility. This book is a small attempt to abide by some of the ethical principles and practices they instilled in me. Tati, this is for you.

THE EMOTIONAL POLITICS
OF RACISM

FACTS AND EVIDENCE
DON'T WORK HERE

Affect. . . . Term [that] connotes any affective state, whether
painful or pleasant, whether vague or well-defined, and whether it
is manifested in the form of a massive discharge or in the form of
a general mood. . . . The affect is the qualitative expression of the
quantity of instinctual energy and of its fluctuations.
                —J. Laplanche and J.-B. Pontalis, *The Language of Psychoanalysis*

To dismiss race as myth is not to underestimate its power. Race, like
religion, is immune to critiques of science and logic because it rests
on belief. And people need beliefs. Although science has discredited
the biological underpinnings of the notion of race, faith rushes in to
seal the cracks, paper over glaring omissions in arrested explanations
of human difference offered by racial ideology.
                —John Edgar Wideman, "Fatheralong"

This book is about the primacy of emotion and affect in contemporary expressions of racial violence and discrimination. I show that emotional rewards and
losses play a central role in shaping how and why people invest in racism, nativism, and imperialism in the United States. Public feelings about "criminality,"
"terrorism," "welfare dependence," and "illegal immigration" are not simply
individual sentiments; they have been essential to manufacturing consent for
military-carceral expansion and the retreat from social welfare goods. The intensification of socioeconomic inequalities, state violence, and punitive control
in the post–civil rights era has largely been achieved through the organization

of public feelings rather than facts. How U.S. publics dominantly feel about crime, terrorism, welfare, and immigration often seems to trump concrete facts and evidence about these politicized matters.

Emotions shape the ways that people experience their worlds and interactions. They give people's psychic realities and ideological convictions (however fictional or unfounded) their sense of realness. Emotions cinch or unravel people's sense of individual and group identity. They help motivate actions and inactions, often in unconscious or preconsciously reflexive ways. Although they may seem fleeting and incalculable, emotions attached to race and sexuality have their own unique logics of gain and loss. Thus emotions function much like economies; they have mechanisms of circulation, accumulation, expression, and exchange that give them social currency, cultural legibility, and political power.[1]

How, for example, might we measure the emotional and psychological impact of losing white cultural dominance in a town where the Latino/a immigrant population suddenly rises? What price might be placed on the emotional high of feeling morally superior to "Arab terrorists"? How do we gauge the impact of collective guilt and shame associated with seeing the photographs of torture at Abu Ghraib, Iraq? How do we quantify the pleasurable thrills or psychological losses involved in a white police officer's sexual and physical violation of a Haitian immigrant? How might the overwhelming affective stigmas generally attached to welfare and public housing accelerate the neoliberal restructuring of New Orleans in the aftermath of Hurricane Katrina? We may not be able to compute such emotional rewards and losses in the same ways that we are able to calculate the monetary advantages and disadvantages produced by racially and sexually discriminatory systems. Even so, socially shared emotions about race and sexuality have recognizable histories of circulation and expression. Because they produce real consequences that often defy reason and evidence, our hesitation to understand emotions as socially shared *economies*, rather than peripheral individuated sentiments, potentially limits the way we conceptualize and approach antiracist struggles for justice.

Emotional economies that are attached to race and sexuality are an important site of inquiry because they have the unique ability to foreclose people's cognitive receptivity. The presumption that we can combat systemic gendered racism, nativism, and imperialism by generating more empirical facts and more reasonable arguments is severely challenged by the reality that people's emotions often prevent and inhibit genuine engagements with knowledge. Any time our emotional structures experience danger, fear, or anxiety—affects that are all too common in discussions of systemic oppression—our capacity to integrate knowledge and participate in communicative acts also tends to diminish. Conversely, our emotional attachments to particular desires, enjoyments, and pleasures can also function to foreclose our willingness to assimilate information and to act on it. As such, in this book I not only try to show the primacy of affect in perpetuating gendered racism, nativism, and imperialism but also argue that we must contend with the distinct operations of affect and emotion if we are to unhinge the embodied and unconscious dimensions of oppression.

My focus on the significance of affective and emotional economies in post–civil rights instances of gendered racism, nativism, and imperialism is not intended to diminish the importance of monetary interests at stake in these systems. The case studies explored in this book show that people's conscious and/or unconscious investments in gendered racial discrimination and violence can rarely be disentangled from localized, national, and global struggles over profits, property, and advantages. Rather, I am interested in the ways that people's emotional and psychological investments compound, mitigate, or sometimes take precedence over their moneyed interests.

Indeed, focusing on the centrality of affect and emotion in systems of oppression helps us explain why many working- and middle-class U.S. constituents across the political spectrum have overwhelmingly endorsed policies and practices that are detrimental to their moneyed interests in the post–civil rights era. These economic losses did not take place all at once, nor were they evenly experienced across different racial groups and geographies. If the effects of these shifts have been detrimental to a majority of working- and middle-class Americans, they have been downright devastating for impoverished communities of color and communities across the globe.

Scholars have extensively documented the complex factors and political activities that have contributed to the expansion of military carcerality, neoliberal economic policies, and social wage retrenchment.[2] Yet the paradox of why Americans have chosen to act against their own economic interests in the post–civil rights era continues to puzzle us. Some scholars claim that U.S. publics are simply ignorant, misinformed, or tricked. Constituents buy into politicians' promises to defend their social, religious, and economic interests (e.g., abortion, the relationship between church and state, the right to bear arms, lower taxes), even though in reality these same politicians enact policies that are economically detrimental to them. Others claim that contemporary U.S. capitalism encourages political apathy in its populace. By preoccupying everyday people with quotidian matters such as working, paying down their debts, and engaging in consumerist culture, the United States cultivates a formal democracy rather than a participatory one. In turn, this allows an oligarchy of ruling elites to manipulate national and global wealth and markets relatively unperturbed.

Certainly, many of these explanations offer partial truths. But they generally leave unexamined the function of public beliefs, fears, and desires in the construction of political will or complicity. More important, they tend to ignore or minimize the distinctly racialized and sexualized aspects of these emotional economies, considering both gendered racial oppression and public feelings peripheral to the ways broader macroeconomic interests and politics are constituted.

By contrast, in this book I argue that hegemonic public fears and stigmas, whose primary threats were constructed as simultaneously color-blind *and* race- and gender-specific, were the central conduits for creating public desires that legitimated state and neoliberal restructuring toward military-carceral expansion and social wage divestment. As I show in the introduction to Part I, post–cold war U.S. military expansion was commonly legitimated through putatively color-blind fears of terrorism, yet this fear distinctly posited "hyperviolent" and "hyperpatriarchal" Arab and/or Muslim men as the embodiment of this threat. Post-1980s prison expansion was explicitly legitimated through purportedly color-blind panics over criminality, yet these fears overwhelmingly associated the threats of crime with Black and Latino "hyperviolent" men who had supposedly abandoned their responsibilities to family and community. By the 1990s the normalized logics of criminality were extended to increasingly target "Latino/a illegal aliens," whereas after September 11, 2001, the idea of "suspicious" Arab, Muslim, and South Asian immigrants residing within U.S. borders further fueled emotional economies of anxiety and fear.

Beginning in the 1980s, Ronald Reagan's successful anti–big government platform initiated widespread divestment from social welfare goods such as affordable housing, education, transportation, environmental protections, and other social services. As I argue in the introduction to Part II, such divestment was primarily legitimated through the racialized and gendered affective stigmatization of what came to be called welfare dependency. Reaganism's demonization of the "cultural pathologies of poverty" claimed to be color-blind but was primarily associated with single Black women with children in visual and discursive practices. Such logics of "undeserving dependency" were flexibly reformulated to also scapegoat Latina women and nonwhite immigrants in the 1990s, when constituents in California voted to partake in the pleasurable powers to exclude undocumented immigrants from what they possessively considered "their" public goods and resources. The Clinton administration's welfare reform policies essentially nationalized these resentments and stigmatizations when it ended state subsidies for documented immigrants and drastically reduced public assistance programs in 1996. As the chapters in Part II reveal, the dominance of these emotional economies eventually came back to haunt those who had thought they were exclusively entitled to the nation's resources and social welfare goods. Neoliberal and state asset stripping left vast majorities worse off economically; yet publics continued to choose to keep their increasingly impoverished states rather than associate themselves with emotionally stigmatized social welfare goods. Rather than suffer the emotional risks of being considered dependent for taking state "handouts," many elected to support privatization, work harder, and incur more and more debt (which deregulation happily enabled banks and lenders to provide at increased limits).

Although numerous state actors, politicians, media representatives, and activists participated in constructing these racialized and gendered emotional economies and sociopolitical shifts, I am more preoccupied with understanding why hegemonic ideologies, fears, and desires appealed to average Americans in the post–civil rights era. How did these beliefs, fears, and desires enable U.S. constituents across liberal and conservative spectrums to shape their sense of racial, gender, and national identity and power? How did they help to exacerbate and assuage their crises or to construct their political purpose or passivity?

My contention is that liberal and conservative constituents were not simply fooled into endorsing policies and practices that gradually proved detrimental to most of them. Rather, dominant American majorities invested in these shifts precisely because the state's proposed remedies to the purported threats of criminality, terrorism, welfare dependence, and illegal immigration seemed to provide solutions to what a lot of people *actually* feared and desired.

Dominant U.S. constituents came to desire and support shifts toward military carcerality because they generated the affective rewards of state protection, national security, and global dominance. These shifts enabled people to experience affectively aggressive thrills and enjoyments through their identification with the state's power, allowing them to vicariously feel the pleasures of punishing, policing, and excluding so-called illegal immigrants, suspected terrorists, and supposedly incorrigible criminals. These shifts offered a sense of psychological, social, and affective righteousness to those who were invested in notions of law and order, just as the stigmatization of welfare dependence amplified emotional investments in individual self-reliance and personal responsibility. State divestments from the social wage gained their legitimacy by rewarding people with a sense of affective superiority over those deemed undeserving. These economies of emotional reward and stigma were overwhelmingly attached to people of color, nonwhite immigrants, undocumented migrants of color, and/or poor people. They worked because they reified preexisting sensibilities and feelings about race, gender, sexuality, class, and national identity, particularly among dominant white middle- to upper-class constituencies.

Popular beliefs and emotions attached to crime, terrorism, welfare, and immigration did not just guide public support for expanding military carcerality and social welfare retrenchment; they also tended to remain impervious to arguments and evidence that proved that the panics over criminality, terrorism, welfare dependence, and immigration were largely manufactured or hyperbolic. In other words, once these manufactured fears and desires situated themselves in U.S. constituents' affective structures and ideological worldviews, they became uniquely personal and crucial to constituents' sense of identity, to how they organized their purpose, and how they justified their actions. Hence, affective economies structured people's beliefs about crime, terrorism, immigration, and welfare in ways that were distinct from the logics of reason.

Racialized fears over losing monetary advantages have a long history of making Americans leap from the logics of reason to the unique operations of emotion. The case studies investigated in this book indicate that beliefs, fears, and desires about crime, terrorism, welfare, and immigration are sometimes expressly compounded by moneyed interests. In post-Katrina New Orleans, for example, moneyed investments in neoliberal development and privatization were reinforced by predominantly white residents' affective contempt for largely Black public housing residents who were demonized for being overly "dependent" on state resources. Together, these moneyed and affective investments produced a conservative and liberal consensus to eliminate structurally sound public housing units whose occupants were overwhelmingly poor elderly people and Black women with children. The propertied interests of predominantly white residents were central to endorsing these spatialized removals. In turn, these propertied defenses also facilitated the moneyed interests of with private corporate developers (see Chapter 3).

At other times, emotional and psychological investments in preserving specific notions of racial, cultural, national, familial, or sexual power and identity became dissociated from or even worked against moneyed interests. Although they initially sought to defend the property values of predominantly white neighborhoods and to restrict rental housing solely to documented residents and U.S. citizens, nativist organizers in Escondido, California, actually hurt some of the moneyed economies of their town because of anti-Latino/a hatred and discrimination. Motivated by affective investments in preserving white American cultural and spatial dominance in Escondido, nativist advocates decided to accept certain monetary losses in order to reproduce psychological and affective investments in whiteness, nativism, and citizenship (see Chapter 4).

Similarly, the embodied psychosexual enjoyments involved in white police officers' literal acts of brutality and sexualized violence against Haitian immigrant Abner Louima might be interpreted as having worked against the moneyed and legal interests of the New York City Police Department and the state, which lost an estimated $8.5 million for Officer Justin Volpe's violation of Louima's civil rights (see Chapters 1). That egregious case of police violence shows that the affective rewards sought through brutal assertions of white patriarchal police authority sometimes trump considerations of state legitimacy and money.

Finally, the interplay between moneyed and affective interests can also produce mixed results. The U.S. military's sexualized torture of Abu Ghraib prisoners produced an international crisis of U.S. state and military legitimacy in Iraq and across the world. As such, the tortures at Abu Ghraib can be interpreted to have worked against American monetary investments in the Iraq War and the war on terror, given that U.S. state legitimacy is often needed to advance economic imperialism. At the same time, the sexualized terror at Abu Ghraib might be read as normative military methods used to gain U.S. dominance in

Iraq. Such dominance can ultimately reinforce the U.S. state's ability to excavate economic benefits through imperial warfare and occupation (see Chapter 2).

I use the phrase *dominant Americans* or *dominant U.S. publics* throughout this book to encapsulate a series of culturally mediated affective assumptions about who is presumed to belong to the United States and who feels entitled to dictate its political future. It is not just that dominant Americans have greater access to political power and representation or that this power often correlates with having greater levels of wealth, income, and social influence. Dominant Americans are generally not questioned about their right to be in the United States; they do not feel that it is necessary to use hyphenated national identities because people generally do not question their American-ness. They do not have to answer questions about where they originated because of linguistic accents. They show up at protests or community meetings feeling entitled to vote, speak, and advocate. They tend to assume that the police and other state agents are there to protect them rather than to violate them. And they tend to assume a natural right to dictate what to do with foreigners, migrants, and other populations they designate unfit for national or community belonging.

Clearly, almost all the affective presumptions and embodied entitlements assumed by dominant Americans correlate with white racial identity and/or U.S. citizenship. Although we may presume that white people are born with such entitlements, it is important to understand that dominant white Americans' embodied organization is also affirmed by projections, external gazes, and cultural assumptions expressed by other people, including people of color. In other words, it is not just that white American citizens give these entitlements to themselves, or that legal and institutional systems constantly reinforce them; the practices of other people award these entitlements to dominant Americans by virtue of not questioning, not disrupting, or not reformulating the cultural associations that coalesce into American-ness = citizenship = whiteness.

Even more complicated is the fact that although many people in the United States do not fit the racial, ethnic, linguistic, stylistic, or religious molds for what is affectively and intuitively presumed to be normatively American, they nonetheless struggle for inclusion in this category and identify with its core definitions and values. They do so for understandable reasons. Being presumed to belong to America gives people social affirmation and much greater access to resources, jobs, and legal rights. Part of the reason I do not use "white American citizens" instead of "dominant U.S. publics" is because I want to account for the political impact created by the identifications and aspirations of those who seek inclusion into American-ness. Immigrants, people of color, religious minorities, people with linguistic accents, and even some poor whites are certainly not affectively assumed to belong to the normative ideals of the United States. Nor do they presume to dictate the fate of others with the same levels of embodied entitlement as white American citizens who are middle and upper class. But their aspirational identification with the rights, resources, economic logics, cultural values, and racial restrictions embedded in current normative definitions of American-ness often reinforces dominant political views and practices. In other words, my phrase *dominant U.S. publics* tries to suggest that whiteness and American-ness manifest in embodied identities; but they are also ideological worldviews and value systems that people of color and minorities can (consciously or unconsciously) reinforce.

INTENTIONAL VS. UNINTENTIONAL COLOR-BLIND RACISM

Emotional rewards and losses attached to contemporary expressions of gendered racism, nativism, and imperialism play an integral role in shaping the generalizable conditions of our time. As such, expressions of gendered racism, nativism, and imperialism are centrally constitutive aspects of post–civil rights cultural, socioeconomic, and political conditions. Giving this central claim credibility, however, fundamentally depends on the degree to which we discredit the widely held belief that the United States is a color-blind society. This popular belief generally claims that the opportunity structure of America is equally open to all people, irrespective of their gendered racial identity. Although white Americans embrace this belief more commonly, young people of color and immigrants also seem to increasingly believe that anyone who works hard in America can achieve socioeconomic mobility and success.[3] How do we examine the function of emotional economies tied to race and sexuality in contemporary realities if a large portion of people believe that systemic forms of gendered racism are nonexistent, insignificant, or irrelevant?

The challenge we face is not that people have stopped talking about race and sexuality. Color-blind terms such as "criminals," "drug dealers," "thugs," "gangsters," "urban underclass," "inner cities," "terrorists," "hijackers," "suicide bombers," "Islamic fundamentalists," "welfare queens," "crack mothers," "hyperfertile mothers," "illegal aliens," "gangs," "drug cartels," and "taxpayer burdens" have become the coded lingua franca used by dominant U.S. publics to talk about race, gender, sexuality, and nationality. Rather, our core challenge is that these putatively color-blind terms are used to espouse the hegemonic belief that the "behavioral deficiencies" of Black, Latino/a, Arab, and Muslim people are the primary cause of these groups' marginalization. Those who believe that Black, Latino/a, Arab, and Muslim people are culturally dysfunctional often believe that the violence, discrimination, and exclusion that these groups regularly experience are either self-induced or deserved.

Such popular beliefs and projections have made it increasingly difficult to understand U.S. racial, nativist, and imperialist violence and discrimination as constitutive features of our crises and realities. Although many concede the existence of exceptional bigots, few acknowledge the persistence of a structure that systematically apportions opportunities and life chances along distinctly racialized and gendered lines. Despite copious evidence indicating worsening or unimproved patterns of discrimination and violence toward people of color, many white people and some people of color believe that these discriminatory institutional practices have been safely relegated to America's past. Nor do many Americans believe that the logics of U.S. *racial* capitalism and imperialism have much to do with current immigration policies, foreign policy, and global militarism.[4]

Eduardo Bonilla-Silva aptly describes this paradoxical phenomenon as "racism without racists." He shows that few people today openly think of themselves as racist or xenophobic, yet they continue to perpetuate racially discriminatory practices. Bonilla-Silva describes how dominant ideologies that construct people of color as "deficient" and "deviant" in the arenas of work, education, parenting, family structures, sexuality, crime, and consumption allow white people and some people of color to resolve the cognitive dissonance suggested by the coexistence of worsening gendered racial inequalities and the idea that gendered racial oppression is no longer a problem. Such ideologies, Bonilla-Silva argues, conceal the actual causes of gendered racial inequalities and allow dominant white majorities to disavow their racist attitudes as well as their active participation in various patterns of discrimination.[5]

The contradiction Bonilla-Silva highlights, between the popular adherence to color blindness and institutional practices that routinely award social and economic advantages on the basis of patriarchal whiteness and U.S. citizenship, leads many of us to presume that people who claim to be color-blind are merely liars. That is, we tend to assume that beneath the evasions of color-blind rhetoric, people ultimately uphold consciously racist attitudes and convictions and these beliefs motivate them to consciously act in discriminatory ways. Indeed, the case studies examined in Chapters 1–4 demonstrate that some people do in fact lie, deny, disavow, minimize, and/or justify what are ultimately explicitly discriminatory convictions and practices. The instances of gendered racial violence explored in this book also show that color-blind rhetoric and policies have been instrumental in concealing people's explicitly racist, nativist, or xenophobic agendas, making it increasingly difficult for antiracist organizers to pinpoint discriminatory patterns and to gain redress.

Although I do not discount the consequences of consciously intended forms of gendered racism, nativism, and imperialism, I am much more preoccupied with explaining how hegemonic economies of emotion guide people to support institutionalized oppression in unconscious and unintended ways. This preoccupation arises from the fact that people rarely change their racist, nativist, or imperialist beliefs simply because they are made aware of their complicity in systemic forms of oppression. In other words, I want to understand why being presented with evidence about the systemic injustices of color-blind gendered racism rarely has the effect of changing the minds and actions of people who are emotionally invested in holding onto their beliefs, identities, and worldviews.

Charles W. Mills defines frameworks that help reproduce oppression in unintended and unknowing ways as the "epistemologies of white ignorance."[6] Mills argues that, if epistemologies are generally understood to mean ways of knowing, the epistemologies of white ignorance are not the absence of knowledge but rather ways of ensuring that the legacy and consequences of global white supremacy are systematically ignored. Stated differently, white ignorance is a social practice that Michael Taussig describes as "knowing what not to know."[7] Like a public secret that a majority of people participate in but rarely articulate in collective and conscious ways, the epistemologies of white ignorance teach us how *not* to understand the ways that systemic racial and gender oppression is reproduced.

Moreover, because U.S. education, media, family, church, and other institutional apparatuses work hard to reproduce the epistemologies of white ignorance throughout U.S. society, these ways of knowing what not to know need not apply solely to white people. Mills argues that "the 'white' in 'white ignorance' does not mean it has to be confined to white people. . . . [Ignorance] will often be shared by nonwhites to a greater or lesser extent because of the power relations and patterns of ideological hegemony involved."[8] These epistemologies encourage everyone to know how to ignore knowledge, information, and testimonies about the histories of advantage and disadvantage predicated on racial, gender, sexual, national, citizenship, and religious classification. They produce the failure to see how the fates of different people are ultimately linked. The epistemologies of white ignorance produce the failure to experience any ethical upheaval about violence and discrimination—or worse, the tendency to morally justify these acts.

Because these epistemologies foreclose people's ability to see and understand how they might be complicit in systems of oppression, they essentially preclude questions of racist intent. How can someone consciously intend something when they cannot see and understand what they are complicit in perpetuating? In sum, Mills articulates the centrality of reproducing structured ignorance to the project of preserving global white supremacy, because pervasive ignorance enables this racial and economic order to persist in the absence of explicit intent and conscious motivation.

I extend Mills's argument by showing that hegemonic emotional economies help to reproduce white ignorance in people's affective, embodied, and reflexive structures, not merely their cognitive ones. Dominant emotional economies often function to foreclose or reduce people's willingness to challenge false beliefs because embodied experiences of fear, phobia, shame, or desire take precedence over cognition or knowledge. When false beliefs are invested with powerful emotions, such emotions significantly influence the extent to which people are open to new information, facts, and evidence, particularly if these prove emotionally challenging or threatening. If the epistemologies of white ignorance generally teach people what not to know, then emotional economies significantly affect the degree to which people are committed to false beliefs and to knowing what not to know.

The relationship between unconscious or preconscious emotional economies and people's conscious cognition has been increasingly clarified by research in social psychology and neuroscience. Social psychologists have confirmed that people's affective and embodied responses to gendered racial signs and cues often take place in the absence of conscious knowledge and intent. It is as though our bodies have their own ways of knowing that are not necessarily congruent with our intentional and/or consciously avowed views. That is, people exhibit particular physiological and affective responses to gender-specific racial signifiers before they have time to make intentional cognitive decisions and often in contrast to self-reporting.[9]

David Amodio notes that psychologists have found that implicit racial associations (i.e., affective responses that precede or bypass conscious thought and intent) are "typically not correlated with self-reported attitudes and beliefs."[10] This contrast has led psychologists to distinguish between "automatic processing of passively learned stereotypic associations [and] self-report measures [which] typically reflected intentionally endorsed beliefs."[11] Across numerous approaches to measuring the implicit racial responses of American research subjects, Amodio found that "a relatively consistent pattern of findings has demonstrated an association of black people with negative African American stereotypes."[12] This is not surprising, but what is significant about these studies is that "these associations are considered to be implicit because responses on the task are either too fast for conscious deliberation or, in some cases, the group prime is presented so quickly that it cannot be consciously perceived."[13] In other words, these studies show that emotional responses are triggered without conscious awareness or intent. Moreover, affective and emotional responses often function irrespective of the presence of intentional control. Finally, Amodio shows that implicit affective and physiological responses tend to be "uncorrelated with explicit racial attitudes and endorsed racial stereotypes."[14]

In a comprehensive review of new research in what psychologists call implicit racial bias, Jennifer Eberhardt writes that "exposing Whites to Black targets, for example, can affect Whites' physiological responses in myriad ways: how their skin sweats, how their hearts pump, how their cortical voltage shift, how their facial muscles twitch, and how their eyes blink."[15] What's more, the simple exercise of imagining an interaction with a Black partner can produce physiological changes in whites. In an imagined cooperative-learning encounter, studies have shown that "Whites exhibited more responses known to indicate negative affect (i.e., increased brow activity and decreased cheek activity) when they imagined working with a Black partner rather than a White one."[16] These physiological responses stand in contrast to the self-reporting measures of the same study, in which whites rated Black partners more favorably than white partners when they imagined working with them.[17]

Eberhardt concedes that social psychology is still not conclusive about the correlation between automatic implicit racial bias and behavioral actions. But she strongly argues that social psychology and neuroscience research confirm the function of affect and physiological responses to racial signifiers as autonomous from conscious intent. The broad implication of this research is that "social variables can influence biological processes" without needing permission from cognitive and conscious awareness.[18]

Social psychologists' contemporary research on implicit racial bias confirms what psychiatrist Frantz Fanon theorized long ago in *Black Skin, White Masks*. As early as the 1950s, Fanon argued that racist cultures organize and reproduce people's automatic affective responses, not merely their consciously avowed attitudes.[19] Fanon's clinical research led him to conclude that feelings had a unique ability to trump facts. In examining white people's preconscious and embodied reflexive fears of Black people, Fanon argued that affect (rather than reason) overwhelmingly determined how people responded to signs and bodies whose meanings in dominant cultures were associated with threats. "In the phobic, affect has a priority that defies all rational thinking."[20] That is, people who experienced phobic emotional responses to Black people were likely to disregard conspicuously available "reasonable evidence" that people of color posed no threat to them in actuality.

The widespread social panics over the perceived threats of criminality, terrorism, welfare dependence, and undocumented immigration in the post–civil rights era are similarly dismissive of reasonable facts and evidence. Although these threats are largely based on historically repeated myths, fallacies, misrepresentations, and hyperbolic and skewed information about Black, Latino/a, Arab, and/or Muslim people, revealing the overwhelmingly fabricated nature of these threats rarely stops people from believing and fearing them anyway.[21] Because phobic emotional responses feel imminent and crucial to survival and the preservation of one's self-identity, people who experience them tend to feel first and perhaps think later.

Importantly, the groups, objects, or ideas targeted by hegemonic economies of emotion are not arbitrarily chosen. Rather, as Fanon theorized, they are over-determined through cultural and political processes of circulation, repetition, and association.[22] For example, processes that repetitively link the threats of criminality, terrorism, welfare dependence, and undocumented immigration to Black, Latino/a, Arab, and Muslim people overdetermine the focal points around which hegemonic economies of emotion coalesce and accumulate. In other words, repetitiously ominous cultural associations tend to teach people—consciously or unconsciously—to fear people of color and to identify with punishing, containing, and dissociating from them. Stories, movies, television programs, news coverage, video games, political discourses, and social interactions help shape how and why Black, Latino/a, Arab, and Muslim people are feared, disregarded, fetishized, admired, and/or revered. As Sara Ahmed argues, what we feel and the intensity of our feelings are shaped by our social and cultural contexts. Furthermore, if these associations increase in frequency and circulation, our feelings about them also tend to intensify. Ahmed argues that emotion "is produced only as an effect of its circulation" between signs.[23] The more that Black, Latino/a, Arab, and Muslim bodies are associated with threats in circuits of cultural exchange, "the more they appear to 'contain' affect."[24] In themselves, Black, Latino/a, Arab, and Muslim people do not carry affective or emotional value; rather, cultural contexts of signification and exchange center them within hegemonic emotional economies. Feelings, then, are not simply individual matters; they are expressly cultural, socially shared, and political.

Because feelings possess the unique ability to trump facts, antiracist organizers and educators who wish to disrupt the epistemologies of white ignorance must contend with the distinct operative logics of emotions. If sound evidence tends to be disregarded by people who feel emotionally threatened by it, then rupturing the epistemologies of white ignorance requires more than reasonable arguments and persuasive empirical studies. Antiracist feminist justice requires creating socially shared *affective receptivity*, not merely ideological or cognitive openness.

To those who suffer daily from the indignities and aggressions of gendered racism, it may seem impossible that people are not always acting intentionally or consciously to gain the economic and sociocultural advantages attached to American whiteness, citizenship, and/or imperialism. In exploring both intentional and unintentional forms of public support for racism, nativism, and imperialism, I do not mean to diminish the violence of consciously intended racist attitudes and acts. Rather, my aim is to show how dominant ways of understanding *and* feeling work together to prevent dominant majorities from seeing that they are implicated and responsible for ending intersecting oppressions.

Indeed, the way we theorize people's investments in color-blind gendered racism, nativism, and imperialism is likely to guide the way we propose to stage our resistance. By and large, scholarly explanations for people's investments in color-blind racism, or what Lawrence Bobo and Ryan Smith call laissez-faire racism, privilege cognitivist frameworks of understanding. Bonilla-Silva and other critical race scholars imply that the work of antiracism requires the disruption of false beliefs and evasive ideologies through sound knowledge of the history and continuing significance of white supremacy as a racial structure. This method presumes that people are cognitively receptive to sound argumentation and accurate information. Yet anyone who regularly discusses racism, nativism, or imperialism with people whose worldviews have been shaped by false beliefs and ignorance quickly finds out that sound evidence and reasonable arguments fail to make a difference to affectively unreceptive people. Even those who think of themselves as cognitively open to new information are often overtaken by affective anxieties and fears when discussing gendered racial oppression. Take, for example, the impact of affective anxieties in white people who fear being called racist; these emotions often prevent our ability to engage in conversations about racism and the ways we are implicated in its perpetuation.

The scholarship on implicit racial bias indicates that antiracist work involves more than changing people's conscious understandings of race and sexuality. It involves creating cultural practices and social relations that reorganize people's unconscious cultural associations and, by extension, their unconsciously embodied affective structures. Indeed, the work of reorganizing these affective structures begins with cultivating greater emotional receptivity to matters that involve race and sexuality. This reorganization of affect demands a reorganization of the ways racial signs are defined and imbued with meaning in public cultures. At the very least, a reorganization of collective emotions about race and sexuality would require a much more complex and diverse spectrum of cultural and social associations with gendered racial bodies, signs, and histories.

In this book I show that emotions involved in expressions of gendered racial violence and discrimination significantly mediate the relationship between conscious commitments and practice. In other words, remaining attentive to the function of emotion and affect allows us to better understand how and why, when it comes to race and sexuality, people unconsciously engage in patterns of denial and disavowal. It also helps us understand why people who consciously profess beliefs in gendered racial equality do not tend to practice what they preach.

THE FUNCTION OF EMOTION
IN IDEOLOGICAL FANTASIES

Understanding how feelings are able to trump facts requires a theorization of the unconscious dimensions of ideology. Without such theorization, the contradictions between what people say and what they do can only be explained as intentional lies meant to conceal underlying motives or interests or as structured ignorance.

Rather than understanding most people today to be ignorant or good liars, philosopher Slavoj Žižek argues that people generally know that their political regimes act unjustly and exploitatively, but they continue to act as though they do not know.[25] Such contradictory behaviors, Žižek argues, indicate that ideology has both an unconscious and a libidinal dimension that allows people to construct their desires and purpose. He introduces the term *ideological fantasy* to explain how frameworks of belief enable people to minimize, justify, or make exceptions for injustices they know are taking place (even if only vaguely or abstractly). For example, liberals tend to minimize racism's significance by believing that systematic patterns of discrimination no longer exist. This belief allows them to minimize the injustices of racism. Alternatively, people's tendency to render racist violence exceptional rests on the belief that U.S. fairness and equality are otherwise normative. Finally, people's justifications of racist, nativist, and/or imperialist acts often rest on the belief that these acts are necessary for the sake of a greater good or that people should be punished for betraying the implicitly sacred and extrapolitical values of the United States. Americans may see that warfare against Iraq and Afghanistan is detrimental, but they believe that it is necessary for the greater good of U.S. society. Or people may understand that stop-and-frisk policing tactics are discriminatory toward Black and Latino/a people yet still believe that these tactics are necessary to prevent crime.

Beliefs function to offer explanations, coherence, and justification for things that are actually fraught with contradiction, incoherence, and gaps in knowledge. They convert incongruent ideas into commonsense truths and smooth over inconsistencies. Moreover, people often inherit their beliefs unconsciously from family, social, and cultural contexts that repeat, deploy, and validate them. This binding structure of belief enables people to inhabit their fantasies, which Žižek, along with Jean Laplanche and Jean Bertrand Pontalis, defines as settings for staging desire.[26]

Rather than understanding fantasies simply as private projections or daydreams, people's fantasies "are effectively shaped, formed and re-formed—but also disrupted or even shattered—by social technologies, practices, and representations."[27] That is, cultural and political contexts help shape the way people inhabit their ideological fantasies, providing the terms and frameworks through which people construct their ideals. Aspiring to these ideal selves, communities, or nations gives meaning and purpose to people's lives. As Jacqueline Rose argues, "Fantasy is not therefore antagonistic to social reality; it is its precondition or psychic glue."[28]

As an ideological fantasy creates the setting for a desired ideal, it constructs this ideal as something attainable. In actuality, however, the ideal is unattainable because, if it were attainable, we would lose the meaning and purpose on which we have constructed our desire and yearning. For example, a Minuteman who patrols the U.S.-Mexico border to prevent undocumented migrants from entering the country may inhabit an ideological fantasy of the U.S. nation as monoracially white. The Minuteman struggles for the ideal of a monoracial culture because he believes this will restore the U.S. nation's peace and prosperity as well as white Americans' racial and cultural dominance. This ideal is never attainable in actuality, but the Minuteman must conceal the unattainability of his ideal to continue having something to desire. The Minuteman constructs his sense of self and purpose through this ideological fantasy and through the constant desire it reproduces because the ideal is always out of reach; acknowledging that the fantasy is unattainable would be tantamount to losing the structure through which the Minuteman constructs his sense of meaning and would result in the death of the desire that defines his self-identity.

The unconscious processes of concealing the ideological fantasy's unattainability—which allow people to continue defining their identities, desires, meaning, and purpose—often involve external projections. Rather than deal with the traumatic reality that their fantasy ideals are unattainable and that their desired pursuits are futile, people tend to project their failure to achieve grandiose ideals onto "persecutory enemies" who are blamed for national political disintegration or communal disunity.[29] For example, the Minuteman who desires a monoracial white nation attributes his community's failure to attain this ideal to undocumented Latino/a immigrants. He projects the cause of losing the nation's Anglo-Saxon culture, language, and resources onto undocumented immigrants and fantasizes that their removal will restore the nation in his image. Such projections allow him to deny the fact that his ideal monoracial white nation is unattainable and therefore allow him to continue aspiring to it. Ideological fantasies are therefore ways of coming to terms with what a given political community deems excessive to its norms and boundaries.

The psychic glue that allows people to inhabit their ideological fantasies is deeply related to emotions. Žižek's theorizes that *jouissance*, or libidinally charged enjoyment, is central to the ways people invest their projections of persecutory enemies with affective value. That is, persecutory enemies are believed to be the thieves of people's enjoyment. The Minuteman who desires a monocultural nation believes that he cannot fully enjoy his nation or his neighborhood as he wishes because Latino/a immigrants are constantly interfering: They speak Spanish and establish bilingual education programs; they open up Mexican restaurants; they consume public education resources. Persecutory enemies are therefore responsible for taking or stealing the enjoyment of those who presume themselves entitled to such pleasure and satisfaction. As Žižek notes, the persecutory enemy is deemed responsible for preventing the community's ability to "enjoy their nations as themselves."[30]

How a community deals with how they feel about specific persecutory enemies depends on two central factors. First, has the dominant political and cultural context overdetermined this enemy as a proper receptacle for releasing collective aggression? Second, what are the acceptable ways in which everyday people are allowed to express their emotions toward persecutory enemies who purportedly steal their enjoyments?

The law and the state centrally mitigate both how people are permitted to express socially shared emotions toward persecutory enemies and which objects or subjects they deem persecutory in the first place. In liberal democracies it is generally understood that citizens relinquish their right to exert violence toward enemies to the state; they are expected to abide by laws that enable the nation's greater good. In exchange, they receive entitlements to the state's protection and resources. Žižek argues that this social contract necessarily makes people believe that only the state can experience the enjoyment of possessing full sovereign power. In other words, state agents are the only people who do not face consequences for actions that are otherwise prohibited to everyday citizens. Because of this, everyday people believe that they have relinquished their access to unlimited enjoyment. Thus the only way to vicariously recuperate the enjoyment derived from sovereign power, or the power to transgress, is by identifying with the state or whoever possesses enough power to access full *jouissance*.

This social contract purports to give people certain benefits, but it also disempowers them. When it comes to dealing with the persecutory enemies they deem responsible for their diminished enjoyment, people are basically left with two options: continue to obey the laws or take matters into their own hands. In the first instance, they can remain law-abiding citizens who relinquish their power to deal with enemies to the state. People may therefore channel their emotions through lobbying or grassroots campaigns that encourage the state to deal with those who are considered enemies in the ways they deem most effective. For example, if they imagine Black and Latino/a people to be domestic criminals responsible for stealing the nation's enjoyment of law and order, they may encourage their political representatives to develop and use "tough-on-crime" policies and practices to neutralize these projected enemies. Alternatively, people can take matters into their own hands and transgress the law by enacting vigilante or interpersonal violence themselves. They may do this because the affect or emotion they feel toward those they project as enemies may trump their reasonable interests to remain law-abiding citizens. More likely, people take the law into their own hands because they do not believe that their political representatives and their state agents will deal with the persecutory enemies in a manner that coheres with their ideals. Such transgressions are common among people who not only see persecutory enemies as thieves of their enjoyment but also disidentify with the ways their state governments are dealing with these enemies. Tea Party members who warn of extralegal uprisings if the current state does not ban abortions or permit the unification of church and state offer contemporary examples of those who no longer feel they can abide by the existing social contract.

Despite such transgressions of the law and the state, most people continue to repress their desires to transgress (and the illicit enjoyment such transgressions yield) by relinquishing their power to the state. In doing so, they obtain the pleasure that comes from transgressing acceptable norms vicariously through the state's authority and practices. Their political allegiance to the state therefore allows them to access the *jouissance* they believe they lost when they relinquished their power to transgress. In other words, identifying with the state's power to transgress allows people to experience guilty enjoyments otherwise deemed unacceptable. Such vicarious guilty enjoyments unconsciously take place each time we watch a movie and feel gratified, satisfied, and happy that state agents (police officers, the FBI, the CIA) were able to contain and neutralize persecutory enemies. People enjoy fantasizing about their sense of power through their identification with the state. They feel not only that they are participating in constructing the greater good of U.S. society but also that their allegiance to the state gets them closer to achieving their ideological fantasies.

Clearly, people who are overdetermined by dominant popular and political culture to be persecutory enemies of national and community enjoyment cannot inhabit ideological fantasies in the same way as those who presume themselves to be entitled to state representation and protection. A Black man constantly subject to police harassment cannot stage his identification with law and order in the same way as a white man who constantly enjoys police protection and preferential treatment. The Black man's experience with the realities of state violence does not allow him to idealize and fantasize his relationship to state power in the same way. But this experience does not necessarily preclude him from identifying with state power when it comes to, for example, projections of Arab terrorism. Identifying with U.S. military power might help the Black man affectively compensate for the disempowerment he suffers at the hands of domestic police authority. Conversely, if he sees a structural continuity between domestic and international state power, the Black man may remain permanently unable to engage in an ideological fantasy of law and order or U.S. exceptionalism.

This theorization of ideology reveals how unconscious beliefs, fantasies, and affective enjoyments function to foreclose people's receptivity to knowledge and

evidence. Unconscious beliefs and emotions do not just structure people's ideological fantasies; they help construct people's sense of self, meaning, and desire.
Relinquishing these beliefs, emotions, and fantasies is tantamount to relinquishing the very bases upon which people construct meaning in their lives. This is
why people often continue to remain complicit in their nation's unjust practices
even though they are aware of the destruction they foster. Projecting the cause
of their failed ideals and enjoyments onto constructed persecutory enemies allows people to evade the work they must do to confront themselves. It enables
people to deny their complicity in or their responsibility to confront their unjust
governments; it allows them to constitute their desires and libidinal enjoyments
through others' denigration rather than engage in the more difficult work of
seeing and feeling how our fates are always already linked to the fates of others.

The threats of criminality, terrorism, welfare dependence, and undocumented
immigration constructed Black, Latino/a, Arab, and Muslim people as the persecutory enemies standing in the way of achieving various national enjoyments
in the post–civil rights era. The ideological fantasy of law and order (explored in
depth in the introduction to Part I and in Chapter 1) imagines a nation free
of crime; but because such crime is overwhelmingly associated with Black and
Latino/a people, it also implicitly means that the law and order nation coheres
with a fantasy of national patriarchal whiteness. The ideological fantasy of American exceptionalism (elaborated in the introduction to Part I and in Chapter 2)
imagines a U.S. nation immune to terrorist threats; but because these terrorist
threats are overwhelmingly seen as residing in the tendencies of innumerable
Arab and Muslim people, this fantasy also implicitly means that U.S. exceptionalism is predicated on a distinctly imperialist mission that demands permanent
warfare. Finally, the ideological fantasy of economic self-reliance imagines a nation of hardworking people free of dependents and parasites who leech off of
U.S. citizens' public resources and government aid. For some, this fantasy goes
so far as calls for the elimination of social welfare resources altogether in order
to reinstate the rugged individualism valued by free markets. But because these
so-called dependents are primarily imagined as Black and Latina mothers with
children, as undeserving undocumented immigrants, or as poor whites who do
not uphold proper work ethics, the ideological fantasy of economic self-reliance
is predicated on privileging white propertied interests and restricting public resources for their exclusive use.

Proposals for how to best deal with the constructed persecutory enemies associated with crime, terrorism, welfare, and immigration often depend on whether people identify with liberal or conservative politics. But there is little disagreement across the political aisle over the core ideological fantasies that organize people's dominant desires, fears, and identifications with state authority. My point here is not that all Americans inhabit these ideological fantasies or that a majority of U.S. constituents necessarily feel the same way about the constructed persecutory enemies at the heart of these fantasies. It is to say that hegemonic ideological fantasies have a way of unconsciously organizing people's emotional economies and actions. Unless these unconscious and embodied aspects are disrupted, their efficiency will likely continue to function.

EPISTEMOLOGIES OF ETHICAL WITNESSING

I try to tentatively answer a methodological question in this book: If hegemonic ideologies, beliefs, and emotions often trump facts and foreclose people's cognitive receptivity to knowledge that disrupts their worldviews, what methods do we use to create greater affective receptivity to historically sound knowledge and engender more desires for justice? That is, how might we diminish the function of false beliefs and emotions taken as truths that encourage us to act in self-destructive ways? In addition to providing correctives to myths, historical fallacies, and reductive narratives, how might emotional economies be reoriented to align with antiracist feminist praxis?

This problem deeply preoccupied Fanon in *Black Skins, White Masks*. All the methods that Fanon considered for rupturing hegemonic ideological fantasies and feelings encouraged by European cultures seemed to lead back to the power of these cultures' *ontological* and *epistemological* frameworks. These frameworks were explicitly structured to disallow any genuine recognition of the complex humanity of people of color. That is, because the ontological and epistemological frameworks of European and American societies needed the myths, fallacies, misrecognitions, and misrepresentations projected onto gendered racial difference to structure their own meanings and identities, people of color were relatively doomed to be persecutory enemies who could only approach and approximate, but never *be*, normatively valued humans within these frameworks. Those who strive for recognition and validation under the dominant ontological frames and values that govern global white supremacy concede a tremendous ethical price. In exchange for validation and recognition as a law-abiding person, as a U.S. citizen, as a "model minority," as economically independent, these ontologies demand our adherence to a value system that constructs our worth through someone else's denigration. Because they offer systematic rewards, incentives, and punishments, the ontological and epistemological frameworks of racist cultures are of course extremely far-reaching. But just because these frameworks are blind to the existence of other ontologies and epistemologies—or consider them illegitimate—does not mean that other epistemologies and ontologies do not exist.

The racial regimes of American or European cultures are not capable of grasping or controlling all relations of power. As Cedric Robinson argues, "The production of race is chaotic. It is an alchemy of the intentional and the unintended, of known and unimagined fractures of cultural forms, of relations of power and the power of social and cultural relations."[31] This means that people have the ability to align themselves in unlikely formations, to traverse unexpected boundaries, to speak from ways of knowing and being that are unknowable or unseen by the epistemological and ontological frameworks privileged by global white supremacy. Shifts in people's imagination, social relations, and orders of power have the ability to collapse fantasy and affective structures that appear immovable and entrenched. These buried or unseen epistemologies and ontologies ethically haunt the public beliefs, fantasies, and feelings that sustain investments in gendered racism, nativism, and imperialism, threatening to lead to their unraveling and collapse. I define these as epistemologies of ethical witnessing.

To see and feel the epistemologies of ethical witnessing, one must do a lot of work to recuperate and emotionally integrate materialist histories that have been thrown into the debris of history, to use Walter Benjamin's phrase. As Robinson and Sandra Harding show, "Any body of systematic knowledge is always internally linked to a distinctive body of systematic ignorance."[32] Although the radical traditions and cultural spaces of ethical witnessing have been vehemently ruptured by state violence, orchestrated economic disasters, neoliberalism, mass incarceration, immigrant detentions and deportations, global warfare, and the political counterinsurgencies of the post–civil rights era, they still offer remarkable frameworks for devising methods that rupture the hegemonic emotional economies of the post–civil rights era. Methods of feeling, seeing, dreaming, and practicing that expose the hegemonic ideologies and unjust operations of racial regimes persist. Their most powerful possibility lies in showing that individualist hoarding, fearful alienation, and social divisions are rooted in historical wounds and traumas that will continue to haunt until they are confronted and redressed. No fantasy or feeling can fully conceal or repress the persistent intrusions of repressed historical memories and sufferings. No masquerade or naturalized system of knowledge and power can completely erase the evidence that lives in the embodied intergenerational memories of the oppressed.

A legacy of justice is rooted in people's memories, visions, and emotional economies, pulsing through U.S. histories of the present and regularly unmasking the legacies of white supremacy. This legacy gives us epistemological, ontological, and affective frameworks for dreaming, desiring, and identifying in ways that not only stand *against* gendered racism but also offer the potential of producing embodied alignments *for* collective racial, gender, and economic justice. Robinson showed how methods of knowing and feeling that are rooted in the legacy of ethical witnessing are evident in countless practices of resistance that make up the Black radical tradition.[33] Gloria Anzaldúa demonstrated how the epistemologies and emotional economies of ethical witnessing generate forms of consciousness and praxis that both contend with the impositions of gendered racism and generate practices of healing.[34] Edward Said marked the persistence of resistance, self-determination, and dignity even in states and spaces of permanent exile.[35] James Baldwin understood that his life's calling was to be a witness to the iterations and negotiations of this legacy of ethical witnessing and justice—to conjure up possibilities for America that it was not yet capable of conceptualizing or demanding of itself.[36] W. E. B. DuBois outlined the epistemologies and emotional economies of ethical witnessing in the unlikely alliances between ethnic white immigrants, brown and Black workers, and the radical abolition vision of "40 acres and a mule."[37] The legacy of ethical witnessing motivated the farm workers' movement in California, where Chicano/a emotional economies became powerful methods for recruiting publics to align with workers' dignity and humanity.[38] This genealogy of justice and ethical witnessing is heard in the voices of Harriet Jacobs and Ida B. Wells, who demanded more than false tones, hypocrisy, and inaction from white Christians complicit in the atrocities of slavery and lynching.[39] This vision lives in the bodies of John Brown and Bill Moore, bodies whose intolerance for white supremacy grew to the point of death.[40] It is this legacy of ethical witnessing that stands as a mirror to a society dominantly committed to its collective destruction.

The legacy of ethical witnessing and racial and gender justice is cumulative, intergenerational, and permanently engaged in struggle rather than utopic. It is transferred and learned both affectively and consciously. The instances of violence and discrimination examined in this book are confronted by powerful methods of feeling, seeing, and practicing that are rooted in ethical witnessing. Those who fought against the violence and denigration of police brutality in New York, against the tortures in Abu Ghraib prisons, against anti-immigrant housing discrimination in Escondido, and against orchestrated abandonment in New Orleans call upon us to reorganize our spaces, practices, embodied reflexes, and desires to align with the actualization of collective dignity and liberation. They encourage us to acknowledge that our fates are linked and that a society that denies the unjust outcomes of its past and present actions cannot stand on ethical grounds. The epistemologies of ethical witnessing seek to make justice irresistible and white supremacy intolerable. So long as we overvalue the power of dominant ontological and epistemological frameworks organized by racial regimes, it is difficult to see why people would want to give up the privileges and structured advantages of whiteness, nativism, and imperialism. But if we locate ourselves in the ontology and epistemology of what Walter Benjamin called "the tradition of the oppressed" or what I call the legacy of ethical witnessing, the collective divestment from the moneyed and affective economies of gendered racism, nativism, and imperialism becomes desirable.

CRIMINALS AND TERRORISTS: THE EMOTIONAL ECONOMIES OF MILITARY-CARCERAL EXPANSION

Who wishes for law and order? Who fears losing safety and protection? Who desires to bring "democracy" to other nations through occupation and military invasion? Who is anxious about losing national power? One of the paradoxes embedded in powerful nations and dominant people is their perpetual insecurity and anxiety. One would think that—precisely because of their economic, racial, national, and/or gender dominance—such nations and people would rest contentedly in their power, prosperity, and authority. After all, Eurocentric cultural dominance in the United States automatically endows white Americans with entitlements that others have to work hard to earn or never even imagine obtaining. Those who unquestionably belong to the nation and possess U.S. citizenship are granted global privileges irrespective of whether they desire them: entitlements such as *not* being presumed an illegal alien or a potential thief at the supermarket; privileges such as *not* being stopped by the police because you are driving while Black or *not* being searched by the TSA airport security officer for the billionth time because you look Muslim.

It seems that those who possess dominance, despite their veneer of authority and entitlement, are simultaneously fearful of losing the coordinates through which they secure their power. Popular complaints about reverse racism against

white Americans or the impending decline of the United States as a global superpower give us insights into the ways people and nations at the top construct
their value, meaning, and purpose. If they describe themselves as disempow-
ered, it is because they remain constantly vigilant about potential threats to
their power and status. Sensing symbolic and concrete shifts in the tide—racial
demographics moving toward the browning of America, China and India's
economic ascent, immigrants gaining rights, the effects of affirmative action
policies, diversity training, Spanish-speaking families, Muslim mosques—they
seek ways to restore their power.

Have they actually lost power? It doesn't matter much. Their feelings and
beliefs warn them that they have or that, if they don't do something, they will
soon lose all the signposts by which they have constituted the value of their
properties and personhoods. Sure, according to all sociological indicators, white
men are still dominant, and the United States is still a global superpower. But
will this always be true? Those who do not experience the automatic entitlements, unearned social privileges, and wealth advantages of the dominant U.S.
publics look at their flamboyant emotional claims of disempowerment in dis-
may. How can people who possess so much believe themselves to be victims?

In this part, I broadly outline two ideological fantasies in the post–civil
rights era that were central in aligning the desires of dominant majorities in
the United States with the state's unprecedented expansion of militarism and
incarceration since the late 1970s. At stake in these ideological fantasies were
real and imagined losses in dominance and power. The projected losses were
psychological and affective as much as they were economic. Domestically, I
explore how dominant majorities' identification with the ideological fantasy
of law and order helped forge widespread support for the expansion of prisons
and policing. In the global domain the reorientation of the ideological fantasy of U.S. exceptionalism toward the threats of Arab terrorism helped secure
public support for proliferating military apparatuses and permanent warfare.

Dominant public identifications with law and order and U.S. exceptionalism
were not natural or inevitable. Nor were these identifications secured through
the same ideas, feelings, and practices of former eras. Rather, they had to gain
their legitimacy above and beyond a range of other possible identifications,
desires, and political futures. Further, whereas one might expect public feelings
about military-carceral expansion to be focused on macropolitical issues such

as preserving national security and stable economies, it turns out that the most powerful fears and desires focused on distinctly sexualized and racialized matters. Concerns over whether Arab men are hyperpatriarchal and hyperviolent were somehow critical to whether the United States would gain any ground against terrorism. Fears over Black men's presumed hyperviolent threats preoccupied those who called for more incarceration. Anxieties over undocumented Latino/a families being too large or Latina women being hyperfertile were central to whether people legitimated a new Immigration Customs and Enforcement (ICE) detention center or advocated for deportations. Such normative preoccupations with race and sexuality indicate that Americans continue to articulate political matters in distinctly familial terms. These racial, sexual, gender, and propertied norms are experienced as deeply important issues through which America's national future is envisioned and struggled over.

THE PUNITIVE EMOTIONAL ECONOMIES
OF CARCERAL EXPANSION

The 1960s–1970s era, much like today, was characterized by crises. Global decolonization movements and domestic freedom struggles forced the U.S. state and dominant white society to make significant adjustments.

Counterinsurgencies irrevocably delegitimized and outlawed explicitly white supremacist laws and discourses in the United States. Mainstream institutions in the South and North, previously set up to exclude people of color through legalized and de facto forms of exclusion, had to adjust their policies and practices. In an intense era of urban riots between 1965 and 1968 following the assassinations of such political figures as Malcolm X and Martin Luther King Jr., numerous cities were set ablaze, warning people of chaos and disorder. Simultaneously, a global economic recession in the mid-1970s was creating rising inflation, stagnant wages, and unemployment in the United States.

The counterinsurgencies that struggled for racial and feminist justice throughout these eras triggered intense fears and insecurities in dominant white majorities. Throughout the 1960s and 1970s such fears motivated white people to move to the suburbs en masse. Taking their wealth and resources with them, they left inner cities to dilapidate and experience the recession in heightened ways. Politicians who witnessed the rise of these fearful emotional economies—

and who were themselves furious over the victories they were forced to concede to civil rights activists—saw a moment of opportunity to reexcavate an old American ideological fantasy, one that promised the restoration of law and order in a time of racial chaos.

This ideological fantasy has long historical precedents. During slavery, it was used to legitimate the violent suppression of slave rebellions in law and practice.[1] Throughout the period of territorial expansion westward, a paternalistic version of law and order justified Native American removal and genocide on the grounds that the indigenous were savage and unwilling to conform to the propertied and market relations of liberal individualism.[2] Post-Reconstruction, vigilante mob violence and lynchings against Black, Mexican, and other non-white people, particularly against men of color, also claimed to be enacted in the name of law and order. Eliminating and controlling the putatively hyper-violent and sexually predatory nature of people of color was deemed critical to the stability of the U.S. nation.[3] Similarly, the convict lease system that emerged in the aftermath of the Civil War, whose convicts rapidly became disproportionately Black, depended on the ideological fantasy of law and order to secure its legitimacy. As the nation's territory and economic power increased in the mid-nineteenth century, the persecutory enemies who were presumed to steal the peace, security, and prosperity of American law and order from dominant white majorities also increased. From Mexican banditry, disease, predatory sexuality, gang violence, and territorial reconquest in the Southwest, Texas, and California;[4] to constructions of Asian "yellow perils" intent on "contaminating" and "subverting" the U.S. empire from within;[5] to Arab sheiks and Islamic fundamentalists intent on swindling Americans out of wealth and power,[6] the ideological fantasy of law and order was yearned for yet always out of reach.

Reformulating Racial Struggles as Crimes

The conservative congressmen of the 1970s who had experienced huge psychological and legal losses to racial justice organizers were confronted with a core challenge in their reexcavation of the law and order ideological fantasy. Old versions of the fantasy almost always identified their enemies in unabashedly racist ways. The moral delegitimation of fascism and racism won by the antiracist freedom movements of the post–World War II era meant that dominant U.S. majorities could no longer define their goodness through white supremacist advocacy. The tide that swept the nation reformulated American goodness as something predicated on racial tolerance, equal opportunity, and fairness. Because changing social warrants no longer allowed dominant U.S. majorities to feel good and righteous about endorsing a type of law and order that was overtly white supremacist, post–civil rights law and order had to be expressed using distinctly color-blind terms.

The conservative congressmen overcame the challenge of reformulating the ideological fantasy of law and order in color-blind ways by introducing what Vesla Weaver calls a "frontlash" of legislation tied to crime. Rather than waiting to respond to the growing momentum of civil rights and feminist gains with backlash legislation, the congressmen's frontlash legislation on crime sought to prevent any more losses to white patriarchal dominance. This issue-based strategy "relied on two mutually reinforcing elements: (1) depoliticization and criminalization of racial struggle and (2) racialization of 'crime.'"[7]

The association between racial justice struggles and criminality had historical precedents in the sedimented emotional economies of white majorities, and the congressmen who initiated the frontlash on crime knew this well. The frontlash movement "became preoccupied with showing that racial discord was neither motivated by police brutality nor did its origins emanate from racial discrimination; rather, it was criminality, pure and simple."[8] The depoliticization of racial struggles meant that people of color's militant protests against exclusion and exploitation in the domains of housing, education, employment, and transportation were reformulated as acts of crime against the nation.

The same actors who had fought vociferously against civil rights legislation, defeated, shifted the "locus of attack" by injecting crime onto the agenda. Fusing crime to anxiety about ghetto revolts, racial disorder—initially defined as a problem of minority disenfranchisement—was redefined as a crime problem, which helped shift debate from social reform to punishment.[9]

Rather than allowing emotional economies to continue aligning with the plight of disenfranchised people of color and women, the frontlash legislators exacerbated white public fears over losing cultural and economic dominance by fostering public perceptions that militant organizing movements (e.g., the Black Panther Party for Self-Defense, the American Indian Movement, the Brown Berets, the Puerto Rican Young Lords, the Red Guard Party, I Wor Kuen) were actually criminal thugs.[10] This criminalization of antiracist struggles depended on concealing the legislators' explicitly racist motivations through color-blind talk about crime. As Julia Sudbury argues:

While overt Jim Crow racism had waning public acceptance in this post–Civil Rights era of Martin Luther Kingesque integrationist policies, criminalization provided a new camouflaged racist language in which code words such as "criminal," "drug dealer" and "welfare queen" could be used to refer obliquely to the racialized "enemy within."[11]

On first view this discursive shift from explicitly racist political discourses to covert and coded discourses may seem trivial. But it arguably solved two significant political problems for the right-wing frontlash congressmen. First, color-blind discourses helped these political actors avoid accusations of state-sponsored white supremacy at a time when such discourses and practices had been widely discredited. Second, color-blind discourses that criminalized racial struggles facilitated a fundamental shift in the ways that dominant white majorities understood the *cause* of existing racial inequalities.

In 1965 it was still possible for President Lyndon B. Johnson to openly admit that white racism and discrimination had crippled the life chances and opportunities of people of color *and* to argue that the state should take affirmative action to redress these past wrongs.[12] Only fifteen years later, the criminalization of racial struggles essentially rendered such political honesty inconceivable. The legitimate grievances of Black, Latino/a, and other communities of color over the ways that U.S. society had socioeconomically excluded and marginalized them for centuries had gradually been converted into illegitimate pleas for special handouts and irrational insurrections against order and authority. State and media discourses that criminalized racial struggles converted urban ghettoes that had been impoverished by racially discriminatory policies and practices into spaces of "cultural pathology" or neighborhoods where people of color's "behavioral deficiencies" were responsible for perpetuating cycles of poverty. The causes of racial inequalities in wealth, income, education, and employment were no longer attributed to the historical patterns of white exploitation and exclusion; rather, they were overwhelmingly ascribed to people of color's "deficits."[13]

Conservative politicians began promoting these reversals in historical realities as early as Barry Goldwater's 1964 presidential campaign. Although Goldwater's campaign failed because public sentiments were still supportive of civil rights struggles, Richard Nixon and Ronald Reagan, who deployed the law and order ideological fantasy in subsequent political platforms, regularly won. Increased public identification with law and order propelled Reagan to the governorship of California in 1966 and Nixon to the presidency in 1968 over Lyndon Johnson. Their insistence that tough-on-crime policies would work to address civic unrest much more efficiently than purportedly soft antipoverty programs began persuading U.S. constituents who feared the spike in urban crime rates between 1960 and 1975 and the political riots that affected numerous cities in 1965–1968.[14]

Capitalizing on Democrats who also favored law and order over antipoverty and racial redress programs, Reagan advanced the next stage of the frontlash movement on crime. Having successfully criminalized racial struggle, Reaganism went on to racialize crime by repeatedly demonizing impoverished Black and Latino/a people. Whereas in the 1960s impoverished communities of color possessed the moral authority of people who were struggling for racial liberation and economic equality alongside third world decolonization movements, by the late 1980s their bodies and faces symbolized the incorrigible criminal enemies of law and order. George H. W. Bush's infamous use of the Willie Horton ad in his 1988 presidential bid against Michael Dukakis refurbished old white fears over Black hyperviolence and sexually predatory aggression; but it also confirmed to Democrats that failing to collude with the frontlash conservative agenda on law and order would result in losing congressional and presidential seats. Subsequently, Democrats and Republicans would forge a powerful consensus over tough-on-crime policies, the expansion of prisons, and the instantiation of punitive policing practices.

If the 1980s had widened emotional economies of fear whose persecutory enemies were overwhelmingly depicted as hyperviolent Black and Latino men and irresponsible crack-addicted Black mothers, the 1990s extended the enemies of law and order to also include undocumented immigrants. A conservative nativist movement sponsored by Governor Pete Wilson convinced California taxpayers, who were facing economic losses as a result of the ever-increasing budget allocations for mass incarceration and other late capitalist crises, to scapegoat so-called illegal aliens for stealing their public resources (see introduction to Part II). Over time, however, the status of being an undocumented immigrant became criminalized. Right-wing calls for securing the U.S.-Mexico border beginning in the 1990s intensified the nativist dimension of U.S. racism and eventually shifted definitions of crime to apply simply to the unlawful presence rather than the acts of undocumented immigrants.

The attacks on the World Trade Center on September 11, 2001, extended nativist suspicions to people who appeared Arab and/or Muslim to the American imagination and were residing in the United States. The FBI's call for Arab, Muslim, and South Asian immigrants to voluntarily declare themselves to state authorities only exacerbated fears over potential enemies within. By 2010, Arizona's SB 1070 blazed new legislative pathways to criminalize, racially profile, and harass undocumented immigrants, and numerous states followed suit.[15]

A new infrastructural component was added to the webs of mass incarceration to contain undocumented immigrants and foreigners suspected of terrorism: immigrant detention centers. Multiplying the very enemies it purported to police through its changes in law and practice, the U.S. state went from operating 18 immigrant detention facilities in 1981 (whose daily average population was 54) to 204 facilities by 2011, with an average daily population of 32,095.[16] In the second term of Barack Obama's presidency, the restructuring of the Department of Homeland Security and bolstered support for ICE have yielded the highest rates of detentions and deportations in U.S. history, routinely targeting Latino/as, Arab, Muslim, and other immigrants of color, severing families, and criminalizing what were formerly considered civic violations.[17]

Simultaneous Deployments of Criminality and Exceptionality in Mainstream Media

It is worth remembering that Reagan, who masterfully and gradually aligned public desires with law and order, was an actor before he was a politician. As such, he understood how processes of affective and emotional identification worked in Americans; he understood what appealed to the sentiments of white majorities who were still the favored voting blocs in U.S. elections. Reagan also understood that wars required theatrical spectacles as much as laws, policing, and incarceration tactics to preserve their legitimacy. Using his knowledge of making movies, Reagan initiated a war on drugs based much more on fabricated spectacle than empirically substantive problems. Media coverage regularly featured the ill effects of Black and Latino/a gangs, gangsta hip-hop, the crack epidemic, and the ill effects of illicit drug use to legitimate the war on drugs. Yet sociological realities indicated that crime rates had started to decline and that most of the problems Reagan demonized were the result of neoliberal shifts in the economy, which damaged working-class jobs and wages in general but devastated urban communities of color in particular. As Jimmie Reeves argues in *Cracked Coverage*, media representations of the war on drugs "redefined the economic turmoil and familial instability accompanying the shift from a manu-facturing to a service economy as simply the consequences of cultural patholo-gies driven by individual immorality."[18] Such depictions of Black and Latino/a cultural pathology were repeated until people experienced virtually automatic bodily fears and phobias in response to these associations.

Yet the media demonization of Black and Latino/a marginalized communi-ties would not have been popularly understood to be about crime (as opposed to racism) if mainstream media had not simultaneously begun to overrepresent law-abiding exceptional minorities on television screens. On the one hand, people were encouraged to vehemently fear Black and Latino/a urban commu-nities; on the other hand, they were recruited to feel affection and admiration for good, law-abiding people of color.

Mainstream media cultivated such emotions of admiration, affection, and affinity by circulating representations of model minority Asian Americans, whose work ethic, quiet cultural values, and familial structures cohered with law and order.[19] They also began airing enormously popular sitcoms such as *The Cosby Show*, *A Different World*, and *The Fresh Prince of Bel Air* as features of everyday life throughout the 1980s and 1990s. Coupled with the rising prominence of such Black neoconservative figures as Justice Clarence Thomas, Ward Connerly, Colin Powell, and Condoleezza Rice, who regularly symbolized their loyalty to the state and to law and order, these media representations allowed white majorities to stage their admiration for law-abiding, respectable minorities as proof of their antiracism.

The overrepresentation of law-abiding and state-identified people of color on *Law and Order*, *CSI*, *Law and Order: SVU*, and innumerable dramas whose plots revolve around preserving law and order, helped to create emotional economies of affinity toward people of color, but only insofar as they were coupled with law-abiding and normative behaviors. Such emotional economies helped to neutralize arguments that white phobic feelings toward inner city people of color had anything to do with racism. Further, pitting the rebellious criminality of the Black and Latino/a urban underclass (symbolized by rappers like Tupac Shakur) against the law-abiding compliance of minorities of color (symbolized by figures like Bill Cosby) helped defuse charges that the war on drugs was a racist war, a claim consistently made in targeted people of color's countercultural narratives throughout the 1980s and 1990s.[20]

The phobic/philic structure of post–civil rights media representations also enabled new patterns of identification and desire among people of color. Historically, Black, Latino/a, and other people of color rarely had an easy identification with state agendas for law and order. In the eras of overt white supremacy and Jim Crow, law and order always meant containing all people of color. Similarly, in the 1960s and 1970s the state's criminalization of racial struggles in the name of law and order was still dominantly understood to mean protecting white constituents' entitlements and power from people of color. By the 1980s and 1990s, however, some people of color had also realigned their identifications and desires with the state's fight against crime and drugs.

Because distinctions between good and bad people were made primarily through discourses about crime rather than race, mainstream media helped promote what Swati Rana calls "majority-identified minorities."[21] That is, people of color whose desires aligned with American hegemonic values and institutional practices (e.g., complying with the law, joining the armed forces, obtaining an education in order to advance neoliberal market capitalism) were rewarded with the affective validation that they were not like people of color who were criminals or illegal aliens. Even as majority-identified minorities continued to face discrimination, dissociations from the affectively stigmatized and feared Black and Latino/a urban underclass were virtually required for people of color who wanted to pursue educational and professional mobility.[22] A stylistic choice such as not pulling up one's baggy jeans had symbolic and literal consequences in institutional spaces shaped by the normative values of patriarchal whiteness. As a result, people of color who wanted greater levels of wealth and income were required to perform their racial identities in ways that demarcated their detachment from the so-called deficient values of the urban underclass. Even celebrities who made their wealth and income through the commodification of the styles and cultures originating from impoverished communities of color (e.g., hip-hop celebrities) got to keep their money and status only if their cultural products did not openly challenge the state's violence and the validity of capitalism. The affective shame and perversity attached to impoverished Black and Latino/a people encouraged emotional dissociations among majority-identified people of color and intensified intraracial divisions along class lines.

Because people of color in the urban underclass were presumed to be persecutory enemies of law and order and were punished accordingly, their disidentification with the state's discourses and agenda was palatable. Indeed, those who affectively disidentified with the ideological fantasy of law and order were not just considered enemies of the state. They were also necessary for creating the affective rewards and enjoyments of those who considered themselves law-abiding and therefore entitled to state protection. The urban underclass was also the referent against which majority-identified people of color who aspired to become normative civic subjects measured their success. Being socially valued, feeling morally righteous, and enjoying the guilty pleasures of enacting punishment by identifying with the state's punitive agenda depended on constructing criminals as immoral, illegal, and deserving of punishment. Access to these affective rewards and enjoyments was no longer exclusively available to whites, because people of color could also experience these enjoyments by identifying with the "good behavior" mandated by law and order. Yet given that criminality was virtually equated in public beliefs with impoverished Black and Latino/a people in urban ghettoes, such affective enjoyments could hardly avoid the pitfalls of their gendered racialization even as they purported to be color-blind. That is, keeping the distinctions between criminal people of color and law-abiding ones clear was a challenge for those who used racial difference rather than acts of a crime as decisive indicators. Such slippages were clear when the law-abiding Henry Louis Gates, a distinguished professor of African American Studies at Harvard, was misidentified as a criminal as he entered his own house and was arrested.[23] Slippages were also clear in the hundreds of instances in which Latino/a, South Asian, Arab, and other U.S. citizens of color were suspected of being undocumented.

Once representations depicting impoverished Black and Latino/a people and undocumented immigrants as criminal gained enough affective intensity through their repeated circulation, the projection of criminality no longer needed any substantive proof or sociological evidence to function as true. That is, because people believed and reflexively felt that criminality was embodied in "those people," they were unreceptive to whatever sociological evidence might otherwise say about crime or the historical and racially discriminatory causes of urban poverty. For example, the FBI's own crime statistics showed that crime rates remained stable or actually declined from 1980 to the present and that illegal drug began declining in the 1970s.[24] According to a 2010 Center for Economic and Policy Research report, "Crime can explain only a small portion of the rise in incarceration between 1980 and the early 1990s, and none of the increase in incarceration since then."[25] Despite these factual realities, publics repeatedly endorsed increasing taxpayer allocations to federal, state, and local expenditures on corrections, which rose from approximately $17 billion in 1982 to $75 billion by 2008.[26]

The post–civil rights racialization of crime meant that criminality was not about a diverse set of individuals who traversed the law. As Lisa Cacho argues, impoverished Black and Latino/a people are not presumed to be law-abiding subjects who might or might not become law transgressors: "As criminal by being, unlawful by presence, and illegal by status, *they do not have the option to be law abiding*, which is always the absolute prerequisite for political rights, legal recognition, and resource redistribution in the United States."[27] The more that the narrow associative repetition between criminality and impoverished Black and Latino/a people in cities circulated in the post–civil rights era, the more the dominant reflexive and automatic affective economies of fear and anxiety mistook their bodies (not their acts) as criminal. Importantly, the more this belief became entrenched in phobic affective reflexes, the more people's cognitive receptivity to sociological facts and evidence diminished. Feelings essentially trumped facts. Substantive evidence offered by those who challenged the injustices of the prison-industrial complex was rendered irrelevant against emotionally charged beliefs.

This is not to say that crime and drugs did not bring *actual* problems to *some* neighborhoods. Neighborhoods where job and business opportunities had been decimated by deindustrialization, urban renewal policies, and white flight experienced a rise in alternative (and criminalized) labor economies, such as drug trade and distribution. In effect, the rise of these economies, particularly among Black and Latino men whose unemployment rates in formal labor markets sometimes reached up to 50 percent, did produce devastating effects, for example, increased gang violence, drug addiction, property crimes, and gun violence. People of color who lived in these neighborhoods and called for increased police presence were generally motivated by the need to protect themselves from these tangible vulnerabilities. Unfortunately, greater police presence was an almost sure way of intensifying, not diminishing, violence in neighborhoods of color.[28]

But the violence and property threats that were tangible in certain inner city geographies were generally far removed from predominantly white suburban spaces. White suburbia was overwhelmingly protected and immune to these realities because of the residents' wealth, resources, and police protection. Despite this, the hegemonic emotional economies and unconscious beliefs attached to criminality functioned to make white suburban publics feel that these threats were just as real and imminent in their lives. Anticipating property and emotional losses as a result of crime, which they equivocated with any increasing presence of Black and Latino/a people in their neighborhoods, these white majorities increasingly desired the protection and security promised by more policing and prisons.

What we had, then, were desires for protection motivated by different social experiences. Poor people might have been motivated to call for increased police presence in their neighborhoods because they were actually vulnerable to violence. Majority-identified people of color may have been motivated to endorse punitive tactics in order to dissociate themselves from demonized people of color in urban locales. White majorities, despite facing few actual threats related to crime, tended to believe that the threats of criminality traveled with the bodies of people of color. As a result, they called for policing and containment practices to ensure their protection, particularly when people of color crossed into what they presumed to be their spaces. Despite these divergent motivations, some conscious and others unconscious, the outcomes tended to reinforce the state's agenda for carceral expansion.

The more that the racially coded political discourses and media representations of Black, Latino/a, and nonwhite immigrant criminality circulated in political discourses and mainstream media representations, the more that U.S. publics endorsed state policies that expanded prison building, policing, border militarization, immigrant detention, and tough-on-crime legislation and sentencing. Conversely, the more prisons the state built and the more resources and labor it allocated to policing and punishment industries, the more the ideological fantasy of law and order grew in affective dominance and value. This vicious and mutually reinforcing expansive cycle between political discourses, media representations, and institutional practices gave birth to what Mike Davis calls "the prison industrial complex."[29]

The intricate web of policy making, federal and state funding, and legislative shifts that contributed to the expansion of the prison-industrial complex beginning in the late 1970s has been well documented.[30] Partnering with private entrepreneurs and corporations who sought to generate profits through prison construction and management, the state initiated a monumental infrastructural shift.[31] Between 1974 and 2000 the U.S. state prison system grew from 592 prisons to 1,023 prisons, an increase of 73 percent.[32] By 2005 the United States had 1,821 federal and state correctional facilities, of which 415 were privately operated.[33] Each new state prison costs between $280 million and $350 million to build.[34] Taxpayer dollars flow where dominant emotional needs overwhelmingly want to allocate them: toward state punitive control and containment.

Of course, these new prisons had to constantly supply the bodies that would justify their purpose and economies. As it built more and more prisons, the state increased policing, arrests, and convictions, particularly for drug-related activities. Between 1982 and 1996 drug commitments to federal and state prisons witnessed a 975 percent increase.[35] Working in conjunction with new drug commitments, judges in the criminal justice system dealt out increasingly longer sentences.[36] Collectively, these policies and practices led to an increase in the U.S. incarcerated population from approximately 500,000 in 1980 to 2.3 million people in 2012. Of this total population, about 60 percent are people of color, with Black and Latino men disproportionately represented.[37]

The remarkable expansion of border militarization and enforcement, immigrant detention and incarceration, and private security industries that supply ever-expanding state surveillance technologies have also expanded the prison-industrial complex. Beginning with the Clinton administration's passing of the Illegal Immigration Reform and Immigrant Responsibility Act of 1996 and vastly extended by the post–9/11 USA PATRIOT Act of 2001, the state greatly widened its capacity to scrutinize, criminalize, and detain immigrants for visa violations or for suspicion of terrorism-related activity. Although the targets of anti–illegal immigrant policies had been disproportionately Latino/as, after September 11, Arab, South Asian, and Muslim immigrants (or those presumed to belong to these groups) experienced routine targeting under counterterrorism policies. Such legislative shifts legitimated the growth of what Deepa Fernandes terms the "immigration-industrial complex": an infrastructural, labor, and technological rise in immigrant surveillance, captivity, prosecution, and deportation sponsored by mass economic investments of both state and private capital.[38]

To illustrate just one aspect of this expansion, the U.S. Customs and Border Protection (CBP) budget in 1986 was a meager $151 million;[39] under the consolidated Department of Homeland Security (DHS), the 2011 CBP budget was $11.4 billion.[40] Immigration and Customs Enforcement (ICE), which is responsible for rounding up and deporting undocumented immigrants within the United States, saw its budget increase from $3.3 billion in 2003 to $5.7 billion in 2010.[41] Responsible for policing and mediating immigrants' entry into the United States, particularly along the U.S.-Mexico border, the CBP has been accused by numerous migrants and human rights groups of gross violations, including the use of rape and sexual assault against undocumented women and asylum seekers, as coercive tactics.[42] Approximately 23,000 immigrants are held in detention on a given day, and more than 900 correctional facilities and ICE detention centers across the country hold 200,000 detainees each year.[43] Despite egregious records of inmate violations, private corporations, including the Corrections Corporation of America and GEO Group Inc. (formerly Wackenhut), have profited handsomely from contracts with the federal government to run immigrant detention centers.[44] When the DHS was created in 2003, it consolidated 22 government agencies to facilitate links between communication and surveillance apparatuses, including intelligence, local police departments, and federal immigration authorities. With a staff of 179,241, the DHS was allocated a first-year budget of $30 billion in 2003. Big and small private corporations competed for lucrative state contracts by providing new surveillance commodities, which were justified as necessary counterterrorism instruments.[45]

Eventually, even poor whites became a target market to feed the demands of the prison-industrial complex. Between 1999 and 2005 the rate of incarcerating white people for drug offenses in state prisons increased by 42.6 percent and the rate of incarcerating Black people for these same offenses decreased by 26.1 percent.[46] This suggests that the effects of military carcerality do not necessarily spare those who—because of their racial, cultural, or economic dominance—assumed that they would evade state punishment and containment.

The definition of persecutory enemies, particularly when articulated through color-blind frames of law and order, has the ability to change in order to target new populations. Under this system, racial privilege does not necessarily secure state protection.

THE EXCEPTIONALIST EMOTIONAL ECONOMIES
OF U.S. MILITARISM

It is worth remembering that U.S.-based racial justice and feminist movements did not wage their challenges to racial capitalism and patriarchy solely on domestic terrains. Rather, organizing against the Vietnam War, winning decolonization movements through pan-African alliances, and building third world liberation fronts against capitalism and imperialism also challenged the hegemony of white patriarchal supremacy globally.[47] The U.S. state sought to neutralize the reach of the crises produced by these international solidarity movements by criminalizing foreign as well as domestic enemies. As Ruth Wilson Gilmore argues:

The more that militant anti-capitalism and international solidarity became everyday features of U.S. anti-racist activism, the more vehemently the state and its avatars responded by, as Allen Feldman puts it, "individualizing disorder" into singular instances of criminality, that could then be solved via arrest or state-sanctioned killings rather than fundamental social change.[48]

If domestic enemies were dominantly associated with impoverished people of color in the United States, foreign enemies were identified in the bodies and demands of anticapitalist and anti-imperialist resistance movements from Mexico City to Paris. Such organized resistance elevated anxieties and fears over communism to new levels, the groundwork for which had been laid by McCarthyism and J. Edgar Hoover's campaigns to remove and neutralize radical activists suspected of having communist ties.[49] If law and order and Black and Latino/a urban criminality created the domestic crises that the state purported to police, communism created the cold war crisis that the U.S. state purported to police internationally. Moreover, it permitted what Gilmore describes as the transformation of the Pentagon "from a periodically expanded and contracted Department of War to the largest and most costly bureaucracy of the federal government," in charge of sustaining a "permanent warfare apparatus."[50] The positioning of Russia as archenemy number 1, along with its communist and socialist allies, justified a massive expansion of U.S. militarism in the aftermath of World War II through the cold war.

The state recruited both liberal and conservative publics to concede to this expansion by deploying the powerful ideological fantasy of U.S. exceptionalism. Donald Pease describes the fantasy of U.S. exceptionalism as a "complex assemblage of theological and secular assumptions out of which Americans have developed the lasting belief in America as the fulfillment of the national ideal to which other nations should aspire."[51] Although there is a lot of variation in the content of this exceptionalism, its function as an ideological fantasy is to secure public consent for extralegal U.S. state practices, or exceptions. That is, the ideological fantasy allows the U.S. state to transgress the laws it purportedly claims to normally uphold for the nation's greater good. The fantasy of U.S. exceptionalism allows U.S. citizens not only to misrepresent their history through romanticized grand narratives of liberal democracy and progress but also to incorporate its violent and discriminatory "states of exception" as acceptable and necessary.[52]

According to Pease, the fantasy of U.S. exceptionalism worked so well for so long because the modern state enlists its citizens to identify with public law as a kind of superego, or ultimate paternal authority.[53] The state's imposition of law establishes the limits of acceptable behavior for its citizens, hence acting as a disciplinary mechanism. In establishing limits, however, the law simultaneously creates the illicit desire to transgress the law. This illicit desire is tied to the enjoyments or pleasures of transgressing.[54] The enjoyment of transgressing the law is particularly pronounced if the transgressor does not suffer the consequences or is not punished; that is, the transgressor gets away with the crime. In order to avoid the state's punishment, one way in which publics can experience the illicit enjoyment of transgressing is by identifying with the state's own ability to transgress. By identifying with the state's sovereign power, individuals can experience a kind of vicarious derivation of illicit enjoyment by imagining themselves as the agents of the state's transgressions.[55]

The fall of communism in the late 1980s and the end of the cold war produced a crisis in the ideological fantasy of U.S. exceptionalism through which public consent for post–World War II American militarism and imperialism had dominantly been secured. Gradually, the new foreign archenemy of the United States coalesced under the rubric of terrorism, a term that in the post–9/11 landscape became virtually synonymous with "Arabs" and "Islam." The ideological fantasy of the new American exceptionalism and its affective economies reorganized U.S. public desires to align with remarkable military expansion in order to placate socially shared fears of Arab and Muslim persecutory enemies intent on undermining U.S. national sovereignty, economic hegemony, and religious and cultural values.

The Shared Affective Structures of Islamophobia and Islamophilia

The construction of Arab terrorism as a new foreign archenemy did not spring out of the blue; its historical precedents in Europe date back to the ninth century,[56] but it also evolved in post–World War II America as the nation escalated its economic interests in the Middle East. These U.S. interests developed in tandem with the dissemination of orientalist political discourses. As Edward Said demonstrates, orientalism encompasses the discourses, myths, signs, and ideas that persistently depict the Orient as undeveloped, inferior, incapable of defining itself, and ultimately something to be feared and controlled.[57] Said notes that American orientalist political discourses portray the Arab as a negative value, not only because of his anti-Zionism but also because of his status as an oil supplier to the West—a status that keeps the developed, democratic world permanently threatened.[58] Meanwhile, a remarkably narrow definition of Islam as a religion that is antihuman, incapable of evolution, and fundamentally authoritarian often serves as the explanation for Arab Muslim extremism. Indeed, the term *Arab Muslim* has "so strangely abstract and diminished a meaning"[59] in the U.S. context that its use tends to convey the central object of U.S. ideological fantasies of exceptionalism rather than a complex denotation used by people who consider themselves Arab and/or Muslim. I note that my analysis focuses on American fantasy constructions of Arab Muslims as signifiers of foreign persecutory enemies, not Arab and/or Muslim people per se.

At the heart of the American orientalist discourses on Arabs, Said claims, are two general themes: "number and generative power. . . . Almost without exception, every contemporary work of Orientalist scholarship (especially in the social sciences) has a great deal to say about the [Arab] family, its male-dominated structure and its all-pervasive influence in [Arab] society."[60] Said notes a silent yet consistently invoked implication in the coupling of Arab male sexual prowess and the *lack* of modern achievement. The argumentative pattern unfolds as follows: (1) The Orientalist recognizes the power of the traditional family in the Arab world; (2) he remarks on the weakness and irrationality of the Arab mind; (3) he declares the Arab's need for a Western hero who will guide the Arab world into modernity; (4) he implies that the panacea of modernization will remedy the failures of the Arab family as an institution, particularly the failures of its premodern and regressive patriarchal structures.

The first silent implication in the logic of these orientalist narratives is that the source of power in Arab societies (because they purportedly lack technological, rational, and cultural achievements) is fundamentally male, sexual, and biological. The orientalist discourse implies that "what is left to the Arab after all is said and done is an undifferentiated sexual drive. . . . The Arab produces himself, endlessly, sexually, and little else."[61] In other words, the Arab man is impotent when it comes to producing structures that will raise the Arab world out of the realm of biological reproduction (animality) into the realm of civilization. Hence, Arab society at large is generally understood as a derivative of Arab male sexuality. But as Said notes, "The absolutely inviolable taboo in Orientalist discourse is that that very [male] sexuality must never be taken seriously."[62] Hence the potency of Arab male sexuality (reduced to the biological) must be disavowed in orientalist political discourses in order to construct the Arab world's need for Western paternalism. This paternalism, as we will see, serves as the ideological backbone of U.S. imperialist occupation and economic investment in the Middle East.

The second silent implication is that Arab women are not subjects in this contest between the United States and the Arab world. The subject of orientalist political discourses is invariably male. As I elaborate in Chapter 2, orientalist constructions of Arab women and Arab women's sexuality function as objects of exchange in the contest for patriarchal power between the imperialist subject (figured as the United States) and the subjects of imperialism (figured as Arabs in the Middle East). Western feminists have invested heavily in their own projections of Arab woman as beings that need to be rescued from patriarchal domination, in effect, unwittingly complying with a paternalistic imperialist logic.[63] This is not to say that violence against women in the Middle East, as much as other global locales, is not a regular feature. It is to say that this construction of Arab women has much more to do with the affective investments of Western women, who gain their sense of worth and redeemable value as caring helpers. As such, they need such victimized Arab women to reproduce their own sense of purpose and meaning.

U.S. political discourses have so consistently fused Arabs with extremist terrorism and reductive notions of Islam that these terms often have the effect of triggering phobic reflexes in Americans. But the phenomenon of Islamophobia created a paradox in U.S. political discourses. On the one hand, anti-Arab Muslim sentiment worked well to justify military expansion to combat America's new foreign archenemy, Arab terrorism. On the other hand, such Islamophobia made it increasingly difficult to uphold the narrative of U.S. democracy, multicultural tolerance, and religious freedom. These values were absolutely critical to reproducing the affective economies that sustained people's investments and beliefs to U.S. exceptionalism. Without the feeling that the United States was ultimately doing something good—spreading democracy, establishing tolerance in extremist locales, and so on—the ideological fantasy of exceptionalism would reveal itself as a concealment for imperialist invasion and racial oppression. To reconcile these paradoxes and secure the feelings that Americans were ultimately democratic people who had to, at times, undertake necessary evils, political discourses made strict distinctions between good Muslims and bad Muslims. As Andrew Shryock has argued:

The exemplary Muslim citizen, member of the tolerant and inclusive (Western) society, has his equivalent in the modern Muslim-majority state, member of a tolerant and inclusive (Western-dominated) family of nations. Lurking behind this formula, thwarting and distorting it, is the "deal breaker": the Muslim radical, the extremist, the terrorist, or, just as problematic, the Muslim person or Muslim-majority state that does not want to be incorporated on those terms.[64]

This distinction has long historical precedents but was specifically disseminated in the aftermath of September 11, 2001. The political agenda of defeating Islamophobia as a way to uphold the image of U.S. exceptionalist democracy and religious tolerance was immediately advanced by George W. Bush in the aftermath of the attacks on the World Trade Center and the Pentagon. In his September 17, 2001, speech at the Islamic Center in Washington, D.C., President Bush declared, "These acts of violence against innocents violate the fundamental tenets of the Islamic faith. . . . The face of terror is not the true faith of Islam. That's not what Islam is all about. Islam is peace. These terrorists don't represent peace."[65] What Shryock calls Islamophilia, or affection for Islam and Muslims as a symbol of racial and religious tolerance, is strikingly similar in structure to Islamophobia. The problem with Islamophobia, Shryock argues, does not lie in pointing out the "empirical presence or absence" of Muslims who may in fact practice or advocate violence, oppress women, hate Jews, and so on. Rather, the key danger of Islamophobia lies in its "essentializing and universalizing quality" and its "categorical stigmatization" of all Arab Muslims under a rubric of naturalized or inherent sameness.[66] Similarly, Islamophilia has the tendency to impose character traits constitutive of the good Muslim that also disregard complexities and contradictions, imposing a perfect sameness between the good Muslim and the values of the liberal democratic state.[67]

If the proposed corrective to Islamophobia in the United States is Islamophilia for good Muslims, we still find ourselves in ideological fantasy territory. Both good and bad constructions of Arab Muslims function to enable different affective enjoyments tied to American national identity and have little to do with Arab and Muslim people themselves. Islamophobia allows certain constituents to feel the enjoyments of punishing bad Muslims for traversing on national sanctity. Islamophilia allows other constituents to gain their sense of moral righteousness by tolerating Muslims who share their values. To confirm such acts of goodness, tolerant and exceptionalist Americans focus on saving women from the claws of Arab hyperpatriarchal extremism or justify U.S. occupations in the Middle East in order to save good Muslims from the hooks of religious fanaticism. Islamophilia also enables certain U.S. publics to reject Americans who are Islamophobic, claiming that they are not the authentic representatives of their nation. However, both Islamophobia and Islamophilia conceal that only those who presume to possess the nation feel entitled to dictate how Muslims should be positioned in it. In other words, implied in the affective politics of how Americans should treat Muslims and Arabs is a presumption of dominance. Specifically, constituents who assume a high degree of national belonging (e.g., white Americans) presume themselves to be what Ghassan Hage calls the "spatial managers of the nation."[68] The process of deciding whether to tolerate or eliminate Muslims suggests not only a struggle about how to order those deemed outsiders but also a struggle over who has the right to spatialize people and in what manner.

Most U.S. constituents relinquished the authority to move Arab and Muslim bodies within and beyond national borders to U.S. immigration and military agents. Without the mutually reinforcing emotional economies attached to expressions of Islamophobia and Islamophilia, the United States would not have been able to sustain the contradictions suggested by proliferating conquest missions and its self-image as a fair, just, and exceptionalist democracy. Without this paradox the numerous proxy wars in Asia, Africa, and Central America that the United States fought throughout the cold war, U.S. involvement in Afghanistan to oppose the Soviet Union, U.S. support of Iraq against Iranian nationalism, and U.S. wars of open aggression would have been reconfigured as authoritarian imperialism.[69]

Those who strongly believe that the U.S. state will fail to effectively safeguard their lives against Arab terrorism tend to take matters into their own hands. As Hage argues, those who engage in personal acts of violence feel that they have lost their privileged relationship to state power and, by extension, that the coordinates through which they secure their belonging are under threat.[70] Sensing that their cultural, political, and racial power is in decline and that the state is not doing enough to preserve the order that grants them these powers, these individuals give in to the excesses of interpersonal violence and vigilantism.

You Too Can Be an Appendage to the State!

Said argues that classical imperial hegemony has always been characterized by the twinning of power (derived through direct dominance) and legitimacy (produced in the cultural sphere). What differs in this era of American hegemony "is the quantum leap in the reach of cultural authority, thanks in large measure to the unprecedented growth in the apparatus for the diffusion and control of information."[71] Televisual news media and films are central apparatuses for the circulation, production, and consumption of the ideas and images associated with Arab terrorism. American films have historically portrayed the Arab man as sadistic, deceitful, and dishonest: a slave trader, camel driver, or moneychanger. The Arab woman's veiled body has been simultaneously eroticized and victimized to enable the heroics of the Western white man and the white Western feminist as rescuers.[72] Such historical narratives established orientalist tropes whose function was to produce and validate a Western civilized identity.

However, some significant shifts took place in the emotional economies cultivated by post–civil rights televisual and filmic representations.

The 1980s began with one of the most widely covered stories in television
history: the Iran hostage crisis, which lasted for 444 days. Nightly television reports of Americans being held by Iranian militants in Tehran shaped and oriented
the U.S. public's imagination toward new state agendas. Symbolizing this new
orientation, President Reagan declared in his inaugural address that "'terrorism'
would replace 'human rights' as the nation's primary foreign policy concern."[73]
The hostage crisis also attached new meanings, associations, and symbols to the
notion of terrorism. As Melani McAlister argues, "These [media] accounts brought
Americans, rather than Israelis, into the primary position as victims—and eventually fighters against—terrorism."[74] Reflecting on the gendered significance of
the Iranian hostage crisis, McAlister argues that media accounts associated the
hostage's families with the private sphere of the American family—a civilian,
feminized sphere that was supposed to be off limits to public and masculinized
militant invasion. The hostage takers were therefore understood to be staging
an attack on the privacy and feminized innocence of U.S. families. As terrorists,
they were transgressing the terms of legitimate warfare, refusing to stay within the
military theater established by official state agendas. Rather than understanding
the hostage crisis within the contested and conflicted history of U.S.-Iranian relations, the hostage takers' illegitimate invasion was attributed to "militant Islam"
as a "single, unchanging cultural proclivity to mix faith with politics, and to express both through violence."[75] Positioning U.S. families as victims was central
to engendering emotional economies that sought to recuperate dominance and
reestablish protection. The U.S. state was figured as the patriarchal protector of
these feminized family spaces, and its weapons were deemed necessary appendages to secure such safety.

The affective frames that relayed the Iran hostage crisis to U.S. families were
reinforced through a new action film genre focused on hostage rescue operations.
Feminized victims in these films encouraged audiences to develop emotional
attachments to masculinized state protection. By reflecting and reproducing
collective anxieties about terrorist threats to U.S. private civilians, these action
films displayed spectacular military rescue and defeat operations as antidotes
to the threats. Films such as *Iron Eagle* (1986), *The Delta Force* (1986), *Rambo*
and its two sequels (1982, 1985, 1988), and *Die Hard* (1988) represented terrorist

enemies from various geographies while foregrounding heroes from the U.S. Army, the Navy Seals, the CIA, the FBI, or the police. As McAlister argues, this film genre posits various plotlines but always centers the "construction of the American family as that which must be saved."[76] As films like *Not Without My Daughter* (1991) seemed to be saying, "The United States' interventionism abroad was justified because this world of personal feeling and domestic ties was threatened from the outside. State-sponsored activities like counterterrorism or military force could be undertaken for the sake of something identified as private—love, the family, revenge."[77]

This film genre shifted in its casting choices from the 1980s to the 1990s. Later films, such as *Navy Seals* (1990), *The Long Kiss Goodnight* (1996), *The Siege* (1998), *Three Kings* (1999), and *Rules of Engagement* (2000), featured more actors of color and (mostly white) women in the roles of U.S. state agents. These Black, Latino, Arab American, and female characters were charged not only with protecting the American family and nation but also with upholding the values that made the U.S. exceptional: its adherence to constitutional and international laws, its commitment to due process, and its refusal to stoop to illegal tactics such as torture. Black, Latino, Arab American, and female state agents were charged with upholding these democratic principles even though it sometimes meant acting against renegade U.S. state agents who found it acceptable to rule by exception rather than law.

Such representational media shifts were significant for two primary reasons. First, representations of Black, Latino/a, and Arab American actors as agents of the U.S. state helped to create ideological and emotional pathways through which to disavow accusations of anti-Arab racism and xenophobia. How could the U.S. state be perpetuating anti-Arab racism when Black, Latino, and Arab Americans were patriotically defending the American family and nation from terrorist threats? This color-blind and racially coded framing allowed U.S. audiences to be drawn into the pleasurable bonds forged when directing aggression against a common Arab terrorist enemy, even if their racial experiences within the United States were widely divergent. Multiracial representations of U.S. military agents reassured Americans that their state was not engaged in morally delegitimized imperialist invasions predicated on white patriarchal Western supremacy.

Furthermore, such multiracial and multigender representations of U.S. state agents encouraged audiences who were historically disidentified with

U.S. nationalism to identify with the state's military and foreign policy agenda. Giving visibility to Black, Latino, Arab American, and female characters as heroes defending democracy and the American family created identification channels that encouraged Black, Latino, Arab American, and female audiences to feel the affective rewards of U.S. belonging, feelings from which they had been historically excluded by white patriarchal supremacy. Of course, this nationalist bond was itself predicated on preserving affective investments in heterosexual patriarchy. Women represented as state agents had to exhibit the hypermasculine bravado normalized by militarism, and queer state agents were representationally absent. The recruitment of audiences of color (especially men of color) to identify with the U.S. state's military agenda was predicated in part on the pleasures of seeing Black, Latino, and Arab American characters in heroic patriarchal roles. Such characterizations had been denied to men of color throughout Hollywood film history, and the affective enjoyment of seeing themselves in patriarchal positions of power did much to forge the bonds constitutive of U.S. patriotism, nationalism, and exceptionalism.

The fantasy of U.S. exceptionalism, however, required a particular form of political amnesia. Not only did it require people of color to dissociate domestic racial antagonisms (e.g., the 1992 Los Angeles riots) from international ones (e.g., the 1992 Desert Storm Operation in Iraq), but it also required divorcing the U.S. state's targeting of impoverished Black and Latino people through the war on drugs from the U.S. state's targeting of Arabs, Arab Americans, and Muslims at home and abroad through the war on terror. As Michael Rogin argues, "The concept of political amnesia points to a cultural structure of motivated disavowal."[78] In other words, investing in the fantasy of U.S. exceptionalism through cultural apparatuses required disavowing the connections between domestic racism perpetuated through law and order state agendas and international racism deployed through warfare and foreign policy.

Institutional Policies and Practices

The ideological fantasy of U.S. exceptionalism and the emotional economies that increasingly desired the punishment and elimination of terrorists legitimated enormous shifts in foreign policy and military tactics during the cold war and post–cold war period. As Mahmood Mamdani argues, one tactic that emerged out of the military losses in Vietnam was to finance covert proxy wars in order to prevent communist alliances between the Soviet Union and emergent nations in Africa, Asia, Latin America, and South America. The CIA supervised low-intensity conflicts that "aimed to undermine revolutionary governments, not just movements."[79] In his 1985 State of the Union address, President Reagan boldly pledged to assist anticommunist forces fighting pro-Soviet governments "on every continent, from Afghanistan to Nicaragua."[80] Such covert, proxy low-intensity conflicts became the main U.S. military strategy in the third world and Central America throughout the cold war era.

Similar tactics would be implemented in the Middle East. Under the Reagan and Bush administrations of the 1980s and early 1990s, the United States would conduct a proxy war in Afghanistan against the Soviet Union (1979–1989), intervene in Lebanon (1981–1983), provide logistical and military support for Iraq in the Iran-Iraq war (1980–1983), covertly sell arms to Iran in the same Iran-Iraq war (the Iran-Contra deal of 1983–1985), bomb Libya (1986), and expand arms sales to Saudi Arabia (1985–1988).

The end of the cold war, along with a heightened focus on defending U.S. economic interests in the Middle East, did not put an end to U.S. support for covert proxy wars and interventions. However, the beginning of the Gulf War in 1991 signaled a shift in foreign policy and military tactics toward a resurgence of open aggression. Through a barrage of air strikes televised for U.S. audiences in ways that were akin to video games, the Gulf War signaled a tactical shift toward a form of U.S. militarism that was concurrently covert, spectacular, offensive, preemptive, and perpetual. As McAlister argues, the first Gulf War finally allowed the United States to move beyond the stigmas of Vietnam, signifying the rise of a new world order led by a multicultural and multiracial army. Such offensive tactics were carried out by U.S. troops that included African Americans and increasingly Latino/as as their frontline soldiers. Meanwhile, Black military leader Colin Powell "served as a dignified and highly visible leader whose no-nonsense approach to winning the war made him an apt symbol of both multiculturalism at home and the New World Order abroad."[81]

This rising public support for the new American militarism paved the way for what would become the endless war on terror declared by George W. Bush in the aftermath of September 11, 2001. The wars in Iraq and Afghanistan along with countless private and covert operations have widened the web of militarism while rapidly eroding the frameworks of international and domestic laws on surveillance, racial profiling, indefinite detention, due process, and human rights. Defense spending since 2001 has increased dramatically. According to reports by the Center for Arms Control and Non-Proliferation, the total defense budget increased by 67 percent between 2001 and 2011, from $432 billion to $720 billion in inflation-adjusted dollars. Over the same decade, the Pentagon's base budget, which does not include war and nuclear weapons funding, has increased by 38 percent, from $390 billion to $540 billion.[82] By 2012, U.S. federal spending on the wars in Iraq and Afghanistan was estimated to have reached $1.4 trillion.[83]

The emotional economies that shaped how people inhabited the ideological fantasies of domestic law and order and international U.S. exceptionalism offered affective rewards, psychological compensations, and guilty pleasures. By projecting real and imagined losses onto criminals and terrorists, U.S. majorities aligned their hopes and desires with the state's agenda, encouraging more punishment, more surveillance, more containment, and more militarism. Predictably, despite an unprecedented proliferation of carceral spaces and military operations, Americans continue to feel insecure, anxious, and afraid. It seems that, contrary to their hopes, military-carceral expansion has only exacerbated societal instability, compounding it with economic decline as a result of the now astronomical spending budgets of corrections, criminal justice courts, immigrant detention, deportations, and military defense. Until public affective structures and identification patterns construct security through frameworks that do not require others' denigration or destruction, it seems that the perpetual insecurities of the dominant, and their yearnings to preserve power, will continue to proliferate alienation and violence as normative states.

CHAPTER I

NEW YORK, NEW YORK: THE RAGING EMOTIONS OF WHITE POLICE BRUTALITY

On the fateful August 9, 1997, evening that Haitian immigrant Abner Louima suffered through the sadistic police brutality of the New York Police Department (NYPD), he had gone to see a popular Haitian band play at a club in East Flatbush. Club Rendez-Vous, located on Flatbush between Farragut and Glenwood, was one of the few places to go see live Haitian compas music. The Brooklyn neighborhood is home to one of the largest concentration of Haitians in the United States. The first Haitian newspaper in the United States, *Haiti Observateur*, was established here in 1971.[1] Haitian restaurants infuse the air with the aroma of fried plantains and pork while animated discussions of politics are heard in Creole and English. Radio Soleil d'Haiti broadcasts news to Haitians from their studio at Nostrand Avenue and Tilden.[2]

By the time Louima immigrated to the United States in 1991, several generations of Haitians had settled in New York City. Seeking reprieve from the political repression and violence of President François "Papa Doc" Duvalier's administration, Haitians used the family reunification pathways offered by the 1965 Immigration Act to bring their relatives to the United States in the late 1960s and 1970s. As human rights violations, poverty, and oppression intensified after Duvalier's son, Jean-Claude "Baby Doc" Duvalier, took power in 1971, people left Haiti using increasingly desperate measures. The arrival of boatloads of undocumented Haitians on the shores of the United States created a refugee crisis throughout the 1980s and early 1990s. Unlike their Cuban counterparts, Haitian requests for political asylum were met with the highest rejection rate of any immigrant group. The refugees were routinely detained and deported by immigration authorities.

The U.S. rejection of Haitians at the end of the twentieth century has a long historical precedent. After enslaved people on the island of Santo Domingo (presently the Dominican Republic and Haiti) successfully overthrew slavery and established a Black republic in 1804, governmental and cultural depictions passionately warned Americans against the menacing ills of Haitian "contamination." At a time when slavery in the United States was justified through popular beliefs in Anglo-Saxon biological superiority, emancipated Black Haitians posed a remarkable threat to its neighboring nation. Their successful slave revolt irrevocably disputed ideologies of Black inferiority and severely ruptured the European worldview that could hardly fathom the possibility of a Black republic. To compensate for these incongruences in the European colonial imagination, the United States constructed Haitians as menacing threats. Officials warned of Haitian "contagion," projecting already existing fears of interracial mixing, or miscegenation, onto their newly emancipated neighbors. They warned that miscegenation would result in the white race's biological degeneracy.[3] They implied that interracial sexual and social relations (particularly marriage) would grant Black people access to property controlled by whites—a threat that would undo the social and economic order of the United States. Taking these threats as real and possible, France and the United States punished Haiti by preventing the island's participation in international trade economies throughout the nineteenth and twentieth centuries. In doing so, the imperial nations essentially guaranteed the Haitian people's impoverishment as a vengeful payback for daring to challenge European hegemony.

Almost 200 years later, U.S. governmental institutions, policies, and media discourses still considered Haitians threatening. Americans were warned that Haitians would infect them with disease, take their jobs, and deplete their social welfare resources. As a result of such ominous projections, among those seeking asylum in the United States, Haitians became the only national group required to take HIV tests. In 1983 Haitians were designated to belong to what the Centers for Disease Control and Prevention (CDC) called the Four H Club (homosexuals, hemophiliacs, heroin users, and Haitians). In 1990 the Food and Drug Administration (FDA) prohibited Haitians from donating blood. A *New York Times* editorial maintained that the "priority" of keeping blood donations "untainted" ranked higher than preventing racial discrimination.[4]

After being categorized as a high-risk group by the CDC and the FDA, Haitians living in the United States faced discrimination, which included losing work, being evicted, and experiencing racially motivated attacks. The George H. W. Bush and Bill Clinton administrations also fueled anti-Haitian sentiments when they instigated forced repatriations in 1991–1992 and 1994 on the basis that "boat people" were economic rather than political refugees. Rising fears over what was termed the Haitian stampede similarly justified the forced removal of Haitian refugees placed in custody at Guantánamo in March 1993.[5]

Defiant of such stigmatizations, Haitians engaged in individual, collective, and political modes of resistance. Through public protests, cultural performances, religious organizations, and *voudou* rituals, Haitians consistently contested the U.S. government's derogatory and demeaning policies. In response to the FDA's stigmatization of Haitian blood, on April 21, 1990, 50,000 demonstrators marched across the Brooklyn Bridge, holding signs that proclaimed, "We're Proud of Our Blood." After similar demonstrations in several cities, including a march in Washington, D.C., from the Capitol steps to the FDA's headquarters, the U.S. government's ban on Haitian blood was rescinded in January 1991.[6]

Cultural practices, music, and Afro-Christian religious rituals have been central to the development of Haitian collective resistance and democracy. Rara street festivals in Haiti bring rural peasant classes and the urban poor together at crossroads, bridges, and cemeteries to perform rituals for Afro-Haitian deities. The cast of characters who have a hand in the six-week-long event includes the captains, priests, queens, sorcerers, musicians, and armies of Rara members as well as the spirits of Afro-Haitian religion, the *zonbi* (recently dead), Jesus, Judas, and Jews.[7] The festivals allow everyday people to bring their views on politics to public spaces.

The Haitian diaspora has recreated aspects of these musical and religious rituals in the United States. After the democratically elected president Jean-Bertrand Aristide was ousted by a military coup in 1991, Rara musicians and their followers played for weeks at the United Nations and in rallies on Capitol

Hill, protesting the attack on Haitian democracy.[8] Rara bands gather regularly in Brooklyn's Prospect Park, using communally produced music and noncommercial performances to call for democracy in Haiti and justice in the United States.[9] They create symbolic forms of opposition to oppressions, building Haitian resilience, survival, and collective solidarity.

When Louima's story of police brutality spread, Rara bands gathered in Prospect Park to stage performances that contested the violence of the NYPD against Haitians and other Black people. Their rituals challenged logics that justified police violence and harassment against Black people in general and Haitians in particular. In doing so, Rara participants in Prospect Park reclaimed spaces, places, and politics in order to assert the dignity and value of Haitian immigrants and other oppressed communities.

GIULIANI TIME

New York City's municipal policies and practices grew increasingly hostile toward people of color, poor people, and Haitian immigrants in the 1990s. Residents experienced significant shifts in policing once Mayor Rudolph Giuliani was elected in 1994. Giuliani largely reversed the governing approaches favored by David Dinkins, an African American mayor who had openly criticized police violence and instituted policies that demanded greater accountability. Only a few months into his term, Giuliani issued Police Strategy No. 5, a policy "dedicated to 'reclaiming the public spaces of New York.'"[10] This policy was established when New York City was experiencing a crumbling urban landscape, abandoned buildings, and a reduction in housing, education, and health care services. Hundreds of millions of dollars in tax-abatement bribes were given to multinational corporations to move into the city or to stay. Everyday workers, on the other hand, confronted soaring unemployment rates up to 10 percent. As the city's housing became less affordable and work less available, public fears over losses in property, jobs, and security increased.[11]

Giuliani skillfully used such social anxieties to pass increasingly punitive policing measures that protected the property interests of the wealthiest neighborhoods and corporations while further disenfranchising the most impoverished populations. Giuliani identified "homeless people, panhandlers, prostitutes, squeegee cleaners, squatters, graffiti artists, 'reckless bicyclists,' and unruly youth as the major enemies of public order and decency, the culprits of urban decline generating widespread fear."[12] The cleanup of the city was to be accomplished by the police, who were encouraged to use proactive and zero tolerance methods. Constraints on police power were dismantled for the sake of reestablishing law and order. Rather than working to create opportunities for the city's most vulnerable populations, Giuliani redefined New York City residents' freedom to be "about the willingness of every single human being to cede to lawful authority a great deal of discretion about what you do."[13]

Giuliani's rhetoric of law and order was coded to suggest that the presence of the culprits posed a threat to commodified or commodifiable property. To justify the culprits' removal, Giuliani and the police had to criminalize and refigure them literally as assaults on public space. As the culprits were criminalized, they became threats to those who had the power to commodify and control public space. The presence of the impoverished people, not their actions, was redefined as criminal. As one of Giuliani's aides argued, "I regard someone approaching someone else, putting them in fear of bodily harm as a criminal act. . . . The police will again be given discretion, trained properly, commanded properly, managed properly to stop that kind of behavior."[14] In embodying a threat to public space, the culprits were systematically removed from what were deemed clean streets but permitted to stay in what the NYPD called dirty blocks or streets—spaces where illicit activities were purposely overlooked by the police. "The analogy is clear: the clean street, the clean body and body politic, clean white public space."[15] The confluence of whiteness, wealth, and commodifiable space defined law and order, whereas the presence of people of color, poor people, and illegitimate immigrants defined criminality.

New York's homeless population (estimated at 100,000 in the 1990s) was cleared out in order to demarcate Manhattan as an attractive location for multibillion-dollar corporations such as Disney. The aggressive Welfare to Work Program cut off thousands of public assistance recipients. Between 1995 and 1998, 363,000 people were taken off the city's welfare roles; spending for child welfare was especially targeted, and recipients could receive checks only if they performed work, usually for the city government. The city replaced thousands of full-time workers with workfare recipients, whose payments translated into below-minimum-wage levels.[16] In this general climate of dispelling populations through restructuring policies that favored the wealthy and big businesses, it was clear that the New York City police, the mayor, and those who supported the mayor's practices were set on applying various disciplinary mechanisms not only inside institutions such as prisons and asylums but also on the level of everyday life and civic space. As Allen Feldman argues:

This externalization of discipline can be measured in a wide variety of phenomena, including the development of what Mike Davis terms *scan-scapes* and *social control districts* and the emergence of the militarized, high technology office building and shopping mall and what are locally termed by the New York City police as *safety corridors*, which are, in effect, sites of police colonization in inner-city neighborhoods. Gounis also has noted the establishment of privatized and volunteer vigilante police forces that patrol such areas as Times Square, Grand Central Station, and the West Village.[17]

A flood of police officers were sent to East Harlem, Hunts Point in the Bronx, Maria Hernandez Park in Brooklyn, and Guy Brewer Boulevard in Queens to close down various public drug markets. These operations, unlike past selective raids and arrests in drug operations, involved complex mechanisms of spatial and bodily control: cordoned street sweeps by police working with the warrant squad to arbitrarily stop and check individuals; temporarily detaining and searching young males found congregating on the streets or gathering in fast-food places; road blocks and checkpoints to stop vehicles; extensive undercover bicycle patrols; huge numbers of police units pulled from throughout the city to make the theatrical surveillance of the state perfectly clear.[18]

This omnipresent surveillance of poor people and of communities of color endorsed by Giuliani's rhetoric of clean public space affected every aspect of daily life for those whose racial identities or class status marked them as assaults. Like African Americans, Haitians and other Black immigrants were constantly imagined as criminals and often presumed as such by the police. Haitian bodies were part of a semiotics that identified them as threatening people who were intent on taking over public spaces presumed to belong to white people and/or American citizens. A 28-year-old Guyanese musician keenly summarized such normalized policing projections as follows:

I am so tired of riding the train, walking down the street, or just standing still, and if cops are around, they will always ask me what I'm doing . . . like I'm bothering them. I would ask them why they are harassing me, but I know that they need very little motivation to shoot me. Giuliani has showed us over and over again that police have the right to shoot black men in open daylight for no reason and that they can get away with it.[19]

These shifts in the political geography of New York City had significant effects on the ways that police officers performed their duties and the ways that they understood the limits of their power. Certainly, not all police officers used Giuliani's zero tolerance methods as an excuse to abuse their authority. But such punitive methods encouraged NYPD officers to feel as though their power should not be challenged. Moreover, such methods fostered a police culture that was increasingly unaccountable to people's integrity and dignity. As Louima recalled, one of the police officers who brutalized him at the 70th Precinct declared, "It's Giuliani time, not Dinkins time."[20]

THE CASE THAT SHOOK THE CITY

Louima and his cousin, Jay Nicholas, had just seen King Kino and the Phantoms play at Club Rendez-Vous.[21] Louima had seen the Phantoms numerous times, and the compas band members knew him by name.[22] The band was important to the Haitian community, particularly following the 1992 release of their song "Cowboy." The song's unabashed critique of right-wing paramilitary troops in Haiti became widely popular, and eventually Kino was forced into exile in the United States. When Kino returned to Haiti in 1993, the Phantoms played to an audience of 60,000 Haitians, and the audience collectively sang "Cowboy" with a little help from its creator.[23] That night, Haitians in Flatbush welcomed the Phantoms, participating in a long collective tradition that testified to Haitian people's resistance to oppression through music.

Louima and Nicholas were about to go home when a fight broke out between two women. Louima and Nicholas got out of their car to see what was going on. As more people spilled out in front of the club, the police arrived. Among the police officers who came to the scene were Officers Thomas Bruder, Charles Schwarz, Eric Turetzky, Justin Volpe, and Thomas Wiese. The cops attempted to disperse the crowd using increasingly forceful tactics and demeaning words. "The party's over, clear the street, go the fuck home!" shouted one cop. Turetzky threatened to kick a pregnant woman in the stomach.[24] The Haitian crowd disobeyed and resisted. They talked back and some of them threw bottles. The crowd grew increasingly agitated, letting the police know that they would not tolerate being disrespected. By virtue of their numbers, Haitians dominated the space. A drunk Haitian man by the name of John Rejouis was verbally confronting Volpe, insisting he had rights. Attempting to prove his authority, Rejouis showed Volpe a badge, indicating that he was a New York City prison guard. In response, Volpe slapped his hand, knocking the badge and Rejouis to the ground. Seeing this exchange, Louima confronted Volpe regarding his treatment of Rejouis. Volpe began pushing Louima away, and tensions rose as Louima refused to budge. Louima was hit and knocked to the ground. Suddenly, Louima's cousin Nicholas sucker punched Volpe on the side of his head, knocking him to the ground. Nicholas took off running. By this time the crowd was shouting, "Fuck these cops!"[25] Police officers who saw Volpe on the ground began chasing Nicholas. Mistakenly thinking that Louima was the one who struck him and that Louima was the one who took off running, Volpe joined the chase.

Patrick Antoine, another Haitian immigrant, was walking in the neighborhood unaware of what was happening at Club Rendez-Vous. Coming up behind Antoine, Volpe yelled, "You fucking guy!" and hit him on the back of his head with a flashlight. As other officers caught up to Volpe, they started beating and kicking Antoine. The officers placed Antoine under arrest, charging him with felony assault, obstructing government administration, disorderly conduct, and resisting arrest.[26] As Volpe and Bruder took Antoine into their squad car, Officers Schwarz and Wiese announced over the police radio that they had in custody the guy who had sucker punched Volpe. Mistaking Louima for Nicholas, they had picked Louima up at Glenwood and Bedford.

Louima arrived at the 70th Precinct around 4 a.m. with a bruised and lacerated body. He had been beaten twice in the patrol car before arriving at the precinct. Schwarz and Wiese presented Louima to Sergeant Jeffrey Fallon at the front desk and began filling out paperwork. Volpe arrived at the precinct shortly after Schwarz and Wiese and saw Louima at the front desk. Furious over the night's events, Volpe walked to the juvenile questioning room, found a wooden broomstick, and cracked it in half over his knee. He placed the bottom of the stick behind a locker and placed the upper half behind the garbage can in the precinct bathroom.

A moment of planning and premeditation? Imagining—so far in fantasy only—what he would do with the upper half of the broomstick, Volpe asked Officer Mark Schofield, who was standing near the front desk, for a pair of gloves. Schofield offered Volpe a pair of leather gloves. At some point Volpe put the gloves on. The court's testimonial record states that as Louima was being processed at the front desk, "his pants and underwear fell to his ankles." However, Louima claimed in an August 14, 1997, interview that "the cops pulled down my pants in front of the desk sergeant. . . . They were grabbing my wallet. They found some money and took it out."[27] When Sergeant Fallon finished the processing, Volpe and another officer took Louima to the bathroom.[28] He had to shuffle because his pants and underwear were still around his ankles. Other officers complied with Volpe's wish to avenge the night's events.

"I kept screaming, 'Why? Why?'" said Louima. "All the cops heard me, but said nothing. What they said to me I'll never forget. In public, one says, 'You niggers have to learn how to respect police officers.'"[29] Once the bathroom door was closed, Volpe picked up the broken broomstick that he had hidden behind the garbage can and told Louima, "I'm going to do something to you. If you yell or make any noise, I'll kill you."[30] Volpe threw Louima to the ground with his head near a toilet bowl and kicked him in his naked groin. As Louima began screaming, Volpe put his foot over Louima's mouth. Volpe and the other officer punched him in the head and body. The accomplice grabbed Louima by the handcuffs and lifted him from the ground. Leather gloves on, Volpe forced the broken broomstick approximately six inches up Louima's rectum. The impact perforated Louima's colon and bladder. "When they pulled it out," Louima said, "it was covered with blood and feces."[31] The Memorandum and Order of *United States of America v. Justin Volpe* states that Volpe held the feces-covered stick in front of Louima's mouth and taunted him. Louima, however, remembered the feces-covered stick, which he believed was a toilet plunger, being rammed into his mouth. Louima's broken teeth bore witness without words.

Volpe slammed the stick against the wall, leaving traces of Louima's feces and blood. With Louima crying in pain, Volpe lifted him to his feet and took him to the same holding cell where Antoine was also being held. Before putting him in the cell, Volpe told Louima that if he told anybody what had happened, Volpe would kill him. Volpe returned the leather gloves he had borrowed to Officer Schofield, who protested that they were soiled. "So wash them off," said Volpe.[32] Schofield washed the gloves and put them on top of a locker to dry.

"I broke a man down," Volpe stated to other cops in the precinct. Taking Sergeant Kenneth Wernick to the bathroom, Volpe showed him the stick used in the sexual assault and declared, "I took a man down tonight." Then Volpe showed the stick to Officer Michael Schoer. Smelling the feces on the stick, Schoer asked, "What is that, dog shit?" "No," Volpe responded, "human shit." Finally, Volpe threw the broom handle into a trash can outside.[33]

Inside the holding cell, Antoine would later describe Louima as so badly beaten that he could not stand up. "He was in really bad shape. His pants were hanging. They even fell to his ankles. He couldn't stand. He looked cold. He kept holding his knees like he was cold."[34] Four hours later, an ambulance took Louima and Antoine to the hospital. The medics, who were required to have a police escort to proceed to the hospital, had been waiting for two hours. At the hospital the police officers told the emergency room doctors that Louima had been injured in a gay bar and found on the street.[35] Later, Louima would recall, "I kept saying, 'Please, God, don't let me die.' I was praying to protect my life because if I died, I didn't know who would take care of my children."[36]

THE PSYCHOSYMBOLIC PUNCH

The retelling of this story of racialized and sexualized violence raises grave questions. Rather than evoking indignation, repeating narratives of gendered racial violence might instead "immure us to pain by virtue of their familiarity . . . and especially because they reinforce the spectacular character of black suffering."[37] As Saidiya Hartman asks:

Are we witnesses who confirm the truth of what happened in the face of the world-destroying capacities of pain, the distortions of torture, the sheer unrepresentability of terror, and the repression of the dominant accounts? Or are we voyeurs fascinated with and repelled by exhibitions of terror and sufferance? What does the exposure of the violated body yield? . . . At issue here is the precariousness of empathy and the uncertain line between witness and spectator.[38]

By narrating Louima's torture, I am unable to avoid processes that potentially reinforce the spectacular nature of Black suffering. There is no guarantee that the retelling of this story will not trigger some people to engage in the guilty enjoyments of voyeuristic sadism or other emotional economies that justify Black people's violation. Yet the retelling can also engender emotional economies of outrage, indignation, and anger that can be used to create resistance.

Those who find such scenes of violence morally indefensible can become collective witnesses who seek redress, healing, and justice.

Significantly, Louima's courage to tell his story created the possibility for others to become ethical witnesses rather than indifferent spectators. Despite Volpe's death threats and other police officers' complicity in covering up the story, Louima began publicizing his story to journalist Mike McAlary of the *New York Daily News* only a couple of days after he was beaten. Louima's audacity and inability to stay silent ruptured structures of discourse and feeling that normalize voyeuristic consumption of violence against terrorized Black bodies. Speaking for himself, Louima refused to have his experience go unacknowledged. This was no easy task, particularly because his admission would have to include the sexual dimensions of the brutality. Louima's testimony was in many ways a continuation of the defiant acts begun at Club Rendez-Vous. Just as Louima had confronted Volpe for insulting Rejouis, he was now staging a massive attack on the NYPD's legitimacy in general and Volpe's authority in particular. After all, it was in some ways incomprehensible that Volpe and the other cops would react with this level of sadistic violence simply because a Haitian man punched a cop.

If we place the police violence within a larger historical context, we begin to see that the punch dealt by Louima's cousin was not the primary threat to Volpe and the other cops. What the cops could not integrate into their worldviews and structures of feeling was the fact that Haitians like Louima had dared to challenge their authority. Because the officers' authority was itself predicated on socially and legally sanctioned white male entitlements, the Haitians' defiance conjured long-established antagonisms between Black communities and white cops. In other words, the threat to the cops' physical safety was minuscule compared with the symbolic threat Haitians posed to American state authority when embodied and executed by white men. The scene at Club Rendez-Vous not only suggested that Haitians were willing to defy law and order agents but that they also would not permit white cops to do whatever they pleased in their neighborhoods. The cops, who had mostly grown up in the white suburbs of Staten Island and Nassau County, viewed the Haitian neighborhood through stereotypically racist projections of criminality and deviance.[39] Their last names—Volpe, Schwarz, Wiese, and Bruder—suggest that they were the descendants of Italian and German immigrants who had chosen the advantages of moving to homogeneous white suburban neighborhoods, spaces where property and social values depended on white people's dissociation and distance from people of color.[40]

Even if people are not consciously aware of it, a people's history lives in their embodied movements, modes of being, patterned responses, and value systems. The punch and the Haitian crowd's defiance were part of a long cumulative history of Haitian resistance to U.S. hegemony. As is well documented, the Haitian Revolution made Haiti the ultimate symbol of resistance in the cultural imaginaries of slave societies such as the United States.[41]News of the Haitian Revolution motivated the U.S. postmaster general to warn Georgia's senator in 1802 that allowing Blacks to be postal riders would breed slave revolts. By acquiring and spreading information, the postmaster cautioned that Blacks "will learn that a man's rights do not depend on his color."[42] Haiti's constitutional disintegration of racial hierarchies and categories threatened the very core of a U.S. society whose vicious maintenance of the color line was integral to preserving white supremacy.[43]

Throughout the nineteenth and twentieth centuries, the United States consistently intervened to keep Haitian people dependent and impoverished. Whether directly occupying Haiti (1915–1934), supporting François Duvalier's dictatorship (1957–1971), or helping overthrow the democratically elected government of Jean-Bertrand Aristide (1991–2004), the United States had consistently destroyed Haitian freedom dreams. In an unending dialectical struggle, Haitian cultures of resistance engendered emotional economies that defiantly opposed oppressive authorities at home and abroad. The grassroots Lavalas movement, which worked tirelessly to elect the Catholic priest Aristide as president and establish policies that benefited poor people in Haiti,[44] as much as the musical protests of Rara bands and followers created ideological disidentification with authoritarian oppression and emotional economies that struggled to align with justice.

The punch to Volpe, then, conjured these cumulative emotional economies of Haitian defiance. But the sucker punch also signified Haitians' symbolic affinity with American genealogies of resistance that challenged the legitimacy of law and order. Throughout American history, law and order campaigns have justified people of color's exclusion from accessing and owning property, prohibited them from voting, and prevented them from exercising basic rights. Law and order has more often than not been the government's code for protecting the interests and entitlements of white majorities. As such, the punch also dislodged the idea that law and order is really about everyone's protection, highlighting the ways people of color are rarely the subjects being protected.

It is as though—in a flash—the punch conjured the long history of struggle against the advantages and authority of white patriarchy and the haunting figures responsible for those uprisings. African fugitives from slave plantations were building maroon communities in Jamaica, the Guianas, Suriname, South Carolina, and Georgia.[45] An alliance among West Indians, Africans, Spanish, Irish, and Native Americans (the "outcasts of the nations of the earth"[46]) were plotting the 1741 New York conspiracy. Nat Turner was rounding up his troops for insurrection. The charismatic Jamaican Marcus Garvey was building a movement for Black political freedom. Ida B. Wells was demystifying the key motivations behind lynching and advocating self-defense.[47] Mamie Till was displaying Emmett Till's mutilated body. Rosa Parks was refusing to give up her seat. Fannie Lou Hamer was testifying on national television about being beaten. Puerto Ricans were building an independence movement against colonizing forces. Black Panther Party members were exercising their right to bear arms in self-defense. These interlocking signifiers testify to the presence of a genealogical legacy of resistance that also engenders affective value, motivating people and cultures who have been obstructed and challenged by white patriarchal power to stay the course.

Of course, I am not suggesting that the police officers thought consciously about historical resistance to white patriarchal power or about Haitian histories of defiance as they brutalized Louima. Rather, their bodies were attuned to responding in accordance with these histories. In the immediate moment the cops simply sought to recuperate their authority, express their vengeance, and reconstitute the psychic organization through which they understood themselves and the world. Each blow the police officers dealt to Antoine and Louima offered an emotional reward and psychic compensation for what the cops felt they had lost at the Club Rendez-Vous scene. But their acts and emotions followed well-established methods for asserting and recuperating white male police authority. Within the white patriarchal logics that Volpe embodied and enacted, any person who defied police authority deserved retaliation.

Importantly, the officers' psychological and emotional interests trumped all other reasonable considerations. The cops' desires to enact immediate punish-

ment and retribution took primacy over the possible long-term legal and monetary ramifications of their actions. Their actions suggest that recuperating what
W. E. B. DuBois called the "public and psychological wages of whiteness"[48] was
more important in that moment than the monetary, legal, or social losses they
might face later on.

UNPROTECTED BODIES

When Volpe came out of the precinct bathroom after raping and beating
Louima, he told his fellow officers, "I broke a man down. . . . I took a man
down tonight." Broke a man down into what? Into an animal? Into a slave?
Into a woman? Into a homosexual? To "break a man down" suggests a shattering
of his symbolic, psychological, and bodily integrity. The acts Volpe performed
to break down Louima followed scripts of sexualized racial violence that have
been repeated numerous times throughout U.S. history against Black people.
The sexual humiliation achieved Volpe's goal of retribution more effectively
than bodily brutality alone.

Volpe sought to feminize Louima for daring to consider himself equal to
Volpe as a man. Anal rape was a way to symbolically castrate Louima of his
manhood and reduce him to what heteropatriarchal societies consider the
naturally subordinate position of women or homosexuals. Forcing Louima to
swallow the phallic object with which he was raped allowed Volpe to regain the
white patriarchal dominance he had lost when he was punched to the ground.
Converting Louima into a feminized subordinate forced to figuratively suck his
dick gave Volpe the maniacal emotional thrill gained from possessing the power
to humiliate and denigrate. But it also allowed Volpe to reconfigure the rape
as something Louima wished. The sadistic sexual violence that forced Louima
to swallow the phallic object constructed "a vision of the castrated black man
as one actively seeking the pleasures of castration."[49] To disavow their perverse
violence, violators like Volpe often construct their victims as both desiring and
deserving of domination. Forcibly situated in a powerless feminized position,
Louima was terrorized into assuming the docile role he had originally refused
to take in relation to white police authority.

Understanding Volpe and the other cops' actions within a white supremacist legacy that regularly used sexual brutality to subordinate Black people

who dared to consider themselves equal shows us that no act of violence is simply individual. Volpe's attempt to strip Louima of the possibility to consider himself an equal man, a rights-bearing human, a father, and a husband illuminates the ways in which emotional responses and actions are culturally inflected and informed. Read through signs of sexual and racial difference, consigning and disciplining Louima to the feminine position is an attempt to avert the threat of masculine sameness (and therefore equality) between white and Black men. To allow gendered sameness between Volpe and Louima would have entailed permitting Louima an equal symbolic claim to patriarchal power, something that would undo the racial hierarchies between men of color and white men. As Robyn Wiegman argues, "In the context of white supremacy, we must understand the threat of masculine sameness [between white men and men of color] as so terrifying that only the reassertion of a gendered difference can provide the necessary disavowal."[50] In other words, Louima had to be symbolically castrated and feminized through rape in order to stop him from being a threat to Volpe's white patriarchal authority.

Volpe's violence hauntingly mimicked the scripted violence of lynching scenes. Fears over Black men's access to citizenship and political and economic power following Emancipation in 1863 eventually led to the rise of ritualized and widely attended lynching scenes.[51] To bind the real and fantasized threat that Black men's political-economic enfranchisement presented to white masculine dominance, the Black male body was constructed as hypersexual, hyperviolent, and prone to raping white women. These mythological constructions justified Black men's violent emasculation and death. The public culture that regularly displayed Black violated bodies on postcards, in newspapers, and through other commodities helped terrorize Black people into socially subordinate positions. Paradoxically, the projection that Black men possess the power to steal white men's full enjoyments and privileges through their hyperphysical and hypersexual power left white masculinity always fearful, tenuous, and lacking. Thus entrapped, the white male finds "in sexual violence the sexual pleasure necessary to uphold both his tenuous masculine and white racial identities."[52]

Even though Volpe's violation of Louima might be interpreted as an attempt to regain the coherence of white heteropatriarchy, Volpe's proximity to Louima's exposed body, particularly in the acts of penetrating Louima's orifices (anus and mouth), suggests the covert presence of a sadistic homoerotic desire.

In lynching scenes white men's unconscious homoerotic desire for the Black male body is generally revealed through the division of the lynched victim's body parts among the mob, particularly among men. Some accounts speak of the division of the genitals and/or body as the culminating scene in what by the turn of the twentieth century had become a ritualized and nationally celebrated form of spectacle lynching.[53] The distribution of the body parts and the genitals became an acceptable form of homoerotic exchange, a communal bonding over "the same penis they were so overdeterminedly driven to destroy."[54]

Similarly, in the 70th Precinct scene, Volpe spectacularly parades the phallic broomstick covered in Louima's blood and feces around the precinct. He recruits other police officers to participate in his sadistic scene. First, he marks the wall of the precinct bathroom with the blood and feces. As he exits the bathroom, he testifies to his fellow officers that he broke a man down. He then takes Sergeant Wernick to the bathroom and shows him the scene of the violation and the stick used in the sexual assault. Volpe then shows the phallic symbol to Officer Michael Schoer. Smelling the feces, Schoer asks if the stick is covered in "dog shit." To this, Volpe responds, "No, human shit." Volpe returns the bloodied gloves he wore while raping Louima to Officer Schofield, as though to communally display the instruments used in the violation. No officer interrupts the scene of complicit consent Volpe creates. This reveals that "the power of racial abuse is not just a sign of pathology, or legal loophole, or failure in police procedure; it is fueled by a culture and community of consent."[55]

But Volpe's wish for absolute mastery could not be publicly endorsed in 1997 with the same unashamed audacity of a lynch mob. In other words, the sadistic homoerotic communal bonding over the instruments used to violate Louima and the shared police power derived from the exchange had to happen in secret and be concealed. Volpe threw the broomstick away, Schofield washed the bloodied gloves, and somebody must have cleaned the bathroom.

Volpe's sexualized acts of racial violence are further complicated by the fact that he was planning to marry Susan, a 26-year-old African American woman who worked as a civilian employee at the 70th Precinct.[56] They had been dating for two years and were living together when the brutality happened. In an August 18, 1997, interview with Mike McAlary of the *New York Daily News* (before Volpe confessed), Susan defended her fiancée. Believing that he was incapable of committing such heinous crimes, Susan described Volpe as different from the other officers at the 70th Precinct who were normatively racist.

"I am an educated woman," Susan declared. "In the police world at that precinct you have to be aware of racism," Susan claimed. "There was nothing from Justin. . . . What color were our children going to be? It's just like Justin tells the guys in the station, 'Susan isn't my black girlfriend. She is my girlfriend, period.'" They had been on vacations together to the West Indies and the Bahamas. They had talked about racism many times. "Cried about it at night," said Susan. Volpe had brought her to his parents' Staten Island home. "I have been to his house many times. His father, Robert, and Justin's mother treat me like their daughter." Susan built a case that Volpe was not racist and therefore incapable of doing what people suspected he had done.

The pressures of being a Black woman engaged to a white cop were heavy enough. Susan regularly faced other Black men's critiques for her partner choice. "The black guys say to me, 'Has he brought you home to meet his parents? It's just sex, nothing will come of it.' . . . Black people will say, 'How can you stand by him and believe he is innocent.'" Such suspicions are based on a long legacy of white men taking advantage of Black women's bodies to assert racial domination over Black people. Cultural projections of Black female hypersexuality have historically functioned to conceal white men's systematic crimes of sexual exploitation during slavery and its aftermath.[57] Innumerable testimonies during the era of Jim Crow also testify to white men's violation of Black women as a way to deny Black men's claims to familial, economic, patriarchal, and legal authority.[58] Of course, the warnings Susan and other Black women confront suggest that some Black men project their resentful emotions for being denied patriarchal authority by white men onto Black women. Telling Black women what they should or should not do with their sexuality suggests that some Black men also long for the social and psychological rewards of male domination, a power often denied to them because of their nonwhite racial identities.

As though to avoid the "I told you so" warnings from Black people, Susan attempted to give incontestable proof that Volpe did not violate Louima. "You can't lead one life and then do that, in the precinct bathroom. Racism isn't some switch you can turn on and off." Despite her defense of Volpe, there were moments in the interview when Susan considered the possibility that he committed the act. "I can't imagine being married to . . ." She couldn't finish the sentence, as though not wanting to pursue the line of thought. McAlary recounted: "This is like the cliché, 'I can't be a racist. Some of my best friends are black.'" Understanding how it sounded, Susan attempted to explain: "I know. But I know he is not an evil person. His life with me would have to be a lie. We are planning on getting married and having children. If Justin Volpe did this, he did it to me and his children."

Susan's comments in her interview with McAlary make it clear that she saw a fundamental connection between herself and Louima on the basis of race. That is, if Volpe beat and raped Louima, Susan would have to retrospectively reconstitute her sexual relations with Volpe through a frame of racialized sexual exploitation and denigration rather than a frame of love and mutuality. Her use of the past tense ("He *did* it to me and his [unborn] children") suggests that she saw a radical incongruence between Volpe's sexual intimacy with her and his violation of Louima.

What enabled the *lack* of contradiction between Volpe's acts of raping and beating Louima and having a relationship with Susan and planning to have children with her? If we consider the historical record, we see that the logics of white patriarchal supremacy are able to reconcile the coexistence of interracial sexual relationships and sexualized racial violence. Under these logics Black men can thwart white men's full enjoyments of patriarchal and sexual privileges. These privileges include having unrestrained access to intimate sexual relations with Black women. Punishing and violating Black men offers a way to eliminate competitive threats to this understanding of white male prerogatives. If the general structure of patriarchy treats women as objects of exchange between men who are fighting to prove their superiority by possessing women, the structure of *white* patriarchy uses Black women as objects of possession to disempower men of color and widen their prerogatives. Such logics create people's sense of value and worth through the denigration and possessive control of others, particularly Black women. Of course, systems of value and worth that do not require others' subordination exist and can be practiced. I am not suggesting that all interracial relationships subscribe to these logics, even if these histori-cally repetitive practices of sexual and racial violence circumscribe the ways that interracial relationships are perceived. But the dominant value system of U.S. society suggests that racial and gender oppression is necessary for accessing a sense of superior value and worth.

"NYPD: SAME AS TON TON MACOUTES"

Louima refused to accept the long legacy of police brutality and sexual denigration legitimated by white supremacist logics without a fight. From his hospital bed, Louima recounted his experiences to McAlary. Demanding an investigation into the night's events, he forced the police officers at the 70th Precinct to account for their roles in the events of August 9. His story implicated New York City's and the nation's public, asking that they position themselves as ethical witnesses rather than passive spectators. As his story became widely read in the *Daily News*, people began organizing.

Haitians immigrants, Haitian Americans, and the larger Brooklyn Afro-Caribbean community raised critical voices against the NYPD. They understood Volpe's rape and beatings alongside a continuum of police harassment and violence against Black immigrant communities. Five days after Louima was tortured, Brooklyn's radio station Radio Soleil was flooded with calls by Haitians who voiced their outrage at Louima's story, claiming it as a systemic problem. "Most people are saying that this is not some isolated incident involving one or two bad cops," summarized Ricot Dupuy, manager of the radio station. "They are saying that they feel it's the entire New York City Police Department."[59] Innumerable testimonies of police violence were articulated. A native of Gambia, Simbala Jauwar, described his encounters with the police: "They've yelled at me, they've kicked me, they've called me n———r."[60] Community leaders substantiated the complaints. Ronald Auberg, a policy analyst for the Haitian Centers Council declared, "The Caribbean community as a whole has experienced many problems with the police. There seems to be no accountability in the Police Department."[61]

To New York communities of color, Louima's story signified the constant threat of arbitrary police brutality. These communities were quite direct in waging a political critique that addressed police brutality as *systematically* targeting people of color. As Manfred Antoine, president of the Alliance of Haitian Migrants, reiterated, "When a Haitian sees a police officer, instead of thinking this is someone there to protect them or serve them, they think this is someone to be careful around, to stay away from as much as possible."[62] Louima's violated body signified what Feldman calls a "sacrificial model of memory formation."[63] The scenario became emblematic, symbolizing "the prescriptive memory of an entire collective."[64] In other words, Louima's story did not signify his wound

alone. It spoke to innumerable stories of police harassment, violence, and killings against people of color that had remained untold and unaddressed.

On August 16, 1997, approximately 4,000 people gathered in front of the
70th Precinct to protest. Signs at the protest reflected the fact that Haitians were
drawing parallels between authoritarian forms of state violence in Haiti and
those in the United States. "N.Y.P.D. same as Ton Ton Macoutes," stated one
poster, referencing the paramilitary troops that enforced Duvalier's dictatorship
in Haiti. This connection enabled Haitian immigrants and Haitian Americans to
realize that the critiques they had waged against authoritarian practices in Haiti
were also pertinent in the U.S. context and specifically apposite to the NYPD's
treatment of Haitians. Jacques Paul, who had arrived in the United States only
three years before, recalled marching in protests in Port-au-Prince, the Haitian
capital. "It was very dangerous. A lot of policemen beat the people and killed
them, and the people were unarmed," he stated. When asked whether he expected
similar problems in New York, he exclaimed, "To find this kind of thing? No!"[65]
But Haitians also articulated the different expectations they had of the United
States as a nation that proclaimed its ideological commitment to civil rights and
democracy as foundational. Pierre Beaux, a Haitian livery cab driver, described
police brutality as "a part of life" in Haiti. "But we're not in Haiti," he said an-
grily. "I have a vote here, and I have rights, and I'll be stone-cold dead before
I'll let anyone take them away. This is what this horrible thing has taught us."[66]

The August 16 demonstration in front of the 70th Precinct also drew connections between the legacy of U.S. anti-Black racist violence and Louima's
case. "KKK must go!" the crowd chanted. "Pig! Shame on You! Seven-O, KKK!"
Drawing parallels between Louima's torture, state-sponsored U.S. violence
against African Americans, and authoritarian violence in Haiti, protesters were
able to unravel the mythology of equality and democracy in the United States
as far as communities of color were concerned.

Although the marches were primarily organized by Haitian organizations
(Haitian American Alliance and Haitian Enforcement Against Racism), representatives from the Irish, Asian, Latino, and Jewish communities pledged their
support for a march across the Brooklyn Bridge at the end of August. Anthony
Stevens, a member of the Council of Dominican Educators, stated that more
than 400 Dominicans from Washington Heights in Manhattan would participate in the march. Referring to interethnic divisions between Dominicans and

Haitians, Stevens declared, "We want to show that in New York there are no divisions between Dominicans and Haitians. We're in this together."[67]

The August 29 protest brought 15,000 people out to protest police brutality. The photographs of the march across the Brooklyn Bridge, where only seven years earlier Haitians had protested the FDA's ban on their blood, show a remarkable assembly of conscious people intent on being ethical witnesses to Louima and other violated Black people. Through their numbers and their racial, national, and linguistic diversity, the protesters created reverberating emotional economies of care that insisted on the sanctity of people of color's bodies and rights. Waving toilet plungers (the object initially believed to have been used by Volpe to violate Louima), the protesters revealed the illegitimacy of the state, the NYPD, and all the hegemonic powers that deemed communities of color criminal and undeserving. Instead, they pointed to the criminality of the state. Explaining the gravity of the plunger as symbol, Haitian student Farentz LeFargee said, "Waving these plungers in the face of the police is a reminder of what happened. The plunger may become a symbol of oppression to Haitians, much as in the same way a lynching rope has become a symbol of oppression to Southern blacks."[68] Protesters played on Mayor Giuliani's "Courtesy, Professionalism, Respect" public relations campaign, reformulating the slogan to "Criminals, Perverts, Racists." Genevieve Lagerre Dazon, a 61-year-old Haitian immigrant, summarized her participation in the protest in fundamental terms. "We are human," she said. "And that was not human. Just not human."[69]

PUBLIC (DIS)IDENTIFICATIONS WITH THE U.S. STATE

Although the wider New York public generally maintained an empathetic attitude toward Louima, not all constituents agreed that police brutality against people of color was ubiquitous or systemic. Whether one took the view that Louima's story represented something normative or aberrational largely depended on whether one belonged to or identified with communities of color. It also depended on whether a person's racial and gender identity was assumed to warrant police protection or symbolized purportedly criminal or alien threats to law and order. It depended on whether one understood America's historical legacies of sexualized racial violence and the collective memories of resisting the terrorizing practices of white supremacy.

Arguing that patterns of police brutality were being exaggerated, William J. Bratton, New York City police commissioner from 1994 to 1996, cited a 1994 study conducted by the NYPD to make the claim that the police force was not excessively forceful. The study "found that although officers made nearly 275,000 arrests in 1993, fewer than 100 people were hospitalized as a result of these encounters. This number includes people who violently resisted arrest—including those who shot at officers."[70] Although Bratton never mentioned race as a central issue in patterns of police brutality, he implied that people of color were suffering from false delusions. His use of statistics attempted to minimize the significance of everyday people's testimonies of police harassment, illegal searches, and arbitrary killings.

Bratton did not mention that the Civilian Complaint Review Board (CCRB) in New York City had received 20,535 complaints against individual police officers from July 1993 through June 1997.[71] This number is likely much lower than actual instances of police misconduct because New York City residents often believe it is a waste of time to file a formal complaint against the police. Because the CCRB's recommendations for reprimanding officers are regularly disregarded by the NYPD, residents believe it is futile to even try to hold cops accountable. Nor did Bratton mention that the Mollen Commission had revealed numerous instances of police officers being "violent simply for the sake of violence" in a report published in 1994.[72] An exchange between the commission's investigators and a police officer working in the Bronx indicated that police officers regularly used excessive force to establish their dominance.

"Did you beat people up who you arrested?"
"No. We'd just beat people in general. If they're on the street, hanging around drug
     locations. It was a show of force."
"Why were these beatings done?"
"To show who was in charge. We were in charge, the police."[73]

Describing the Internal Affairs Division of the NYPD as a "do-nothing agency," the Mollen Commission report also described instances of a group of officers engaging in rape and terror. Police officers "raided a brothel in uniform, ordered the men to leave and the women to line up. The cops then picked their victims of choice and proceeded to terrorize and rape them without compunction."[74] Because such instances of terror, torture, and rape were regularly left unaddressed and unprosecuted, the Mollen Commission concluded that police brutality emboldened NYPD cops by making them feel invulnerable. The emotional rewards derived from exercising limitless and unchecked methods of terror gave officers a sense of invincibility. Such emotional rewards may have also produced feelings of guilt, shame, and remorse over time. But in police and legal cultures where brutality is collectively condoned, such moral reminders are unlikely to change actions.

Systematic patterns of police brutality and arbitrary killings are purposely obfuscated by the state. The Justice Department does not keep data on instances of police brutality.[75] This not only makes it difficult to makes sociological arguments but also helps to diminish and disaggregate the testimonies of those who are most affected. Patterns of police violence are converted to aberrational instances of individuated disorder. By contrast, independent organizations that keep track of police killings confirm the testimonies of the most affected. In 1997 the Stolen Lives Project reported 27 fatal killings by the police in New York City alone.[76] Since four officers shot 41 rounds of ammunition at Amadou Diallo while he was reaching for his wallet in 1999, Stolen Lives has listed an additional 239 fatalities at the hands of the NYPD.[77] Most of the stolen lives are young Black and Latino people.

Even when cops are prosecuted for brutality, guilty verdicts are extremely rare. Because local district attorneys who regularly depend on the police to prosecute their cases are responsible for investigating police misconduct, the officers' actions are rarely found to be legally excessive.[78] The defendants almost always argue that they were acting in self-defense. As the world witnessed in the 1992 Rodney King trial, the police officers, the prosecution, the judges, and the jury worked to convert King's brutalization into police self-defense by emphasizing King's previous police record and staging his body as a threat to the police officers—projections that could only be believed under conditions of white paranoia that normatively understand Black men as inherently criminal.[79]

The extremity of violence against Louima and the massive public outrage he helped create through his early testimonies made it difficult for state representatives to treat this case as they usually did. Louima's rectal wounds did not lend themselves to being interpreted as acts of self-defense on the part of the cops. What's more, Louima had no previous criminal record, was working as a security guard, and was a married family man with a wife and child. His delegitimation on the basis of a past record of crime therefore proved difficult. The Haitian community's mass protests had done much to sway the court of public opinion in Louima's favor.

Once it became increasingly clear that Louima's story was true, state representatives such as Mayor Giuliani and Police Commissioner Howard Safir publicly vowed to hold the officers accountable and to break down the "blue wall of silence" of the 70th Precinct. The NYPD, and by extension the state apparatus, was forced to align itself with Louima to regain its legitimacy. Louima's torture took place in the middle of a mayoral election, and newspaper accounts continued to expose the police's attempts to cover up their tracks. King Kino and the owners of Club Rendez-Vous, who had received a ticket for disorderly conduct the day after Louima was brutalized, exposed the NYPD's attempts to portray the club as a place that condoned violent gay sex. On August 16, 1997, Kino played again at Club Rendez-Vous, adding a verse to the song "Cowboy" to show that the NYPD cowboys had the same violent spirit as the paramilitary cowboys in Haiti.

The way I see it, the cops are like a group of guys who are against the people. To me, it become [sic] no different than the Ku Klux Klan—racists that hate people, that think they have the power to hit you on the head, slap you in the face, kick you in the butt. They can do whatever they want . . . So, I look at them like a gang like that . . . The same police brutality we had in Haiti since I was a kid was the same police brutality that I meet in 1997 in front of a club where I'm playing. So I make no differences. The same U.S. government that sent people to train people in Haiti for police brutality is the same government that has the worst police brutality. But I never heard a story that they put a stick in someone's butt in Haiti.[80]

Despite Giuliani's public relations campaign vowing to address dirty cops, the Haitian community exposed him as the leader who time and time again sanctioned police harassment and violence.

Midway through his trial Volpe confessed to raping Louima, and on December 19, 1999, he was sentenced to 30 years in prison. Charles Schwarz was initially sentenced to 15 years in prison for violating Louima's civil rights. However, the U.S. Court of Appeals for the Second Circuit overturned Schwarz's conviction in 2002 on the basis that he was denied a fair trial.[81] As a result, Schwarz served only a 5-year sentence on a perjury charge and was released in

2007. Thomas Wiese and Thomas Bruder, charged with conspiracy to obstruct a federal investigation, were also initially convicted on March 9, 2000,[82] but a federal appeals court overturned their convictions in 2002 on the grounds of insufficient evidence.[83]

Volpe's conviction gave communities of color in New York the sense that a little bit of justice had been served. Holding a cop accountable for an egregious police brutality case against a Black man was a legal novelty in New York. As a result, the communities that protested the NYPD's violence achieved a certain collective satisfaction. Louima's case symbolized a victory for all the police brutality victims whose suffering had gone unnoticed or had failed to afford legal recognition or compensation. Louima continued to be an advocate against police brutality, appearing with Al Sharpton after Sean Bell was killed in 2006. He used his settlement money, the largest in New York City history, to establish the Abner Louima Foundation, which funds children's education in Haiti.

Communities that supported Louima largely framed their visions of justice through the law. Because of long historical patterns of denying people of color legal forms of redress, obtaining legal recognition for Louima's suffering was prioritized in the demands of oppositional communities. But such demands for accountability and remunerative redress still looked to the state for solutions, reinforcing the idea that the criminal justice system was the primary venue through which to obtain justice. Consciously or unconsciously, such legal frames for justice continue to reinforce emotional economies of revenge and punishment. Volpe's incarceration was supposed to be the punishment for his transgressions, but this hardly interrupted dominant ideologies and structures of feeling that equated justice with punishment. Framing justice through the law diminished possibilities for imagining other forms of justice. Ideas for restorative justice that did not involve incarceration but still created forms of accountability to Louima and other victims of police brutality were not articulated. Although Louima received monetary rewards for his unspeakable suffering, it is unclear whether this compensation was capable of creating a mode of healing that did not reinforce normative public appetites for revenge and punishment. So long as publics equate justice with punishment, even when it comes to people like Volpe, it is unlikely that the state's extralegal tactics and the normative violence in U.S. cultures will be overhauled.

To ethically witness Louima's story means to engage in an act of translation, one that reads the specter of racial and sexual violence in a way that cultivates the complex legibility of the one who suffers. The act of ethically witnessing Louima's story entails an emotional disengagement from the pleasures of aestheticized spectatorship. But it may also mean disidentifying with state-sanctioned forms of punishment and incarceration in order to imagine other forms of individual and group accountability. Being an ethical witness means cultivating indignation and resistance toward racial and sexual violence, but it also means critically imagining how to undermine the public emotional patterns and institutional structures that perpetuate its existence. It means creating modes of community accountability that do not reinforce a state and legal apparatus that is constitutively predicated on violence and the injustices of mass incarceration. In other words, ethical witnessing demands that we imagine forms of justice that do not reinforce the state apparatuses that perpetuate the very oppressions we are trying to critique. It demands that we posit a basis for social relations rooted in dignity and mutual interdependence rather than the pleasurable enjoyments of punishment, however deserved that punishment may be. The story of Abner Louima, a story of inconsolable and inexpressible suffering, hopefully teaches us to participate in cultivating an ethics of care wherein the dehumanization of others not only becomes unjustifiable but also undesirable.

CHAPTER 2

ABU GHRAIB, IRAQ:
THE EVASIVE EMOTIONS
OF U.S. EXCEPTIONALISM

Seven years after the police brutality case of Abner Louima, a spectacular display of U.S. military abuse and torture punctured the American public sphere. The 2004 Abu Ghraib scandal severely shattered the grand narrative that the war on terror was bringing democracy to Iraq. Although abuses had been reported as early as November 2003, the display of photographs of sexualized torture and sadistic denigration on CBS's *60 Minutes II* in April 2004 exposed the scandal to global communities.[1] An internal military investigative report leaked to *Salon* magazine revealed that 1,325 photos and 93 video clips of suspected Iraqi detainee abuse were taken between October 18 and December 30, 2003. Of these pictures, 660 were images of adult pornography, 546 photos contained suspected dead Iraqis, and 29 photos showed U.S. army soldiers in simulated sex acts.[2]

A flurry of shock, shame, state explanations, investigations, and prosecutions followed the initial display of photographs. Seymour Hersh's investigative reporting in the *New Yorker* and subsequent book, *Chain of Command*, as well as Mark Danner's *Torture and Truth*, offered extensive accounts of the sequence of events, trials, and prosecutions related to the Abu Ghraib prison tortures. These writers argue that, contrary to official claims that these were the isolated acts of a few soldiers, the torture and abuse of Iraqis were sanctioned by Defense Secretary Donald Rumsfeld, the Bush administration, and top military generals.[3]

By revealing the egregious underpinnings of U.S. imperialism in the Middle East, the visual display of such sadistic acts disrupted public identifications with U.S. exceptionalism. The belief that the United States is uniquely suited to lead "backward" authoritarian nations toward the "progress" of liberal democracy has long defined the structure through which the United States has justified its military missions abroad.[4] This time, however, instead of witnessing evidence of U.S. freedom and democracy, publics witnessed a nation whose soldiers were engaged in rape, racist denigration, and sadism. American publics certainly knew that militarism and warfare in Iraq wreaked violence and destruction. But they were not prepared to see the ugliness of morally reprehensible extra-legal tactics. The tortures at Abu Ghraib demanded that Americans confront all aspects of U.S. militarism as well as the logics that sustain their own national, racial, and sexual identities.

Immediately following the display of Abu Ghraib photos, official state responses claimed that these were the aberrational acts of a few American soldiers amid otherwise honorable military operations. A public relations strategy primarily deployed by the Bush administration,[5] Defense Secretary Donald Rumsfeld,[6] senior military officials such as former defense secretary James R. Schlesinger,[7] and the report that Lt. Gen. Paul T. Mikolashek presented to the Senate Armed Services Committee[8] vehemently denied that sexualized torture was a state-sanctioned war tactic. The tortures and murders were euphemized as abuses and humiliation, and the apologists claimed that order would be restored once the perpetrators were punished. The state refused to concede that top military officials and Defense Secretary Donald Rumsfeld were well aware of what was happening at Abu Ghraib. The state also disavowed that it systematically used torture in violation of international law.[9]

The state's claims were largely discredited by news sources. Mounting evidence suggested that military abuses in Iraq were prevalent and systemic.[10] In addition, a *Wall Street Journal*/NBC News poll indicated that the American public generally did not believe the state representatives' defense. The poll found that "55% of respondents believe that U.S. military commanders in Iraq or U.S. government officials played [a] role in the decision to 'abuse and torture' Iraqi prisoners in U.S. custody at Abu Ghraib prison."[11]

Abu Ghraib created a crisis in the U.S. state's legitimacy. Like Abner Louima's 1997 police brutality case, Abu Ghraib suggested that state-sponsored sexualized racial violence was a normative modality of warfare. Yet even as U.S. publics generally did not believe the state's claims that this was a case of a few bad apples, constituents' investments in the ideological fantasy of U.S. exceptionalism proved too deep to create mass opposition to the war on terror. Although factions of Americans saw Abu Ghraib as a clear example of the wider ills and global insecurities wreaked by U.S. militarism and imperialism, liberal and conservative majorities tended to use well-established mechanisms of displacement and disavowal to quell the crisis.

ORIENTALIST PROJECTIONS

Raphael Patai's 1973 book, *The Arab Mind*, was used to develop the torture and sexual humiliation techniques inside the Abu Ghraib prison in Iraq. *The Arab Mind* also served as a key text in the cultural instruction of American soldiers deployed to the Middle East. Norvell DeAtkine, director of Middle Eastern Studies at the John F. Kennedy Special Warfare Center and School in North Carolina, claimed that "his troops find the cultural knowledge—everything from how Arabs feel about their language to their sense of time—more than useful."[12] DeAtkine also admitted that "at the institution where I teach military affairs, *The Arab Mind* forms the basis of my cultural instruction. Over the past 12 years I have also briefed hundreds of military teams being deployed to the Middle East."[13] Unsurprisingly, DeAtkine wrote the introduction to the 2001 edition of Patai's *Arab Mind*. In the months before March 2003, the discussions of prowar Washington conservatives focused on the notion that Arabs have a heightened vulnerability to sexual humiliation. The two themes that took precedence in these discussions were that Arabs only responded to force and that their biggest weaknesses were shame and sexual degradation.[14]

As an orientalist text, *The Arab Mind* tells us much more about American stereotypical constructions of Arab culture and Arab people than it does about the complex historical forces that shape U.S. politics and militarism in the Middle East. Orientalist ideologies and stereotypes, which imagine the Middle East as radically different, inferior, and culturally regressive compared to the West, structure the remarkably racist and reductionist generalizations made in

The Arab Mind. As Edward Said has demonstrated, orientalist projections are repeated ad nauseam in European and American texts and discourses, making them appear as truths. As they circulate, orientalist constructions and stereotypes gain emotional value. Emotional economies of fear attach themselves to these projections, making Americans reflexively think that Arabs are inherently dangerous and therefore persecutory enemies intent on obliterating the U.S. nation. By contrast, paternalist emotions feed on stereotypes that Arabs would be lost without American assistance and guidance. Although orientalist stereotypes and emotions tend to be externally projected toward bodies that Americans imagine as Middle Eastern, they also generate internal economies of reward and pleasure for Americans. By projecting political regression and sexual deviance outwardly, Americans are allowed to affirm their interior national, familial, racial, and sexual identities as superior and exceptional. Consequently, U.S. imperialist interests in the Middle East are concealed or justified by socially shared emotions attached to orientalist constructions.

In *The Arab Mind* the Arab world is depicted through generalizations about Arab people's sexuality, child-rearing practices, and family structures. The family structures are implicitly compared to American sexual, gender, and family ideals and norms, which are assumed to be superior and progressive. Patai takes U.S. national exceptionalism for granted, but he demonstrates this exceptionalism through constructions of Arab "deviance" in formative sexual and gender development. As in other orientalist texts, Patai assumes that Americans are exceptional because they are at the forefront of civilization and history. They have presumably surpassed problems such as gender inequality, religious fanaticism, and patriarchal formations of the family—all markers of "uncivilized" or regressively fundamentalist peoples and cultures. Meanwhile, race (invoked by such vague terms as "Arab society," the "Arab world," and "Islam") functions as a master signifier that consolidates these sweeping stereotypes of deviance, taking them as inherent characteristics that define all Arabs. By transforming U.S. orientalist and racist projections into the embodied traits that all Arabs possess, Patai lays out the many reasons that Arabs in the Middle East failed to join the progressive movement of history led by the exceptionalist United States.

Patai constructs Arab men as sexually pathological. He traces this condition to Arab child-rearing practices. He claims that because the Arab mother's relationship to her son is essentially incestuous, Arab men are predisposed "to accept the stereotype of the woman as primarily a sexual object and a creature who cannot resist sexual temptation."[15] Patai's projections of sexual pathology regularly appear in counterterrorism discourses, which similarly project Arab women's "bad mothering" as the root cause of "bad family structures" that lead to "psychological compulsions that effectively determine and fix the mind of the terrorist."[16]

Whereas Patai's orientalist discourses focus on the bad Arab mother to construct the idea that Arab boys will inevitably develop a sexually pathological psychic structure that later manifests in both hyperaggression and hyperpatriarchy, other orientalist discourses focus on the supposed bad Arab father. In an online article for the conservative forum *FrontPage Magazine*, titled "The Sexual Rage Behind Islamic Terror," Jamie Glazov claims that the Arab father causes Arab boys to become sexually pathological. Because they are socially segregated from women, Glazov claims, Arab men "succumb to homosexual behavior" and pedophilia. Glazov argues that the word *homosexual* does not exist in Arab culture because male-on-male incest, rape, and pedophilia are so normative that they are not understood as transgressive acts. "Having sex with boys, or with effeminate men, is seen as a social norm. . . . An unmarried man who has sex with boys is simply doing what men do."[17] And in case one does not quite understand what this reveals about Arab sexuality, Glazov concludes that "sex in Islamic societies is not about mutuality between partners, but about the adult male's achievement of pleasure through violent domination."[18]

Patai also makes claims that homosexuality is normative in the private spheres of the Arab world, but he does not see it as a central cause of family pathologies. Like Glazov, Patai regards homosexuality as a sexual outlet resulting from the cultural restrictions on sexuality in the Arab social sphere. He sees homosexuality as a symptom rather than a cause of sexual pathology. He argues that the pathologies introduced from early childhood to puberty (presumably through the mother and Arab culture in general) lead Arab men to become latent rapists in their adult life, which is why men and women in Arab cultures must be kept separate. Remarkably, Patai asserts that this is the Arab male's tacitly assumed self-image.[19] Moreover, Patai claims that Arabs families believe that they have to segregate the sexes because women's sexual urges are too uncontrollable to trust such encounters.[20] Such orientalist projections of Arab hypersexuality and perversity render various forms of symbolic and literal violence against Arab people illegible or simply deserved. In constructing Arab male sexuality as excessively deviant, the orientalist presumption is that Arabs would enjoy acts that Americans would consider violent and morally objectionable. According to the orientalist imagination, humiliating Arab men requires excessive and hyperviolent sexual acts because they are so attuned to sexual perversions. By extension, the abnormal perversities that orientalists project on Arab female sexuality imply that she is also in need of correction. Simultaneously, her subjection to Arab male domination and perversity construct her as being in need of rescue.

The second central fantasy projection in *The Arab Mind* focuses on Arab children's (especially boys') unique relationship to force and corporal punishment. Patai claims that corporal punishment is common in the Arab family and is used to make children submit to the authority of the Arab father.[21] Beyond punishment for disobedience, "the father's heavy hand, the rod, the strap, and, at least among the most tradition-bound Bedouin tribes, the saber and the dagger" are meant "to harden [the Arab boy] for his future life."[22] But it is unclear for what future Arab boys are being prepared, because later Patai argues that Arab men are incapable of action and achievement. It is as though the exertion of force onto Arab children is enacted solely for the purpose of reproducing the authority of the Arab father and, by extension, the Arab family's extremist patriarchal structure.

ShrinkWrapped, a blog by a psychoanalyst who claims that he is attempting "to understand our world," draws even more explicit connections between children's corporal punishment in Arab culture and Arab men's purported tendency toward violence and patriarchy. In a November 1, 2006, post titled "Arab Culture and Democracy," the blogger claims not only that practices such as group circumcision and beatings lead to increased tolerance and propensity for violence in Arab culture, but also that they lead to cognitive difficulties.[23] Later, the blogger makes a deterministic link between child-rearing practices, irrationality, aggression, and the impossibility for Arab culture to sustain democratic processes and civil society.[24]

A respondent to *ShrinkWrapped*'s November 1 post considers the psychoanalyst's deterministic arguments and comes to the conclusion that the only solution for eliminating such pathologies in the Middle East—pathologies that always threaten to contaminate the United States—is to wage genocide.[25] According to this respondent, the notions of inherent and incorrigible Arab pathology and irrational aggression are sufficient reasons to justify such expendability.

Claiming that Arabs are stuck in a compulsive repetition of aggression and violence, *ShrinkWrapped* then invokes a third projection common in orientalist discourses. Because of their cultural and sexual pathologies, Arabs are presumed to be inherently unable to progress economically and mimic the development of Western cultures. This third projection ostensibly claims that sexual pathology in Arab societies, particularly the prevalence of hyper-patriarchal practices, deterministically affects the lack of economic progress in the Arab world.

In *The Arab Mind* Patai concocts a similar theory by drawing on another orientalist text, McClelland and colleagues' *Achievement Motive*.[26] This book draws connections between permissiveness and strictness in child-rearing practices, achievement motives, and national economic development. Patai supports Dr. Edwin T. Prothro's arguments in *The Achievement Motive*; Prothro argues that "differences in rate of economic development in different countries might be attributable not to natural resources, available investment capital, or technological skills alone, but also to the amount of achievement motive found in the inhabitants of that nation."[27]

Prothro's anthropological research sought to prove the validity of this hypothesis by comparing the children of three groups: Armenian Orthodox Gregorians, Greek Orthodox Arabs, and Sunni Muslim Arabs. These groups stand in for the more general groups of Christian Armenians, Christian Arabs, and Muslim Arabs, respectively.[28] The need for achievement (and hence the motivation behind economic development) in the children of these groups, Prothro's study found, was highest among the Armenians and lowest among the Sunni Muslims. One explanation given for this difference is that, compared with Christian Arab mothers, Sunni Muslim mothers do not foster their children's independence. Implicit here is the Muslim mother's unwillingness to let go of her erotic and incestuous relationship with her son. But the key reason both Patai and Prothro give for this difference centers once again on the role of the father in child-rearing practices. "It thus appears that in the high-achieving group, the father is a more remote figure than in other groups; lower paternal control is correlated, in Lebanon as in America, with higher achievement."[29] Patai's logic claims that if the Arab father were less patriarchal and controlling, achievement among Arab children would increase. Because this is not generally the case, the implication is that Arab cultures need American interventions in the Middle East to advance economically. Presumably, Americans would offer "correctives" to Arab cultures by introducing them to just the right degree of patriarchal control, to "proper" child-rearing practices, and sexual norms that are best suited for economic and civic progress.

Edward Said argues that orientalist discourses must never take Arab male sexuality and Arab enumerative power seriously. This structure of disavowal helps neutralize any possible challenges Arabs might make to American white paternalist and patriarchal authority. By understanding political regression and economic underdevelopment in the Middle East to be directly linked to Arabs' sexual deviance, perversity, and "uncivilized" practices, U.S. orientalism assumes that Arabs cannot rise above primitive biological reproduction (enumerative power) into civilized cultural and economic development. This disavowal constructs the Arabs in the Middle East as permanently in need of U.S. control, intervention, or rescue. Moreover, it helps Americans who identify with these constructs to feel good about themselves, because they are presumably supporting the U.S. military in bringing morally righteous ideas and practices to what are deemed uncivilized locales.

If dominant ideas and emotions about Arab male sexuality claim that their pathologies create hyperpatriarchal formations of the family, spread aggressive irrationality, diminish economic achievement, and prevent the creation of civil society, U.S. orientalist stereotypes situate Arab women somewhat differently. Patai claims that Arab families generally neglect their daughters. A girl's crying "evokes little attention—since one is not supposed to pamper a girl."[30] She is weaned much earlier than boys; she is devalued, considered shameful to the parents from birth, and becomes a cause for apprehension later in life, "lest she, by infringing the moral code, bring shame and disgrace upon her father and entire family."[31] Patai describes the Arab woman as so entrapped in the extremity of Arab hyperpatriarchy that she is not even conscious of her own oppression. As the biological and cultural reproducers of the traditional Arab world, particularly as the primary caretakers of children, Arab women are imagined to be completely submissive to the demands of Arab men.[32]

Patai repeatedly emphasizes that the honor of the Arab father and family rests on the Arab woman's *ird*, a word Patai translates to mean a woman's
honor, itself predicated on her sexual propriety. According to one Algerian
writer, Mouloud Feraoun, whom Patai quotes to support his claims, Arab men's
"honor was buried in the vagina as if it were a treasure more precious than
life."[33] The protection of women's chastity, Patai argues, becomes an obsession so great in Arab culture that "an entire way of life has been built around
it, aiming at the prevention of the occurrence of a situation which might lead
to a woman's loss of her sexual virtue, or which might enable a man to cause
such a loss."[34] Veiling, the seclusion of women, keeping women uneducated,
and female circumcision are all measures taken to protect Arab women's sexual chastity. Arab men's view of Arab women, according to Patai, is that they
are "like animals, highly sexed and willing to have intercourse with any man.
That is all they care about."[35]

The end of Patai's chapter "The Realm of Sex" reads like orientalist erotic
fiction, oscillating between extreme Arab sexual prohibitions to limitless Arab
sexual desires. In the second section of the chapter Patai discusses the association between sex and sin instilled in Arab children, and in the third section
he speaks of eleventh- and twelfth-century practices of limitless sexual "freedom and hospitality": Arab men who were not jealous of their wives sleeping
with other men, sexual laxity, orgies—stories based on the traveling journals
of early European orientalists. So, on the one hand, male control of and obsession with women's chastity literally organizes family life, the gendered
division of space, social practices, and manners. On the other hand, these
prohibitions create the popular impression that Arab women's lust is greater
than men's. Again, rather than positing this as his view, Patai claims that it is
Arab women's *self-image*.[36]

A victim of Arab patriarchy, but a highly sexualized one, the Arab woman
vacillates in Patai's narrative between meek doe and sexualized erotic object.
As though proclaiming a prophetic vision, Patai claims that a time will come
when "the West will be accused of an entirely new type of 'sexual' imperialism,
which will denote to opponents of innovation perhaps the most vicious, because
most insidious, attempt of the West to impose itself upon the Arab East." He
concludes with certainty that "just as all the protests against Western cultural
imperialism are of no avail . . . one can expect that ultimately the Arab mind

will have no choice but to accept Western sex mores."[37] The march of Western progress, it seems, is irreversible and apparently irresistible.

Largely because of the overwhelming predominance of Western fantasies of the harem and the veil[38]—which timelessly relegate Arab women to the realm of the private and the sexual—orientalist discourses render Arab women's rights to citizenship and their participation in public affairs virtually invisible. These projections posit the Arab woman as someone who must be educated about her own oppression by Americans and thereby—with an air of evangelism mixed with the cry of the die-hard feminist imperialist—saved.[39] Under this emotional and ideological structure, the Western patriarch is needed to challenge the extremist hyperpatriarchy of Arab men, and the American woman is needed to educate Arab women about their oppression and to tame their hypersexuality and abnormal child-rearing practices.

But U.S. orientalism also constructs Arab women as an absence. This absence is not just constituted through the disappearance of Arab and Arab American women's testimonies in U.S. public discourses on the Middle East. It is in the terrain *between* "the imperialist subject and the subject of imperialism"[40] that the Arab woman becomes a voided absence. Figured simply as the symbol of conquest rather than a person with agency and will, the Arab woman becomes the emptied terrain on which the imperialist Western male subject and the Middle Eastern subject of imperialism stage their contests for power.

The U.S. obsession with Arab women's veiling, or *hijab*, after September 11, 2001, symptomatically reveals this American imaginary and emotional structure.[41] From Laura Bush's radio address on "gender apartheid" in Afghanistan under the Taliban in 2001,[42] to the feature on *60 Minutes II* titled "Unveiled," which aired in October 2001,[43] to *Time* magazine's November 2001 feature "Headgear 101,"[44] the issue of Arab and Muslim women's veiling entered American public discourse as a matter of grave concern and as a symbol of Arab countries' oppression of Arab women.

Gayatri Spivak points out that European imperialism often symbolizes its dominance by defying native customs. She cites the British passage of a law prohibiting the Indian native custom of *sati* as an event that was meant to symbolize the "civil, good society" introduced by British imperialism.[45] In contemporary politics saving Arab women from the purported oppression of the veil would symbolize that the civil, good society of American democracy was finally advancing amid the chaotic conflicts in Iraq.

Americans' emotionally charged desires to unveil the Arab woman as a way to symbolize the victory of U.S. democracy have produced grave consequences for women in Iraq. Iraqi women have been confronted with increasing pressures to wear traditional dress. Previously heterogeneous practices related to the *hijab* have become increasingly homogenized in Iraq. Because Iraqi women's veiling or unveiling signifies who is winning in this imperialist contest, adherence to traditional dress symbolizes Iraqi opposition to U.S. imperialism. An Iraqi woman, using the pseudonym Riverbend, described the intensified control of Iraqi women's bodies in her award-winning blog *Baghdad Burning* as follows:

You feel it all around you. It begins slowly and almost insidiously. You stop wearing slacks or jeans or skirts that show any leg because you don't want to be stopped in the street and lectured by someone who doesn't approve. You stop wearing short sleeves and start preferring wider shirts with a collar that will cover up some of your neck. You stop letting your hair flow because you don't want to attract attention to it. On the days when you forget to pull it back into a ponytail, you want to kick yourself and you rummage around in your handbag trying to find a hair band . . . hell, a rubber band, to pull back your hair and make sure you attract less attention from *them*.[46]

In this battle between men, Iraqi women oscillate between two binary allegiances that prove equally unsatisfactory. Either she refutes U.S. imperialism and accepts reactionary native traditionalist impositions, or she refutes native impositions and symbolically accepts U.S. imperialism. In such impossible polemics, "The figure of the woman disappears, not into pristine nothingness, but into a violent shuttling that is the displaced figuration of the 'third-world woman' caught between tradition and modernization, culturalism and development."[47]

The U.S. soldiers who carried out the tortures and denigration practices at Abu Ghraib knew that displaying the sexualized terror of imprisoned Iraqi men and women was an effective way of symbolizing U.S. imperial domination and conquest over Iraq. But in the complicated symbolic terrain whereby the United States had to conceal such overt forms of terror in order to preserve the ideological fantasy of U.S. exceptionalism and democracy, these overt displays of military conquest and imperial domination backfired.

UNVEILING IMPERIALISM

Writing from the other side of the world and in physical proximity to the Abu Ghraib prison, Riverbend offered consistently incisive critiques of the U.S. occupation. On the day the Abu Ghraib photographs were released on Arab television networks, she wrote the following entry.

Friday, April 30, 2004
THOSE PICTURES . . .
The pictures are horrific. I felt a multitude of things as I saw them . . . the most prominent feeling was rage, of course. I had this incredible desire to break something—like that would make things somehow better or ease the anger and humiliation. We've been hearing terrible stories about Abu Ghraib Prison in Baghdad for a while now, but those pictures somehow spoke like no words could.

Seeing those naked, helpless, hooded men was like being slapped in the face with an ice cold hand. I felt ashamed looking at them—like I was seeing something I shouldn't be seeing and all I could think was, "I might know one of those faceless men . . ." I might have passed him in the street or worked with him. I might have bought groceries from one of them or sat through a lecture they gave in college . . . any of them might be a teacher, a gas station attendant or engineer . . . any one of them might be a father or grandfather . . . each and every one of them is a son and possibly a brother. And people wonder at what happened in Falloojeh a few weeks ago when those Americans were killed and dragged through the streets.[48]

Riverbend disrupts structures of seeing that transform suffering into an abstract aesthetic exercise by forcing us to think about the intimate social and familial networks of the Abu Ghraib prisoners. Situating them within the everydayness of life creates affective identification with the Iraqi prisoners. That the prisoners might have crossed paths with Riverbend at work, college, grocery stores, and gas stations or that they might be part of larger family networks suggests that she links her life and fate to theirs. Riverbend can identify and suffer with the prisoners at Abu Ghraib because she understands that she is not immune to the arbitrariness of violence, paranoia, and chaos that characterizes struggles for power in Iraq. This is fundamentally what it means to be implicated in someone else's suffering. Structurally, she sees that her own struggle within the context of occupation cannot be dissociated from what the prisoners faced.

Unlike the shame expressed by dominant U.S. publics, which largely focused on the way Abu Ghraib made the United States look to the rest of the world, Riverbend's shame is connected to the prisoners and their families. She feels shame for them as though she too is suffering the humiliation. And she intuits shame for things that the photographs do not display but that the knowledges of the oppressed recognize. "It's beyond depressing and humiliating . . . my blood boils at the thought of what might be happening to the female prisoners,"[49] Riverbend writes. Indeed, photographs released in 2006 did display sexualized images of female prisoners at Abu Ghraib; numerous reports of rape against both female and male Iraqi prisoners emerged as well. Hence for Riverbend the photographs symbolized what people in Iraq already knew. "Everyone knew this was happening in Abu Ghraib and other places. . . . Seeing the pictures simply made it more real and tangible."[50]

Riverbend's shame is followed by anger and rage. She too wishes for the punishment of those who carried out the tortures and derived sadistic pleasure from the aesthetically sexualized scenes of violence.[51] She wishes to quell her humiliation by engaging in the tactics of an eye for an eye. She wishes that the U.S. torturers will also suffer from the intergenerational repercussions of pain and humiliation. But she wishes this only momentarily. Ultimately, Riverbend's narrative is preoccupied with considering what modes of ethical recognition and witnessing are possible in the contexts of militarism, warfare, and occupation. She knows that there is no real sense of justice in vicious exchanges of war, where every instance of violence escalates into greater violence. Indeed, a few days later the beheading of Nick Berg was televised and the eye-for-an-eye exchanges between the subjects of imperialism and imperial subjects continued, locating the tortures at the Abu Ghraib prison within the context of permanent states of emergency. It is from this perspective that Riverbend critiques the Americans' shock at seeing the Abu Ghraib photographs.[52] As an ethical witness, Riverbend refuses to accept the logic of sadistic violence, sexual abuse, rape, and punishment as historical norms or necessary facets of U.S. warfare purportedly enacted in the name of progress. Addressing the U.S. military but also the U.S. public, she states:

Friday, May 7, 2004
JUST GO . . .
You've seen the troops break down doors and terrify women and children . . . curse, scream, push, pull and throw people to the ground with a boot over their head. You've

seen troops shoot civilians in cold blood. You've seen them bomb cities and towns. You've seen them burn cars and humans using tanks and helicopters. Is this latest debacle so very shocking or appalling? . . .

I sometimes get emails asking me to propose solutions or make suggestions. Fine. Today's lesson: don't rape, don't torture, don't kill and get out while you can—while it still looks like you have a choice. . . . Chaos? Civil War? Bloodshed? We'll take our chances—just take your Puppets, your tanks, your smart weapons, your dumb politicians, your lies, your empty promises, your rapists, your sadistic torturers and go.[53]

Riverbend uses frameworks of interpretation and structures of feeling that reveal U.S. imperialism's exacerbation of fundamentalism in the Middle East, the proliferation of gendered and racial oppression, and the pursuit of capitalist profits through warfare. These frameworks rupture orientalist projections of Arab terrorism and extremism that render military violence legitimate or necessary. Riverbend appeals to structures of feeling whose ethical potential lies in a demand to divest from violence altogether.

THE CONSERVATIVE RESPONSE

In stark contrast to Riverbend's frameworks of seeing and feeling, conservative American publics tended to be unapologetic about the Abu Ghraib tortures or expressed amazement that they would raise such public outrage. As a guest on MSNBC's *Imus in the Morning*, Jay Severin, a nationally syndicated talk radio host and a major media pundit, claimed, "We took terror prisoners, and we treated them essentially to a week in Las Vegas. I have to pay good money to have that done to me."[54] Severin could not figure out what the fuss over Abu Ghraib was all about because, in his view, the photographs displayed prisoners who "walked around naked. Big deal."[55] Severin's comments associate the Abu Ghraib tortures with the commodified pleasures and vices of Las Vegas. By reifying the tortures into carnivalesque sex acts, Severin and other conservatives explicitly displayed the emotional gratification they felt in witnessing the sexual subjugation of America's archenemy, "the Arab man."

Before the release of the photographs, Severin had contributed his opinion on how to deal with Muslims in the United States by stating, "I think we should kill them."[56] He encouraged the circulation of aggressive hatred toward Muslims and Arab people while fostering American callous desires for their elimination. Conservative constituents who identified with Severin's orientalist views were able to vicariously feel the satisfactions of an American dominance that had finally shed its guise of benevolence and returned to overt aggression. This was particularly important for Americans who thought that the U.S. military was getting soft.

On his May 4, 2004, show, radio talk host Rush Limbaugh associated the tortures with fraternity pranks, claiming that the U.S. soldiers were simply releasing aggression. "I'm talking about people having a good time, these people, you ever heard of emotional release? You ever heard of need to blow some steam off?"[57] That same day, *Weekly Standard* online editor Jonathan Last agreed on CNBC's show *Dennis Miller* that "worse happens in frat houses across America . . . bad pictures with some guys playing naked Twister. It's bad, but we don't want to get too crazy."[58]

This notion that perhaps the abuses should not have happened but that Americans should not overreact with outrage became a theme in conservative media. This rhetoric buttressed itself repeatedly with the notion that what happened at Abu Ghraib was minuscule compared to the atrocities waged by the Arab world. Fox News talk show host Sean Hannity reinforced this theme in his loud and retaliatory question to Rosie O'Donnell on the ABC show *The View*. "Are we better off with Saddam captured and the mass graves and rape rooms closed, yes or no?"[59] Evading the fact that rape and sexual violence were central to the Abu Ghraib tortures, Hannity fueled public emotional economies of revenge, retaliation, and resentment toward Arab, Muslim, and Iraqi people. A comments thread in the *Mudville Gazette*, a website frequented by former and current American soldiers, reiterated Hannity's reaction to Abu Ghraib even more explicitly.

Imperial Crusader: This whole story is absurd. That the media are obsessed with America's enemies being photographed naked, while these same enemies chop off people's heads, burn people alive, and intentionally target civilians, is the biggest outrage of all.

. . .

Old Glory: I don't see what the big deal over this is. It might be a little unsavory that some guys get tortured, but they are fighting against us trying to take our freedom and our lives.

. . .

Papa Ray: Torture by giving the prisoner, what he has always wanted, but could not do because of his religion is not torture, because it gives him the excuse to do it and know that, it was not of his own free will, so Allah will give him a free ride to his virgins with no punishment. If you don't believe me, visit some of the Arab, Middle Eastern Porno sites.

. . .

Harry: As we know, in New York City they would pay good money for the treatment at Abu Ghraib in their fancy clubs. Being led around on a leash in the nude by a cute chick is worth a lot of money there. . . . Well, some of the wealthier ones have "torture chambers" in their homes.[60]

The dominant discourses espoused on conservative websites and blogs revealed that a faction of the U.S. public unapologetically viewed the tortures at Abu Ghraib as necessary and justifiable. This justification was constructed through the conviction that the only way Americans could win the fight against the unpredictable violent extremism of so-called Arab terrorists was to engage in extralegal warfare tactics, perpetually maintaining a state of emergency that transgressed international agreements on the limits of warfare, torture, and human rights. In other words, it was argued that Americans should suspend democratic principles and moral standards until the war on terror—a war without end—was won.

In addition, some conservatives were explicit in expressing the sadistic pleasure they derived from Iraqi men's sexual humiliation (widely portrayed through the use of the broader term "Arab men"). Consider the prevalence of orientalist stereotypes about Arab male sexuality that mirror Patai's projections in Papa Ray's comments. Papa Ray imagines that the sexually repressed Iraqi prisoner secretly wishes for his own sexual humiliation, having no permissible outlet in Arab culture to express or exercise his sexual desires. Here we see again that the American construction of the sexually pathological Arab man allows Papa Ray to convert sexual violence imposed by U.S. soldiers into Iraqi prisoners' own covert sexual desires. Further reflecting Patai's disavowals in *The Arab Mind*, Papa Ray argues that this is not his own fantasy projection but rather the Arab man's own self-professed image, as evidenced by Arab and Middle Eastern pornography sites.

Meanwhile, Harry argues that liberals are hypocritical; they complain about Abu Ghraib but engage in similar sexual perversions in New York City's "fancy clubs." In making this analogy between liberals and the prisoners at Abu Ghraib, Harry seamlessly bypasses questions of power and consent. Like Jay Severin,

Harry equates sexual abuses enacted by U.S. soldiers at Abu Ghraib with the commodities of sadomasochistic pornography and prostitution. Harry aligns himself with an imagined normative heterosexuality that is purportedly free of the sexual perversions of liberals and Arabs alike. This construction gives Harry the gratification of being morally justified and sexually proper, even as he voyeuristically participates in the speculative pleasures of the sexualized violence through which American freedom is wielded.

The conservative response expressed support for U.S. militarism and imperialism without the concealments and obfuscations evident in the state's official disavowals. If the state claimed that the Abu Ghraib tortures were unacceptable, conservatives unabashedly retorted that sexual violence and humiliation were simply part of war. In this sense conservatives were not interested in perpetuating a rhetorical discourse that oxymoronically insisted on humanitarian warfare in Iraq. Even if the Abu Ghraib tortures were deemed illegal, conservative media outlets and Internet comments focused on the idea that public outrage over Abu Ghraib was unpatriotic and injurious to the American efforts to win the war on terror.

The emphatic declarations expressed in such conservative responses betray a nostalgia for a time when white supremacist, anti-immigrant, xenophobic sentiments could be openly articulated and enacted in America. The nostalgia expresses a deep frustration with the idea that the U.S. nation cannot do things the way it did in the pre–civil rights era. Conservatives associated the state's inability to openly advocate for the annihilation of its enemies in Iraq with what they characterized as the sissyfication of America. This concern suggests that conservatives take orientalist stereotypes of Arab sexual prowess, enumerative power, and hyperpatriarchy quite seriously. Conservative blogs insisted that soft liberals were imposing unnecessary prohibitions on Americans with their political correctness. Because of the so-called liberal media, Americans were no longer free to express their xenophobia, patriarchy, and racism forthrightly.

This frustration nostalgically wished for a prefeminist America, idealized through images of white suburban middle-class families in the 1950s, a time when women knew their place. Severin suggested as much when he criticized President Bush for apologizing for talking tough.

[President Bush] was essentially begging Oprah and Dr. Phil to forgive him for speaking like a man because he said "wanted dead or alive." I mean, you know, be a man.

You're the commander in chief, not the fruit in chief. Don't apologize to people for speaking tough in a time of war.[61]

This wish for Americans' return to a time when overt forms of masculine aggression were socially acceptable understood the Abu Ghraib sexual humiliations and tortures as a move in the right direction. Many conservatives claimed that U.S. soldiers who aggressively punished Arab enemies intent on destroying American freedom and lives needed to be celebrated, not condemned.

The emotions attached to such conservative responses seemed to repeatedly invoke a sense of loss in American white patriarchal authority. Presumably, to this faction of the U.S. public, supporting the war on terror meant reconstructing an American polity that was tired of dealing with the assaults dealt by antiracist, feminist, antiwar, anti-imperialist, queer, and third world liberation movements.[62] The war on terror was a new opportunity to reconstitute the logics and narratives of white patriarchal supremacy, this time against Arabs. Fantasizing themselves as appendages of an American military apparatus that used extremist heteropatriarchal methods, conservatives revealed that they had made important libidinal investments in U.S. imperialism. By supporting the extralegal tactics of Abu Ghraib, they reasserted their own sense of sexual prowess, patriarchal control, and national and/or racial supremacy against the tide of losses since the 1960s.

THE LIBERAL RESPONSE

In liberal public discourses the state's "aberration" defense was generally challenged. Unlike conservatives who minimized or justified the sadistic abuses, most liberals condemned the Abu Ghraib tortures. Liberals repeatedly articulated responses of outrage, shock, shame, and concern. They condemned the Bush administration's and other conservatives' mishandling of the war in Iraq. They pointed to President Bush's lack of justification for initiating the war in Iraq, the U.S. state's deviation from the Geneva Convention's prohibition of torture, the lack of due process for prisoners detained in Iraq and at Guantánamo Bay, and the general erosion of civil liberties and intensifications of presidential power after the September 11, 2001, attacks on the World Trade Center and the Pentagon.[63] Academic scholars similarly focused on legal and military policy shifts to the right, arguing that these set the conditions for the extralegal tortures at Abu Ghraib.[64] Whereas conservatives were explicit about their affective enjoyments in seeing the Arab enemy shamed and humiliated, liberals tended to express shock and shame while simultaneously falling short of condemning the larger structures of violence endemic to U.S. militarism and imperialism in the Middle East.

Liberals commonly negotiated the national shame raised by the Abu Ghraib photographs by blaming the Bush administration and conservatives for mismanagement, corruption, and excess in the war on terror and the war in Iraq. Conservative bloggers who justified the Abu Ghraib tortures were attacked by liberal bloggers who questioned conservative constituents' state of mental health. Calls to impeach and incarcerate President Bush and his conservative allies were one of the most commonly invoked solutions that liberals proposed after Abu Ghraib, as illustrated by the following online comments posted on the liberal website, Think Progress.

Jay Radal: [Rep. John] Murtha needs to call Bush and Cheney to resign or the Congress must impeach both of them! Americans want prison terms for them!

. . .

Clyde the Ripper:
Don't shut down the cells at Gitmo!
What better place to put the Bushco?
They can argue all night
Over who has the might
To to [*sic*] tell the rest of the Repugs where to go.

. . .

Rebel in CA: My thoughts exactly. I believe Abu Ghraib should remain open as well, so the Iraqi's can "waterboard" Dead-Eye Dick and the rest of the Bushco, or walk 'em on leashes with cigarettes dangling from the corners of their mouths a la Lindy whatever her name was.

. . .

IraqVet, responding to Clyde the Ripper's comment: I COULD NOT have put it any better! What a NOVEL idea! Worthy of recognition in CONGRESS! I for one would welcome THAT legislation. The thought of seeing Barbara and Lynn crying their eyes out would be pure poetic justice for all of the mothers who have only solace from a flag draped coffin.

. . .

John Gilpins: As far as I'm concerned, the Abu Ghraib chapter changed peoples' perception of this war. We were supposed to be the "good" guys but we weren't. The "integrity" Bush was trying to push went down a rat hole. Just like the billions of dollars we are spending is going down a rat hole.

When a few, or more than a few, Bush administration officials are in jail, I hope we can verify that the prison is open for business. Don't worry officials! We, the American taxpayers, will make sure the prison is open. PRISONS!!!!![65]

This exchange, and many others like it, indicates that both liberal and conservative responses to Abu Ghraib tended to adhere to a logic that uncritically considered incarceration and bodily punishment the best ways to obtain justice. Although they disagreed over who should be punished and incarcerated, they agreed that these forms of triage would restore their respective ideals of American democracy. These logics evaded questions about the effects that such popularly accepted modes of punishment, containment, and elimination produced in the U.S. body politic. Few liberals challenged the general exacerbation of violence, trauma, and alienation that these American notions of justice perpetuated, particularly in the lives of people of color in the United States. To evade the fact that such systems of punishment, incarceration, and removal inevitably bled into the broader cultures of the national body, liberals held onto the protective fiction that ridding themselves of conservative pathologies such as the Bush administration would restore their nation to health. If conservatives adopted a similar logic of punishment and triage toward pathological Arabs and Muslims, liberals reified this logic with conservatives in mind.

Patricia J. Williams argues that such logics of triage evade the fact that all forms of destruction (overt or passive), containment, and punishment produce collective consequences that affect the dominant as much as the oppressed. "The Malthusian nightmare has never been a simple matter, I think, of letting someone else go hungry, or of letting someone else die. It is a matter of amputation—that's the metaphor I'd rather use. And one can't cut off one's leg and pretend it never belonged."[66] Dominant liberal and conservative logics seemed to agree that amputating criminal pathologies through incarceration (widely accepted in the liberal response) or eliminating terrorists by means of warfare (widely accepted in the conservative response) would protect the healthy American body politic. Constituents across the political aisle seemed to believe that the infrastructures that quarantined pathologies (prison) or amputated them (war) were natural and necessary. Believing that the healthy were safer and better off through such practices of triage, the collective hardly noticed that they could not comply with the violence and atrocities of these systems and remain unaffected.

Illuminating this logic of punishment and triage helps us to see that the emotional, ideological, and material infrastructures out of which Abu Ghraib emerged had been established long before the tortures and abuses were exposed.[67] As I argued in the introduction to Part I, emotional economies of fear tied to largely fabricated panics over criminality and undocumented immigration had already produced public desires for increased policing, mass incarceration, border militarization, detentions, and deportations within the United States. The logic of triage, which justified the incarceration or violation of Black, Latino/a, and poor people who were considered pathological in order to preserve the healthy, was simultaneously deployed toward foreign populations. Both dominant and marginalized Americans were solicited to identify with U.S. exceptionalism and militarism against the threats of Arab terrorists. The sense of value derived from identifying with the superiority of the United States offered various forms of psychological and emotional compensation for Americans who otherwise felt devalued or threatened. People who invested in notions of U.S. citizenship and belonging that were predicated on the simulated and actual enjoyments of punishment and triage necessarily dissociated themselves from resistant traditions that had opposed the practices of U.S. imperialism, warfare, and racial capitalism as well as the underlying logics that sustained them.

LIBERAL INVESTMENTS IN U.S. EXCEPTIONALISM

When liberals discussed the evident sexualized racial violence depicted in the Abu Ghraib photographs, they conjured other examples of American atrocities. While some liberals reinforced the logic of justice as punishment by calling for the imprisonment of conservatives, other liberals drew connections between Abu Ghraib and the normalcy of violence in U.S. culture, particularly in domestic prisons.[68] Lynching photographs, sadomasochistic practices in pornography, the torture scenes on Fox TV's drama *24* were all invoked to demonstrate the prevalence of torture and sexual violence in U.S. culture. However, invoking other forms of sexualized racial violence (whether real or fictional) rarely elicited calls for the end of U.S. militarism overall. The copious evidence of violence outlined by liberal commentators on Abu Ghraib did not seem to seriously perturb underlying emotional investments in the idea that the United States nonetheless continued to offer the best model of democracy.

In the 1930s philosopher Walter Benjamin argued that fascism became popularly embraced in Europe in part because "in the name of progress its *opponents* treat [fascism] as a historical norm."[69] Benjamin was referring to people who were shocked at the destruction brought by warfare, capitalism, and fascism in Europe yet simultaneously believed that these practices were normative and necessary for the sake of progress. He critiqued the conceptions of history adopted by fascism's opponents as much as its proponents. Such understanding of history, Benjamin argued, takes the degradation of the oppressed for granted and implicitly justifies increasingly violent states of emergency. So long as people are outraged at the by-products of warfare, capitalism, and fascism but continue to take these as historical norms, the opponents of these systems will remain complicit in their persistence.

Similar conceptions of history were implied in U.S. liberal responses to Abu Ghraib. Although many expressed shock and outrage at the by-products of U.S. militarism, capitalism, and racism, liberals tended to remain attached to historical narratives of American democracy that were not only progressivist but also exceptionalist. Despite the conspicuous tortures at Abu Ghraib, it was generally assumed that the violence of militarism and the exploitation of capitalist development were necessary (if at times unfortunate) undertakings in bringing about democratic progress in the Middle East. The evidence of sexualized racism depicted in the photographs symbolized a regressive moment in this progressivist narrative of history. The assumption that various forms of oppression are inevitable historical norms is evident in a comment made by rstybeach266 condemning the tortures on the liberal website Media Matters for America. Responding to Jay Severin's declaration that U.S. soldiers had essentially treated Abu Ghraib Iraqi prisoners to a week in Las Vegas, rstybeach266 argued:

The idea that our enemies torture our prisoners, or that the US has tortured individuals in the past, does not suddenly give us the right to torture anyone. Every incident of torture IN THE PAST should be looked at with scorn. This is the exact reason we list these incidents in history books, so that we DON'T REPEAT THEM, simply because it is not a just policy. The US and its citizens feel that the United States is above all of these countries we have issues with, the US feels it has the obligation to make these countries BETTER, more like us. The overall consensus among civilized nations, and any rational person can tell you, torture is wrong. We as a nation should be setting the HIGHEST of examples when dealing with any military situation, considering the fact that we have the most powerful, sophisticated, and expensive military ever known to mankind. Torturing POWs or possible terrorists is wrong.[70]

This commentator argues that Americans must condemn torture at Abu Ghraib precisely because they are superior to "uncivilized" nations. Each instance of past American violence, the respondent seems to claim, should be used to make America more progressively righteous. In such a historicist narrative, the violent states of emergency experienced by the oppressed become lessons that give those who practice them the opportunity to evolve and become less violent. The unjustified suffering of the oppressed is taken for granted as something that will always exist, not as something that people believe can actually stop taking place at all. This preserves the conception of history that Benjamin was critiquing almost a century earlier, accepting the violence integrally constitutive of the systems of warfare, capitalism, and racism as historical norms. Of course, these are observable realities. However, in assuming that these oppressive acts are natural and inevitable, they function to foreclose imaginaries that create modes of being that are not integrally predicated on denigration, violence, and exploitation.

Emotional expressions of shame permeated liberal responses but were not generally expressed in relation to the violations that Iraqi prisoners suffered at Abu Ghraib. Rather, the shame focused on how these tortures made Americans look to the rest of the world. Liberals repeatedly expressed shame over the ways Abu Ghraib damaged America's global reputation. When another series of Abu Ghraib photographs was released in February 2006, debates again ensued regarding the impact they would have on America's international standing. As for those who were responsible for what happened at Abu Ghraib, the majority view was that political responsibility did not fall on Americans but rather on governmental and conservative leaders. Consider the following exchange on the blog of the listener-supported radio station WFMU (Jersey City, New Jersey):

Mike D.: The freedoms we enjoy, and most specifically the freedom to vote, also come with responsibilities. My point is that the responsibility for what happened is not limited to Bush, his Administration, or the military. It's on all of us, there's no getting around it.

. . .

Nextstop: I dispute the use of a key word by Mike: "Responsibility."
I am not responsible for Abu Ghraib.
I am, however, ashamed.

. . .

Chris: It's true. I'm FOR western civilization and all of its values. I never defended what went on at Abu Ghraid [*sic*], I simply noted that it is wrong to see it as an indictment of our nation. That is what militant Islam does and neither you nor I nor any other decent citizen of a free nation supports the acts of those animals that are now (thankfully) in prison.[71]

As is evident in this exchange and many others like it, shame over the tarnished image of America after the Abu Ghraib photographs were released did not disrupt the general liberal and conservative consensus that the United States was morally superior to the absurdly broad imposition described as militant Islam. By tracing the contours of the liberal public sphere, we can see that the Abu Ghraib photographs were interpreted through frameworks that took orientalist constructions of Arab hyperaggression as true. Such ideological and emotional assumptions functioned to preserve liberal investments in U.S. exceptionalism and to justify warfare and racial imperialism as necessary political-economic infrastructures for the sake of progress, albeit with greater limits to state power.

Another way to manage the ruptures in dominant national self-perceptions was to express empathy. In general, liberal respondents did not express empathy for the Iraqi prisoners or Arabs who suffered as a result of the war in Iraq. Rather, they felt distressed when imagining themselves or one of their family members in similarly tortured positions. This form of empathy tended to diminish the specificity of the Iraqi prisoners who had been violated, suggesting that there were limits to the publics' emotional identifications with Iraqis. Expressing the sentiment that one was sorry about what happened at Abu Ghraib and that most Americans would never endorse such tortures helped to quell anxieties about the wider implications of the tortures—namely, that they were extensions of normalized U.S. cultures of racial and sexual violence that implicated everyone, not just a few bad apples. On the one hand, such expressions of empathy created possibilities for publics to disidentify with U.S. militarism and violence and question the general illegitimacy of U.S. imperialism. On the other hand, expressing empathy offered a disavowal mechanism for liberals to distinguish themselves morally from conservatives and Arab extremists alike. Saying that one felt bad for what happened at Abu Ghraib but failing to engage in any war resistance practices functioned to reify the moral goodness of the U.S. liberal subject without disrupting the apparatuses of warfare. Feeling good for feeling bad discouraged public engagement in antiwar actions, substituting feelings of empathy for the labor of resistance.[72]

Indeed, there was such prevalent public ignorance about Middle Eastern nations and cultures that even if one conjured up facts and evidence with which to contest these widely shared beliefs and emotions, one would be hard pressed to find them in dominant news media. In *Culture and Imperialism*, Said demonstrates that cultural, discursive, and political-economic American structures purposely eliminate settings that foster disidentifications with the ideological fantasy of U.S. exceptionalism. "There has not yet developed a discourse in the American public space that does anything more than identify with power."[73] That is, public investments in U.S. exceptionalism can hardly be ruptured in the absence of alternative epistemological and emotional frames of understanding. Such ruptures would not only have to produce forms of collective consciousness that question the validity and necessity of U.S. global warfare rather than debating which military tactics are legitimate or illegitimate, but would also have to stop treating sexualized racial violence and sadistic torture as historical norms and unfortunate by-products of progress.

This liberal complicity with U.S. warfare, capitalism, and racism—even if unconsciously held—was widely normalized through media representations and narratives that had long trained U.S. constituents to enjoy simulated exercises in violent destruction. We might return to Benjamin's last paragraphs in "The Work of Art in the Age of Mechanical Reproduction" to think through the effects produced by cultural processes that aestheticize and spectacularly trivialize the suffering of enemies. In that essay, Benjamin claims that humankind's "self-alienation has reached such a degree that it can experience its own destruction as an aesthetic pleasure of the first order."[74] In other words, processes that foster alienation conceal the fact that destroying others is also a way of destroying ourselves. Like Rosa Luxembourg in *The Accumulation of Capital*, Benjamin understood imperial warfare as the desire to expand capitalist modes of production, markets, and surplus labor populations in order to increase possibilities for surplus capital.[75] But he argued that this expansion was made acceptable to populations through cultural apparatuses that converted the violent processes inherent in these systems into aesthetic enjoyments. The aestheticization of violence helps to profoundly detach us from the consequences we produce in other people's lives. In turn, such radical social alienation allows us to overtly or guiltily enjoy others' suffering because our capacity to feel connected to distant enemies is radically diminished. Profound forms of alienation are required of both imperial subjects and the subjects of imperialism in order to make them comply with the violent processes of warfare and the death economies of security, punishment, imprisonment, and the intelligence industries.

Social alienation is concealed from consciousness through simulated enactments of violent aggression that offer immediate libidinal and psychosexual rewards. We might remember that the realm of American culture—video games, movies, television series, fairy tales, novels—regularly stimulates emotional economies of fear toward Arab enemies and offers viewing audiences affective satisfaction through the enemy's simulated violent destruction.

Joel Surnow, co-creator and executive producer of the popular counterterrorism television show *24*, unabashedly admits that he toys with such public fears and enjoyments: The show is "ripped out of the Zeitgeist of what people's fears are—their paranoia that we're going to be attacked. . . . There are not a lot of measures short of extreme measures that will get it done. . . . America wants the war on terror fought by Jack Bauer. He's a patriot."[76] Describing the show's numerous torture scenes (67 over 5 seasons), Howard Gordon, the co-creator and executive producer of the show, declared, "Honest to God, I'd call them improvisations in sadism." Gordon admits that these sadistic scenes are concocted by the writers' own imaginations.[77] The show, watched by liberals and conservatives alike, redeploys patterned orientalist projections articulated by authors like Patai but adds an important dimension. The show aims to align the television audience's emotions and identification with Jack Bauer, the American patriot. It does so by producing affective rewards and enjoyments when the Arab terrorist enemy is killed, compounding these emotional effects by the 24 hours that wind down to a ticktock beat on the screen. Each episode has to incrementally increase the aestheticization of violence to conjure up the affective pleasure of destroying the terrorist enemy. The spectators' affect is structured according to the presumed goals of American militarism.

As Jonathan Beller argues, such cinematic exercises in aestheticizing violence against constructed Arab persecutory enemies train U.S. national subjects to consider themselves extensions of the military state apparatus.

This conceptualized machinic interface of state and subject is "the military-industrial complex," which seems at first glance simply to name a set of material social relations of intertwined state and corporate interests that are in the obvious if sometimes lamentable business of killing people, but also names (in a whisper) the accommodating and totalitarian psychosis of socially sanctioned mass murder, along with *an ostensibly untranscendentable aesthetico-moral rubric of violence and self-destruction, and therefore an ontology and a metaphysics.*[78]

Liberals adopted national identities that accommodated socially sanctioned mass murder by endorsing the aesthetic-moral rubric of U.S. exceptionalism. Considered inviolable and untranscendentable, the idea that the U.S. nation was destined to lead other nations toward the progress of democracy minimized or disavowed the extent of global self-destruction and alienation perpetuated by American warfare and racial capitalism.

Like their conservative counterparts, some liberals also revealed emotional investments in the simulated enjoyments of sadistic violence that are regularly encouraged by the ideological and affective logics of triage, punishment, and incarceration. Instead of imagining Arab terrorists as the objects of torture, liberals engaged in fantasies that punished conservatives. Consider the following exchange among liberal commentators responding to Jay Severin's claims that Iraqi prisoners were essentially treated to a week in Las Vegas:

defkon_1: Sounds like a good reason to start up a collection to send Jay to Las Vegas and have him treated like the AG prisoners. I'll personally pay for him to be hog-tied and smeared in his own feces. Who else is in?

. . .

pete592: I'll throw in some blindfolds, vicious barking dogs, a camera, and some electrodes for his fingers. Maybe if we're lucky, we can find some smiling soldiers giving the "thumbs up" to complete the package.

. . .

Lynn: don't forget the guy on guy naked pyrimid [*sic*].

. . .

rufus t firefly: Defkon. Sounds good to me. I'll bring a camera so we can take some candids of electrodes being hooked up to his genitals. I'm especially looking forward to seeing Severin, Limbaugh and all the rest of the AG and "Club Gitmo" apologists all trussed up in one big sweaty smelly pyramid of some good ol' fashion prison love. We'll leave the hoods off this time, though. "Squeal like pig for me, boy!"

. . .

pete 592: LOL. . . . Let's show Limbaugh what a real "fraternity prank" is.

. . .

iflurry 8094: What happens in Abu Ghraib . . . stays in Abu Ghraid [*sic*].[79]

To condemn the Abu Ghraib tortures, the liberal respondents ironically articulated fantasies that reified and replenished the affective pleasures of punishment and triage encouraged by U.S. militarism and incarceration. Such exercises not only allowed liberals to displace responsibility for what happened at Abu Ghraib onto conservatives but also allowed them to gain affective rewards through simulated acts of sexualized punishment and humiliation without having to avow their investments in such economies of pleasure.

ETHICAL WITNESSING FROM THE TRADITION OF THE OPPRESSED

Benjamin understood that the misrecognized and invisible epistemologies of the oppressed were vital to rupturing the grand narratives of historicism and progress offered by the powerful and elite. Benjamin took what most writers discarded as the debris of history to reveal the collapses, contradictions, and juxtapositions of history as moments filled with both danger and the opportunity to collectively organize against oppressive structures. As Neferti Tadiar argues, the opportunity to rupture oppressive ideologies and practices "lies in the daily exercise of our creative capacities to remake the world, in the acts of living in ways that depart from the orthodox dreams of our world-historical, real-politik time."[80] The tradition of the oppressed teaches us to "attend to the cultural resources that people have drawn upon and invented in their daily struggle to prevail over the small and grave, intermittent and relentless acts of repression, debasement and dispossession directed against them."[81]

The refusal to participate in the logics of denigration, dehumanization, and destruction conspicuously revealed by Abu Ghraib entails challenging the underlying structures of seeing and feeling that made its institutional emergence possible. It means disidentifying with the logics of imperial warfare that purport to bring about national protection and security but only exacerbate global destruction. It means thwarting the logics of triage that justify the removal, punishment, and containment of people deemed pathological and imagining other forms of collective accountability and redress. It means rupturing cultural modalities that aestheticize human suffering or encourage us to take pleasure in simulated acts of violent denigration. It means cultivating emotional economies and practices that value humanization, freedom, and dignity over profits and hierarchical orders of power. As Tadiar argues, "Such vital work depends on the freeing of our imaginations from the hold of existing realities, which naturalize the presence and necessity of all the apparatuses of social regulation and expropriation supporting the global order, from states and prisons to military forces and labour markets."[82]

Those who interrogate the connections between global militarism and domestic incarceration see that these apparatuses offer us pseudoversions of security. In reality, they construct the very objects they purport to police. By perpetually disseminating fears of terrorism to accumulate public aggression toward Arab and Muslim people and nations in the Middle East, the apparatuses of U.S. militarism, punishment, and incarceration proliferate gendered racism, social alienation, fear, and insecurity as permanent features of twenty-first-century lives.

Although they were marginal, epistemological frameworks of seeing and feeling that countered such discourses of security were reflected in U.S. public discourses. *Village Voice* writer Richard Goldstein highlighted how U.S. public emotional investments in the pleasures of imperialist domination and in the logics of triage and punishment were fundamental to the perpetuation of oppression through U.S. militarism. In his article "Stuff Happens! Don't Call It Torture. It's Just a Broomstick up the Butt," Goldstein seems to invoke a parallel between the NYPD's brutality and sexualized rape of Abner Louima in 1997 and the Abu Ghraib tortures, even though Louima is not mentioned.

One reason why these photos are such a sensation is that they are stimulating. Especially the image of that woman grinning over a pyramid of naked men. She's the Phallic Female, watching guys parade around naked and jerk off before her. This really gets the kitten-with-a-whip crowd drooling. And when it comes to sadistic pleasure, there's nothing like forcing a man to give a simulated blowjob or take a peg-leg–sized anal probe. Shit, you won't even see that on *Oz*.

But that's the great perk of war. You can unleash the darkest reaches of your libido. Murdering, mutilating, and raping are all part of the adrenaline rush—and nothing feels better than that forbidden thrill in the name of God and country.

The most distressing thing in those photos from Abu Ghraib was also the least remarked upon. That soldier standing over his prostrate prisoners, holding his thumb up, was wearing surgical gloves. Was he afraid of being contaminated by his victim's blood, feces, semen—or just their humanity? We'll never know. But it's an astonishing symbol of what America is becoming: a nation where suffering is tolerable—even pleasurable—as long as the shit doesn't get on our hands.[83]

The writer deduces from one detail in an Abu Ghraib photograph a logic that equivocates U.S. justice with incarceration, bodily harm, rape, humiliation, punishment, and pleasure. Presumably, U.S. state agents enact their punishments and amputations on those they consider pathological without wanting to get their health contaminated or stained. Although Goldstein does not make propositions for ways of seeing and feeling that would rupture the underlying logics of triage and punishment, he is unique in arguing that the destruction of warfare, capitalism, and racism should not be treated as historical norms or as necessary collateral damage for the sake of progress.

Yanar Mohammed, co-founder of the Organization for Women's Freedom in Iraq, likewise strengthened frames of understanding and feeling that challenged the logics and practices that justified an ever-expanding U.S. military industrial complex. Exposing the fallacy of American support for democratic and anti-patriarchal measures, Mohammed noted that the United States has consistently sustained groups that increased the levels of fundamentalism in Iraq rather than groups who were fighting for democratization. "The freedom-loving people of Iraq . . . the women's groups, the labor groups, the youth groups, have never been supported. . . . We see all the support going to the misogynist groups, to those who are—who have inhumane agendas. And this was the occupation of Iraq. This is what it's about: the Talibanization of Iraq. This is what we have witnessed."[84] Mohammed follows this comment with a call for the immediate end to the U.S. occupation in Iraq as a necessary precondition to beginning the process of imagining another possible future.

This other future, for Mohammed, needed to be determined by Iraqi people without the imposing interventions of U.S. warfare and foreign policy interests.

There will be some chaos for some time, but because the extremists do not have the strong support from the people that they should have—most of the support came from either surrounding countries or the big powers in the world. The U.S. administration prefers to see moderate, so-called moderate, Islamists in power, and what's moderate about somebody who looks at women as less than men, about someone who thinks that people belonging to other sects of Islam are less of human beings, and about someone who has no accountability. . . . The people of Iraq are still an integrated society. The youth do not want to see the extremists in power. We will have the dynamics that will make it work, be it by election, be it by the grassroots, who will bring about the democratic sense into the country.[85]

Mohammed implicates herself in a future hope for democracy in Iraq. This is not the democracy touted by the Bush administration, the conservatives who clearly enjoy the sadistic pleasures of warfare, or even the liberals who claim innocence and exceptionality in the face of permanent U.S. global warfare. This is a democracy whose future cannot be charted and whose pathway cannot be legislated by imperial domination.

Iris Marion Young proposes a model to encourage a shared sense of political responsibility for stopping and disrupting globally interlocking systemic oppressions.[86] Unlike individual forms of harm, systemic oppressions implicate everyone in their structures. For example, because U.S. residents pay into a tax system that funds U.S. militarism, they are implicated in the oppressions perpetuated by the armed forces but are not necessarily individually responsible. Rather than resorting to liability models that seek to identify individual perpetrators in order to seek monetary rewards or punishment as compensation, Young proposes a political responsibility model that suspends individualized or group-based politics of blame for systemic oppressions in favor of holding everyone responsible for the outcomes produced by their habituated, unconscious and conscious practices. This future-looking politics of responsibility motivates people to act against injustices less out of a general concern for suffering than "on the more specific grounds that we are connected by our actions to the processes that cause injustices for others."[87] In other words, by accepting Martin Luther King Jr.'s axiom that injustice anywhere is a threat to justice everywhere, shared and diverse forms of political responsibility have the potential to diminish the emotional rewards people derive from channeling aggression toward those they define as pathological. Rather than simply replace the content of who is pathological and who is healthy, people need to divest from the very logics and emotional economies that equate punishment and triage with justice. To do so, people need to create modes of belonging, accountability, and justice that are not predicated on someone else's denigration and dehumanization. This is of course possible, but it is difficult to practice so long as we remain invested in the aestheticized pleasures of violence and the cheap thrills of feeling superior over deprecated enemies.

Tricia Rose reminds us that "justice is an intimate matter. It is a social commitment that is lived in interpersonal, intimate exchanges. Intimate justice is a social commitment that works to ensure that we have the freedom to love, and can express our love to be free."[88] Public investments in U.S. imperialist supremacy, concealed by forms of conservative displacement and liberal disavowal, demonstrate that the military-industrial complex is not just about macropolitical economic structures. It is also about emotional rewards, psychological losses, and intimate desires. Ethical witnessing depends on a notion of political responsibility predicated on an ethics of care for the ways we are implicated in producing others' suffering, even if that suffering is taking place as far away as Abu Ghraib, Iraq.

WELFARE DEPENDENTS AND ILLEGAL ALIENS: THE EMOTIONAL ECONOMIES OF SOCIAL WAGE RETRENCHMENT

Economies of fear attached to criminality and terrorism encouraged many people to call for more prisons, more punishment, and more militarism. As legislators sought to allocate increasing amounts of taxpayer revenue to the budgets and infrastructures of military carcerality, they argued that the state's other half—the social welfare state—had grown too big. Neoliberal advocates claimed that big government was stagnating American development. They claimed it was encouraging U.S. constituents to remain childlike. Spoiled by Big Daddy Government, constituents purportedly refused to grow out of their dependency on state-subsidized goods and into economically self-reliant adults.

Beginning in the late 1970s and early 1980s, neoliberalism, a system that favors less regulation over markets and less taxation over big businesses and wealthy elites in order to increase their profit margins, sought to triage aspects of government that offered sustenance and services. If the parts of the state that offered life-sustaining goods to people were not reduced or cut off, neoliberalism's proponents argued, American workers would become lazy. Government's function, they argued, was to punish and protect. Taxing big businesses and regulating markets for the purposes of redistributing resources to U.S. residents in the form of assistance programs for poor people, health care, environmental protections, education, transportation, and affordable housing were deemed wasteful spending.

Such neoliberal arguments reformulated an ideological fantasy of economic self-reliance that had long been central to American identity. Not all forms of economic self-reliance were considered legitimate, however. To gain social validity, economic self-reliance had to be obtained individually rather than collectively or with governmental help. Second, self-reliance had to be earned through hard work and legal means. Despite the fact that such strict criteria would have invalidated most multinational corporations and banks, Wall Street finance firms, and wealthy elites whose self-reliance was largely obtained through theft, inheritance, government bailouts, and/or illegal means, public focus rarely shifted vertically to interrogate what the wealthiest sectors were doing.[1] Instead, U.S. publics sought to prove their self-reliance by distinguishing themselves from those at the socioeconomic bottom. When it came to work and economics, the phrase *welfare dependency* became a condensed signifier indicative of everything self-reliant Americans were not. People who were welfare dependent were shamed for their insolence and indigence and presumed to be parasites feeding on taxpayers' hard-earned money. Such shaming economies yielded affective rewards of superiority, solidifying an embodied sense of value in those who believed that the poor had only themselves to blame for their marginalization.

There was one more caveat. Public goods that U.S. constituents across the political spectrum continued to desire and legitimate (K–12 education, Social Security payments, Medicare insurance, libraries, public parks) were to be restricted in their use. After all, if Americans' hard-earned dollars subsidized these social welfare goods, why should immigrants, who were deemed illegitimate illegal aliens and who were presumed to evade income and property takes, benefit from them? Undocumented immigrants may be hard workers, the rhetoric went, but this did not entitle them to the limited and diminishing resources the nation offered.

Thus began a thirty-year struggle to privatize public goods previously subsidized through taxation systems that asked corporations, big businesses, and everyday Americans to contribute to the collective social wage. State capacities that offered services that sustained lives were gradually reduced, and the rates at which big businesses and wealthy elites contributed to the collective economic safety net of U.S. society progressively decreased. Things got worse overall for most working- and middle-class Americans, but impoverished communities of color were stripped of public assets and their entitlements with even greater ferocity.

Those who fought for neoliberal restructuring and social wage divestment traded in the currency of affective stigmatization and valorization to shape public desires and fears. Rather than arguing on the basis of facts and evidence, politicians and pundits told publics that dependency was shameful and that undocumented immigrants were parasitic; they validated individualist aggrandizement at the expense of others and rewarded possessive and competitive corporate endeavors even as the rest of American workers suffered. The emotional economies of social wage divestment were therefore critical to widening income and wealth gaps. Although most U.S. constituents unwittingly supported neoliberal shifts that increasingly eroded their national economic interests, wealthy municipalities regularly won localized movements to restrict the use of public goods for themselves only. Rather than share public goods with poor neighborhoods and people deemed dependent, wealthier neighborhoods and municipalities regularly demonstrated what George Lipsitz describes as "cultural commitments . . . that promote hostile privatism and defensive localism as suburban structures of feeling."[2] By devaluing modes of being that value collective interdependence and sharing, such commitments encouraged wealthier homeowners to "capture amenities and advantages for themselves while outsourcing responsibilities and burdens to less powerful communities."[3] These suburban structures of feeling constructed America's impoverished citizens and undocumented immigrants living in inner cities as persecutory enemies who stole their enjoyments and quality of life.

THE SHAMING ECONOMIES OF WELFARE

The social contracts of traditional liberal democracies are predicated on the assumption that states have a responsibility to take care of national subjects' basic needs by offering subsidies for health care, education, affordable housing, transportation, environmental protection, parks, libraries, and emergency services. In the United States the safety net offered by publicly subsidized social welfare goods is relatively new. Much of the infrastructure for subsidized health care, education, labor and environmental protections, and retirement pensions became available only in the 1930s and 1940s, after long working-class struggles.[4] State regulation of markets to prevent corporate monopolies were instituted largely after it was determined that the 1929 stock market crash could have been prevented if capitalist greed and wealth inequalities had been tempered. Even as social welfare goods expanded in the post–World War II era, people of color were routinely excluded from their benefits until the 1960s.[5] Midcentury freedom movements incorporated welfare rights, fair housing, and educational equity as part of their economic, gender, and racial justice agendas. The grassroots National Welfare Rights Organization forced states to change eligibility and procedural rules that had excluded Black citizens and to raise benefits and increase availability of benefits to female-headed households.[6] The Fair Housing Act of 1968 finally prohibited racial discrimination in mortgage lending and real estate markets. Coupled with President Johnson's War on Poverty and other affirmative action programs meant to redress the historical exclusion of Blacks, Latino/as, and other people of color in education and employment, these gains appeared to move in progressive directions.

Yet these were short-lived victories. The links between feminist racial justice movements, the War on Poverty, and affirmative action programs that acknowledged the state's responsibility to redress past wrongs faced vehement opposition from many white publics.[7] By the time an economic recession hit in the 1970s, those who had been the disproportionate and sometimes exclusive beneficiaries of these goods (primarily white Americans and men) were fearful of how this widening social wage would affect their status and their wallets. State processes necessary for instituting antipoverty programs, adding Social Security payments for women, desegregating public education, and offering Medicaid for the poor were projected to cut into their entitlements and require higher taxes.

By the late 1970s homeowners were revolting against increasing taxes. California's Proposition 13 passed with populist support, cutting homeowner and business property taxes and inspiring similar measures in other states. Although Proposition 13 focused on reducing or capping property tax rates in California, the antitax populist sentiment engendered demands for reductions in other types of taxes as well. Indeed, the homeowners' revolt was largely ignored until a group of wealthy business elites got involved. Led by Howard Jarvis, business elites saw a great opportunity to capitalize on homeowners' antitax sentiments, enabling them to pass measures that reduced business taxes as well. After adding provisions that would reduce taxes on business properties, these elites put a lot of money behind ballot initiatives such as Proposition 13.

By 1981 Ronald Reagan's anti–big government and antitax platform would similarly capitalize on middle-class Americans' economic anxieties over inflation and increasing taxes by passing the Economic Recovery Tax Act of 1981. Although it appeared to serve middle-class homeowners' interests, the Recovery Act overwhelmingly favored the wealthiest families and corporations. As Clarence Lo argues in *Small Property Versus Big Government*, "Ronald Reagan's secret was his ability to appeal to blue-collar and middle-class voters on economic issues even as he pursued a program to benefit corporations and upper-income earners."[8] Indeed, "Only 7 percent of the benefits went to families who then earned less than $20,000, but numbered one-half of all families."[9] The legislation also reduced taxes on business investments and depreciation, but these did not favor small businesses. Rather, the legislation awarded 80 percent of its benefits to the 1,700 largest corporations.[10]

Reagan's success depended on a public secret that enjoyed demonizing and shaming people who were poor. Such shaming was directed at those deemed white trash because of their supposed unwillingness to conform to proper work ethics and family values. But the greatest shaming and demonizing was reserved for Black and Latina mothers who were receiving public assistance in the form of housing, food stamps, and Aid to Families with Dependent Children (AFDC) cash stipends. The structures of feeling that endorsed the demonization of women of color were deeply sedimented in U.S. historical narratives and ideologies. But in the aftermath of the civil rights movements, they had to be reformulated as cultural pathologies rather than biological inferiorities.

The political process of converting the legitimate economic demands of people of color into self-inflicted cultural pathologies began just as freedom movements were gaining ground. A 1965 report by Senator Patrick Moynihan and the Department of Labor myopically focused on the supposedly nonnormative structure of Black families as the cause of Black economic marginalization.[11] Moynihan argued that Black women's matriarchal dominance was preventing Black economic mobility because Black men were not being allowed to take their proper place as heads of households. Moynihan's argument had incredible affective appeal. Rather than holding white majorities accountable for their complicity in producing racial inequality through exclusionary and discriminatory practices in housing, employment, education, and society, Moynihan's discourse directed dominant white majorities' emotional economies to engage in the pleasures of scapegoating intraracial family dynamics for systematic poverty.

For Black women Moynihan's discourse had an incredible "damned if you do, damned if you don't" effect. On the one hand, compared to white patriarchal family ideals, Black women were considered too independent. By extension, Black men were positioned as not manly enough to be the dominant breadwinners or to discipline Black women into their "proper" subordinate gender role. Affectively, both white patriarchal society and Black men were encouraged to derive aggressive enjoyments from demonizing and disciplining Black women's independence, but for different reasons. To regain patriarchal authority over Black women's purportedly hyperindependent defiance, Black men were urged to compensate for insecurities tied to patriarchal manhood through Black women's subordination. By contrast, white people who sought to affirm themselves as sexually proper and normative families needed Black women's independence as a referent for nonnormativity.

On the other hand, Black women were blamed for reproducing poverty; hence they were simultaneously accused of being too dependent on the state's social welfare. Under this formulation the U.S. government was positioned as the paternal figure supervising Black matriarchal family structures, in which Black men were figured as absent fathers. Through public assistance the state reproduced white supremacist notions of benevolent paternalism, because Black families putatively could not take care of themselves without paternal state assistance. The state symbolically became the patriarchal authority that was going to usher Black men and Black women into a proper family structure that was not feminized or infantilized as dependent. In reality, public assistance programs were grossly insufficient for getting anyone out of poverty.

The charge against Black women's dependency on the state helped regenerate emotional economies of shame. By associating nonpatriarchal family structures (female friendships; communal forms of living and child rearing; multigenerational households; lesbian, gay, bisexual, or transgender partnerships) with immorality and personal failure, such shaming economies encouraged impoverished Black women and families to turn their anger and blame inward on themselves. Rather than understanding such family formations as methods of survival and resilience in the face of gendered racial oppression and state-sanctioned impoverishment, Black women's survival strategies were demonized as causing Black communal failings. As black feminist scholars Angela Y. Davis, Patricia Hill Collins, Kimberly Springer, and Dorothy Roberts have extensively argued, demonizing Black women as nonnormative in their sexuality, fertility, and family practices allowed white majorities to avoid loosening their tight and largely exclusive grip on institutional access to economic wealth, political power, and social privileges.[12]

Economies of shame attached to welfare dependency also recruited some Black people to participate in the stigmatization of public assistance and other social services. In particular, Black men who felt the wounds of emasculation as a result of their diminished abilities to provide economically sometimes focused their political energies on reasserting Black patriarchy and individual independence. Moynihan's political discourse refueled the erroneous assumption that Black women took jobs away from Black men and fed cultural projections of Black women as domineering and aggressive. As Springer demonstrates, "Black women did not usurp black men's jobs, because black women occupied gendered positions in the sex-segregated job market. . . . The so-called black matriarchies were far from financially stable without black men's second income."[13] But the political discourse of Black matriarchy as a central cause of Black men's emasculation trumped the empirical realities of sex-segregated labor markets and the fact that Black women were actually at the bottom of the economic ladder compared to both white people and Black men.[14] Projecting Black women as emasculators endowed them with a malefic power they did not actually possess.

Such dominant and intraracial projections set the stage for constructing one of Reaganism's central domestic persecutory enemies: the welfare queen. Intent on building public support for cutting social welfare services in order to support free market neoliberal policy shifts during the 1980s, Reagan popularized the image of Black women who drove Cadillacs and exploited state bureaucracies through welfare fraud to avoid doing honest hard work. This stereotype did not encapsulate most Black women's experiences; most Black women continued to work because public assistance stipends were insufficient to make ends meet. Nonetheless, the circulation of political discourses about welfare queens and the idea that state assistance encouraged lack of personal responsibility created a socially shared emotional economy that aggrandized contempt for the poor in general and Black women who received state assistance in particular.

The expanding negative affective economy tied to Black women's welfare dependence worked in tandem with increasing anxieties and fears over Mexican-origin women's reproductive practices and the economic burdens of undocumented immigration. Correlations were drawn between a growing Latino/a population in the West and undocumented immigrants' supposed freeloading on publicly subsidized state resources. Because Latino/as were racialized as illegal aliens intent on stealing American jobs and taxpayer-subsidized goods irrespective of their immigration status, the reproductive practices and migratory patterns of Latino/as came under increased scrutiny.

By the late 1970s "a host of interests converged that collectively created a watershed period in the social construction of Mexican-origin women's fertility as problematic."[15] As Elena R. Gutiérrez demonstrates in *Fertile Matters*, this was a period in which a growing number of U.S. government officials, demographers, population control activists, and medical professionals "were concerned with curbing the birthrate as a means to avoid overpopulation. The reduction of fertility rates became the primary means through which advocates hoped to control the impending 'population bomb,' placing women's fertility (and thus, their bodies) at the center of national interest."[16] Although the rising birthrate was putatively a national concern that applied to all women, Mexican-origin women's fertility came under special scrutiny as social scientists began to draw connections between U.S. population increases, the higher fertility rates of Mexican-origin women, and undocumented immigration. Such links were specifically made in states such as California, where the population had increased by 27 percent during the 1960s and 1970s.[17]

Despite such anxieties about overpopulation, studies showed that the nation had reached its lowest ever average birthrate of 2.03 children per family by 1972.[18] This rate more than complied with the zero population growth rate advocated by population control activists and government officials. As Gutiérrez argues, social scientists discovered that rather than experiencing population growth, "the nation was actually undergoing a population *shift*, with birthrates among poor whites and nonwhites remaining significantly higher than their more affluent counterparts."[19] In other words, population control experts and government officials expressed subtle and not-so-subtle anxieties over the fact that America's demographics were becoming increasingly nonwhite and working class.

Politicians capitalized on rising public anxieties over Latino/a population growth in the West and Southwest by constructing perceptions of "an impending catastrophic situation of world poverty brought about by excessively fertile women and an immigrant invasion from Mexico."[20] The racialized and gendered projection of welfare dependence functioned as a culturally constructed receptacle for public anxieties about the declining white population and the economic recession of the late 1970s. The projected dependence of Latina women on needs-based assistance and the anticipated taxpayer burden ushered in by undocumented immigration functioned to fuel an affect of indignation and possessiveness in Americans who were facing rising unemployment and stagnant wages. In fact, Black and Latina women's children and undocumented immigrants had little to do with the causes of poverty and the national economic recession. But the projection of welfare dependence worked extremely well to build public consent for economic agendas that sought to reduce needs-based assistance programs and subsidized public goods in order to implement neoliberal economic policies.[21]

The projection of welfare dependence afforded compensatory psychological and affective rewards to U.S. publics who were feeling threatened by anticipated losses of white demographic, political, racial, and cultural privileges. U.S. publics who were angry about actual economic losses were encouraged to direct this aggression toward the least powerful rather than to notice the ways in which state policies and private forces were restructuring the U.S. economy to favor the wealthiest sectors. Focusing public attention and emotions on Black and Latina public assistance recipients worked exceedingly well to cultivate political consent for policy shifts that would make the rich richer while making it appear that the state was actually serving working- and middle-class (white) Americans.

These myths of Black and Latina dependence and familial and sexual non-normativity became so popularly entrenched in public emotional and ideological structures that sociological evidence about the actual factors that contributed to upward mobility in the post–civil rights era was persistently refuted or ignored. As Thomas Shapiro has extensively demonstrated, "Inheritance is more important in determining life chances than college degrees, number of children in the family, marital status, full-time employment, or household composition."[22] Although wealth and inheritance have persistently proven to be the most significant forces in determining people's life chances and opportunities in the post–civil rights era, U.S. publics are repeatedly encouraged to inhabit an ideological fantasy of economic self-reliance predicated on concealing the ways discriminatory policies and practices in lending, real estate markets, education, transportation and employment have enabled white Americans to build inheritance while overwhelmingly denying these same opportunities to people of color.

The argument that cultural and behavioral deficiencies caused poor Black and Latino/a people to remain in poverty became prevalent even among those oppressed and targeted by Reagan's gendered and racial demonology. In the general public domain, however, welfare dependence was soon equated with an identity that was antithetical to the traditional American values of hard work, personal responsibility, and individual self-sufficiency. The negative affective value attached to public assistance programs for the poor would encourage publics to unwittingly advocate for slashing *all* social welfare programs and public goods.

The Clair Huxtable Media Effect

For white publics the projection of welfare dependence grew in emotional value as media representations of Black welfare queens, crack mothers, and pregnant undocumented Latinas crossing the U.S. border increased their circulation in the 1970s and 1980s. In a social context of vanishing jobs, stagnant wages, and rising costs in health care, housing, and education, the New Right coupled the burdensome problem of welfare dependence with the notion that poor Black and Latino/a communities were fraught with impoverished family values, immorality, criminality, and sexual deviance. This "not only released members of the white majority from any sense of responsibility for the many sins of their fathers, but it gave them reason to feel that they were the 'truly victimized.'"[23] Rather than seeing themselves as responsible for redressing the injustices of the economic exploitation and exclusion of people of color, white majorities constructed themselves as victimized taxpayers who were burdened by parasitic, lazy, or illegal dependents. In yet another uniquely American inversion of empirical realities, Black and Latino/a communities who had faced centuries of slavery, labor exploitation, economic marginalization, and legalized racial discrimination were constructed as privileged; they supposedly received handouts and special favors through public assistance programs and affirmative action policies.

Whereas reporters in the western United States increased coverage of what Immigration and Naturalization Service director Leonard Chapman described as the "silent invasion" of undocumented Latino/a immigrants,[24] CBS news documentaries such as "The Vanishing Family: Crisis in Black America" selectively emphasized the pathological sexual behaviors that kept teenage Black mothers in Newark, New Jersey, poor and on welfare. News coverage of Mexican immigration was often coupled with overpopulation discourses and resentment over waning taxpayer resources. By the 1990s pregnant Mexican migrant women intent on crossing the border to gain the entitlements of U.S. citizenship figured prominently in news reports and anti-immigration campaigns. Black mothers' reproductive practices suffered from unprecedented levels of scrutiny as news coverage of Reagan's war on drugs featured irresponsible crack mothers who could not take care of their drug-addicted children, once again emphasizing taxpayer resources expended on the undeserving.[25] As Herman Gray shows in *Watching Race*, the coupling of television images of Black Americans and Latino/a undocumented immigrants "overrunning the borders and apparently competing for shrinking resources . . . made it seem as if (white) America were being attacked from within and without."[26] Whereas Black and Latino men were generally figured under the sign of criminality, Black and Latina women were figured under the sign of hyperfertility, sexual deviance, and welfare dependence.

The general consensus among both conservative and liberal publics that the social problems in poor Black and Latino/a communities were rooted in behavioral, familial, and sexual pathologies would not have been as persuasive had media representations not offered positive racial counterparts to the welfare queen, the crack mother, and the hyperfertile Latina. Symbolized through such representations as *The Cosby Show*'s graceful Clair Huxtable, the poised news anchor Connie Chung, and the self-made entrepreneur Oprah Winfrey, audiences were taught that women of color who purportedly upheld American family values of sexual normativity, responsible work ethics, and a willingness to assimilate into U.S. culture would be validated rather than demonized. Impositions that demanded a politics of respectability of women of color had long historical precedents.[27] However, in the context of the post–civil rights era, representations of respectable women of color effectively concealed the fact that political economic conditions made it increasingly impossible for impoverished Black and Latino/a families to adhere to heteropatriarchal family models and achieve economic self-reliance, if Black and Latino/a people desired such models in the first place.

The expanding prison-industrial complex and the rise in militarism were swooping up young Black and Latino men from impoverished communities en masse. If men of color between the ages of 18 and 34 were not being locked up by the police and the criminal justice system, they likely were getting recruited for the frontlines of America's armed forces. Shrinking employment opportunities in urban geographies and the expansion of militarism meant that by 2010, African American, Latino/a, Asian/Pacific Island, and Native American soldiers made up 30 percent of active duty members and 24.1 percent of the selected reserves. Because of a lack of educational opportunities, men of color were disproportionately concentrated in low-ranking positions.[28] Police killings and intracommunal violence were similarly involved in the tragic removal of men of color from their familial and neighborhood networks.[29]

As a patterned consequence, Black and Latina mothers were not only left to care for children and elderly people but also faced increased burdens to keep their families afloat economically. As William Darity and Samuel Myers argue, "At least one of the central causes for the decline in two-parent families in black communities appears to be the reduction in the supply of economically able men suitable for the roles of husband and father. . . . We contend that black men have become less useful in the emerging economic order; they are socially unwanted, superfluous and marginal."[30] In other words, men of color of marriageable age were not simply decreasing demographically. Because emotional and materialist economies were rendering them less desirable, their attractiveness for marriage was also waning, usually in direct proportion to their economic marginalization. The popular myth that Black women were choosing female-headed households over marriage to remain eligible for state assistance was overwhelmingly unfounded.[31] As projected myth, however, Black female welfare dependence engendered emotional rewards for those invested in the ideological fantasy of economic self-reliance and heteropatriarchal family models that were too big to relinquish. In other words, because this projection functioned to displace anxieties over the decline of heteronormative patriarchal families throughout U.S. society, substantive evidence offered by scholars such as Darity and Myers were trumped by emotional economies and beliefs.

Deepening Poverty

The freedom movements of the 1960s and early 1970s produced emotional economies that created public identification with the plight of the most marginalized and excluded. During those decades, moral arguments that decried the injustices of overt racial and economic exclusion gained significant affective value. Because of this public support, state representatives were able to institute some policies intended to begin redressing past wrongs. President Johnson's Great Society initiatives instituted new programs, such as Medicare and Medicaid, or expanded old ones, such as Social Security, unemployment compensation, food stamps, and public assistance. Cumulatively, these antipoverty programs reduced the percentage of poor Americans from 18 percent in 1960 to 9 percent in 1972.[32] The education, housing, health care, job training, and affirmative action policies instituted under the auspices of the War on Poverty increased African Americans' opportunities and access, setting the stage for an emergent small Black middle class during the late 1970s and 1980s.[33]

The Reagan-Bush era sought to reorient public feelings that identified with the struggle for racial, gender, and economic justice. Emotional economies that popularized dissociative contempt toward poor Black and Latina mothers and toward Latino/a undocumented immigrants gave the New Right and Reaganism the legitimacy they needed for social welfare retrenchment. As Linda Faye Williams demonstrates, such retrenchment eliminated policies and programs that had a disproportionately large Black and Latino/a clientele and benefited the working poor. For example, the 1981 Omnibus Budget Reconciliation Act not only ended public service jobs programs that had been used to increase the ranks of municipal employees but also removed 400,000 people from the food stamp program. Likewise, President Reagan terminated all funding for new subsidized housing and increased the required rental contribution of public housing residents by 5 percent. Overall, public housing expenditures declined by more than 40 percent during the Reagan-Bush era.[34]

In 1988 the Reagan administration passed the Family Support Act, which legislated broad workfare requirements for mothers receiving public assistance. It also granted states the authority to introduce restrictive rules and requirements to meet various behavioral conditions in order to maintain aid eligibility.[35] The convergence of the war on drugs and welfare retrenchment likewise resulted in increased criminalization of drug-dependent mothers. Elaborate and unprecedented punitive policies disproportionately affected poor Black and Latina mothers, who were more likely to be scrutinized because of their contact with state agencies.[36] Moreover, states overwhelmingly refused to increase the cash value of AFDC benefits to keep up with inflation. "Between 1970 and 1994, with inflation taken into account, the median maximum monthly state benefit for a mother with two children on AFDC rolls dropped by 47 percent."[37]

Reagan also introduced stricter eligibility requirements for unemployment benefits, cut Medicaid benefits for the working poor, and eliminated the minimum benefit for low-income Social Security recipients. Together, these policy shifts had the effect of increasing poverty among poor people of all races, although they disproportionately affected Black families headed by women. Between 1979 and 1989, one study found that "among families with children, 63 percent of the increase in the poverty population could be attributed to governmental policy. . . . However, government policy accounted for 87 percent of the increase in poverty for black female-headed households."[38]

By the 1990s emotional economies were severely disidentified with public assistance programs for the poor. One might argue that hegemonic feelings toward welfare recipients were downright contemptuous. The Clinton administration mirrored these sentiments through national policy, passing the Personal Responsibility and Work Opportunity Reconciliation Act (PRWORA) in 1996. This act would abolish AFDC and replace it with block grants to states called Temporary Assistance to Needy Families (TANF), essentially returning widespread authority to the individual states.[39] Because dependency had been fused with poor Black people and Latino/a undocumented immigrants in dominant majorities' imagination and emotive structures, the 1996 welfare reforms were seen as publicly desired remedies to protect economically self-reliant and deserving taxpayers from those who were considered undeserving and illegitimate.

One major effect of PRWORA was to reduce the number of families receiving means-based assistance and introduce mandatory work requirements for recipients. According to the Center on Budget and Policy Priorities, in 1996, when 6.2 million families with children were facing poverty, 4.38 million families were receiving some type of assistance. By 2010, 7.26 million families were facing poverty in the United States, but only 1.98 million families were receiving assistance. This was a 55 percent decline following PRWORA's enactment.[40]

Another major policy shift introduced by PRWORA was to make both documented and undocumented immigrants ineligible for a wide array of public assistance programs. This exclusion of immigrants from public assistance came at a time when most new immigrants were coming from Latin America, the Caribbean, and Asia. This merger materialized when several of the key tenets of California Proposition 187—a ballot initiative that sought to deny undocumented immigrants all public benefits, education, and health services—worked their way into PRWORA and the 1996 Illegal Immigration Reform and Immigration Act. These reforms made undocumented immigrants ineligible to receive most public health services and benefits and made documented immigrants ineligible for the first five years they resided in the United States.[41]

The ideological fantasy of economic self-reliance and the emotional economies that shame public assistance recipients not only function to mask the material and economic shifts that have increased poverty in the post–civil rights era, particularly for single Black and Latina mothers with children. This ideological fantasy and its affective corollaries also function to reify white American family ideals in a time when whiteness, heteropatriarchy, and nuclear family formations are themselves in crisis. The affective economies of contempt and paternalism generated through the demonization of welfare dependence yield enormous affective and psychological value for those who feel threatened by shifts in racial demographics, changing family formations, the definition of marriage, and economic power structures. These fantasies and feelings afford modalities through which to derive a sense of pseudosuperiority and enjoyment. By identifying with the state's ability to sever those it deems too costly, U.S. constituents enjoy expressing racialized and gendered aggressions toward impoverished communities of color in particular and poor people in general. Deriding and denigrating Black and Latina mothers for their purported laziness, hypersexuality, and hyperfertility allows American taxpayers to imagine themselves as increasingly victimized and validated by normative ideals. As these emotional economies increase their circulation, middle- and upper-class people of color are also recruited to adopt affective economies of contempt for poor welfare recipients. By extension, poor people are encouraged to internalize the shame and stigma imposed on them and to lose sight of the ways in which systemic forms of discrimination and disenfranchisement work to deepen their poverty.

Affective investments in the fantasy of economic self-reliance, meritocracy, and deserving taxpayers had the effect of producing wide liberal and conservative support for social wage retrenchment. Slowly, such policy shifts unevenly eroded the economic security of all working- and middle-class Americans, including white Americans.

THE EXCLUSIONARY ECONOMIES OF NATIVISM

The ideological fantasy of self-reliance was predicated on excluding and dispossessing dependent U.S. citizens who purportedly deprived the national body of its full economic potential. But this fantasy also directed its exclusionary sentiments toward foreigners. Nativists define their sense of national identity, self-reliance, and security in terms of the perceived threats posed by people whom they deem alien or inassimilable. Because for most of America's history cultural belonging and substantive citizenship have been overwhelmingly correlated with white identity, nativism in the United States has deep historical entanglements with racist ideologies that seek to exclude nonwhite immigrants from entry into the United States from with civil rights and economic entitlements.[42] The legal category of "illegal aliens" was established in the 1920s and 1930s through restrictive policies that "established for the first time *numerical limits* on immigration and a *global* racial and national hierarchy that favored some immigrants over others."[43] Capitalist desires for cheap nonwhite immigrant labor have competed with nativist desires to preserve European heritage and white numerical dominance. Although these opposing desires have been present since the nation's origins, their negotiation in the post–civil rights era required some important shifts.

Because the moral delegitimation of white supremacy no longer allows nativists to argue for immigrant exclusion on the basis of biological or cultural inferiority, post–civil rights discourses have sought to fulfill the ideological fantasy of national self-reliance through the removal of "bad" immigrants, depicted as engaging in various forms of illegality. The bad immigrant crosses national borders without documentation, participates in informal labor economies that do not contribute to income taxes, engages in criminal activities, refuses to speak English and to adopt American values, and expropriates public resources meant for legal residents and U.S. citizens. Moreover, the bad immigrant also has decidedly gendered associations, adding stigmatized notions such as teenage pregnancy, hyperfertility, "too large families," and nonnormative sexual economies or alternative family models (e.g., multigenerational, woman-centered) to a composite projection of social ills. Although these projections appear color-blind and are articulated largely through constructions of illegality, bad immigrants are invariably imagined as nonwhite. There is no national imaginary that projects groups of white immigrants as bad or threatening to U.S. national self-reliance and security in the post–civil rights era.[44]

Although bad immigrants are associated with immigrants of color, "exceptional" immigrants of color may earn the designation of good immigrants. To earn this designation, immigrants of color must be law abiding in the way they enter and stay in the United States, work hard, refuse public assistance, pay taxes, uphold traditional (heteropatriarchal) family structures, and seek assimilation into U.S. national culture by speaking English and adopting American values. Those who argue for the presence of good immigrants in the United States tend to support a multicultural ideal of national self-reliance and law and order; but they still presume that they are entitled to control the ways this multiculturalism is spatialized and expressed. In other words, they still assume that they are the spatial managers of the nation who determine the standards and values to which immigrants are expected to conform.[45] As such, the multicultural national ideal as much as the monocultural one relies on notions of identity and belonging destined to engage in exclusionary and possessive investments.

Emotional economies of nativist contempt often surge during fiscal crises and economic recessions. For example, immediately following the national economic recession of the mid-1970s, politicians and pundits often scapegoated undocumented immigrants from Mexico for stealing American jobs and taking advantage of social welfare resources.[46] To divert U.S. publics from focusing on the ways deregulation policies were destabilizing the middle and working class in the late 1970s, state politicians and wealthy elites often stoked nativist emotional economies. As a result, public fears over losing national economic benefits were misdirected toward powerless immigrants, and the detrimental effects of neoliberal shifts stayed in hiding.

Nationalist fears over economic losses to immigrants are not the only factors motivating the possessive and exclusionary desires of the ideological fantasy of self-reliance. Nativist emotional economies also surge in periods of economic prosperity and stability. Struggles to exclude and dispossess bad immigrants are also motivated by fears over losing white cultural dominance and the pleasures of asserting entitlements exclusively available to those who are presumed to belong. Post-1965 shifts in the nation's population demographics, impacted primarily by Asian and Latin American immigration, raised fears over the ways in which white population declines would affect whites' cultural and political dominance. Between 1981 and 1990, "immigration's net impact on population growth rates doubled from previous decades, accounting for 39.1 percent of the nation's population growth."[47] By 2010, census forecasts predicted that nonwhite and multiracial families would outnumber whites by 2042.[48] Despite the overwhelming power that whites continued to possess in institutional positions and political realms, the population growth of nonwhite majorities as a result of immigration and higher birthrates helped instigate widespread desires to stop immigration through border militarization, restrictive immigration policies, and the deportation of undocumented immigrants from within national borders. As mentioned, population shifts also motivated the rise of possessive desires to deny immigrants' use of public goods such as education, health care, and subsidized housing.[49]

Responding to this sense of impending losses in white hegemonic power, since the 1970s far-right nativist activists and organizations have ascended to lofty positions in political and policy circles of influence. The core of nativist organizing and state policy making is made up of John Tanton, of the Federation for American Immigration Reform (FAIR), U.S. Inc., and Numbers USA; Kris Kobach, formerly an attorney for FAIR and the Immigration Law Reform Institute and currently the secretary of state of Kansas; Barbara Coe, of the California Coalition for Immigration Reform and the Council of Conservative Citizens; Glenn Spencer, of Voices of Citizens Together and the American Border Patrol; Joseph Turner, of Save Our State (SOS); Dan Stein, Roger Conner, and Cordia Strom, of FAIR; Paul Ehrlich and Garrett Hardin, of Zero Population Growth (ZPG; now Population Connection); and Lawrence Pratt, of English First and the Council for Inter-American Security.

Most of these organizations and leaders have explicit links to white suprema-cist or neo-Nazi groups or espouse these philosophies internally.[50] Funded by right-wing foundations such as the Pioneer Fund, the Heritage Foundation, and the Laurel Foundation, this network of nativist proponents has found sympathizers in various political leaders. They have funded and organized cam-paigns that have resulted in remarkably punitive and restrictive anti-immigrant policy outcomes, such as the English Only movement, California's Proposition 187, Arizona's 2004 Proposition 200 (which requires residents to show birth certificates or passports to receive public services or vote), and Arizona's SB 1070 (which criminalizes undocumented immigrants).[51] Most recently, nativist proponents have passed HB 2281 (which eliminated the Mexican American/La Raza Studies Program in the Tucson Unified School District).[52] However, because of the moral illegitimacy of overtly white supremacist discourses, these nativist proponents have become increasingly sophisticated at strategically veil-ing their views.

The ingenuity of post–civil rights nativist groups was to cultivate anti-Mexican and anti–undocumented immigrant sentiments in color-blind and coded rather than explicitly racist ways. John Tanton was particularly astute at understanding that public support had to be garnered through discourses about scarce economic and environmental resources, overpopulation, and illegality rather than through old discourses, which projected nonwhite immigrants' cultural, racial, or biological inferiority. Along with other political strategists, Tanton developed frames that argued for immigration restrictions because it made good economic common sense; preserved environmental resources and sustainability; prevented the social ills of overpopulation, teenage pregnancy, state dependency, and multilingualism; kept state resources in the hands of de-serving, hardworking taxpayers; and halted increases in crime and deviance. In internal organizational memos Tanton emphasized time and again that effec-tive messaging would produce the desired outcomes of strengthening nativist and population control agendas.

But not everyone who invested in anti-Mexican and anti-Latino/a nativist emotional economies was motivated by blatant white supremacist views. Indeed, the effectiveness of these color-blind, gendered, and racially coded discourses lay in their ability to recruit moderates, liberals, and immigrants themselves to identify and support exclusionary policies and outcomes based on their sense of economic loss and eroding natural resources, the moral righteousness of being law abiding and self-sufficient, and their heteronormative family ideals.

Exclusionary emotional economies attached to undocumented immigrants have become so effective that many pro-immigration advocates now stage their counterarguments by emphasizing the benefits of what are deemed good immigrants. Pointing to the strong work ethic of immigrants, their taxpayer and other economic contributions, the need for low-wage Mexican, Latino/a, and Asian American labor in U.S. agricultural and factory production, and immigrant contributions to community revitalization, pro-immigration advocates have often contributed to the stigmatization of so-called bad immigrants. This pro-immigrant political strategy has unwittingly strengthened nativist and far-right agendas. It has effectively concealed the fact that undocumented Latino/a, Caribbean, Asian, and African migration is a by-product of detrimental neoliberal policies enacted by the United States, Europe, the International Monetary Fund, the World Bank, and the World Trade Organization in various nations of the global South.[53] It has also rendered illegible the fact that the U.S. economy actually seeks to keep undocumented immigrants dispossessed and powerless in order to continue exploiting their labor in various industries. Finally, such emotional disidentification with purportedly bad immigrants fails to acknowledge how racialization processes create enormous slippages between good and bad immigrants. Immigrants' racial identity can always trump their good behavior. Because the spatial managers of the nation presume the right to designate who is good and who is bad and because this designation is always entangled with racialized and gendered classification systems, good immigrants can become bad in arbitrary ways. For example, after the attacks of September 11, 2001, Arab, Muslim, and South Asian immigrants who were previously considered economically self-reliant good immigrants got moved to the category of bad immigrants presumed to pose threats to national security.

Perhaps the most disheartening effect of the rising dominance of nativist fantasies, feelings, and state discourses about undocumented immigrants is the way that Latino/a, Asian, African, Caribbean, and other immigrants have themselves been encouraged to participate in economies of shame, stigmatization, and blame tied to criminality, welfare dependence, and illegality. To distinguish themselves as good immigrants, Latino/a, Asian, Caribbean, African, and other documented immigrants have sometimes taken hard anti–undocumented immigrant positions. Not wanting to be perceived as illegal or dependent on welfare or as taxpayer burdens, some immigrants have elected to adopt extreme stances on self-reliance, hard work, and personal responsibility. Such stances, particularly when Latino/a, Asian, African, or other immigrants of color hold them, effectively reinforce a dominant public climate that discourages immigrants to feel entitled to public goods they have helped subsidize. Although these immigrants are admirable for their self-determination and networks of familial and communal self-reliance, such "pull yourself up by your own bootstraps" endorsements ultimately support neoliberal and conservative agendas that seek further privatization and divestment from social welfare safety nets.

Dangerous Waters and Other Overwhelming Feelings

Overwhelmingly, media representations equate undocumented immigrants with Mexican immigrants and other Latino/as. Although East Asian, South Asian, African, and Caribbean immigrants have also been scrutinized for their effect on Anglo-American hegemony, these immigrant groups have generally been peripheral in media coverage on undocumented immigration (perhaps with the exception of Haitians). Using tropes such as "invasion," "brown tide," "taxpayer burdens," "criminals," "overpopulation," "hyperfertile," "welfare takers," and "environmental erosion" to frame debates and ideas, mainstream news media coverage in print, television, and radio has increasingly centered on the arguments and policy recommendations of the nativist organizations mentioned earlier. Mainstream media have helped to reproduce emotional economies of xenophobia, hate, fear, and anxiety during increasingly economically insecure times, providing fallacious but emotionally satisfying pathways through which publics can channel and assuage their anxieties. Because nativist agendas are often ideologically aligned with neoconservative movements that seek to privatize health care, education, transportation, parks, libraries, and universities, U.S. constituents who align with anti-immigrant agendas also tend to support economic policies that weaken the social wage and the overall stability of working- and middle-class people.

When it came to coverage of undocumented immigrants in the 1970s, *U.S. News and World Report* repeatedly disseminated alarmist headlines such as "How Millions of Illegal Aliens Sneak into the U.S." (July 22, 1974) and "Border Crisis: Illegal Aliens Out of Control" (April 25, 1977).[54] Metaphors used in 1970s coverage included describing the U.S.-Mexico border as a war zone and immigrants as staging an invasion. Thanks in large part to Tanton and ZPG's organizing efforts, the discourses of overpopulation, scarce social services, and competition for scarce jobs became commonsense assumptions in public debates about immigration. Indeed, Leo Chavez found that issues tied to Mexican immigration in 10 popular national magazines were resoundingly alarmist and maintained this perspective between 1965 and 1999.[55]

Immigration coverage in mainstream magazines and newspapers temporarily subsided after the passage of the Immigration Reform and Control Act of 1986, which required employers to attest to their employees' immigration status and made it illegal to knowingly hire or recruit unauthorized immigrants. By granting amnesty to certain seasonal agricultural workers and to undocumented immigrants who had entered the United States before January 1, 1982, the act temporarily quelled nativist anxieties through processes of incorporation. By the early 1990s, however, a new nativist wave permeated media representations. The conduit, of course, was California's Proposition 187, which sought to deny undocumented immigrants public education, prenatal care, and other social services.

In examining more than 100 articles published on Proposition 187 in the *Los Angeles Times*, Otto Santa Ana shows in *Brown Tide Rising* that the central metaphor used to describe immigration focused on "dangerous waters" and that secondary metaphors focused on "war," "animals," and "the body."[56] Santa Ana understands metaphors in media coverage and public discourse to be reflective of the "basic, embodied values of the dominant social order." He argues that the primary concern among California's constituents was not economic. "Rather, [California governor Pete] Wilson capitalized on the sense of increasing loss of sociocultural preeminence among his core constituency, as the *rising brown tides* ostensibly reshaped the Anglo-American hegemonic order."[57]

Media coverage of Mexican and Latino/a undocumented immigrants from the 1970s to the 1990s tended to solidify nativist affective economies of contempt, stigmatization, repulsion, and exclusion. But these nativist movements did not take place without remarkable grassroots opposition. Large pro-immigrant mobilizations took stances against Proposition 187 under the campaign slogan "No to S.O.S."[58] Although they did not achieve enough support to stop Proposition 187, grassroots immigrants' rights organizers began to recognize the increasingly nativist and racist attacks they faced in the form of new criminalization processes of undocumented immigrants. In 2006 the immigrants' rights movement gained significant ground as millions of people throughout U.S. cities protested the Border Protection, Anti-Terrorism, and Illegal Immigration Control Act of 2005, which passed in the U.S. House of Representatives but failed in the Senate. The bill, HR 4437, proposed raising penalties for undocumented immigration and classifying anyone who helped someone enter or remain in the United States illegally as a felon.

These significant pro-immigrant mobilizations instigated a remarkable backlash in the mainstream media. In a report examining all 2007 episodes of *Lou Dobbs Tonight*, *The O'Reilly Factor*, and *Glenn Beck*, the Media Matters Action Network found an overwhelming focus on undocumented immigration. Seventy percent of *Lou Dobbs Show* episodes, 56 percent of *O'Reilly Factor* episodes, and 28 percent of *Glenn Beck* episodes in 2007 discussed undocumented immigration. Throughout the episodes these media figures, their guests, and their often factually erroneous reporting repeated two dominant myths. The first myth made links between undocumented immigration and rising levels of crime. Dozens of segments featured specific cases of undocumented immigrants who committed crimes, leading to an overwhelming news overrepresentation of crimes committed by undocumented immigrants relative to actual crime statistics.[59] The second myth disseminated by these shows was that by overusing social services and by not paying taxes, undocumented immigrants were economic burdens on U.S. society. One in four episodes of *Lou Dobbs Tonight* in 2007 featured the depiction of illegal immigrants as taxpayer burdens.

By repetitively linking notions about crime waves, out-of-control borders, drug cartels, disease-ridden immigrants, taxpayer burdens, reconquest, and NAFTA superhighways to Mexican undocumented immigrants, Dobbs, O'Reilly, Beck, Savage, and other media figures strengthened the emotional value of nativism. These discourses, representations, and fallacies allowed embodied and preconscious affective responses of rage, fear, and anxiety to be directed toward nonwhite immigrants, particularly Latino/as. Such releases yielded affective enjoyments because they resolidified a sense of exclusivity and superiority to national belonging. Worse, affective satisfaction was derived from having the cultural, political, and racial power to exclude. This was a satisfaction only those who were culturally dominant could enjoy without facing severely detrimental consequences.

Institutional Policies and Practices

Nativist organizations, paleoconservatives, and media figures have worked together to enact significant social welfare policy shifts predicated on immigrant exclusion in the post–civil rights era. First, nativist and racist desires to preserve white numerical hegemony have specifically targeted the reproductive capacity of Mexican-origin, Latina, Black, and other women of color. Mexican-origin and African American women suffered egregious violations by being coercively sterilized by doctors at the Los Angeles County–USC Medical Center (LACMC) between 1968 and 1974. Convinced by population control advocates that Latina and Black women's hyperfertility would threaten white majorities and cause undue burdens on U.S. social services, doctors and nurses at LACMC performed more than 180 forced and/or coercive sterilizations while these women were in late stages of labor.[60]

Not without irony, several sections of Proposition 187 were transplanted into the 1996 PRWORA. The fatal brew of anti-immigrant and antiwelfare public feelings thus produced outcomes that sought to simultaneously curtail the constructed threats of Black and Latino/a welfare dependence, overreproduction, criminality, and taxpayer burdens, which were by then converging and overlapping in the public imagination. Indicating the expansion of a surveillance state, individual states and public housing agencies were required to report personal information on noncitizen benefit recipients to the Immigration and Naturalization Service (now the Department of Homeland Security).[61]

The overlapping projections of welfare dependence and undocumented immigration in the 1990s also worked with expanding notions of criminality to punish Black, Latina, and other women of color involved in drug use while pregnant or in other illegal activities. State policies of reproductive control that disproportionately affect women of color and poor women include handcuffing women to their hospital beds while they were giving birth, charging them with child neglect of their unborn fetuses, and coercing them into having Norplant implanted (Norplant, now discontinued, was a birth control method lasting five years that was found to have significant side effects).[62] Similarly, the intersectional economic and interpersonal forces that motivated some Latina women (both documented and undocumented) to engage in nonviolent crimes, particularly related to the drug trade, made them increasingly vulnerable to arrest, conviction, and incarceration during the never-ending war on drugs.[63] As antiracist reproductive rights scholars and activists have persistently demonstrated, women of color who are poor are rendered vulnerable to state, interpersonal, and reproductive violence because they embody and signify multiple threats to hegemonic ideological fantasies.[64]

Although instituted with poor (documented and undocumented) women of color in mind, the cumulative effects of anti–social welfare and anti-immigrant legislation ultimately affected all women. As became evident in the 2000s, attacks on all women's reproductive rights have become increasingly normative, with conservatives seeking the reversal of legal abortion in both law and access, the abolishment of federal funding for institutions such as Planned Parenthood, and restrictions on contraception and other reproductive health care services.[65] Regrettably, white women who advocate for reproductive and women's rights but fail to see how these are historically and contemporarily related to public and state support for population control, criminalization, and immigration policies that target women of color have a limited understanding of how and why all of women's reproductive rights are currently under attack. Precisely because these policies are color-blind, they eventually bleed into larger national logics on reproduction, family planning, and women's rights.

In addition to endorsing color-blind institutional racism, antiwelfare, anti-immigrant, and pro-criminalization policies have intensified patriarchal cultures that want to restrict women's control over their bodies. This is evident in the degree of white patriarchal conservative backlash to what were once considered established women's rights (e.g., the right to abortions). Believing that such patriarchal attacks are divorced from nativist and racialized population control politics makes it appear as though the war on all women's bodies and reproductive rights sprang out of nowhere. In actuality, such punitive measures had long been rehearsed and legitimized consistently through color-blind practices that targeted poor women of color with children. After 40 years they have seeped into the commonsense logics of the larger national body.

All the evidence presented in this introduction suggests not only that persistent racial and gender discrimination, exclusion, and vulnerability to premature death are enacted through color-blind policies but also that those who feel real or perceived losses in white patriarchal authority, cultural dominance, or economic wealth are not likely to divest from these nativist economies unless they radically shift the modalities through which they construct their sense of identity, coherence, and power. So long as notions of national identity are predicated on the affective enjoyments of exclusivity, possessive individualism, and justified violence, the devastation caused by nativist investments is not likely to disappear.

In their new configurations, ideological fantasies of self-reliance predicated on eliminating the invented burdens of welfare dependence and undocumented immigration excavated old racialized and gendered fears and enjoyments but reformulated them through color-blind frames. U.S. constituents enjoyed directing various forms of stigma, contempt, and aggression toward those deemed undeserving and illegitimate in order to deem themselves economically self-reliant, law abiding, and culturally valuable. In doing so, they sought to recuperate their psychological and affective coherence. Ironically, however, these desires endorsed systemic shifts that further exacerbated their insecurity.

Over time, such antiwelfare and anti-immigrant emotional economies helped to accelerate state divestments from affordable housing, education, community development, parks, libraries, and transportation in order to compound corporate profits and the financial portfolios of the richest people. Such antiwelfare contempt also created favorable political conditions for increased privatization and deregulation. Anti–big government public feelings helped support the quiet counterrevolution taking place through revisions to the U.S. tax code that favor the propertied classes, neoliberal trade agreements that exacerbate workers' displacement and exploitation across the globe, the deregulation of finance capital, and spectacular victories of multinational corporations for greater profits. While publics were focused on the color-blind and racially coded panics over welfare dependence and undocumented immigration, these economic policy shifts gradually increased alignments between the U.S. state and private finance capital, moving us further and further away from the collective benefits of the social wage.

CHAPTER 3

NEW ORLEANS, LOUISIANA: THE DEMOLISHING EMOTIONS OF NEOLIBERAL REMOVAL

In Spike Lee's documentary *When the Levees Broke*, Phyllis Montana Leblanc, a Black resident of New Orleans East, tells the story of how she survived Hurricane Katrina and its aftermath. In her tone and testimony she expresses utter disbelief at the U.S. government's abandonment of New Orleans residents during the storm of August 2005 and its callous treatment of displaced victims after the hurricane. She attempts to convey the terror, betrayal, and hopelessness of the experience. As she tells her story, Lee overlays Leblanc's narrative with a montage of images and sounds that are particular to New Orleans and the Gulf region. Images of people yelling for help on rooftops, of dead floating bodies, of filth and desperation at the Superdome, of armed military troops on highway bridges, of helicopters rescuing children and women in baskets, of the flood in 1927, and of Hurricane Betsy in 1965 make associative connections between former and contemporary suffering and disenfranchisement. Feeble attempts by FEMA's Mike Brown, President George W. Bush, and Department of Homeland Security chief Michael Chertoff to euphemize the government's failed response intersect with and juxtapose the testimonies of indignant, traumatized, and dispossessed Katrina survivors. Set to the blues music of the Mississippi Delta and the irreducibly unique movements of New

Orleans culture, Lee's mix of sounds, images, official government narratives, and survivors' testimonies seems to point to a single persistent demand: The suffering of thousands of displaced people in New Orleans must be recognized and rectified.

The story of New Orleans before and after Hurricane Katrina conjures up frameworks, fractures, and feelings situated within a historical dialectic of oppression and resistance particular to the Mississippi Delta yet intricately tied to larger dynamics in the United States. The astute geographer Clyde Woods describes the dialectic of the Mississippi Delta as the historical struggle "between Bourbonism and the Blues."[1] On the one hand, the ebb and flow of this dialectic is characterized by unimaginable acts of violence to preserve hierarchies of racial power and property. On the other hand, it speaks to persistent demands for communal justice, interdependent social development, and human dignity.

To preserve their hold on propertied and political power historically linked to the plantation economies of slavery and the worldviews of white supremacy, the Bourbon class has used some of the most extreme forms of institutional racism to perpetuate "hostile privatism and defensive localism" in the Mississippi Delta.[2] Bourbonism seeks to hoard the property and social advantages that have been historically correlated with patriarchal whiteness through the reproduction of gendered racial segregation, population control, and removal practices. But complex counterinsurgencies built to resist the economies of death favored by Bourbonism continue to thwart this greedy pursuit.[3] Innumerable acts of resistance, alliance, flight, armed rebellion, cultural ritual, and musical creation in New Orleans and the Mississippi Delta make up the worldviews, value systems, and intracommunal ways of relating that characterize what Woods calls "blues epistemologies" and the "Blues agenda."[4] In addition to providing an extensive archive of testimonies that remain generally invisible or illegitimate to dominant historical narratives, Blues epistemologies offer people who are the targets of gendered racial exclusion, exploitation, violence, and elimination methods of resistance rooted in Africanist, Native, interethnic, and intercultural practices of communal sustainability. In the worldviews expressed through the Blues agenda, the struggle to create material conditions that would allow displaced Black and poor people to return to New Orleans was intimately linked to the fight to maintain the "emotional ecosystems" of support, social networks, communal interdependence, and cultural rituals that made up the epistemology of the Blues.[5]

Housing became a central site for staging the struggles between Bourbonism and the Blues in post-Katrina New Orleans. This struggle became particularly acute when the Department of Housing and Urban Development (HUD) and the Housing Authority of New Orleans (HANO) announced plans to demolish 5,100 public housing units just as New Orleans was experiencing a massive crisis in affordable housing.[6] The state of Louisiana estimated that 55 percent of the damaged homes in New Orleans were rental properties, with approximately 82,000 rental homes sustaining severe damage.[7]

Almost a year after the storm, landlords faced extremely high repair costs for several reasons. First, homeowners' insurance rates rose dramatically after Katrina, inflating landlords' mortgage payments.[8] Second, new building codes and requirements to elevate homes one or two feet above floodplain levels sometimes added significant costs to rebuilding.[9] Third, private insurance claims did not necessarily cover the entire cost of repairing rental units, forcing landlords to use savings for repairs that would likely be reflected in higher rental rates. Fourth, government assistance for rebuilding was limited, took a long time to obtain, and favored the repair of rental units that catered to higher-income tenants.[10] For example, Louisiana allotted $869 million in Community Development Block Grant funds to a small rental property program that gave forgivable loans to small private landlords if they rented to tenants at 80 percent, 65 percent, and 50 percent of the area median. But the application process for this program was not made available to landlords until January 2007. Before 2007, Congress had not allocated any resources to rental housing for people with incomes below 30 percent of the area median (this would translate to people whose earnings were $15,690 per year in the Greater New Orleans Region (New Orleans, Metairie, and Kenner).[11]

As a result of this severe shortage of rental properties and the high costs of rebuilding rental units, fair market rents in New Orleans rose by 50–80 percent after Katrina.[12] Essentially, this meant that the poorest renters (those below the 30 percent area median) were least likely to find affordable rental housing in the private markets of post-Katrina New Orleans. Indeed, by 2007 the homeless population in New Orleans had doubled, with 12,000 people living in tents in front of the mayor's office and under bridges.[13] This affordable housing crisis disproportionately affected poor Black women with children and elderly people. Before Katrina 77 percent of households in public housing in the New Orleans area were headed by women, which included homes with women living alone or with others. Of people who occupied units subsidized with Section 8 vouchers, 88 percent were woman-headed households.[14] Despite this remarkable shortage in affordable housing, HUD/HANO and the New Orleans City Council supported the demolition of the structurally sound "Big Four" complexes: B. W. Cooper, C. J. Peete, Lafitte, and St. Bernard. According to internal HANO documents, the costs of demolition and redevelopment were estimated at $450 million more than repairing the public housing units and $174 million more than upgrading them.[15]

Making matters worse, by 2006 predominantly white parishes with higher property values had already implemented several municipal ordinances to prevent poor people from seeking rental housing in their neighborhoods, particularly if they relied on Section 8 vouchers. In other words, the replacement of public housing units with Section 8 vouchers forced residents to seek housing in the private market, which was decisively and legally hostile to them. St. Bernard Parish, for example, passed Ordinance SBPC 670-09-06, which stated, "No person shall rent, lease, loan or otherwise allow occupancy or use of any single-family residence located in an R-1 zone by any person or group of persons, other than a family member(s) related by blood within the first, second, or third direct ascending or descending generation(s) without first a Permissive Use Permit from the St. Bernard Parish Council."[16] Because 93 percent of St. Bernard Parish's residents were white, the blood relatives ordinance essentially sought to prevent mostly Black people and other people of color in search of rentals from moving into white homes in St. Bernard Parish.

A resolution in predominantly white Jefferson Parish similarly called for a limitation on low-income housing within its borders, and the city of Slidell, Louisiana, sought to pass a zoning ordinance that would limit multifamily development within its borders.[17] Testifying before Congress, James Perry, the executive director of the Greater New Orleans Fair Action Housing Center, noted "that in the case of Jefferson Parish, a Parish council person has made repeated attacks on poor people and all but proclaimed poverty as illegal in the Parish. The actions by the Parish suggest the need for an 8th protected class under the Federal Fair Housing Act—income."[18] In privileging homeowners, single-family units, and blood relatives, Perry argued that housing and zoning ordinances functioned to discriminate against and exclude poor people who were renters, particularly if they were people of color.

In response to these struggles over exclusionary municipal ordinances and public housing, liberal and conservative discourses in more than 280 *Times-Picayune* letters to the editor published between 2006 and 2009 overwhelmingly reflected hegemonic logics and sentiments. Contributors contrasted "homeowners," "hard-working taxpayers," and "family-oriented households" with the purported ills and threats of "Section 8 tenants," "renters," "crime," "public housing residents," and "the poor." The letters expressed public feelings of defensive localism, hostile privatism, and paternalist good intentions toward public assistance recipients. Such emotional economies encouraged dominant publics to actively participate or passively comply with local and state policies that sought to remove and abandon poor people who relied on subsidized housing in New Orleans, most of whom were Black and female.

NEO-BOURBON EMOTIONS: THE DEFENSIVE LOCALISM OF HOMEOWNERS' QUALITY OF LIFE

In the most prevalent racialized narrative that justified the removal of poor people from New Orleans, homeowners claimed to be defending their quality of life. In a letter to the editor of the *Times-Picayune* favoring the St. Bernard Parish blood relatives ordinance, resident Stephanie Caruso claimed, "It's not a race issue. It's a quality of life issue and a property value issue."[19] Resident Chris Holmes similarly reinforced the distinction between homeowners and renters by saying, "In an attempt to preserve the integrity of our neighborhoods and our home values, our parish government enacted a reasonable rental ordinance. . . . We want to live in an area dominated by owner-occupied homes."[20] Here was an instance of the epistemology of white ignorance at work—a process of knowing what not to know in order to preserve a worldview and identity. As George Lipsitz has tirelessly demonstrated, higher property values and the good quality of life in specific neighborhoods significantly correlate with white racial homogeneity and middle- to upper-class households. Such correlations were purposely created through racially discriminatory housing policies in both private markets and government mortgage lending and housing programs. In arguing that quality of life and property values had nothing to do with race, Caruso and Holmes perpetuated color-blind myths rather than historical facts. They resolved incongruences between their beliefs and patterns of racism that could only be reconciled if they lied to themselves or stayed willfully ignorant. Because property values in New Orleans had everything to do with the racial makeup of the neighborhood and because the phrase *quality of life* was a coded phrase for white geographic dominance, both letter writers expressed a sophisticated disavowal of their complicity in racial discrimination in order to defend their propertied worth and ideological worldviews.

Similarly denying or ignoring the historical correlation between white people's quality of life and the racial exclusion of people of color, homeowner Julie Landry claimed that she was "proud of St. Bernard for wanting to maintain its affordable, but also stable family-oriented atmosphere."[21] Constructing a distinction between poor renters who were presumably not family oriented and the people in her neighborhood, Landry concluded that she was tired of people "who attribute our desire for stable, family-oriented neighborhoods to racism!"[22] Landry's argument that renters are not family oriented is entirely illogical unless it is taken together with her disclaimer about racism. Her preemptive attempt to deny that the St. Bernard's ordinance has anything to do with racism suggests that quite the opposite is true; otherwise she would not feel the need to make the defensive claim. If "family oriented" functions as a code for normative whiteness, and "renter" as a code for people of color who are poor, Landry's arguments make sense insofar as they repeat the stereotypical claim that low-income people of color do not adhere to normative family structures. Intent on not sharing resources and spaces with anyone who does not fit characteristics implied by the phrase *family oriented*, Landry callously strove to block people who were deemed undeserving from basic life resources such as housing.

Other letter writers claimed that they were fighting to maintain their way of life, projecting that renters would bring waves of crime with them. "St. Bernard Parish is a community where people buy houses next door to their parents and where we can allow our children to play in front yards without fear of crime," claimed resident Donna Kathmann. Cognizant of the racial implications, she continues, "We simply don't want our neighborhoods to deteriorate because of renters, no matter what their race."[23] Because 93 percent of St. Bernard Parish residents were white, they revealed that both monetary and emotional investments in whiteness were at stake in these projections. Their identities were predicated on possessively defending their propertied resources but also on alienating themselves from people of color.

The same set of letters to the editor often expressed fear and disdain for residents using Section 8 vouchers or living in public housing complexes. Letters contrasted the working poor who paid market rents and those who received Section 8 vouchers, presumably because the latter were assumed to be unemployed or unwilling to work.[24] Numerous letters equated people who received Section 8 vouchers with criminality and nonnormativity. Letter writer Chris Vogler claimed, "Wherever you have low-income, Section 8 buildings, there is litter, crime and noise. It's very scary to hear of plans to spread this type of housing all over the city and suburbs." Implying that he wished to preserve race and class segregation, Vogler concluded, "The theory that spreading low-income housing around the city may help combat social ills that lead to crime is a very dubious one at best."[25] Chris Roberts, District 1 councilman of Jefferson Parish, similarly claimed, "History tells us that Section 8 developments, like standard pubic housing projects, are crime incubators—destructive to a decent quality of life and economic development."[26] In using the phrase *crime incubators*, Roberts conjured up old stereotypes that associated Black women's reproductive capacities with giving birth to boys who grew up to reproduce crime and nonnormative families. Because most of public housing and Section 8 recipients were Black women with children, the municipal public official transformed Black women's historical resilience in the face of interlocking racial, gender, and class oppressions into dependence and deviance. The official designated himself a paternal authority intent on keeping Black women's reproductive habits and families away from white normative patriarchal families and neighborhoods.

State officials similarly reinforced the defensive localism of white property owners and the segregationist logic of neo-Bourbonism. Louisiana Republican representative Richard Baker quickly situated himself as a spokesman for the Bourbon agenda. In the immediate aftermath of the hurricane, Baker unabashedly stated, "We finally cleaned up public housing in New Orleans. We couldn't do it, but God did."[27] Following Baker's logic of triage, white Louisiana state representative John LaBruzzo reexcavated Jim Crow–like population control policies that targeted Black women's reproduction. In 2008 LaBruzzo announced that he was studying a plan that would pay impoverished women $1,000 to have their tubes tied in order to "reduce the number of people that are going from generational welfare to generational welfare."[28] Using color-blind discursive tactics to evade charges of gendered racism, LaBruzzo preemptively defended himself by saying, "It's easy to say, 'Oh, he's a racist.' The hard part is to sit down and think of some solutions."[29] Largely because of the collective organizing power of the Women's Health and Justice Initiative and scathing critiques from feminists of color, such as Shana Griffin of the New Orleans Women's Health Clinic, LaBruzzo's proposals for racialized and gendered population control did not manifest as actual policy.[30]

At lightning speed, Baker, LaBruzzo, and other supporters of gendered racism masquerading as defensive localism amplified emotional economies of contempt toward low-income Black people, particularly for Black mothers maintaining single-parent households. Supporters of neo-Bourbonism demonstrated the ways in which conscious and unconscious investments in white patriarchal supremacy for profit, gain, or a psycho-emotional sense of superiority helped to perpetuate radical forms of social alienation. The alienation of the neo-Bourbon bloc suggested levels of disconnection and dissociation from people of color deep enough to justify egregious forms of removal, control, or elimination. As Woods appositely remarks:

The portrayal of working-class African Americans and their communities as deviant and pathological is the product of a deviant and pathological strain deeply embedded in American thought. It is a sickness masquerading as science. It makes the creation of new social disasters seem logical and profitable while simultaneously encouraging the celebration of human misery.[31]

Investments in property, profits, and racial supremacy are not only causally linked to Black marginalization but also centrally constitutive of dominant white identities. As we have seen, threats to neo-Bourbon property and wealth are often experienced as threats to psychological and social identities, worldviews, and values whose roots are embedded in white supremacist logics, even though few people would consciously describe themselves as such. These affective and moneyed investments are heavily constructed through fallacies and historical inversions. The affirming notions of white propertied people's self-reliance, familial normativity, meritocracy, and hard work stand on a stack of accumulated lies taken as truths. Any attempt to undo these lies depends on whether white people are emotionally receptive to hearing the testimonies offered by people of color. Such receptivity, at the least, requires a reduction in the emotional defenses that possessively guard white worldviews and spaces.

HISTORICAL REALITIES, INVERTED PERCEPTIONS

Racial and gender stereotypes are difficult to disrupt because people can confirm what they believe to be true in observable realities. For instance, some of the claims that New Orleans homeowners and city council members made about public housing and Section 8 residents were evident across the city and confirmed by empirical studies. Sociologists such as Douglas Massey and Nancy Denton have shown that people who live in neighborhoods with concentrated poverty and racial segregation do experience higher crime rates, higher school dropout rates, higher health risks, higher rates of teenage pregnancy, and higher levels of vulnerability to violence.[32] On virtually every indicator of social well-being and human development, Louisiana's poor ranked at the bottom compared to the other 49 states and the District of Columbia.[33] Scholars have also shown that geographies of concentrated racial poverty pose major obstacles to accessing employment, transportation, amenities, healthy food options, banks, and other services that improve stability and increase opportunities.[34] Projections about people who lived in New Orleans public housing or used Section 8 vouchers showed that dominant publics were conscious of the conditions that poor people faced in general and that working and workless Black people confronted in particular.

These public projections and feelings, however, tended to grossly misread the root causes of poverty and the systemic processes through which they were reproduced. Instead of linking the structural oppressions of concentrated poverty in Black communities to the history of purposeful Bourbon exclusions and violence, dominant stereotypes about public housing and Section 8 residents maintained that these oppressions were caused by the inherent behavioral, cultural, and familial deficiencies of poor people, particularly of African American women and men.

The feelings attached to color-blind, gendered, and racially coded narratives that warned of the purported threats of public housing and Section 8 residents functioned to foreclose people's receptivity to historical facts that reveal how white advantages are legislated and accumulated. Neo-Bourbon whites in Louisiana and New Orleans had long secured their safety, higher property values, higher tax bases, better schools, and better businesses and amenities through policies and practices that purposely marginalized and excluded Black people and other people of color. As Daphne Spain demonstrates, from the 1890s until the 1950s, New Orleans "began adopting the residential patterns of large northern cities. Blacks became increasingly concentrated in the central city while whites settled the newly drained land surrounding the initial settlement."[35] Although technological innovations in land draining allowed New Orleans to expand, entrenched Jim Crow segregation policies ensured that only whites could take advantage of new housing in newly drained areas, such as Jefferson Parish and St. Bernard.[36] Federal and private restrictions on lending and the fact that discrimination against Blacks was still overtly expressed and legal "were actually decisions to create white neighborhoods."[37] Moreover, the expansion of public transportation during the era of Jim Crow meant that Black employees no longer had to live in proximity to white employers. Conversely, whites could move farther from the city but still commute to commercial districts.

By 1950, "fifty-seven percent of all blocks had less than one percent black housing units, while eight percent had less than one percent white."[38] Even those blocks that had higher levels of racial integration correlated with significant inequalities. For example, the median Black-owned home was valued at $3,800, whereas the median home owned by whites was valued at $10,000. Blacks were concentrated in dilapidated buildings that lacked plumbing and were overcrowded.[39] The establishment of HANO in 1937 and the construction of more than 10,000 federally subsidized units by 1956 intensified racial segregation in New Orleans. Public housing complexes were racially segregated under overtly discriminatory federal policies. Even after public housing was legally integrated, complexes remained intensely segregated and disproportionately populated by Black people as a result of their economic marginalization. Public housing units contributed to greater concentrations of Black people in the Seventh Ward (St. Bernard Projects, built in 1942 and expanded twice), the Central City Third and Second Wards (Calliope Projects/B. W. Cooper Apartments and the Melpomene Projects/Guste Apartments), and the Eleventh Ward (C. J. Peete/Magnolia Projects). Urban renewal projects in the 1960s, such as the construction of the interstate highway and the Superdome, were largely responsible for displacing and concentrating Black people in the Ninth Ward, where the Desire Development (built in 1949) and the Florida Projects (completed in 1946) were located. By 1977, 46 percent of Black voters lived in the Seventh and Ninth Wards.[40]

Black people lived in these concentrated enclaves largely because of housing discrimination practices by banks, real estate agents, the Federal Housing Authority, the Veteran's Association, and mortgage lenders.[41] Together, these entities used both overt and covert methods to persistently steer Black people away from white neighborhoods and into substandard housing stock. They denied Black people rental apartments in white neighborhoods and refused to give mortgage loans to qualified Black applicants who sought to become homeowners. They charged higher rents to Black people for overcrowded and substandard units. Such patterns of racial discrimination and higher housing costs for poor Black people reflect national patterns of systemic marginalization through housing, or what Lipsitz calls the "racialization of space and the spatialization of race."[42]

Public housing complexes were also occupied by Black residents at higher rates than whites because extreme racial discrimination in employment sectors and suburbanization rarely allowed Black people to attain subsistence-level incomes. As Martha Mahoney argues:

The relationship flowed from housing discrimination to lack of access to employment. The phenomenon operated in three ways. First, blacks incurred higher time and money costs to commute to jobs, discouraging them from pursuing employment. Second, blacks possessed less information about distant jobs. Finally, employers located outside the ghetto sometimes discriminated against blacks because they feared potential resentment from whites if blacks moved to the suburbs with comparable jobs, or because they, as employers, felt no pressure to avoid discrimination.[43]

During economic crises, such as the oil bust of the 1980s, these correlations between Black unemployment, substandard wages, and spatialized dissociation from wealth and opportunities grew even more obvious. By 1992 the median family income for Blacks in Louisiana was 52 percent that of the median white income, a gap that was wider than it had been in 1968.[44] In terms of measuring assets, white households possessed as much as ten times the net assets of the median black household.[45] Among public housing residents, 74 percent were below the poverty rate, and only 60 percent of working-age residents in these neighborhoods were linked to the labor market.[46]

White people's resistance to the Supreme Court mandate to end school segregation after the 1954 case *Brown v. Board of Education* similarly helped exacerbate Black economic marginalization and concentration in New Orleans. Rather than implement school integration, whites persistently advocated for school closures or moved their children to private establishments.[47] White people's desires to preserve monoracial neighborhoods correlated with preserving higher property tax bases (because of higher valued homes); in turn, such tax bases were essential to establishing and funding good schools, which were jealously reserved for white children's advancement. This caused radical differences between Black children's educational opportunities and those enjoyed by whites.

Residential racial segregation coupled with high rates of poverty makes Black people extra-vulnerable to numerous interlocking and mutually reinforcing oppressions in the arenas of housing, education, employment, transportation, health, and criminal justice. Homeowners who believe and feel that Black people's so-called welfare dependence warrants protective policies of defensive localism radically conceal this history. Such stereotypes and feelings grossly disavow the ways that unearned white property advantages protected by what Woods calls "social-spatial-racial enclosures" are linked to Black impoverishment.[48] Such enclosures function to entrap Black people in geographies and economies that are increasingly stripped of public resources yet are inundated with policing; they also function to enclose spaces of advantage, opportunity, and safety in order to reserve these sustaining resources solely for whites.

BLUE EMOTIONS: RESISTING ORGANIZED ABANDONMENT AND REMOVAL

Blues people had always been the central bloc to resist the predominantly white propertied classes of the Mississippi Delta, whose wealth accumulation had long depended on systemic racial discrimination in housing, education, and employment. Although this struggle between the Bourbon agenda and the Blues agenda had been taking place long before Katrina hit New Orleans,[49] the displacement of hundreds of thousands of families who adhered to Blues epistemologies meant that resistance was difficult to organize. Without the people's presence, the Blues agenda—which demanded the right of return, dignity, the restoration of networks of mutual support, and the restoration of public assets that helped the disenfranchised—was difficult to achieve.

Despite the dispersal and displacement of Blues people throughout the country, public housing residents, civil rights advocates, musicians, lawyers, and national allies built a significant campaign to stop the demolition of the Big Four public housing projects and to revoke the discriminatory municipal housing ordinances. The organizers called for immediate affordable housing options for low-income Black people who had been displaced and for poor people who had been impoverished into homelessness. Some organizers emphasized that most of the displaced public housing residents were Black women with children and the elderly, making the crisis of affordable housing a gendered form of racial and class discrimination. The activists demanded guarantees for one-to-one replacement housing in the event that the government proceeded with the demolitions, and they sought public housing residents' inclusion in redevelopment plans. By December 2007 a remarkable grassroots coalition was supporting the fight to stop the Big Four demolitions.[50]

Contrary to the cognitive denials produced by the hegemonic public feelings of defensive localism, the coalition was not demanding a return to the conditions of concentrated poverty, violence, unemployment, deep residential segregation, dilapidating housing units, and the malaise that these conditions helped to perpetuate. Rather, the coalition, which would eventually become the People's Hurricane Relief Fund, vehemently advocated for the repair of existing public housing in New Orleans because they sought to create material conditions that would enable displaced and impoverished people to come home to New Orleans. As Rachel E. Luft argues, "Organizers carefully chose the term *right of return*. They used it to expose return as a contested process and to assert that it was the government's responsibility to ensure it."[51] Public housing residents and organizers' held well-founded suspicions that the state, local official leaders, and private developers did not have the interests of impoverished and displaced residents in mind when they were drawing up redevelopment plans for mixed-income housing. Such suspicions were based on the dysfunctional practices of HUD/HANO, the evasive tactics of the New Orleans City Council, and collective memories of previous policies that resulted in gendered racial discrimination, dispossession, and displacement in New Orleans.

HUD/HANO, Mayor Ray Nagin, and the New Orleans City Council part-
nered with private construction companies seeking to profit from privatized
reconstruction plans and failed to challenge federal policy that increasingly
sought to divest from public housing. Their consensus to raze the projects was
reached through a process that was hostile to democratic procedures and bla-
tantly excluded public housing residents' input. In February 2007 a lawsuit filed
on behalf of public housing residents Yolanda Anderson, Gilda Burbank, Allen
Harris, Donna Johnigan, Odessia Lewis, Emelda May, Sylvia Moten, Emelda
Paul, Hilda Johnson, Cynthia Bell, Lolita Gibson, Nicole Banks, Judith Watson,
Gloria Williams, Mary Ann Wright, Catrice Doucet, Linda DeGruy, and Kim
Paul temporarily forced the state to halt the demolition process.[52] Residents
were represented by a team of attorneys, including Bill Quigley (lead attorney);
Royal Judson Mitchell Jr. (Loyola Law School Clinic); Adam H. Morse, Anne C.
Fitzpatrick, and Ross B. Bricker (Jenner & Block Law Firm, Chicago); Anita
Sinha, Jill Tauber, Judith A. Browne, and Monique L. Dixon (Advancement
Project, Washington, D.C.); and Tracie L. Washington (Louisiana Justice Institute, New Orleans). Together, the multiracial and multiethnic coalition of public housing residents, attorneys, and activists repeatedly advocated for the right
of return, challenged rampant housing discrimination, and sought to prevent
further public asset stripping. By filing lawsuits and offering the perspectives of
impoverished New Orleans residents to Congress and independent news media
outlets, attorneys Quigley and Washington brought the Blues agenda into public view.[53] Even while winning temporary legal gains, both lawyers understood
that the greatest battle would be in the court of public opinion and sentiment.
Outlining the tactics used by the Coalition to Stop the Demolitions to fight the
state's injustices on the independent media show *Democracy Now!* Tracie Washington emphasized that legal actions were limited in their ability to foster justice.

Legally, we go to court. That's how we've been challenging every wrong in the city of
New Orleans, every violation of civil rights. But at the end of the day, Amy, at some
point we've got to challenge the hearts and the morals of these folks, because there are
not enough of us to keep running to court. So somehow we've got to get to, you know,
a critical mass of people, where they are all telling the government that it's wrong, so
that the government will stop on its own. I mean, at the end of the day, that's what's
going to have to happen in the city, so that we can have social justice and equity.
Otherwise, you know, we just can't keep suing every single day. They'll wear us out.[54]

Washington understood that the struggle to restore the human, civil, and economic rights of the displaced and dispossessed in New Orleans and the fight to preserve public assets such as affordable housing were contingent on public desires and demands. Without the local and national political will to endorse these demands, lawsuits and court battles would eventually favor homeowners, the propertied class, and the state's alliance with private developers.

As the struggle continued throughout 2007, the state's desired outcome of organized abandonment through federal housing policy became increasingly conspicuous when HUD refused to make guarantees for one-to-one replacement of the public housing units scheduled for demolition. In her testimony on Capitol Hill, Washington outlined HUD/HANO and private developers' reconstruction plans based on documents filed with the Louisiana Housing Finance Agency. Public housing in New Orleans was to be replaced by what Washington called "newer and fewer" apartments.

St. Bernard [now Columbia Parc on the Bayou] will be reduced from 1,400 apartments to 595. Of these, 160 will be for public housing, 160 will be tax credit mixed income, 145 will be market rate units; CJ Peete [now Harmony Oaks] will be reduced from 723 existing units to 410 units. Of these, 154 will be for public housing, 133 mixed income, 123 market rate units; BW Cooper will be reduced from 1,546 units to 410. Of these, 154 will be for public housing, 133 mixed income, 123 market rate units; Lafitte will be reduced from 896 units to just over 500, with fewer than 1/3 of the units eligible for public housing residents.[55]

Because female-headed households, with women living alone or with others, made up a large majority of public housing residents and Section 8 recipients in New Orleans (77 percent and 88 percent, respectively),[56] these plans would have the most detrimental effects on poor Black women with children and the elderly. Yet there was no legal requirement for developers to provide a guarantee to replace each demolished public housing unit in the new mixed-income redevelopments, although organizers fought for one-to-one replacement guarantees. In June 2007 Louisiana senator Mary Landrieu and Connecticut senator Chris Dodd introduced the Gulf Coast Housing Recovery Act (S 1668). Aligning themselves with the public housing activists, Landrieu and Dodd proposed legislation that would require redevelopment projects to provide one-to-one replacement in Gulf Coast states affected by Hurricanes Katrina and Rita. But the proposed bill was met with vehement opposition by neo-Bourbon senator David Vitter (R-LA) and the neoliberal agendas of the Bush administration and HUD secretary Alphonso Jackson.[57]

NEOLIBERAL EMOTIONS: THE HOSTILE PRIVATISM OF ECONOMIC SELF-RELIANCE

As the Blues people staged direct actions, legal challenges, and song-filled protests to keep the public housing units in order to facilitate poor people's right of return, dominant New Orleans publics emphasized rugged individualism, self-reliance, and personal responsibility. These publics generally thought that, irrespective of their traumas, troubles, and resources, New Orleans residents were not entitled to government subsidies for housing and that all forms of public assistance for poor people should be eliminated. They expressed emotional hostility toward anything communal, publicly owned and shared, or collectively distributed, favoring instead a guarded hostile privatism.

New Orleans resident Mark Alan Zelden argued that poor people's dependence on government subsidies was the primary cause of poverty and crime. Presumably speaking from a liberal stance, Zelden claimed:

One need not be a right-wing Reaganite to know the system of public housing in New Orleans was highly damaging to the fiber of this great city before Katrina. . . . Any person who suggests we should just touch up St. Bernard or Cooper is a partisan hack with no soul or severely misplaced compassion. I drove through many of these developments on a regular basis before Hurricane Katrina. Most were not conducive to raising young children with a chance to be taxpaying citizens in adulthood. . . . Can we really be surprised that, when people can rent housing for less than $100 per month, they would do so in perpetuity if allowed? The trail of devastated families is too long to simply wave away with clichés about poverty or lack of educational or economic opportunities. Until people are told there are limits to everyone else's taxpayer generosity, we will continue to see examples of senseless violence. Are we truly ready to say enough?[58]

Zelden dismissed evidence that showed how the lack of educational and employment opportunities severely affected poor people's ability to ascend economically, deeming such claims as worn-out clichés. Instead, he argued that behavioral problems of dependence bred environments that were not conducive to "raising young children with a chance to be taxpaying citizens in adulthood." Zelden erroneously assumed that public housing residents did not work and were therefore not taxpaying citizens. Factual evidence showed that most New Orleans public housing residents (most of whom were Black women) worked in service labor economies or in informal labor economies; they had paid more than their fair share of taxes.[59] Zelden contemptuously projected public housing residents to be childlike. Presumably taxpayer generosity had caused them to engage in tantrumlike behavioral cycles of senseless violence. He argued for a severe, heavy-handed disciplinary approach of cutting public housing residents off, presuming that this would forcibly enable them to become self-sufficient. Aside from these deeply hostile and paternalistic assumptions, Zelden's narrative conjured up an entrenched historical narrative that considered Black people incapable of governing themselves and therefore in need of (white) paternal authority, supervision, and discipline.[60]

Zelden and the other New Orleans publics who argued for the hostile privatism of self-reliance paid little attention to the conditions that constrained and limited poor Black residents' ability to obtain living wages, safe and affordable housing, good education, and adequate health care. When Zelden wrote his letter in 2007, public housing exemplified only one site where impoverished New Orleans residents were experiencing discrimination, dispossession, and denigration.[61] Issues that were compounding the public housing crisis included rampant fair housing violations unchecked by federal review;[62] heightened levels of environmental hazards and toxic waste in predominantly Black low-income neighborhoods;[63] continued disinvestment from and neglect of public education;[64] the closure of public hospitals that served the uninsured and the poor;[65] unpaid insurance claims; slow and insufficient payments to homeowners under the Road Home Program that disproportionately affected working-class homeowners;[66] and federal legislation that disproportionately distributed rebuilding funds to homeowners and tax credits to developers without implementing any measures for low-income affordable housing.[67]

The ideological fantasy of economic self-reliance, hard work, and personal responsibility was held together by one of the biggest neoliberal fallacies of the post–civil rights era, namely, that the end of legalized racial discrimination meant that U.S. society now afforded people a free market of equal opportunity. This false belief was held intact by socially shared emotional investments that became more important than factual realities. The sense of being superior to those who had no choice but to rely on public assistance offered psychological rewards that were invaluable in a society that equated self-worth with wealth and class status. Even if people did not possess wealth, not being dependent on public assistance was a way of indicating that at least they were not at the bottom of the social ladder. Such emotional rewards—predicated on shaming poor people—reinforced the momentum of neoliberalism.

As publics became more and more invested in the ideological fantasy of self-reliance or sought to avoid the social shame associated with being poor, they also became increasingly opposed to stigmatized welfare goods such as public housing. Neoliberal advocates who sought to contribute less and less to the social wage had largely won a tax code counterrevolution in the late 1970s. The social stigma of welfare dependence functioned to unburden the wealthiest classes of their responsibility to contribute to infrastructural public goods. Meanwhile, the investment in self-reliance burdened working people with more and more private costs and fees. As the United States entered the twenty-first century, the wealthiest 1 percent of the U.S. population owned nearly half of all the stocks, bonds, cash, and other financial assets of the nation. The richest 15 percent controlled almost all the country's financial assets, suggesting that wealthy interests monopolized a market that called itself free. The 28,000 wealthiest people in the United States received more income than 96 million of the poorest Americans.[68]

Such color-blind equal opportunity mythologies sustained by economies of emotion that defend individual self-reliance and stigmatize collective public assets also masked the fact that people's ability to recover from the devastation of Katrina was overwhelmingly contingent on residents' access to resources and wealth. Because overtly discriminatory policies in the past had severely skewed opportunities for wealth accumulation toward whites, recovery resources were available to white New Orleans residents at much greater rates. White people's access to homeownership beginning in the 1930s was critical to their ability to transfer wealth to subsequent generations, to provide sizable tax bases for well-funded schools, and to accumulate savings that would sustain them even if they faced health and economic crises. Because wealth tends to compound rather than diminish over time, the wealth gap between people of color and whites has been widening as the baby boom generation comes into inheritances from their predecessors. Sociologist Thomas Shapiro estimates that between 1990 and 2020 the white baby boom generation will inherit $7–$9 trillion. Although many white Americans believe that their inheritance was acquired through their ancestors' hard work and personal responsibility, Shapiro and Lipsitz demonstrate that in fact "almost all of that money is rooted in profits made by whites from overtly discriminatory housing markets before 1968."[69]

In New Orleans white residents' wealth and resource advantages derived from past racial discrimination enabled whites to repair or rebuild homes damaged by Hurricane Katrina. Maps that aggregate the number of demolition permits, sales of lots and/or damaged homes to the state, and unoccupied residential addresses indicate that predominantly white neighborhoods have been repopulated at higher rates and rebuilt faster than predominantly Black low-income neighborhoods.[70] The new spatial geography of post-Katrina New Orleans suggests that white wealth and resources accrued from past generations have everything to do with people's ability to invest in the ideological fantasy of self-reliance while demonizing those who are not afforded the same unearned advantages.

This is not to suggest that white people in New Orleans did not suffer trauma, devastation, and economic losses as a result of Hurricane Katrina. Certainly, one cannot adequately measure or compare human losses and suffering. But the hostile privatism of self-reliance functioned to conceal the ways that white people in New Orleans were able to recover from the Hurricane's devastation less because of their individual hard work and resourcefulness and much more because they possessed wealth advantages linked to historical and contemporary patterns of racial discrimination.

Elected officials in New Orleans, many of whom were African American, often compounded fallacies of dependence disseminated by enfranchised and propertied white residents. When African American New Orleans City Council president Oliver Thomas stated, "We don't need soap opera watchers all day. We need people who are coming back if you are able,"[71] he endorsed the hegemonic construction of public housing residents as lazy and unproductive. His words reinforced the myth that people could just pull themselves up by their bootstraps while denying the realities of remarkably low wages, the absence of good jobs, and racial discrimination in employment. Thomas demonstrated that one did not need to be white to endorse the neo-Bourbon and neoliberal agenda. Indeed, a common feature of post–civil rights politics is to use African Americans and other representatives of color as frontline mouthpieces for neoliberalism in order to neutralize accusations of systemic gendered racism. Elected representatives of color who furthered the neo-Bourbon and neoliberal agenda either through direct support or through their passive complicity included African American HUD secretary Alphonso Jackson, Mayor Ray Nagin, and city council members James Carter, Cynthia Hedge-Morrell, and Cynthia Willard-Lewis. All these Black elected officials supported reconstruction plans whose outcomes would be detrimental to poor Black parents and to working-class people in general.

Thomas's comments also revealed that the logics and interests of the neo-Bourbon class worked in concert with those of the neoliberal class. The neoliberal class was not as blatant in expressing its racist contempt for New Orleans Blues people. Neoliberal interests in enhancing privatization, in stripping public housing assets for private gain, and in amplifying the wealth accumulation of the already rich were articulated as something that would benefit a majority of New Orleans residents who were tired of being "generous" toward "undeserving" people. If the neo-Bourbon class derived affective pleasure from excluding Black people from their neighborhoods through overtly discriminatory housing ordinances, the neoliberal class engaged in the cool affective logic of economic triage. They sought to eliminate the poor because they were deemed to be costly burdens on middle- and upper-class potential profits. Even though Black maids, housekeepers, and food service workers in New Orleans made up a large contingent of public housing and Section 8 residents,[72] these working people were deemed bad for business, bad for the revitalization of the tourist economy, and bad for the development plans of big corporations.

Like the neo-Bourbon class, the neoliberal class's hoarding of wealth, property, amenities, police, and political control at the expense of the homeless and the poor was justified through the emotional and cognitive denial that privatization and deregulation exacerbated Black and poor people's disadvantages and suffering. If the neo-Bourbon class unabashedly disavowed their racist intent to remove poor Black people by claiming that these were acts willed by God, the neoliberal class orchestrated acts of removal through housing policies that were replete with rhetorical good intentions, administrative procedural violence, and terrible outcomes.

ESCALATING RESISTANCE

By November 2007 the courts ruled to allow HUD/HANO to proceed with the demolitions, although there were still no guarantees for one-to-one replacement of demolished public housing units.[73] Still, organizers persisted in producing public alignments with the plight of poor people, single mothers with children, and the elderly. The multiracial coalition of local and national resisters offered radically different logics than those offered by neo-Bourbon and neoliberal defenders. They cultivated emotional economies rooted in the people-focused democratic traditions and worldviews of the Blues epistemology. The coalition fought for humanization, dignity, and self-determination in a hostile political climate that favored profits, social alienation, and gendered racial demonization. Rather than concealing systemic gendered racial discrimination and dispossession, the coalition unmasked it at every turn. Rather than allowing themselves to be the pathologized or pitied, the coalition exercised their right to assemble and organize, physically blocking the demolitions with their bodies and loudly contesting the normative business of the New Orleans City Council and HUD/HANO at public meetings.

Whatever neoliberal and neo-Bourbon state and private alliances could not achieve through undemocratic and corrupt policy making, they sought to achieve through state-sanctioned violence. Early in the struggle, activists who had been in the middle of a 17-day occupation of a building at the St. Bernard project to prevent its demolition were raided by a SWAT team. At 2:30 in the morning of January 31, 2007, they were terrorized at gunpoint.[74] Public housing activist Sharon Jasper would later face eviction and battery charges as punishment for her political engagement.[75]

Almost a year later, in mid-December 2007, public housing advocates attended the event "A Party with a Purpose," which included families, children, food, and dancing to the music of the Hot 8 Brass Band. They were met with police brutality, harassment, civil rights violations, and arrests.[76] Persistent demands from public housing residents and activists as well as calls from Congress members such as Representative Nancy Pelosi and Senator Barack Obama to halt demolition until residents had been more directly engaged did not seem to faze the New Orleans City Council too much.[77]

On December 20, 2007, hundreds of activists attempted to enter a city council meeting where council members would be voting on whether to proceed with the demolitions or halt them in order to have more time to engage residents in redevelopment plans. Although the council chambers still had many empty seats, the police closed and locked the gates, blocking hundreds of people from entering. As protesters shook the gates to try to gain access, police pepper-sprayed the crowd and tasered individuals. The protesters used direct action to pull on the closed city council gates yet did nothing to harm police officers. Despite this, the fact that protesters dared to take over the city council space and property warranted, in the minds of the police, a violent response to them. Here, the police considered the city council property more important than the protestors' bodies. Meanwhile, inside the chambers the Blues people demanded that the council open the gates to allow citizens in. Even though they used only their voices to make these demands, police officers inside the council chambers attacked and tasered Sess 4-5, a community activist and hip-hop artist who had been regularly involved in the protests. As people tried to prevent the police violence against Sess 4-5, they too were violently taken down, shoved, or arrested by the police. Police violently yanked on one Black man's dreadlocks to hold him back from defending Sess 4-5. Black and white women were pushed and shoved out of the way. The multiracial police force dealt with their fears over the crowd's power with overcompensations of force.[78]

Several insights are revealed by the unnecessary violent police response at the December 20, 2007, city council meeting. First, the state increases its use of violence when its legitimacy is crumbling. The Blues people showed that the interests motivating the public housing demolitions were profit-driven rather than people-driven. Kali Akuno, executive director of the People's Hurricane Relief Fund at the time, made this crystal clear the day after the protests at the city council meeting.

My interest is basically trying to . . . stop this neoliberal destruction that we see taking place in New Orleans and the complete privatization of all of the different services within the city, housing being, I think, the most critical of them, public housing being kind of the cornerstone of that. But there's an affordable housing crisis in New Orleans, of which the public housing is just one particular element of it. It's the most critical element, because public housing will stabilize rents in New Orleans. And folks should know their rents have gone up three times since the storm, and it's basically pricing . . . working people and African people, on the whole, out of the city. But this is just one particular piece of this whole program.

Public hospitals are also being shut down and set to be demolished and destroyed in New Orleans. And they've systematically dismantled the public education system and [are] beginning demolition on many of the schools in New Orleans—that's on the agenda right now—and trying to totally . . . turn that system over to a charter and a voucher system, to privatize and just kind of really go forward with a major experiment, which was initially laid out by the Heritage Foundation and other neoconservative think tanks shortly after the storm. So this is just really the fulfillment of this program.[79]

The Blues people's resistance to this systematic denigration eroded the city council's, the mayor's, and HUD/HANO's legitimacy. They showed the nation that private developer interests and corporate investments in New Orleans were being defended through policies whose effects produced Black people's removal and working people's abandonment.

Second, the fact that the city council closed the gates before the council chambers were filled indicates that they preemptively sought to foreclose the people's resistance, protests, and voices. The municipal and state representatives' fear indicates that they knew they were doing something wrong but were justifying it as necessary. Such violent defenses suggest that city council members and the police knew they were about to defend something that was morally indefensible. Yet their emotions of contempt for the protesters and their desires to preserve their worldviews and identities resulted in a unanimous city council vote to proceed with the demolitions.[80]

LIBERAL EMOTIONS: THE WELL-MEANING PATERNALISM OF MIXED-INCOME HOUSING

Not all publics in New Orleans invested in the hostile privatism of neoliberal self-reliance or in the color-blind and racially coded defensive localism of neo-Bourbon homeowners. At times, publics advocated for the elimination of public housing because they sought solutions to the extreme vulnerabilities produced by concentrated poverty in racially segregated spaces. Such liberal-minded views on planning efforts sought to aid public housing residents in finding better opportunities. Liberals often expressed good intentions to help those who faced extreme levels of marginalization. Yet these claims were also entangled with paternalistic emotional investments characteristic of the sentimentalist foundations of charities. Such emotional investments derive psy-

chological and emotional rewards on the basis of being morally good toward
the poor. Yet these investments rarely work to transform the larger conditions
that reproduce racialized and gendered impoverishment.

For example, Representative Chris Roberts of Jefferson Parish's District 1
argued that the best way to help low-income people is "by placing them in supporting, mixed-income, diverse settings under proper oversight."[81] Such public
desires to help the poor were often coupled with demands for greater surveillance,
supervision, and policing. The conviction that public housing projects needed
to be replaced with mixed-income developments had guided HUD/HANO
policy making since the 1980s. Beginning with Reagan's massive reductions in
spending on low-income housing, federal and state agents consistently advocated for private mixed-income developments as a way to diffuse the poverty that
tended to concentrate in public housing complexes. During the 1980s, federal
expenditures for subsidized public housing were slashed from $31.5 billion to $6
billion. Federal appropriations for low-income housing were cut by 80 percent,
and federal dollars allocated toward financing new low-income housing were
reduced from $4 billion to $400 million.[82] During the Clinton administration
and the George H. W. Bush administration, government low-income housing
programs were increasingly eliminated, shifting the delivery of affordable housing to the private sector. Mixed-income housing projects, for which developers receive tax breaks in exchange for allocating a particular number of units to
low-income residents, had to reconcile for-profit development strategies with
affordable housing provisions.[83]

Support for the elimination of public housing in favor of mixed-income
developments had already been cultivated in public ideologies and emotional
economies long before Hurricane Katrina hit New Orleans. HUD/HANO,
the New Orleans City Council, and numerous New Orleans residents claimed
that allowing poor, predominantly Black and female residents to return to the
existing public housing projects would mean returning the city to crime rates
that would be detrimental to property values, economic redevelopment, middle-
and upper-class safety, and the revitalization of the tourist industry.

In keeping with its paternalistic overtone of telling the poor what is best for
them while excluding them from planning processes, HUD/HANO would not
be dissuaded from its commitment to replace public housing complexes with
mixed-income developments, despite the crisis in affordable housing. HUD/

HANO proceeded with its plans despite a long record of fair housing advocacy that had repeatedly shown that mixed-income developments were largely detrimental rather than helpful to the poor. This extensive evidence suggests that the HUD/HANO and New Orleans City Council decision to demolish the public housing units was motivated by something other than the desire to improve poor people's lives.

Mixed-income developments have largely failed poor people in New Orleans for a number of reasons. For one, strict occupancy rules, the express goal of which is to keep mixed-income properties marketable, are often used to evict low-income residents from mixed-income developments. For example, former public housing residents living in New Orleans' mixed-income River Garden development (which replaced the demolished St. Thomas housing project in 2004) often felt as though they were "suspects in their own community," in large part because of the heavy police presence in River Garden.[84] Don Everad, director of Hope House (a neighborhood organization, located across from River Garden, that assists low-income residents), noted, "I think it's mostly management's idea on that they have to control the public housing crowd to satisfy the non-public housing residents."[85] Everad acknowledged that safety was important for all the residents but stated that at times poor residents' encounters with the police "has just been pure harassment."[86]

In addition, the desired mixing of classes often fails because of moderate- to middle-income residents' social and cultural refusal to live alongside low-income people, particularly if these groups differ racially. "The biggest complaint really is just the feeling of not being respected, the feeling of being watched all the time," Everad said. "It's less than a specific thing. It's the sense of having to be on guard all the time."[87] Everad testified to the ways in which former public housing residents became feared in mixed-income developments. Emotional expressions of fear, contempt, surveillance, and policing were directed toward them, contributing to their exclusion and marginalization.

In his congressional testimony, the executive director of the Greater New Orleans Fair Housing Action Center, James Perry, declared the St. Thomas mixed-income redevelopment a failure. "I am on record in the past as calling the St. Thomas River Garden HOPE VI Redevelopment a failure. I would reiterate that concern and note that HUD has stated that this failure is the model for the future of public housing in New Orleans and America. I call on you to reverse this effort immediately."[88] River Garden had originally promised to make 775 units available to low-income people (down from the 900 units of St. Thomas). In the end, however, River Garden made only 300 low-income units available for former St. Thomas residents, radically abandoning the responsibility to provide affordable housing.[89] After Katrina, HANO leased public housing units at River Garden to non–public housing residents, violating its 2003 agreement.[90]

Following a trend begun by post-Fordist free market and antiwelfare policies, federal and state policies contradictorily pretend to reconcile developers' private for-profit interests with public interests that serve the most marginalized. In fact, such policies mask the orchestrated ways in which public assets are stripped to serve the interests of private capital. Subsidizing private mixed-income development projects that use publicly funded tax credits and incentives has largely benefited private developers and property owners, not low-income people. As James Fraser, former executive director of the Greater New Orleans Fair Housing Action Center, has documented:

The empirical research on mixed-income redevelopment of distressed urban neighborhoods to date suggests that the overwhelming majority of benefits have been realized by private-sector developers, local government, and other stakeholders who are in the position to benefit from place-based revitalization, while many low-income households—possibly in many ways that policy research has not revealed—have, at the very least, been underserved.[91]

To cultivate consent for such private-public alliances that benefit the wealthy and the interests of homeowners while further marginalizing the poor, state and local agents relied on hegemonic stereotypes and feelings that constructed public housing and Section 8 residents as pathologized people who needed to be corrected or removed.

Liberal sentimentality or affective pity for the Black poor, even if well meaning, operated through different disavowals and denials than those popularized by paleoconservatives and neoconservatives. Still, they contributed to similar outcomes. Rather than advocating for removal and triage, this liberal class advocated disaggregation and dispersal into mixed-income units without considering the larger processes that would once again entrap the Black poor in social-spatial-racial enclosures. The liberal bloc persistently underestimated or disavowed the significance of housing discrimination, lack of affordable housing, and racial steering in the private market.

For one, liberals did not consider where the displaced and homeless were supposed to live while the public housing units were being demolished and the mixed-income units developed. Liberals also did not consider that possessing a Section 8 voucher in a private market that was hostile to low-income renters—particularly those of color—was rather useless. Such vouchers were particularly useless in a city where the rental housing stock had been radically reduced and the rent prices had increased by as much as 50 percent. Moreover, liberals did not understand that their advocacy for surveillance and policing in mixed-income units to counteract what was deemed improper behaviors functioned as a method of displacement. They simply assumed that low-income people should conform to their middle-class value systems and their cultural and social ways of being in the world.

Finally, their investments in saving the poor by telling them what was best for them revealed emotional economies of paternalism and sentimentality that functioned to prevent deep introspective analyses of the ways in which charity models generally fail to acknowledge the systemic patterns of white advantage that are causally linked to Black people's poverty. In other words, these emotions clouded liberals from seeing that Black poverty is not simple misfortune but often a consequence of intergenerational racial discrimination patterns. Feeling bad for the poor but simultaneously advocating for their surveillance, correction, and control kept many liberals in New Orleans from confronting the ways they helped to reinforce both the organized abandonment of predominantly Black poor residents and the racialized and gendered impoverishment they purportedly sought to ameliorate.

THE RICH CULTURES OF STIGMATIZED SPACES

The Blues people knew, felt, and experienced something that the liberal, neo-liberal, and neo-Bourbon people could not see and feel—or something they refused to see and feel. Had the liberal, neoliberal, and neo-Bourbon people permitted themselves to be emotionally and cognitively receptive to the perspectives, values, and social praxis of the Blues people, they would have been forced to shift identities historically built on valuing property over people. They would have had to abandon emotional economies that encouraged dissociative contempt and/or paternalism for people whose lives were so deeply affected by interlocking systems of oppression.

The myths proliferated by the stereotypes and stigmas tied to welfare dependence and criminality dismissed the fact that New Orleans public housing projects were sites that had nurtured renowned cultural producers and political activists. Although they faced premature forms of death through state-sanctioned and interpersonal violence, poverty, environmental hazards, lack of health care, and atrocious education, public housing residents also possessed archives of knowledge that generated incisive social critiques and democratic praxis.

Hip-hop artist Sess 4-5, who grew up in the Ninth Ward's Desire public housing development, offered critiques of oppression through such songs as "No Surrender, No Retreat."[92] In his lyrics Sess 4-5 outlines the traps of poverty in order to undo the stereotypes of dependence, but he also conjures up the spirit of revolution situated in New Orleans public housing geographies by referencing the history of Black Panther organizing for self-determination and self-defense against police violence at Desire in the 1970s. Like his political predecessors, Sess 4-5 continued the tradition of fearlessness as he repeatedly confronted police violence and harassment in the course of the public housing struggle.

Former Black Panther Malik Rahim, who co-founded Common Ground in the Ninth Ward, an organization that evolved into a network of groups helping people with health care, recovery, and reconstruction, continued to struggle for Black self-determination post-Katrina.[93] Describing the terror and abandonment in the immediate aftermath of Katrina in his September 1, 2005, statement, "This is Criminal," Rahim foreshadowed the public housing struggle: "When you see all the poor people with no place to go, feeling alone and helpless and angry, I say this is a consequence of HOPE VI. New Orleans took all the HUD money it could get to tear down public housing, and families and neighbors who'd relied on each other for generations were uprooted and torn apart."[94]

Like Rahim, former Black Panther Althea Francois, an organizer with Safe Streets/Strong Communities and with Critical Resistance South and coordinator of the New Orleans chapter of the National Coalition to Free the Angola 3, continued fighting for the Blues agenda by contesting the death economies of mass incarceration and the egregiously racist policing of New Orleans until she died on Christmas Day 2009. When told of her passing, Robert Hillary King, of the Angola 3, invoked Matthew 25:35, stating, "'I was hungry and you fed me, was thirsty and you gave me drink, was in prison and you visited me.' Althea fed us with hope. She had an enormously giving spirit that we will all deeply miss."[95]

The Calliope (B. W. Cooper) housing project was the home of a remarkable array of New Orleans musicians, including Master P, C-Murder, the Neville Brothers,[96] and local bounce artists such as Glenda "Goldie" Roberts and Chev Off the Ave. These musicians not only mix sounds, dances, and beats organically endemic to New Orleans cultures rooted in Africanist, Native American, French, Spanish, and Caribbean convergences but also attest to the ways that music and dance in New Orleans are matters of spiritual and physical survival. The economies of pleasure engendered by New Orleans musicians and dancers provide reprieve, escape, and physical release from the economies of death and destruction that Blues people regularly confront.

As rapper Mia X (Mia Young), who had lived at the Lafitte and the St. Bernard public housing projects, stated, "Unlike anywhere else, we need our culture for our survival—we need to listen to second line . . . we need to listen to bounce music."[97] Mia X describes her music as tribal, in part because of her connection to New Orleans Mardi Gras Indians, a group of African Americans who dress up in elaborate costumes during Mardi Gras, represent long-held Black cultural traditions in New Orleans neighborhoods, and function as mutual aid societies that help members with medical bills, funeral expenses, home repairs, or lost wages.[98] Allison "Tootie" Montana, a revered Mardi Gras Indian chief who suffered a heart attack while protesting police murder and vigilante violence at a city council meeting in June 2005, was a distant cousin of Mia X.

These social networks, ecosystems of emotional and material support, were critical to the survival and resilience of poor Black people in New Orleans. They drew from long African American legacies of making something out of nothing and of turning to communal networks of support in times when the state exercised organized abandonment.

Harold Battiste, legendary founder of AFO Records, grew up in the Magnolia Projects (C. J. Peete) in the 1940s near the famous Dew Drop Inn on LaSalle St. As bounce artist Magnolia Shorty raps, "M-A-G-N-O-L-I-A, that is the home where the soljas stay." The numerous hip-hop artists who grew up there, including Juvenile, Turk, Soulja Slim (previously Magnolia Slim), Ruda

Real, Jay Electronica, and B.G., repeatedly reference the Magnolia projects in their music, videos, names, and tattoos. Similarly, bounce artist Katey Red titled her 1999 album *Melpomene Block Party* in order to locate herself inside the geography of the New Orleans Melpomene public housing complex.

The significance of place is repeatedly evoked in New Orleans hip-hop and bounce music to testify to the violence and oppression residents have witnessed in their lives as well as to celebrate the social networks that enabled their resilience and perseverance. The common call-and-response practice of shouting out all of the New Orleans wards and public housing projects by name is reflected in one of the earliest bounce songs produced by Gregory D and Mannie Fresh, "Buck Jump Time," and continued in songs such as "Nolia Clap," by Juvenile.

Aw yeah! You know the baseline in the background, baby!
New Orleans, you know what time it is? (Buck jump time!)
[Hook]
That Calliope (Buck jump time!)
That Melpomene (Buck jump time!)
Magnolia (Buck jump time!)
St. Thomas (Buck jump time!)
Lafitte (Buck jump time!)
That Iberville (Buck jump time!)
Desire (Buck jump time!)
That Fischer (Buck jump time!)

To outsiders, calling out the names of New Orleans public housing projects may seem trivial. But to those who are situated inside the social networks, violent traumas, oppressions, creative cultures, and methods of resilience that characterize New Orleans housing projects, the process of naming one's place is deeply significant. It grants affirmative recognition to people who are otherwise denigrated, demonized, and devalued. It enables processes of ethically witnessing experiences borne out of centuries of discrimination and marginalization. It generates validity for residents' dignity to persevere despite the oppressions that come with poverty. It affirms the significance of interdependence and interpersonal connections to survival and transformation.

Activist Shana Griffin, who was actively involved in the Coalition to Stop the Demolitions, explains the links between public housing, intersecting oppressions, and possibilities for resistance.

I spent 23 years of my life in the Iberville Public Housing Development, so it shaped not just my life work, but my identity, in terms of me identifying as a Black feminist. . . . Being in that environment, I was also acutely aware of relationships between poverty, substance abuse, inter-relationship violence, institutional racism, savage inequality around education, as well as the over-policing of communities of color. . . . But it is also one of the strongest communities to live in. That people can be denied to return to their communities of origin, city of origin . . . Are they just expected to start over? How can you just start over when your safety net has been destroyed? Your family, your friends, your neighbors, your church, your schools are gone? . . . And the culture shock! New Orleans is more of a Caribbean city than any city in the South, or any other city in this country. It is a completely different culture. And there is just this expectation that you will adjust quickly. . . . We need to be talking about sustainable human development. People have the right to return to a city that has quality affordable housing, and schools with the supplies they need to educate our kids.[99]

As part of the New Orleans chapter of INCITE! Women of Color Against Violence, Griffin was instrumental in bringing to light the gender-specific effects of racism in the response to Katrina and its aftermath.[100] Along with women such as Charmaine Neville, who bravely testified after being raped while trying to survive flooding and federal abandonment,[101] Griffin opened dialogue on "the intersection of violence perpetrated upon marginalized communities, both by external social forces and by those within our communities."[102] Insisting that the interlocking violence of the state and from the community converged primarily on the bodies of women of color, INCITE! called for community accountability and for the end of all Black people's criminalization. The organization interpreted the organized abandonment of public housing residents through the rubric of population control policies.

Population control policies, such as the destruction of affordable housing, denial of health care, lack of environmentally safe public schools, and lack of other critical community services, intentionally block particular people—especially poor women of color—from returning home. These policies create a *forced* migration and displacement of people of African descent and other people of color from New Orleans.[103]

Griffin and INCITE!'s commitment to the ethics of communal accountability and healing manifested in on-the-ground mechanisms for "facilitating women's access to safety and health care as it builds a political base for revolutionary change."[104] These women looked to meet the immediate needs of their communities to build interpersonal bonds and communities of consciousness. After several years of organizing, the New Orleans Women's Health Clinic (NOWHC) opened on May 1, 2007. It provided much needed health services for low-income women in New Orleans and incorporated "an analysis of the root causes of the current health care crisis into the services it provides."[105] The organizers of INCITE! continue to launch initiatives that focus on contesting the effects of rape and domestic abuse, overpolicing and incarceration, environmental racism, and lack of access to health care.

How do we become ethical witnesses to the resilience, self-determination, dignity, and democratic visions of New Orleans Blues people? How do we learn to privilege people over profits? How do we reshape our identities so that our unconscious and conscious investments in patriarchal white supremacy, social alienation, and violence become intolerable? The emotional economies prevalent in the epistemologies and practices of New Orleans Blues people replenished courage, healing, interdependence, and sustainability. These vital feelings and visions countered the death-producing economies of neo-Bourbonism, neoliberalism, and liberal paternalism. Sunni Patterson, a poet from the Ninth Ward whose family is deeply rooted in New Orleans, repeatedly articulated and disseminated the emotional economies and worldviews foregrounded by the Blues agenda. In her poem "We Made It," Patterson walks us through imagery and emotions that testify to the daily atrocities of racism, sexual violence, indignities, and state-sanctioned degradation. She does not hesitate to articulate how governmental violence intersects with intimate and interpersonal violence, seeing all such conditions as originating from roots of oppression that live both within and without. But Patterson does not end her testimony at the scene of unspeakable violence. Instead, she reminds us of our shared responsibility toward creation, toward building each other's regeneration and determination.

So I'm from a stock
that pitch cocktail bombs and hand grenades.
We pour cayenne pepper around the perimeter of a building

to keep the police dogs at bay.
I'm the Panther Party
in the Desire Housing Projects in New Orleans.
I'm nigga turning the gun on the National Guards.
Take a long, long look.
I'm a cook in the kitchen
asking the missus to taste the dinner
take a long, long sip,
'cuz death ain't always this good.
It's eyes popping out they sockets.
It's a lifeless body rocking backwards and forwards.
It's a boy stabbed forty-seven times
in front the church house.
It's a man forty-three years old,
stuffing his penis in a nine-year-old girl's mouth,
naw, death don't always taste good
just don't sound like something I want to eat often.
I hear them say
it was like a train came through the room
left mama so depressed she was unable to move
until this one day.
A few months after the hurricane.
Husband and child found the trinity bloody in bed.
His wife, his son, his other daughter was dead,
and on the end table there was a letter that read,
"I couldn't stay here,
not for one minute longer,
and it made no sense for me to leave here alone,
'cause who would take care of my babies
with they mama gone?"
I'm telling you, death ain't always good.
It'll leave you fending for water and food.
It'll riddle up your body in the Audubon Ballroom
They'll El-Hajj Malik el-Shabazz you,
crown you King, then dethrone you in a Lorraine Hotel.

They'll disfigure your body to where folks can't tell
if you Emmett Till or not,
tell the mama, "Keep that casket open,
let all the world see it ain't just burning in Mississippi."
Hell, it's hot wherever you be,
from the rooftop to the cell block,
step on up to the auction block,
bend over,
touch your toes,
son, show your teeth,
lift her titties,
examine his balls,
now, this damn near sound like a hip-hop song,
but it's slavery at its peak,
a circus for all the freaks.
They'll warn you, "Caution when you speak,"
can't afford the truth to leak,
but will say "Blessed are the meek
and are the ones who make peace
and are the ones who are persecuted
for the sake of righteousness,"
for we say theirs is the kingdom,
earth is their inheritance.
So no matter how treacherous,
they'll try to trap us in them trenches,
and they'll dig deeper ditches,
but all that matters is this.
It's like which side will we pick,
or which path will we choose.
It's either win or lose,
'cuz death don't come in vain,
not for us to remain enslaved
or our spirits to remain in cages.
It comes so we might be courageous
to fulfill our obligation to our God and all creation,

stand in determination,
able to look death right in the face
and say we made it,
we made it,
we made it,
we made it.[106]

Patterson understands the necessity of conjuring a long history of Black resistance from the Middle Passage to the present. Choosing her words carefully, Patterson knows that words are not simple echoes in the air; they make worlds materialize and replenish spirits. For her, the movement between word, body, and spirit always has the potential to overcome, to afford affirmative recognition, and to transform death economies into sustainable living realities.

So I'm glad to say I'm of this stock that can come forward . . . even in the midst of all of the tragedy and the chaos, that the spirit is so triumphant, . . . that we can work to make things happen, that we can work to make things move, that . . . our minds are strong and intact. We might be crazy every now and again, . . . but the main thing is to have hope, is to have faith, is to have love, and know that we've overcome so many things. Like our elder says, . . . we're products of the ones that they couldn't kill, and we're here because we couldn't be killed. That's the only reason why we sit here right now, because we can't be killed. What type of DNA is that to have that run through your body, that in the midst of all of these Middle—and this was no different from Middle Passage or anything else, the same tactics.[107]

In being an ethical witness to the oppressed people of New Orleans, Patterson shows that the emotional economies and cosmologies rooted in the epistemology of the Blues hold the potential to conjure up a more just world.

CHAPTER 4

ESCONDIDO, CALIFORNIA: THE EXCLUSIONARY EMOTIONS OF NATIVIST MOVEMENTS

The Southern Poverty Law Center (SPLC) reported that between 2003 and 2006 racially motivated hate crimes against Latino/as (regardless of immigration status) rose by 35 percent nationally and by 50 percent in California.[1] The scripts of racial violence resemble each other in formulaic patterns. Of the numerous incidents described by the SPLC, the attack on David Ritcheson, 16, mimics the sexualized racial violence against Iraqi prisoners at Abu Ghraib and Haitian immigrant Abner Louima with striking resemblance.[2] Along the U.S.-Mexico border the everyday harassment and violence perpetuated by U.S. government agents are compounded by the presence civilian vigilante groups, such as the Minuteman Project and the American Border Patrol. Believing that government entities are no longer willing to defend their national ideal, these nativist vigilante groups strive to preserve white numerical and cultural supremacy in the United States. In 2011 Shawna Forde and Jason Bush, of the nativist group Minuteman American Defense, were sentenced to death for the murders of Raul Flores and his 9-year-old daughter, Bisenia Flores, in Arizona.[3] Such egregious violations signify the intensity of living under conditions that are conducive to small and large expressions of nativist aggression against people of color deemed foreign or threatening.

These overt forms of nativist violence have taken place alongside much more covert forms of anti-immigrant exclusion and disenfranchisement throughout the post–civil rights era. The covert forms are generally not expressed through overtly white supremacist language. Rather, they take place through the dry, quotidian procedures of city council meetings, legal discourses, and local measures. They are expressed through color-blind talk about so-called illegal aliens, or people who are presumed to be in violation of the law by virtue of their presence rather than their actions. One hundred sixty-four anti-immigration state laws were passed across the United States between 2010 and 2012.[4] By using a term such as "illegals," elected state and municipal representatives count on the way this word triggers a series of assumptions that barely need argumentation or clarification before they are taken as truths in the imaginations and embodied emotions of dominant U.S. majorities. Those who advocate exclusionary ordinances count on normalized post–civil rights beliefs and feelings that undocumented immigrants are undeserving of resources such as education, health care, housing, and DMV identification cards. Municipal and state politicians count on the normalized idea that at least some of their residents are invested in a possessive, exclusionary, and racialized form of nationalism that supersedes their interests in preserving human rights. Local procedures that legitimize anti-immigrant exclusion and marginalization claim to be about upholding the law, but this veneer betrays deeper interests that are at once racialized, gendered, economic, and emotional.

Municipal ordinances that seek to deny undocumented immigrants rental housing have become a significant site for staging antagonisms about the future of America's national character. Controlling space is an integral process in the development of localized power relations. In particular, space circumscribes and informs people's notions of belonging, participation, and safety. Space determines the extent to which people are presumed to be national agents who influence the governance of localized and national structures or the objects these structures seek to control.

As of 2009, 105 localities in 29 states had considered anti–illegal immigrant ordinances. Of these, 42 localities have passed measures containing housing restrictions.[5] The origins of these ordinances can be traced to the 2005 Illegal Immigration Relief Act drafted by Joseph Turner, the nativist leader of Save Our State (SOS).[6] Although the city council of San Bernadino, California, failed to pass Turner's proposed ordinance by a 4–3 margin, this did not deter SOS's leader from establishing a model that other municipalities could follow.

Turner's endeavor proved remarkably successful. On July 13, 2006, only a few months after the San Bernadino measure failed, Hazleton, Pennsylvania, became the first municipality to adopt an anti-immigrant housing ordinance.[7] Hazleton's ordinance was longer and more detailed than Turner's original measure because nativist attorneys Kris Kobach and Michael Hethmon helped redraft it. At the time, Kobach worked as senior counsel for the Immigration Reform Law Institute (IRLI) and Hethmon was IRLI's director. The IRLI is the legal arm of the Federation for American Immigration Reform (FAIR), an anti-immigrant organization founded in 1979 by John Tanton and currently led by Dan Stein. Since its inception, FAIR has thinly concealed its white supremacist agenda to preserve the dominance of America's European character, culture, and population by advocating restrictions against undocumented immigrants. They have also masked their goals to keep America white through the misuse of environmental rights discourses, framing their opposition to immigration as a concern over overpopulation. Working tirelessly to manufacture public panics, FAIR has been at the forefront of instituting anti-immigrant legislative restrictions and exclusions at federal, state, and municipal levels.[8] With the support of IRLI and FAIR, Kobach and Hethmon adapted Turner's idea and found a loud advocate in Hazleton's mayor, Lou Barletta.

Ordinances that deny housing to undocumented immigrants are part of a new nativist strategy developed by FAIR and IRLI; the aim of this strategy is to foster what these groups call the self-deportation of Latino/a immigrants and other immigrants of color.[9] FAIR and IRLI are interested in restricting or excluding immigrants of color from basic rights within the United States generally, but because Latino/as make up the majority of undocumented immigrants in the United States, the two organizations have implemented this strategy in predominantly white small town locales with growing Latino/a populations. By denying undocumented immigrants the basic things they need to function (driver's licenses, identification cards, rental housing, health care services, and education), FAIR and IRLI hope that both documented and undocumented Latino/as will self-deport back to their countries. Although the nativist organizations do not explicitly state this, it is a logical conclusion tó make for two reasons. First, given that many Latino/a families have both documented and undocumented members, ordinances and restrictions on undocumented immigrants inevitably affect the lives of documented immigrants as well.[10] Second, these nativist organizations know that a person's Latino/a appearance and identity, *not* their immigration status, determines whether she or he will be suspected of being undocumented. As such, any restrictive measure against undocumented immigrants prominently relies on racial and linguistic profiling for its implementation.

FAIR had to develop legal strategies that targeted undocumented immigrants in part because explicit exclusion on the basis of national origin, race, or ethnicity is no longer legally defensible in post–civil rights America. According to Hethmon, ordinances that proliferated throughout America's small towns offer important field tests for determining the legal limits of restricting undocumented immigrants' rights. The more these municipal field tests proliferate across the nation, the more they broaden public support for formalizing restrictions against undocumented immigrants at the state and national level.[11] Kobach and Hethmon were instrumental in drafting Arizona's SB 1070, which gave local and state police officers the power to arrest undocumented immigrants for civil violations of immigration law.[12] Although the Supreme Court revoked most of SB 1070 in its June 2012 ruling, it upheld the "show me your papers" provision that allows the state to instruct its police to check the immigration status of people they detain.[13]

But the self-deportation movement sought to achieve much more than an overhaul of long-established legal precedents in immigration, fair housing, and constitutional law. It sought to create exclusionary emotional economies that legitimized the policing, surveillance, harassment, and rejection of Latino/a immigrants and other immigrants of color. Although the nativist movement lost many legal battles along the way, it gained tremendous ground in the court of public opinion. There is no evidence to date that the self-deportation movement has reduced the number of immigrants in the United States, particularly those who are undocumented. But there is ample evidence that their efforts have amplified anti-Latino/a emotional economies that foster racialized divisions and hatred. Asked how he would respond to the accusation that anti-immigrant ordinances create climates of fear, Hethmon responded, "I say: Well, yeah, it's not great. But it's the best choice."[14] The anti-immigrant legislative tactics that FAIR and local municipalities use have been instrumental in fostering emotional cultures that advance nativist ideas and practices in both conscious and unconscious ways.

Anti-immigrant ordinances have mainly been proposed and/or adopted in locales where rapid increases in the foreign-born or Latino/a population have occurred since 2000.[15] These population shifts (rather than the actual number of immigrants of color in the locale) often instigate racialized fears that undocumented immigrants will become strains on municipal resources. Yet the locales where anti-immigrant ordinances passed are generally not experiencing high unemployment rates. Approximately two-thirds (68 percent) of the locales that passed anti-immigrant ordinances between 2006 and 2009 had unemployment rates at or below the national average in 2000.[16] Indeed, some of the small towns or suburban municipalities that passed such ordinances experienced economic revitalization as a result of the consumerism, small businesses, and tax contributions of growing Latino/a populations.[17] Latino/as often moved to these small town and suburban municipalities because they had heard that employers there were willing to hire undocumented workers[18] or because they sought affordable housing and services they could not obtain in more expensive cities.

ESTABLISHING PENALTIES FOR THE HARBORING OF ILLEGAL ALIENS IN THE CITY OF ESCONDIDO

Once an agricultural town 30 miles north of San Diego, Escondido has been transformed in the last 20 years by suburban development. Because of the rising costs of housing in San Diego, Escondido became one of the last areas offering relatively affordable units in San Diego County. The pull factors of affordable housing and good labor opportunities contributed to the 25.9 percent growth in Escondido's Latino/a population between 1990 and 2010. During that period, Escondido's Latino/a population increased from 23 percent to 48.9 percent of the total population. Meanwhile, whites of non-Hispanic origin went from a slight majority of 49 percent in 2004 to a minority of 40.4 percent in 2010.[19]

On October 18, 2006, the Escondido City Council adopted Ordinance 2006-38R, "Establishing Penalties for the Harboring of Illegal Aliens in the City of Escondido" (hereafter called the EPHIA ordinance), which was introduced by council member Marie Waldron. During the June 2006 Republican primary for the 74th Assembly District seat, Waldron's campaign focused largely on restricting undocumented immigration, and the San Diego Minutemen, a nativist vigilante group, enthusiastically endorsed her candidacy.[20] To garner political support for the anti-immigrant ordinance, Waldron made paranoiac claims that "illegals" were exposing American schoolchildren to diseases such as tuberculosis and leprosy, even though county health officials stated that there was no evidence to support such a claim.[21] Waldron also attributed increased local costs in education, criminal justice, and city infrastructure to the presence of what she described as illegal aliens. She cited no empirical studies or statistical research to support her claims. Waldron's lack of concern for facts and evidence is unsurprising, given that the terrain of politics depends primarily on triggering and shaping affectively charged beliefs.

The key argument of the EPHIA ordinance is that the undocumented are more likely to create poor housing conditions in Escondido, which would in turn contribute to increased crime. This accusation is based on the assumption that the undocumented are less likely to report problems in their dwelling units because of their immigration status. They are also presumed to be more likely to live in overcrowded units without official rental and tenant agreements.[22] Some of these assumptions are based on data obtained from a study conducted by the National Latino Research Center at California State University, San Marcos. The June 2006 study, *Mission Park Community Survey: Escondido, California*, involved a three-year participatory-action research process on the east side of Escondido and was intended to influence the city's planning strategies and resource allocation.[23]

The authors of the survey examined two census tracts where 71 percent of the residents were Latino/a to study quality-of-life indicators, including education, language barriers, overcrowded and deteriorating rental housing conditions, and property and violent crimes. They found that eastside residents faced the typical challenges of racially segregated neighborhoods with high concentrations of poverty. The life chances and opportunities of Latino/as and other poor residents in Mission Park were severely affected by lack of access to good education, lack of availability of well-paying jobs, lack of decent housing, and language barriers. They also found a profound disconnect between Latino/a community members and local institutions and agencies. The policy recommendations of the survey included increasing affordable housing in Escondido, expanding educational enrichment programs, increasing the availability of information about resources and social services (particularly in Spanish), and developing a family resource center and a center that supported women and mothers. Importantly, the survey did not examine immigration or citizenship status. As a result, the problems described in the survey were never correlated with undocumented immigration.[24]

Instead of arguing for improving structural conditions in housing, education, health, civic engagement, and employment in the predominantly low-income Latino/a neighborhoods, city council members who supported the EPHIA ordinance inverted the survey's intent. Citing the survey's evidence of poor housing conditions, overcrowding, and crime on the east side, nativist proponents argued that these problems were essentially caused by undocumented immigrants. Moreover, these problems were predicted to spread, burdening the city's infrastructure. The ordinance was meant to preemptively stop this from happening by giving the city the authority to punish landlords who were willing to rent to the undocumented. The ordinance concluded: "It is in the best interest of and will serve and benefit the health, safety and welfare of the public and law-abiding business entities and property owners to adopt policies and procedures to deter and prevent the harboring of illegal aliens, and criminal activity by illegal aliens."[25] Residents and municipal officials who advocated for the ordinance sought to apply the harboring provision in immigration law to landlords. This provision stated that any person who "knowing or in reckless disregard of the fact that an alien has come to, entered or remained in the United States in violation of the law, conceals, harbors, or shields from detection such alien in any place" would be penalized.[26]

After much contestation and debate by Escondido residents, the EPHIA ordinance was passed by a 3–2 council vote. Council members Waldron, Ed Gallo, and Sam Abed voted in favor and Mayor Lori Hold Pfeiler and Councilman Ron Newman opposed. Evidence did not seem to matter much in the ideological worldviews of EPHIA supporters, but emotions ran high on both sides of the debate.

The plaintiffs who filed suit against the ordinance argued that Escondido's ordinance violated constitutional, immigration, and fair housing laws and precedents.[27] For starters, the plaintiffs argued that it was impossible to see how Escondido residents and landlords could file complaints against undocumented immigrants without discriminating on the basis of race, ethnicity, and/

or national origin, as fair housing law requires. Although the ordinance stated that landlords could not accuse someone of undocumented status primarily or solely on the basis of race, ethnicity, or national origin, the ordinance was silent on how landlords might otherwise identify an undocumented immigrant. Moreover, well-established legal precedent concluded that the enforcement of immigration laws fell under federal, not state or local, authority.

Immigration enforcement procedures are complex, have a separate court system, and follow protocols that require extensive training and understanding of immigration law. In requiring the reporting of suspected undocumented immigrants, arguably the EPHIA ordinance transferred such authority to city officials, who were vastly ignorant of immigration proceedings and the law.[28] As numerous legal scholars have argued, the ordinance also went against many other well-established legal precedents in immigration, fair housing, and constitutional law.[29]

If the EPHIA ordinance violates a number of legal precedents, then its enforcement guidelines border on absurdity. The guidelines state that "any official, business entity, or resident of the City" can send a signed written complaint to the city describing an alleged violation of the ordinance. Essentially, this encourages policing and spying by anyone who suspects that an undocumented immigrant is seeking rental housing.[30] In coded ways the ordinance would likely create conditions in which any Latino/a person perceived to be undocumented would become a target of suspicion. Upon receipt of such a complaint, the ordinance states that the city would then verify the immigration status of the person seeking to lease or rent a dwelling unit by using a federal database.

Therein lies the first absurdity: Such a federal database does not exist.[31] Ordinance supporters simply wished for a database that could provide accurate and up-to-date information about every documented immigrant and nonimmigrant visitor in real time. To date, no database can offer such information. The federal database that employers use to verify work authorization (E-Verify) checks solely for work authorization. This authorization can be dissociated from a person's immigration status. For example, a person who is applying for political asylum, someone seeking a change in status because he or she married a U.S. citizen, and a temporary student all may be considered legal residents without necessarily having the authorization to work. E-Verify is part of a larger program used to check the status of immigrants applying for social welfare benefits called Systematic Alien Verification for Entitlements. Through auditing, these databases have been found to be full of errors and to provide inconclusive responses with regard to immigration status that "disproportionately work to the detriment of noncitizens and naturalized citizens."[32]

Upon verifying the immigration status of the suspected renter by using a database that does not exist, the ordinance's enforcement provisions claim that landlords would then have ten days to evict the renter or else the city would suspend the business license of the landlord. This guideline explicitly conflicts with state laws controlling eviction proceedings and cancellations of existing tenancy.[33] Because EPHIA enforcement guidelines offer no hearings or other procedures that would allow renters to contest the city's findings regarding their immigration status, the U.S. District Court ruled that the ordinance would likely subject landlords to lawsuits, causing them irreparable harm.[34]

NUESTRA AMÉRICA

A few weeks before the EPHIA ordinance was approved by the Escondido City Council, about 400 people stood outside City Hall with signs. On October 4, 2006, a line of 30 officers and deputies suited in riot gear stood between pro-ordinance supporters and those who opposed the measure; later, the police officers configured themselves into two lines, separating the two factions of protesters by a 20-foot gap.[35] At the rallies before the vote, ordinance supporters were predominantly white and opponents were predominantly Latino/a.[36] At one point, the spatial arrangement that divided the pro-immigrant and anti-immigrant protesters sonically converged as both sides simultaneously began chanting, "USA! USA! USA!" In this ironic moment, both sides made claims on the American nation on fundamentally different bases.

The proponents of the EPHIA ordinance were invested in an ideal of American national identity that was first and foremost defined by white hegemony, the English language, and the right to exclude. Wearing red, white, and blue and waving American flags, the San Diego Minutemen and ordinance supporters reiterated their refusal to share space and resources with anyone they deemed foreign or illegal. Whenever they uttered those words, they did not imagine white Canadians. Rather, they based their resentments and rage on the fear that Mexicans and other Latino/a immigrants were in the process of repossessing land, power, and culture that they viewed as theirs. They defended a vicious convergence of white American culture, property values defined by the exclusion of people of color, and the paternalist presumption that they were entitled to tell "foreigners" what to do and where to be.

The largely Latino/a group opposing the ordinance was also making claims to Escondido and the American body politic, but they did so using different historical foundations and epistemologies. Theirs was a claim signified by *nuestra América*, a phrase excavated by Vicki Ruiz from Jose Marti's 1891 essay on the fight for Cuban independence. Marti's essay "not only locates cognition of imperialism among those who feel its weight but also points to a new paradigm of 'the Americas.'"[37] That paradigm has much more to do with "the history of transnational interactions—spaces of dialogue, linkages, conflicts, domination, and resistance" than it does with a notion of American history defined by Anglo-Protestant traditions and a restrictive notion of U.S. citizenship predicated on whiteness and exclusion. *Nuestra América* fundamentally recognizes the integral presence of Latina/os in creating the United States and the Americas and reinscribes U.S. national identity with "Latinos as meaningful actors."[38]

Ruiz identifies many historical moments through which to tell the stories of Latino/as becoming second-class citizens divested of property, political power, and cultural belonging. She recounts stories of Mexican dispossession and disenfranchisement with the passing of the 1848 Treaty of Guadalupe Hidalgo and the western movement of Anglo settlers. She tells of Puerto Rican and Cuban independence movements stalled by the 1898 Filipino-Cuban-Spanish-American War and the rise of American imperialism. She narrates the emergence of civil rights consciousness in 1948 as 500,000 Latino World War II veterans returned home to find racial segregation and denigrating treatment. The cumulative transfer of Latino/a consciousness across generations and spaces would establish the organizational foundations of the Chicano movement, and radical labor organizers such as Luisa Morena would spark the intersecting justice politics of Chicana feminism. And that consciousness would forge radical alliances between Mexican Americans and African Americans through such cases as *Perez v. Sharp*, in which an African American man and a Mexican American woman established the legal precedent for *Loving v. Virginia*, the U.S. Supreme Court case that struck down all prohibitions against interracial marriage.[39] Such historical moments, Ruiz argues, "are suggestive of the ways Latino history recasts and complicates constructions of [American] empire and citizenship."[40]

Those who opposed Escondido's anti-immigrant ordinance articulated claims of belonging to the Americas using multiple symbols and discourses. Some held signs of America's prototypical painting of a white, blue-eyed Jesus alongside pictures of Nuestra Señora de Guadalupe. The merger of prominent American and Mexican Christian images seemed to suggest that the ordinance was immoral and incongruent with Christian principles. It quietly highlighted the hypocrisy of Americans who claimed to be Christians yet advocated anti-Latino/a hatred and exclusion. Alternatively, the two symbols suggested that the moral values upheld by a majority of Latino/a immigrants' were congruent with America's Christian foundations. By extension, perhaps they were meant to signify Latino/a immigrants' willingness to assimilate into the United States based on shared Christian values. The figures of Nuestra Señora de Guadalupe and Jesus Christ gazed toward the ordinance proponents, raising questions about the ethics of the measure.

Other signs held by the opponents of the ordinance pointed explicitly to the racism and nativism it encouraged. One protester's sign read "USA = NAZI," evoking affiliations between the ordinance's fascism and an American police state. Another protester held a sign with a picture of Councilwoman Marie Waldron covered by a stop sign; underneath it read, "Stop Racism!"[41] The presence of Latina and Latino youth at the rally was particularly noticeable. Of all the protesters against the ordinance, they were the most vocal, fierce, and confrontational. They simultaneously ridiculed the EPHIA supporters and took them to task. "We make America!" one teenage boy yelled while a teenage Latina waved her finger vigorously as she challenged the supporters across the police line. Escondido's Latino/a youth had already become attuned to the value of protest in March 2006, when 200 Escondido students walked out of their schools to demonstrate against Arizona's proposed legislation to make undocumented immigrant status a criminal felony.[42]

Repeatedly, opponents articulated that the EPHIA ordinance had racist implications and detrimental effects. Bill Flores, a retired assistant sheriff and a member of the human rights group El Grupo, debunked the purportedly color-blind claims of the ordinance. "The easiest, largest, and most vulnerable section of the brown community is the undocumented, so the city council is going after them. The truth is that there are so many brown people that the political establishment can see the writing on the walls. They see the demographics are changing and they know that the political power is changing and they don't like it!"[43] By making the racist and nativist motivations of the ordinance conspicuous, protesters created spaces of mutual recognition and affirmation. They delegitimized the idea that the ordinance's actual purpose was to distinguish between law-abiding people and undocumented immigrants in order to preserve the well-being of the city. Rather, protesters revealed that white supremacist ideologies undergirded arguments for preserving Escondido's property values through Latino/a exclusion. Pointing out that targeting the undocumented would inevitably affect legal Latino/a immigrants as well, an opponent wrote, "It's embarrassingly obvious that the only people the council are trying to target are the Hispanic citizens that live here, legal or illegal."[44]

The nativists who defended the ordinance expressed both fear and rage toward the local Latino/as, the American Civil Liberties Union, and fair housing organizations that contested the ordinance. They feared that their ideological fantasy of a U.S. nation predicated on the right to exclude nonwhite foreigners was quickly fading. They feared that the shifts in racial, linguistic, and cultural demographics ushered in by the rise in the Latino/a population would cause losses in their propertied wealth. They feared that they were losing their ability to control the cultural aspects of their city and its aesthetics. They dealt with these fears by refusing to collaborate, cooperate, and co-create a new U.S. nation with Latino/as. They expressed rage and evaded moral inconsistencies. The aggressive enjoyments tied to nativist ideologies organized the nativists' sense of purpose, desire, and identity through the power to exclude and penalize.

The protesters were also diverse in the stances they took and the methods they used to oppose the ordinances. Some began organizing for greater Latino/a representation on the city council. Some defended the need for quiet forms of assimilation and law-abiding behavior among Latino/as. They imposed heavy demands on themselves to act properly, believing that good behavior would make it less likely that they would be targeted and criminalized. Others, particularly the Latino/a youth, were unafraid and outspoken. They used confrontational tactics and felt protected by the solidarity of like-minded Latino/a youth. But all of them defended Latino/a people's right to be present in *nuestra América* and to be treated with dignity in the nation they had helped define.

ILLEGAL ALIENS AS TAXPAYER BURDENS

Escondido's nativism mirrored hegemonic ideologies and emotional econo-mies commonly proliferated by national debates on immigration. As I argued in the introduction to Part II, contemporary nativism often focuses on immi-grants as fiscal burdens. The crises introduced by the increased consolidation of global corporate power and wealth under neoliberalism have caused economic instability for all working- and middle-class Americans. Because racial poli-cies offered disproportionate protections to working- and middle-class white Americans from job and housing insecurities during the post–World War II era, these groups were unaccustomed to economic vulnerabilities that working-class people of color had persistently confronted. As costs in education, health care, and housing increased while wages and state subsidies diminished in the post–civil rights era, social anxieties over economic decline increased. Rather than assigning the causes of economic instability to the exploitative schemes of ruling elites, multinational corporations, and government deregulation, na-tivists mistakenly and myopically attributed the national economic decline to immigrants, particularly those who were undocumented.[45]

Only one day after Escondido's ordinance was adopted, Councilman Sam Abed, himself an immigrant from Lebanon, reinforced the rhetoric of im-migrants as fiscal burdens on the Fox News television talk show *Hannity & Colmes*. Without citing any specific studies to support his claims, Abed stated that undocumented immigrants were costing Escondido taxpayers $12 million per year.[46] Abed portrayed undocumented immigrants as usurpers of economic resources, such as public education, criminal justice proceedings, and emer-gency health care services, implying that only documented immigrants and U.S. citizens were entitled to these resources.

Although economic interests seemed to drive Escondido's nativist move-ment, something much more complex seemed to be at stake. When probed by Alan Colmes about undocumented immigrants' monetary and labor contribu-tions to the U.S. economy, Abed was evasive. His silences were instrumental in fostering a structure of cognitive and emotional ignorance about immigrants in general and undocumented immigrants in particular. Abed did not talk about the ways American corporations and factories purposely hire undocumented workers to maximize their profits. He did not discuss U.S. employers who rely on undocumented workers to fill labor demands that Americans are unwilling to meet.[47] Abed did not talk about the ways undocumented low-wage labor helps to keep U.S. food and commodity prices low. He did not talk about the millions of dollars that undocumented immigrants contribute to Escondido and to the U.S. economy through their consumerism, sales and income tax contributions, and payments of municipal fees.[48] Abed also did not offer a macroeconomic view of why social welfare resources such as education, health care, and other municipal services had been shrinking over the past 40 years. Nor did he mention that municipal resources in cities such as Escondido were more likely to be scarce because of changes in the tax code rather than because of the burdens of undocumented immigrants.[49] Abed also did not highlight how U.S. neoliberal policies such as the 1994 North American Free Trade Agreement had directly caused the displacement and obsolescence of innumerable Mexican and Latin American agricultural workers, forcing them to seek work opportunities in the United States. Nor did Abed mention the ways in which these neoliberal policies had helped decrease workers' wages in Mexico and the United States alike.[50] In short, Abed was largely silent on the complex political-economic factors involved in Latino/a undocumented immigration and the ways these factors often benefited U.S. businesses and increased corporate power while damaging all workers' rights and wages in the United States and globally.

Instead Abed stated, "The impact on our culture, on our sovereignty, on our education and our health care has been tremendous."[51] He added that 95 percent of the residents of Escondido supported the effort.[52] This percentage of supporters would later be determined to be invalid.[53] Careful to conceal the racist overtones implicit in Abed's comments, Fox News host Colmes reiterated, "So [the harboring of undocumented immigrants] is a bad idea for economic reasons, as you have pointed out. There are reasons not to do this but purely economic reasons in the community."[54] But it was clear that "purely economic reasons" were not alone in driving Escondido's nativism. Abed contended:

We have heard the liberal views of pushing for liberal border [*sic*], come on over, and demand your benefits, demand education, demand social services and demand citizenship. I think the historic mistake that the Hispanic community did in April and May [was] going down and demanding these—these benefits from us. . . . I am a legal immigrant. I came to this country. I respect the law. I embrace the culture. I speak English.[55]

In using the term "Hispanic community" rather than "undocumented immigrants," Abed unconsciously reveals the reflexive equivocation in his mind
between undocumented immigrants and Latino/as. The Hispanic community's purported resistance to embracing American culture and to speaking
English presumably renders them illegitimate national residents even if they
are documented. In insisting that the Hispanic community should not feel
entitled to demand benefits, education, services, and citizenship "from us,"
Abed implies that Latino/as are not authentically American unless they adopt
the normalized styles, values, and cultures of American whiteness. Numerous
EPHIA ordinance proponents made similar equations between undocumented
immigrants and the Hispanic community, linking the rise in Latino/a populations with declines in property values, quality of life, wages, schooling, and
other services; they even mentioned the prospect of "Mexican re-conquest"
of the Southwest.[56]

The EPHIA ordinance was founded on a powerful and well-established
rhetoric of injury, suffering, and harm popularized by dominant white majorities who were confronted with significant shifts in America's racial and
cultural demographics. Even though most ordinance supporters held more
privileges and advantages than undocumented immigrants in virtually every
economic, political, educational, and social domain, the ordinance encouraged
them to feel victimized and entitled to exclude those who had transgressed on
their way of life: "The harboring of illegal aliens in dwelling units in the City,
and crime committed by illegal aliens harm the health, safety and welfare of
legal residents in the City."[57] This emotional sense of victimization trumped
all sociological facts about Latino/a immigrants in Escondido. To achieve the
emotional and psychological coherence of white victimization, despite a history of racial advantages and privileges, nativists used a set of ideological and
affective denials.

Ordinance supporters commonly denied that color-blind measures caused
racist outcomes. Because the Escondido ordinance focused on illegal immigrants
rather than race- or ethnic-specific groups, publics were encouraged to believe
that the measure had nothing to do with gendered racism or anti-Latino/a discrimination. Jim Brabant, an Escondido resident and landlord, dismissed the
notion that racism was endemic to the ordinance. "Thank you for not giving
in to the baseless charges of racism. There are a lot of good people in this city

who heartily support what you are doing. The chaos of the border may be the purview of the federal government, but its effect is on our cities."[58] In saying this, not only was Brabant able to disavow his complicity in producing the ordinance's racist outcomes while gaining the emotional and propertied rewards yielded by exclusion and exclusivity, but he also reified himself and other ordinance supporters as good, moral subjects. Dictating who belongs in a neighborhood, housing complex, or workers' center offers nativists a psychological sense of dominance, entitlement, and righteousness. Even if legal battles are lost, the affective compensation gained by advocating for immigrant exclusion is acutely important to those who conceptualize themselves as victims and righteous defenders of the nation.

Ordinance proponents often insisted that their support for the measure was motivated by their respect for the law. "This is not about racism," public commentator Charles Mallon told the city council on the night the ordinance was proposed. "This is about whether you're here in this country legally or illegally. If you're here illegally, you're an illegal alien, not an immigrant."[59] But Mallon's preemptive insistence that "this was not about racism" suggests that he was already engaged in the emotional labor of denial and disavowal. A person does not need to preemptively defend something as nonracist unless an affective sense of (perhaps unconscious) guilt is already present. In other words, someone who acts and speaks with a clear conscience does not need to engage in the affective labor of preemptive defenses.

The ordinance's color-blind rhetoric and focus on undocumented immigrants' illegality motivated a small faction of documented immigrants of color to support the ordinance. As I argued in the introduction to Part II, the popular distinction between documented "good, law-abiding" immigrants versus "bad, illegal" immigrants affords new pathways for Latino/as and other people of color to identify with nativist measures. Waving an American flag outside the Escondido City Council chambers, proponent Claire Vanaelstyn stated that the ordinance was "just common sense," adding that to enforce some laws, some people may need to be questioned more than others. "'I'm Filipino. I don't mind if they ask for documents since I look brown.'"[60]

People of color who identify with color-blind forms of nativism can also situate themselves as victims. By investing in the idea that national resources and entitlements should be reserved solely for those who have citizenship or legal residence, they can construct a sense of national belonging and inclusion against those deemed to be unacceptable illegal aliens. Such processes of gaining inclusion through others' exclusion have long historical precedent. Documented immigrants who are themselves vulnerable to being excluded and discriminated against on the basis of race, ethnicity, or language but desire the advantages of national belonging have often participated in nativist or racist violence against newly arrived immigrants or the most demonized racial groups.[61] In doing so, they become morally complicit in the U.S. nation's long historical record of nativist and racist exclusion, even if the racist component is staged through color-blind discourses about defending the law.

At the Escondido City Council public hearing meetings held before the or-dinance's adoption, a small number of Latina/os expressed their support for the ordinance.[62] Among them was Claudia Spencer, who represented an organiza-tion called Hispanic Voices Against Illegal Immigration.[63] A native of Mexico, Spencer met her American husband, Michael Spencer, through a personal ad and eventually became a U.S. citizen. Using her Mexican background to au-thenticate her claims, Spencer joined the Minutemen Project, warning against the potential ills that "illegals" would bring from Mexico to the United States. "I realized that America had freedom, honesty," Spencer said. "All these people, these illegals, are abusing this. Americans are giving them everything and they are incapable of saying, 'I broke the law.' Instead they are saying, 'I came to your country illegally and I want to wave my Mexican flag.'"[64]

After Spencer gave a long speech against undocumented immigrants at a day-labor site and later appeared on the Fox News show *Your World with Neil Cavuto*, she was contacted by officials from the nativist organization FAIR. FAIR worked with Spencer to organize a group of Latino/as opposed to giving undocumented immigrants amnesty, called You Don't Speak For Me. As the group's vice-chair, Spencer took her nativist advocacy nationwide, working to recruit other Latino/as and immigrants of color to oppose undocumented immigration.[65] In 2006 the organization was claiming 3,000 members and at-tending hearings on Capitol Hill, having gained the support of Representatives Walter B. Jones (R-NC), J. D. Hayworth (R-AZ), Brian Bilbray (R-CA), and Virgil Goode (R-VA).[66]

Michael Spencer continued to protest against day-labor sites in San Diego through the Vista Citizens Brigade, which was itself part of a wider coalition called the San Diego Citizen's Brigade. The Brigade's stated mission was to defend Arizona's SB 1070 law after the San Diego City Council passed a resolution against it. The coalition's organizations included several vigilante Minutemen groups who had taken immigration enforcement into their own hands and espoused expressly white supremacist views.[67]

Although this faction of Latino/a supporters of the Escondido ordinance was small compared to the majority of Latino/as who opposed it, their existence suggests that the reformulation of post–civil rights nativism in color-blind terms is useful for fostering divisions among Latino/as and other people of color. The outcomes of this reformulation are twofold. First, it conceals the ways in which the government's partnership with the wealthiest classes and corporations is largely responsible for producing economic vulnerability in the United States and across the globe. Second, it discourages the formation of multiracial and multiethnic coalitions that fight those at the top of the hierarchies instead of scapegoating each other. Intraracial or interethnic divisions staged on the basis of legality versus illegality often generate small advantages and benefits at others' expense. For example, for documented Latino/as, advocacy against undocumented immigrants can generate momentary psychological affirmations and pragmatic rewards based on the power to exclude and to make claims to national belonging. In the long-run, however, immigrants who stage such nativist defenses of American culture, language, and values help reproduce a racialized order of economic stratification that privileges whiteness and reinforces the social alienation produced by extreme inequality.

NO HUMAN IS ILLEGAL

The Escondido housing ordinance became a local platform for staging nativist responses to the largest pro-immigration rallies in U.S. history. Between March and May 2006, 3.7 to 5 million people took to the streets in more than 160 cities across the country to demand immigrant rights.[68] The demonstrators originated from Mexico, Central America, Latin America, South America, the Caribbean, Asia, the United States, and numerous other countries. The crowds had been galvanized to protest by HR 4437, a piece of legislation that would have made it a felony to have undocumented status in the United States. Akin to the 1850

Fugitive Slave Law, the bill also proposed to impose felony penalties on anyone who provided aid or assistance to undocumented immigrants.[69]

May 1, 2006, was deemed the largest day of protest in U.S. history. Demonstrators took over streets in more than 100 cities. Huge turnouts in Los Angeles, San Diego, Chicago, New York, and Washington, D.C., virtually shut down the cities. Protesters waved American and Mexican flags and held signs demanding amnesty, full rights for immigrants, and the end of deportations and detentions. "No Human is Illegal" and "A Day Without an Immigrant" represented the demonstrators' two core demands. The first called for an end to the criminalization of undocumented people's bodies and presence. The second commanded recognition and respect for immigrants' labor, cultures, and contributions to sustaining the U.S. nation regardless of whether or not they were documented.

The immigrant rights demonstrations were coupled with an economic boycott that encouraged supporters across the country to refuse to work, buy, sell, or attend school on May Day. Nativo Lopez, national president of the Mexican American Political Association, stated that organizers were planning on using Mahatma Gandhi's principle of noncooperation in order to force Congress to pass legislative reform that discontinued immigrant exploitation, criminalization, and punitive control.

The immigrant friends and family will essentially say, "I will not cooperate with a system that abuses me today, by offering my labor. I will withhold my labor today. I will withhold my consumption today. And I will participate in marches again, demanding the burial of H.R. 4437 and any similar type of legislation and a demand for full immediate, unconditional amnesty for all immigrant workers."[70]

The boycott was particularly successful on the West Coast, where traffic in the ports of Los Angeles and Long Beach was down 90 percent and 72,000 middle and high school students were absent from Los Angeles schools. Factories such as Tyson, Cargill, and Perdue Farms were closed for the day, with over 20,000 workers absent. A human chain in Phoenix, Arizona, blocked Walmart and Home Depot stores. Another human chain formed on Canal Street in Manhattan, New York, with immigrants chanting, "We Are America!" The southern border was basically shut down as a result of Mexican people's participation in a national May Day boycott.[71] As more than 2,000 students walked out of City University of New York (CUNY) colleges on May Day, they reminded people that the 10,000 undocumented students who attended CUNY paid double the tuition that U.S. citizens contributed and were largely ineligible for financial aid.[72]

The historic protests emphasized the central role that Latino/a and other immigrant workers have in the U.S. economy. Their boycott made evident that a large part of U.S. factory, agricultural, shipyard, construction, transportation, sanitation, landscape, child care, and elder care work literally could not function on a daily basis without documented and undocumented immigrant labor. Immigrants and their supporters made clear that their contributions to the nation entitled them to share in national rights, protections, and resources. The most radical factions demanded unconditional amnesty for all undocumented people currently residing in the United States. They specifically refused to support guest worker programs, which had historically contributed to furthering immigrant labor exploitation and marginalization. They demanded a stop to border militarization, deportations, and detentions. They rejected penalties on employers who hired undocumented workers. Demonstrators argued that such policies only intensified a punitive and exclusionary nativist culture that relegated immigrants, particularly those without papers, to shadow economies and subjugated social positions in U.S. society. They explicitly argued that only amnesty would offer immigrant workers the protections of labor laws, minimum wages, and the right to unionize.

The protesters—a collage of multigenerational families from numerous countries, races, ethnicities, and cultures—stood in stark visual contrast to antiimmigrant members of FAIR, Numbers USA, the various Minutemen vigilante groups, and other nativist organizations, who were predominantly white and aged.[73] Sending visual messages by waving flags from many different countries, but especially the flags of Mexico and the United States, protesters symbolized their allegiance to the American national body, but not at the expense of their own cultural, ethnic, gendered, and racial identities. This represented a political position quite different from immigrants' protests of previous eras. This was not an assimilationist politics predicated on deracinating oneself from one's native cultural traditions and language. Rather, it posited a notion of American national identity and belonging predicated on complex identity formations fraught with transnational and indigenous allegiances, multiple cultural influences, and racial mixture.

FEARING LATINO/A OVERPOPULATION

To Abed and other nativists in Escondido, these protests indicated immigrants' resistance to embracing the Anglo-Saxon foundations of the country, the English language, middle-class values, and submission to law and order. When the EPHIA ordinance was first proposed on August 16, 2006, Councilman Ed Gallo used metaphors of invasion, inundation, overcrowding, and multiplication to justify his support for the ordinance: "Make no mistake, folks. We're being invaded." Fueling economies of racial fear, he added that Southern California was slowly becoming a jurisdiction of Mexico.[74] Gallo's metaphors were reinforced by about a dozen San Diego Minutemen supporters who had come to the meeting carrying signs that said, "Stop Mexican Invasion: terrorists, gangs and criminals."[75]

Councilman Ron Newman countered Gallo's hyperbolic claims, arguing that the ordinance was a platform for political opportunism (Newman, Pfeiler, and Waldron were up for reelection the following November). "We've had no petitions, no inundation of e-mails," stated Newman. "No one is demanding we do something today. This is not about undocumented people in our community. This is about politics. The Hispanic community is being used as pawns."[76] But Waldron, Abed, and Gallo's metaphors of invasion and inundation offered powerful emotional rewards for Escondido's predominantly white ordinance supporters. The belief that Latino/a immigration and family reproduction would cause overpopulation in the United States had become increasingly popular. At times, such fears were explicitly articulated in public comments at city council meetings. Margaret Liles of Escondido, for example, commented at a city council meeting that "America should concentrate on controlling the birth rate and overpopulation."[77] But even when overpopulation was not overtly mentioned, it was consistently implied in discourses about "overcrowding" that would "multiply in the future" to "harm" Escondido's residents.

The projection of Latino/a overpopulation can be traced back as far as the 1930s, when the Great Depression instigated renewed nativism against Mexican immigrants. Eugenic discourses associated Latina reproductive practices with the spread of genetic inferiority and the decline of the Anglo-Saxon race.[78] The projection was resurrected again in the late 1960s and early 1970s when medical and scientific communities as well as the American public grew increasingly concerned about birthrates and increasing immigration rates. Paul Ehrlich, author of the 1968 treatise *The Population Bomb*, argued for birth control measures (compulsory, if necessary) and pressed for tax reforms that would discourage reproduction. He created a powerful population control lobby and linked overpopulation to a decline in U.S. environmental resources and quality of life. FAIR's founder, John Tanton, similarly began focusing on the links between overpopulation, reproduction, and immigration once national birthrates began declining in the 1970s. Unsurprisingly, Ehrlich, Tanton, and other population control proponents' arguments were explicitly concerned with Mexican women's reproductive practices, non-European immigration, and the persistent threat of alien invasion.[79] But these arguments about overpopulation were often deployed using environmentalist and social scientific discourses that did not always reveal the white supremacist ideologies that motivated Ehrlich's and Tanton's advocacy for population control.

The social science community became deeply concerned with explaining the statistical deviance of Mexican women's fertility rates in the 1970s because it was suspected that Mexican families did not follow reproductive patterns associated with white American assimilation and acculturation. Medical communities' concerns over ideal family size had taken their cue from demographic, sociological, and population research studies. In 1969 sociologists Benjamin Bradshaw, Frank Bean, and Harley Browning were the principal investigators of the Austin Fertility Survey, which was the first study to focus on factors that influenced Mexican American fertility rates. As Elena Gutiérrez argues, the study suggested that "the cultural context within which Mexican American women bore children was the most salient variable in understanding their fertility."[80] The survey disproved long-held beliefs that religion and socioeconomic status were the key determinants of Mexican-origin women's fertility rates. Instead, the study concluded that "the high fertility rate of Mexican-origin women was a function of some indeterminate yet resilient aspect of Mexican culture."[81] For population control advocates this ephemeral yet resilient cultural factor was understood as a form of racial and ethnic Latino/a difference that was intransigent to American assimilation.

The politics of these research questions indicates that social scientists were attempting to understand something that they had already deemed aberrant compared with what were considered normative reproductive patterns (implicitly understood as white American). But it also suggests that researchers helped construct the associations that linked purportedly overreproductive Latinas and Mexicanas, U.S. economic regression, a diminishing white population, and environmental erosion.

The national media amplified public fears over Latina women's reproductive rates once social scientists announced the so-called deviance of Mexican women's fertility. Notorious for making broad generalizations on the basis of race rather than nationality, dominant majorities saw Mexican women's reproduction as a signifier for Latina/o overpopulation more generally. Media coverage of "pregnant pilgrims" in the mid-1970s featured Mexican women crossing the border while in labor. Such representations encouraged Americans to invest in emotional resentments toward Latinas, who were presumably stealing American citizenship for their children in order to access resources subsidized by U.S. taxpayers.[82]

Constructing Latina and Mexican women's reproduction as deviant allowed people to assert their own reproductive normativity. By extension, projecting Mexican and Latina women's reproductive aberrance allowed Americans to assuage anxieties caused by the fact that white American gender ideals and patriarchal family structures were themselves in crisis. Predominantly white feminist movements that were challenging long-held assumptions about gender, family, and reproductive ideals had created a crisis in patriarchal hegemony. Concurrently, Black, Chicana, Asian American, and third world feminist movements had raised serious challenges to patriarchal values that were entangled with investments in white supremacy. Projecting Latina reproductive deviance as a threat to white American families, economic resources, and cultural ideals functioned to assuage the social destabilization that whites were experiencing, particularly as white men's power and authority were being challenged on numerous fronts. In other words, locating nonnormativity in Latina women and families offered Americans an emotional mechanism through which to evade the insecurities they felt about themselves. Although these projections gave Americans short-term emotional reprieve through their aggressive projections toward Latinas, it only deepened the unattended wounds of gender, racial, and familial crises in the long term.

Deeply connected with Latina and Mexicana overreproductive fertility rates was a projection of the Mexican or Latino/a family as too large. Aside from causing overpopulation, nativists argued that Mexican evolution lagged behind the modern American nuclear family. Such views had been expressed by demographer Peter Uhlenberg, who studied the relationship between population and modernization. In 1973 Uhlenberg argued that "the reproductive level achieved by Mexican immigrants in 1960 was characteristic of all white women in the United States in 1860. Thus, the average family size of first generation Mexican Americans is equal to that of other American families during the early stages of the industrial revolution."[83] The point was almost always the same: The white American nuclear family was the ideal toward which all other racial and gender family formations should aspire.

Today, fears over Latino/a overpopulation continue to be amplified by numerous nativist organizations under the rubric of environmental concerns. Although some of these organizations appear to have environmentalist agendas as their primary focus, they are financially supported by U.S. Inc., an umbrella organization created by Tanton in 1982 to further nativist agendas.[84] Nativist organizations posing as environmental organizations include Zero Population Growth (now Population Connection), founded by Paul Ehrlich in 1968; Negative Population Growth, founded in 1972; Population-Environment Balance, founded in 1973; and Californians for Population Stabilization, founded separately in 1986 and funded by U.S. Inc. beginning in 1996.[85] Along with nativist organizations like FAIR, the California Coalition for Immigration Reform, Numbers USA, and U.S. English, these organizations have been critical in furthering California's English-only movement and passing Proposition 187[86] and numerous subsequent anti-immigrant measures.

In framing immigration as environmental concerns over the effects of overpopulation, consumption, and natural resources, nativists successfully created new alliances with liberal groups. In April 1998 the well-established Sierra Club experienced a rift when a faction of its members argued that the club should take a formal position on immigrant restriction. The club members voted to take no position on adopting a comprehensive population policy that called for reductions in reproduction and immigration (60.1 percent).[87] This meant that almost 40 percent of the heavily liberal environmental group had been convinced to align with white supremacist and/or color-blind nativist agendas that seek to restrict predominantly nonwhite immigrants from entering the United States. A faction of the Sierra Club made it a point to state their racialized views on the intersections between overpopulation and immigration. Lindsey Grant and Leon F. Bouvier, authors of the Sierra Club book *How Many Americans*, argued in an August 10, 1994, opinion piece in the *Los Angeles Times* that "the impact of population growth will be the most lasting legacy of our current immigration policies."[88] After comparing U.S. population growth rates to those of India, China, and the third world, they proceeded to conclude the following:

We find the idea of another doubling of U.S. population thoroughly frightening. Consider the impact on many of the nation's current problems: urban decay and unemployment; energy dependence, nuclear waste and sewage disposal; loss of biodiversity and resistance of agricultural pests and diseases to pesticides and medicines; acid rain, climate change, depletion of water resources, topsoil erosion, loss of agricultural lands and destruction of forests, wetlands and fisheries, to name just some. . . . We must persuade our national leaders that, while the problems of Haitian boat people and other would-be immigrants are heart-rending and real, they cannot be solved by sacrificing our own future.[89]

Grant, Bouvier, and other advocates of immigration restriction endorsed triage, dispossession, and disenfranchisement in the name of saving Americans. To determine the effects of overpopulation (i.e., to calculate how much of the American body politic to cut off or prevent from entering), advocates of population control use a formula known as the $I = PAT$ equation, developed by Paul Ehrlich and Jon Holden. The formula oversimplifies complex variables and factors by equating the impact (I) of humans on the environment to the product of the number of people (P), the amount of goods consumed per person (A), and the pollution generated by technology per good consumed (T).

This formula does not differentiate between the environmental pollution created by people acting on behalf the greatest purveyor of toxic hazards (the U.S. military or oil companies) and the waste created by poor people living in the United States. The formula eliminates fundamental differences in who has the greater or lesser power to pollute the environment. As such, the equation overemphasizes population numbers and deemphasizes how U.S. oil and hydrofracking companies, nuclear power plants, and the weapons produced for armies across the world create radically disproportionate environmental hazards. As H. Patricia Hynes argues, "Complex, close-grained social and political factors that identify *who* among the universal P is responsible for *what*, and the *how* and the *why* behind much pollution—such as the military, trade imbalances and debt, and female subordination—are outside the scope of this formula."[90] Because wealthy industrialized societies such as the United States are responsible for most of the consumption and pollution across the globe and because poor countries in the global south are responsible for the largest percentage of populations, Hynes questions whether we can equivocate the environmental impact of the poorest 1.1 billion people to the consumption and technology of the wealthiest 1.1 billion.[91] The Malthusian principle embedded in the $I = PAT$ formula is that constraining the reproduction of the poorest (including Latino/as from Mexico) will permit larger consumption patterns for the wealthiest.

Although the EPHIA ordinance claimed to be about the harm that undocumented immigrants caused to Escondido's housing units, it ultimately reinforced public feelings that the city's carrying capacity for Latino/as had been exceeded. As Lisa Cacho argues, this spatial and racial logic "assumes that the nation itself is raced as white with Americans and immigrants of color permitted residence. Through this logic, racial tolerance and intolerance merely refer to different thresholds or different limits as to how many people of color count as 'too many.'"[92] A report by the Immigration Policy Center corroborated Cacho's argument, noting that increases in the foreign-born and Latino populations of ordinance locales "probably plays a stronger role than the actual number of Latinos or immigrants in shaping popular perceptions of an immigration 'crisis.'"[93] The desire to displace excessive and undesirable Latino/a populations was motivated by an embodied perception that Escondido's threshold of racial tolerance had been residentially exceeded.

THE SPATIAL AND AESTHETIC IDEALS OF (WHITE) HOMEOWNERSHIP

Exclusionary emotional economies grew so powerful in Escondido that even after a U.S. District Court blocked the EPHIA housing ordinance in November 2006, city council members proposed to restrict the multiplication of what they deemed to be undesirable populations through a new ordinance that would restrict parking. The June 2007 parking ordinance used another form of administrative violence, the aim of which was to preserve the aesthetic and spatial ideals of predominantly white suburban residents who felt threatened by the growing Latino/a population. The Escondido parking ordinance was modeled after similar measures in wealthy California communities such as San Gabriel, Pasadena, and Menlo Park. Residents who favored the 2007 parking ordinance repeatedly claimed that Latino/a overpopulation was violating white neighborhood aesthetic standards and spatial ideals.

- At night the street is FULL! We can't tell who is supposed to be there and who isn't, as in "Neighborhood watch."

- It will help clean up the streets and improve the neighborhoods.

- House next door to me and three others on my street have at least 8–12 cars each; it is an ugly eyesore.

- An eyesore is generated in some areas by the excessive street parking.

- Residential streets packed with parked vehicles seems to be a sure indication of a decaying, blighted area.

- I want the quality of this city restored and if it means a strict policy to enforce street parking, I am all for it.

- It's about time that something is done about the overcrowding of the streets. With Multi-Family-Illegal-Alien Houses everywhere, some with 8 or 9 cars parked in the yards, driveways and overflowing into the streets this new law is long overdue.

- The primary cause of excessive on street parking is to [sic] many residents living in one unit. This needs to be dealt with first.

- Can they do something about the cars that are parked and dripping oil and marking up the streets?

- A parking ordinance would more than increase the value of property.[94]

Escondido residents who favored restrictions in parking as a way to limit the Latino/a residential population expressed fears and aggressions common to people who are feeling under siege. Such discourses of harm, infringement, and injury were mobilized in defense of property, familial, and aesthetic ideals historically constructed to correlate with predominantly white small-town or suburban America.[95]

Such spatial and aesthetic ideals promote emotional investments in conformity. These ideals implicitly take whiteness, patriarchal family structures, and middle-class homeownership as personifying the epitome of social value and demand that people mold themselves to these standards if they are to be considered worthy. These ideals leave little room for racial heterogeneity and complexity, cultural variation, mutually interdependent economic models, and alternative family formations. They rely on a value system that invariably requires the exclusion and devaluation of all people and practices that do not fit into its normative standards.

This is not to say that immigrants are somehow entirely removed from these investments and ideals. Because these constitute the implied preconditions of achieving the American dream, many immigrants who come to the United States feel compelled to fit into the standards of whiteness, nuclear family models, and middle-class homeownership. At the same time, the exclusionary and restrictive emotional economies of contemporary nativism notify immigrants that, regardless of the precision with which they adhere to these American ideals, the impossibility of assimilating into whiteness racially, culturally, linguistically, or stylistically always leaves them vulnerable to exclusion, violence, or denigration to varying degrees. In other words, immigrant conformity to these ideals may shift or widen the definition of whiteness, but it does not change the structure through which it assigns value and worth to people. Inherently, the historical emotional and ideological structure of propertied whiteness continues to require hierarchies, alienation, and exclusivity rather than cooperation and interdependence.

In many ways the ideological and emotional battle over who is fully valued and recognized in the United States is as old as the nation. Whereas exclusion and inclusion were overtly determined through racial, class, and gender identity in the past, the use of color-blind frames that are implicitly racialized, classed, and gendered in the post–civil rights era creates new pathways for complying with nativism. We might very well value people who are law abiding, but if we are not aware of the ways in which nativist ideologies and emotions have appropriated this notion to justify the exclusion and denigration of undocumented immigrants of color, we become complicit in logics and practices whose outcomes are unjust irrespective of our intent. We might believe in the idea that the United States has limited resources and that its citizens should be the primary beneficiaries of these resources, but if we do not understand that immigrant labor and U.S. global economic exploitation have a lot to do with why the United States possesses such resources, we unwittingly become complicit in a system that requires others' exploitation for our consumer comfort. These views may be popularly accepted, but this does not mean that they have moral and ethical integrity.

THE ETHICAL PROPOSITIONS OF THE IMMIGRANT RIGHTS MOVEMENT

Nations tend to experience increased levels of violence when state legitimacy is in crisis. Similarly, social antagonisms rise when once-accepted norms begin to lose their credibility. Although contemporary nativist violence and exclusion may be disheartening to pro-immigration advocates, the fact that dominant white majorities and other nativist proponents are expressing vehement collective insecurities over the rise of Latino/a, Asian, Caribbean, and African immigration can also be understood as a moment of opportunity. Such ruptures in the social fabric offer organizers the opportunity to create emotional economies that foster justice rather than fear. Emotional economies that humanize and dignify the labor, cultures, families, and languages of present-day immigrants have the potential to lessen everyone's social alienation. In other words, each time we work to transform a society predicated on immigrant exclusion, racial and gender hierarchies, possessive individualism, and social separation toward greater mutual interdependence and care, we create new possibilities for transforming the entire U.S. society as well as its transnational interactions.

By encouraging Americans to create transformative emotional economies and just practices that honor people's dignity, the immigrant rights movement has placed children at the center of its struggles. As Amy Goodman of Democracy Now! noted the day after the historic May 2006 demonstrations, "The people in these rallies across the country—sometimes I feel like I'm at a daycare rally, there are so many children. I mean, infants in strollers, kids waving their American flags. You see whole families that are marching along arm in arm. I had never seen anything like this in protest in this country."[96]

Focusing on immigrant children helps us to develop what Mike Davis calls a "human needs agenda."[97] Concentrated on the future, such agendas are already motivating new labor movements across America to care for their families in dignified conditions. Amid the nativism of the 1990s, immigrant workers developed intricate organizing networks and waged campaigns at the grassroots level, in part because traditional labor unions refused to organize undocumented workers. Davis argues that "the militant, creative organizing campaigns of the janitors, hotel workers and drywall workers kept hope alive in L.A. during the tough years of the 1990s and helped train a new generation of activists."[98] Cautioning against the tendency of labor organizing to mortgage its future to the electoral and increasingly anti–New Deal commitments of the Democratic Party, Davis argues that the new labor movement would be wise to follow "the principle that a hegemonic politics must represent a consistent continuum of values: it must embody a morally coherent way of life."[99] In other words, the immigrant rights movement has to struggle to improve the labor, legal, and social conditions of its most vulnerable members. In doing so, it will refute a framework that reinforces the good immigrant/bad immigrant dyad that unwittingly complies with the racially targeted criminalization of the undocumented and of immigrants of color who are deemed terrorist threats.

Indeed, immigrant rights advocates have demanded more than rampant poverty, miseducation, imprisonment, poor health care, ICE raids, immigrant detentions, and policing for their children. They have regularly revealed the effect of detentions and deportations on the lives of immigrant children with undocumented parents. Immigrant rights organizers challenge the moral vapidity of the richest nation in the world, whose current hegemonic values endorse the criminalization of families and the abandonment of children.

The organizational frameworks of exchange, dialogues, and actions initiated by the contemporary immigrant rights movement not only disrupt public emotional investments in post–civil rights nativism but also generate new sensibilities, identifications, and worldviews that sustain people's commitments to racial and gender justice. Through ethical witnessing and mutual recognition, the immigrant rights movement produces ways of seeing and feeling that confront the color-blind and pseudo-environmentalist reformulations of traditional nativism. Even if fleeting, even if at times fraught with contradictions along racial, class, gender, and ethnic lines, the immigrant rights movement materially enables forms of recognition based on the knowledge, experiences, and intuitions of the aggrieved. It gives those claims affective value and credence. The movement creates spaces of political hope and empowerment, creating forms of investment and praxis that are not predicated on keeping up the denials, disavowals, and displacements of nativism. The organizing, protests, community meetings, and direct actions of the Border Angels, of the Justice for Janitors campaign, of the Undocumented and Unafraid movement, of the IDEAS chapters at numerous schools, of the DREAM activists, of the Labor/ Community Strategy Center and the Bus Riders Union and innumerable other grassroots organizations across the nation create ways of being and seeing that rupture the isolationist individualism, hostile privatism, and racialized violence encouraged by post–civil rights nativism.

In 2014 Escondido once again made national news for its nativism. Anti-immigrant protesters in the nearby city of Murrieta, California, blocked federal immigration buses that were transporting migrant children who were fleeing violence and poverty in Central America; the children were being transported to a Southern California border patrol station, but the Escondido City Council voted to deny the migrant children shelter. Self-righteous nativist emotional economies had evacuated the possibility of finding sympathy for some of the most vulnerable children in the world.

The nativists' hatred had an unintended consequence. It demonstrated to pro-immigrant organizers the futility of trying to have a reasonable conversation with nativists who would rather turn away children and spit on pro-immigrant advocates than give up their worldviews and self-interests.[100] Moreover, it demonstrated to a wider American public that the logic of nationalist self-preservation through nativist exclusion invariably leads to racial violence and moral bankruptcy. Everyone who witnessed the ways in which Escondido's nativist emotional economies ultimately led to hardened hearts and hateful actions was forced to contend with whether they wanted to continue endorsing a form of American nationalism that was predicated on gendered racial violence, exclusion, and denigration.

THE OTHER SIDE
OF SOCIAL DEATH

The number of fatalities resulting from gendered racial violence and discrimination in the United States and across the globe keeps growing. Its frequency and intensification is palpable. Everyday my eyes travel across the names of too many deceased and wounded bodies. Too many families overpowered by grief stare back. It is as though the entire world is shifting, like we are on the verge of some type of reckoning where we have to decide which side of history we are going to stand on. Complicity and passivity do not seem like viable options anymore. Decisions have to be made about whether we are going to act for what is right or remain complicit in a sinking boat of collective self-destruction.

State lies and justifications are no longer holding. In the violent summer of 2014 the world offered us increasingly stark evidence of the injustices of racialized and gendered warfare, militarism, immigrant detentions and deportations, police killings, incarceration, and deepening poverty. The faces of more than 400 children and 2,000 people killed by Israel's attack on Gaza in the span of six weeks express stark testimonies of the effects of ongoing warfare. Pakistani, Yemeni, and Afghani families whose members have been killed by pilotless drones demand to know if the United States will ever end its thirst for global dominance. The United States is bombing Syria as militarization continues to escalate in the Middle East. The gazes of Central American children being turned away by nativists in Murrieta and Escondido, California, suggest that U.S. society has reached a new level of moral bankruptcy in immigration matters. Deportations are at their highest rates in history, splitting up families and devastating lives. The symbolically raised arms of Black people confronting militarized riot police as they protest the shooting of Michael Brown in Ferguson, Missouri, are at the very least demanding that cops stop uttering lies and denying a systemic problem rooted in gendered racism. A grand jury's failure to indict police officer Darren Wilson on November 24, 2014, suggests that the state's refusal to confront systemic racism and violence continues. But the thousands of people who protested across the United States in the days following the grand jury's announcement visualizes a tide of collective consciousness and action that not only refutes state lies but also seeks to create new ways of existing in the world.

Only a year earlier, during the summer of 2013, the verdict in George Zimmerman's vigilante killing of Trayvon Martin pierced our ears, tightened our chests and stomachs, and moved our feet into the streets. We were not surprised that the courts acquitted him. By then, not-guilty verdicts for police officers, security guards, and vigilantes who were responsible for murdering young Black and brown people had become commonplace. But this does not mean that we were not outraged.

Three days after the verdict, our grassroots collective in Ithaca, New York—a small upstate college town geographically surrounded by prisons—organized a vigil for Trayvon Martin. Members of the collective, the Shawn Greenwood Working Group (SGWG), came together in 2012 to fight the intersections of systemic poverty, racism, militarized policing, and mass incarceration. Our working group chose its name in remembrance of a young Black man, Shawn Greenwood, who had been unjustly killed by white Ithaca police officer Brian Bangs on February 23, 2010. The choice to symbolically defend a Black man who was a working father but also had a criminal record received community criticism and opposition. We confronted this criticism with educational workshops on the ways in which segregated Black poverty created extra-vulnerability to policing, violence, and incarceration. SGWG understood that unless we defended the lives of criminalized people of color against institutional practices and ideologies that justify capitalizing on their bodies, we would simply reinforce logics that rendered the lives of criminalized people disposable.

Like hundreds of people who took to the streets to protest the Zimmerman verdict, the SGWG and many people in Ithaca came out to honor Trayvon Martin and to challenge the state and the criminal justice system's refusal to offer any form of recognition for his unjust killing. We wanted to create a space in which people could testify and express feelings about the realities of gendered racism in the United States without censorship. If the state, the law, and the criminal justice system were unwilling to acknowledge the systemic nature of racial violence in the United States, we would grant this recognition to ourselves.

On July 17, 2013, people marched through Ithaca with black balloons and a banner that read, "We Empower Ourselves to Protect Our Children." SGWG members created the slogan to symbolize our distrust of state agents, whose institutions clearly did not offer protection to children of color. Standing above pictures of Trayvon Martin and Shawn Greenwood, spoken word artists Dubian Ade and Devon James recited a co-written poem titled "For Trayvon." They asked for the spiritual presence of Martin, Greenwood, Amadou Diallo, Sean Bell, and all people who had been unjustly killed. They offered a paradigm for revolution that was fundamentally anti-assimilationist. Ade and James wanted more than oppressed people's access to capitalist institutions that perpetuated global exploitation. They wanted more than people of color's access to positions of power in governmental institutions that perpetuate violence and the interests of wealthy elites. They suggested instead that "the revolution will dismantle the American psyche."[1] Ade and James made the audience feel as though they had power inside themselves to build collective justice. They reminded people that they were part of long ancestral traditions of courage, resistance, and ethical witnessing.

Performance artist and poet Sophia Terazawa followed Ade and James with a recitation of "You Know Her." Drawing connections between the violence suffered by Trayvon Martin, violence against Asians and other people of color, U.S. militarism and colonialism, and patriarchal logics, Terazawa did not permit the crowd any affective distance from the responsibility to remember the red record of atrocities across the diasporas. In weaving cross-generational and cross-geographic testimonies of violence together, Terazawa insisted on the collective power of remembrance. Her poem concluded with the piercing insistence of the following verses:

The system has not failed!
It is here, alive in her bones, the Brown, the Black, the Yellow, the Red, and
the Gold, the Third World Left,
the Gaza Strip Mamis throwing their bodies over sons,
Filipina sisters taking bullets browned and blackened under sky
that was once cradled by spirits of young dark brothers,
Somalian daughters pointing at empty throats,
singing hymns to Black fathers, Queens of Tiananmen Square.
The system has not failed!
It is here, in her body, the Brown, the Black, the Yellow, the Red, and
the Gold, the Third World Left,
shadow speakers,
tongues forked foreign and American, untranslatable,
incinerated, spreading its fever like a virus.
The system's success is international,
border-crossing immigration of violence.
You know her in the way she knows Trayvon Martin.
31 years ago in Detroit he was beaten to death by a baseball bat and white paranoia.
You know her.
15 years ago she witnessed a white man and his young son castrate her father.
You know her.
You know her.
Young men of color killing each other in Los Angeles, New York City, Houston,
   Oakland, Chicago, you know her, Cambodian against Black against Latino
   against Black against Black against Korean against Chinese against Black against
   Black against Black against Vietnamese.
So what of Trayvon and the movement of my community, my
Asia America?
Vincent Chin
Bang Mai
Joseph Santos Ileto

Anil Thakur

Thao Q. Pham

Ji-Ye Sun

Naoki Kamijima

Won-Joon Yoon

Mukesh Patel

Jim Loo

Luyen Phan Nguyen

Zhen Bo Liu

You know her in the way she calls spirits of her brothers,

young brown and mango and rice paper bodies,

growing up to be men

at the wrong place, at the wrong time,

come rolling over the mountain

and join the spirit of one more,

of one more Diaspora.[2]

Following the vigil for Trayvon Martin, the SGWG conducted a series of teach-ins that contextualized contemporary instances of police and vigilante racial violence within the historical legacies of white supremacy. Conceptualized in collaboration with Felice Blake, the teach-ins connected racial violence to anti-Black and anti-Latino/a lynchings, to immigrant labor exploitation, to defenses of white property, to divestments from public goods, and to military-carceral expansion. The "Teach-ins for Trayvon" raised the collective consciousness of Ithaca's community members and allowed people to offer testimonies about the ways these matters manifested locally. Although some believed that militarized policing, mass incarceration, immigrant detentions, and warfare were distant from the pristine and wealthy liberal town, anyone who had their eyes open could see and feel the impact of all these state practices within the span of 100 square miles.

U.S. military drones that killed people in Pakistan, Afghanistan, Yemen, and other parts of the Middle East were launched from a base located only an hour away from Ithaca. Two members of the SGWG, James Ricks and Clare Grady, worked alongside other antiwar organizers in the Upstate Coalition to Ground the Drones and End the Wars to contest U.S. militarism at its tangible roots. The group's regular protests against drones at the Hancock Air Base in Syracuse,

New York, resulted in Kafkaesque misuses of the law. The base commander, Col. Earl Evans, took out an order of protection against the protesters, most of whom were over 40 years old and politically committed to nonviolence. By abusing a legal instrument generally used to protect people from domestic and interpersonal violence, the state indicated its rising paranoia toward antiwar protesters when it sentenced Clare Grady's sister, Mary Anne Grady Flores, to one year in jail for violating the order of protection while taking a picture.[3] Grady and Ricks were also repeatedly arrested and sentenced to short periods of time in jail for violating the order of protection. Incarcerating nonviolent grandmothers and grandfathers was a clear sign that the state's political legitimacy was crumbling.

As these local protests against militarism and drones continued, the SGWG and other community members began organizing opposition to a proposal to expand the Tompkins County Jail. The project proposed to add seven more cages to the existing jail, which would cost $1.5 million (if interest on the borrowed public funds was factored into the overall cost). We felt that the infrastructures of state containment and control—including local jails—proliferated community, interpersonal, and state violence. Adding cages would do absolutely nothing for people's healing and well-being. Incarceration has proved time and again to deepen individual and social sickness, not remedy it. If our county was going to borrow funds to build public infrastructure using our taxpayer dollars to secure its debts, we wanted to build schools, hospitals, roads, and transportation. Not without irony, during our struggle to stop the jail expansion, the Ithaca City School District announced that it would have to slash its school budget by $6.1 million because of New York State's retreat from its promise to subsidize the local budget. Here was a local case of more investment in punitive incarceration and divestment from social welfare goods.

At the many county legislature public meetings we attended, organizers in the Coalition to Stop the Tompkins County Jail Expansion and community members made arguments about the ill effects of mass incarceration. We gave extensive evidence of the criminal justice system's institutionalized racism, its unprecedented consumption of taxpayer dollars, and its complete failure to create real forms of security. We gathered copious amounts of data that showed that these trends were mirrored in our local community. We showed that policing in Tompkins County affected people of color and poor people disproportionately. We argued that the county's money would be much better spent addressing alcohol and drug addiction, mental health problems, joblessness and racial discrimination in formal labor markets, lack of education, and youth services.

We were met with unfeeling stares. Evidence, facts, and heart-wrenching testimonies by people who had been detrimentally affected by incarceration failed to shift most of the legislators' voting positions.

It was as though we were speaking to deadened souls. Evidence, facts, and reasonable arguments proved totally useless in shifting these legislators' affective structures and ideological worldviews. To them, we were noise and nuisances. They waited for us to fill the publicly allowable time slots for comments so that they could vote and do what they already had set out to do. Their emotional emptiness and lack of responsiveness to testimonies of suffering were a profound display of quotidian complicity in administrative violence. As is typical of people who have direct legislative power to affect lives, most of the county legislators claimed that they were powerless. The New York State commissioner of corrections, who had threatened to pull the county's variance that allowed the jail to operate beyond its capacity, was supposedly pressuring them to show progress for addressing overcrowding. Even though they could not predict incarceration rates in the future, the legislators contended that the jail expansion would eventually reduce taxpayer costs incurred by having to board people elsewhere. They paternalistically and sentimentally argued that keeping people in Tompkins County's jail would give them access to resources not available in other counties, making these jails more "humane." When community members proposed numerous alternatives to incarceration that could reduce the local jail population and save the county money, the ideas were rejected. The proposed alternatives did not follow the false and simple equivocation preferred by the county: that more cages would reduce outside boarding costs.

During those public meetings and protests, this book project kept staring back at me. As I witnessed the legislators' embodied indifference and emotional intransigence, I confirmed once again that evidence and reason fail to make a difference to bodies and minds that are affectively unreceptive. We were battling emotionally entrenched structures that held intact ideologies, beliefs, and worldviews, not empirical evidence. The coherence of the legislators' ideologies, beliefs, and worldviews relied on rejecting all testimonies that threatened to unravel it. The struggle was therefore deeply personal, because the SGWG and the Coalition to Stop the Tompkins County Jail Expansion ultimately demanded a shift in the paradigms and investments through which the legislators and dominant white liberal majorities in Ithaca understood their racial, gender, and class identities. In asking them to shift their paradigms of interpretation, we were ultimately asking people to give up who they were, or who they had constructed themselves to be. This was the unconscious danger that most of the legislators' affective structures were attempting to prevent at all costs.

The socially shared belief that people who commit crimes deserve to be punished through confinement and removal repeatedly blocked our arguments. I can only conclude that the vengeful enjoyment people derive from having the power to punish others creates a formidable psychic and affective glue that upholds this belief in U.S. society. We were not able to disrupt the legislators' and the dominant liberal community's emotional investments in this belief in order to cultivate receptivity for the idea that there were other ways to hold people accountable for the ways they had wronged others. We were also not able to convince the legislators that it made more sense to address the root causes that disproportionately cause poor people and people of color to end up in jail than to invest in a system proven to deepen problems. I suspect that most people refuted such logical solutions because they did not want to align themselves with people who were associated with poverty, criminality, or social deviance. It was as though people believed that defending poor and criminalized populations of color would result in their own social devaluation.

From October 2013 to May 2014 the SGWG and the Coalition to Stop the Tompkins County Jail Expansion managed to convince only three legislators (out of fourteen) to vote against the bond resolution that would fund the expansion. Leslyn Clairborne-McBean and Kathy Luz Herrara, the sole Black and Latina representatives on the legislature, pushed to at least delay the expansion project until alternatives to incarceration could be fully explored. Carol Chock, a white legislator, also voted against it after initially supporting the project.

CREATING SUSTAINED MOTIVATION
FOR THE STRUGGLE TOWARD ANTIRACIST JUSTICE

The organizing efforts of the SGWG and the Coalition to the Stop the Tompkins County Jail Expansion taught us invaluable lessons about antiracist struggle. Time and again we witnessed that feelings and beliefs trumped facts. Time and again we saw that people were afraid to relinquish the paradigms and beliefs that structured their worldviews and that this prevented them from aligning their actions with justice. Time and again we learned that elected representatives, legislators, police, and military officers—irrespective of their individual sentiments, goodness, and perspectives—were likely to follow logics, procedures, and practices whose outcomes were overwhelmingly unjust toward poor people and people of color in the United States and across the globe.

These organizing experiences made me reflect deeply on the methods we tend to use in antiracist justice struggles and how we might be more effective in shifting institutional injustices. One methodological tendency in localized antiracist struggles is to address demands for change toward legislative bodies and elected representatives. This is in many ways logical. After all, Tompkins County legislators held the power to authorize the jail expansion or stop it; military commanders at Hancock Air Base could stop drones or deploy them; police officers in Ithaca could use racist intimidation and militarize our lives through the use of SWAT forces or divest from these practices. I realized, however, that there is a core difference between making demands of state representatives and depending on them to effect change. Indeed, we learned that when the court of public opinion changes to support justice, legislators and laws will have no choice but to offer concessions. The potential of our antiracist struggle was restricted by our own emotional attachments to the idea that legislative bodies and state representatives are committed to fostering democratic practices.

Such investments in the idea that the state is democratic prevented some organizers from accepting evidence that quite the opposite was true. Although some police officers, representatives, and legislators certainly work to move the state's practices toward democratization, the overwhelming momentum of current state infrastructures, laws, and governing practices are set up to produce distinctly undemocratic and unjust outcomes.

The emotionally entrenched belief in U.S. democracy and exceptionalism often motivates antiracist and antiwar organizers to miss opportunities to direct their energies toward communities. Certainly, communities are also invested in dominant ideologies about criminality, terrorism, welfare, and immigration to varying degrees; but they do not have direct roles in upholding these through legislative and procedural practices. Antiracist organizers who witnessed the legislators' emotional intransigence and accepted that they were likely to support the unjust goals of the state reconfigured how they participated in the legislative spaces. Instead of speaking to elected representatives, they increasingly focused on speaking to people who were affectively receptive and therefore more likely to help us oppose the jail expansion.

As organizers began to direct their public comments toward each other rather than legislators, they symbolized their defiance toward county representatives who were clearly unwilling to hear the evidence and testimonies they offered. At one meeting one activist turned her back to the legislators to speak to the community. In response, the chair of the county legislature, Michael Lane, interrupted her, vehemently demanding that she direct her comments to the legislators. Lane's disproportionate anger to the minimally defiant act indicated that the tactic of recognizing ourselves, as opposed to relying on elected representatives to give us validity, was critical to building communal empowerment and rupturing the fiction that the state is capable of offering democratic praxis.

At another meeting, when protesters refused to stop testifying about a police brutality case against a local lesbian woman, the chair threatened to remove the speaker from the chambers. As protesters increasingly refused to abide by the state's extremely constrained rules for making public comment, which never allowed for an actual conversation, legislators became visibly agitated. County legislator James Dennis told the audience at one point that as a former teacher, he would ask the antijail protesters to go to the "time-out chair" for their behavior.[4] Dennis's incredible reaction confirmed not only that his affective structures were calloused and paternalistic but also that we were not likely to convince people who showed so little regard for collective testimonies of suffering.

As I witnessed the legislators' emotional intransigence and moral indifference, I thought about what James Baldwin had explained to his nephew decades earlier in a letter titled "My Dungeon Shook." Describing how white people in power routinely refuse to confront their complicity in perpetuating systemic injustices against Black people in America, Baldwin offered the following advice to his nephew:

There is no reason for you try to become like white people and there is no basis whatever for their impertinent assumption that *they* must accept *you*. The really terrible thing, old buddy, is that *you* must accept *them*. And I mean that very seriously. You must accept them and accept them with love. For these innocent people have no other hope. They are, in effect, still trapped in a history they do not understand; and until they understand it, they cannot be released from it. They have had to believe for many years, and for innumerable reasons, that black men are inferior to white men. Many of them, indeed, know better, but, as you will discover, people find it very difficult to act on what they know. To act is to be committed, and to be committed is to be in danger. In this case, the danger, in the minds of most white Americans, is the loss of their identity.[5]

It may seem strange for Baldwin to claim that the greatest danger in the minds of white people, or those identified with the ideologies, benefits, and advantages of whiteness, is the loss of their identity. But if we understand identities as condensed configurations of the emotions, beliefs, worldviews, and practices that make up who we are, we can see how testimonies that threaten the stability of this configuration have the potential to create embodied responses that feel akin to dying. Baldwin's advice to his nephew is terribly difficult to swallow. Why should oppressed people bear the burden and responsibility to accept their oppressors with love? Why should the oppressed have compassion for dominant white majorities' refusal to accept a history that shows them complicit in denigration and destruction?

Reading Baldwin's arguments across his numerous reflections on racism and violence in the United States helps us to see that he is hardly saying that Black people should turn the other cheek to white majorities who continue to consciously or unconsciously endorse systemic racism. Rather, Baldwin is interested in developing resistance methods that offer oppressed people psychic integrity and spiritual strength. As he wrote about innumerable acts of unspeakable racist violence, Baldwin came to see that if oppressed people did not release the rage, anger, vengeance, and shame produced by white supremacy, these emotions would eventually result in their own misery, self-destruction, and self-devaluation.

According to Baldwin, the advantages gained by white Americans through their complicity in institutional racism have a price. This price is conspicuous in the social alienation, spiritual emptiness, and moral bankruptcy prevalent in the lives of many white Americans. Baldwin did not believe that white racism was unidirectional, producing negative effects solely in the lives of people of color. He understood systemic racism as something that made the entire U.S. society sick, including white people. As such, when Baldwin advises his nephew not to become like white people, he is encouraging him to release negative affects such as anger, shame, rage, and revenge. Failing to do so puts the oppressed at risk of becoming as spiritually ill and morally bankrupt as those who oppress.

My attentiveness to Baldwin's advice and to Audre Lorde's forewarning that "the master's tools will never dismantle the master's house,"[6] helped me learn to engage in our antijail movement differently. I realized that fighting oppression requires enormous amounts of understanding and compassion for those who remain unmoved by oppressed people's suffering and demands for justice. Exercising such compassion did not mean that we agreed with people who wanted to remain complicit in institutional oppression! It also did not mean that we repressed feelings of anger, rage, and exasperation. Rather, it meant that we engaged in practices that facilitated our emotional sustenance rather than our gradual exhaustion. Feeling permanently hostile and angry toward unmoving people—even when such emotions are justifiable and war-ranted—has wearing effects in the long term. If anger turns to hatred, its poison will not be unidirectional but will likely bleed into interpersonal dy-namics and organizing methods that encourage authoritarianism, miscommu-nication, and factionalism. Working on having compassion for alienated and morally bankrupt people as well as for organizers who are at varying levels of understanding gendered racism creates emotional sustenance. Not having to perform the intense labor that tightly held hatred, anger, and hostility neces-sitate makes room for other feelings and better listening. It allows people to focus on both spiritual and psychological forms of empowerment. Such emo-tional sustenance allows organizers not only to build opposition to injustice but also to develop new ways of seeing, feeling, and relating. As the hip-hop group Rebel Diaz told us when they came to perform at Ithaca College in 2013, "Don't just oppose. Propose!"

Gradually, we expanded our antijail organizing to community and educa-tional spaces, where we could build support for opposing mass incarceration through conversation, personal testimonies, historical examples, poetry, music, and of course, parties. These spaces felt infinitely different from the legislative chambers. Our repetitive insistence that mass incarceration worked to deepen our collective sickness and that we were all responsible for addressing the root causes of poverty, gendered racism, and unjust policing slowly shifted the ways that some Tompkins County residents felt about mass incarceration and crime. Most important, it affirmed the experiences of people and families who had been directly affected by incarceration. At an event titled "Community Conversation: The Local Impact of Incarceration," formerly incarcerated Black men, as well as mothers whose partners were in prisons and jail, talked about the stigma and shame attached to criminality and getting locked up. Through our collective ethical witnessing, which repeatedly testified that something more sinister than individual behavioral deficiencies was taking place in America, we attempted to diminish these emotional economies of shame and stigma, replacing them with communal forms of empowerment and support.

Students who had been coming to the community protests created their own spaces by staging a "Know Your Rights Week" on April 21–25, 2014. Dubbing themselves Juice after the movie featuring Tupac Shakur, Ithaca College students organized a screening and discussion of *Fruitvale Station* as a way to discuss the injustices of national and local police and security guard killings of people of color. Students invited SGWG member and respected community leader Gino Bush to speak to students about his experiences on death row in many upstate New York prisons as well as his undying commitment to drug addiction recovery, forgiveness, spiritual healing, and community activism. They mobilized people to attend talks and workshops conducted by prison abolitionists Ruth Wilson Gilmore and Craig Gilmore during their visit to Ithaca that week. And they mobilized people to attend another prison abolition talk by Angela Davis hosted by Cornell University the next day.

In empowering themselves to organize under their own terms, members of Juice, the SGWG, and the Coalition to Stop the Tompkins County Jail Expansion worked together to create social spaces predicated on emotional economies that valued the lives of people targeted by policing and incarceration. These spaces were concerned not only with discussing the problems that plagued the lives of people of color and poor people but also with building structures of feeling and relating predicated on oppressed people's resilience, creativity, dignity, and contributions.

Because the SGWG and the Coalition to Stop the Tompkins County Jail Expansion faced persistent rejection from the legislators and a final vote authorizing the funding for the jail expansion, we confronted the challenge of sustaining our movement. I learned that our inability to sustain antiracist struggles is often linked to the ways we frame our organizing visions. People often join a struggle because they believe in fighting for a specific cause (to stop the jail expansion, to stop the drones, to stop racist policing). When their cause suffers losses because state representatives engage in the normative business of refusing them recognition, activists often experience emotional exhaustion and defeat. They become skeptical that organizing efforts make a difference.

Our focus on winning specific campaigns rather than creating sustained and sustaining antiracist praxis sometimes misguides our organizing. Every campaign win can later become appropriated to produce injustice. Take, for example, the feminist movement's victory to grant legal recognition to gender-specific issues in prisons. This victory is now being used by the state to argue for expanding "gender-responsive" prisons, perpetuating logics that expand mass incarceration instead of imagining other possibilities for redress and accountability. Strategic adjustments by the state, antagonistic political forces, and numerous other factors create the chaos in which we work. I learned again that justice is not a static thing we achieve once and for all. It is something that has to be persistently struggled for on the basis of shared principles as conditions change.

Those who see themselves on a lifelong journey to uphold principles of justice and to build life-sustaining outcomes eventually understand that victories can become losses and that losses can galvanize movements. I learned from my cocreators in the SGWG that the point is simply to struggle for justice, honesty, respect, integrity, and love. We struggle because we find white supremacy intolerable. We struggle because we find U.S. warfare, mass incarceration, and immigrant detention unjustifiable. We struggle because we see how gender and sexual violence destroys families and communities. We struggle because we cannot accept the ways economic inequalities limit impoverished people's creative power and potential. These were the shared principles and feelings that sustained our commitments to organizing.

People call us fools. Pragmatists call us naïve. Skeptics laugh at us. But we are comforted and motivated by the fact that, at the very least, we try to abide by our principles. We do this imperfectly and always incompletely. When we try not to engage in the labor of hatred, denial, disavowal, guilt, and projection; when we reveal the lies repeated by white heteropatriarchal supremacy; when we do not reject the fact that we are all complicit in systems of denigration and destruction in some way; when we do not shy away from our social and political responsibility to end oppression—that is when the process of struggling for justice begins to offer an unchartered sense of liberation, an unlegislated experience of freedom, and a mutually interdependent place to belong.

NOTES

INTRODUCTION

1. Sara Ahmed argues that emotions are an effect of the circulation between particular signs and meanings and that these constitute "affective economies." See Sara Ahmed, "Affective Economies," *Social Text* 22, no. 2 (2004): 117–39; and Sara Ahmed, *The Cultural Politics of Emotion* (New York: Routledge, 2004). For an overview of scholars who theorize public feelings, see, Ann Cvetkovich, "Public Feelings," *South Atlantic Quarterly* 106, no. 3 (Summer 2007): 459–468.

2. On the expansion of military carcerality, see, for example, Ruth Wilson Gilmore, *Golden Gulag: Prisons, Surplus, Crisis, and Opposition in Globalizing California* (Berkeley: University of California Press, 2007); Michelle Alexander, *The New Jim Crow: Mass Incarceration in the Age of Colorblindness* (New York: New Press, 2010); Christian Parenti, *Lockdown America: Police and Prisons in the Age of Crisis* (New York: Verso, 1999); Julia Sudbury, ed., *Global Lockdown: Race, Gender, and the Prison-Industrial Complex* (New York: Routledge, 2005); and Mike Davis, *City of Quartz: Excavating the Future in Los Angeles*, new ed. (New York: Verso, 2006).

On social wage retrenchment, see, for example, Linda F. Williams, *The Constraint of Race: Legacies of White Skin Privilege in America* (University Park: Pennsylvania State University Press, 2003); Michael K. Brown, *Remaking the Welfare State: Retrenchment and Social policy in America and Europe* (Philadelphia: Temple University Press, 1988); Marisa Chappell, *The War on Welfare: Family, Poverty, and Politics in Modern America* (Philadelphia: University of Pennsylvania Press, 2010); Robert Lieberman, *Shifting the Color Line: Race and the American Welfare State* (Cambridge, MA: Harvard University Press, 1998); Jill Quadagno, *The Color of Welfare: How Racism Undermined the War on Poverty* (Oxford, UK: Oxford

University Press, 1994); and Kenneth Neubeck and Noel A. Cazenave, *Welfare Racism: Playing the Race Card Against America's Poor* (New York: Routledge, 2001).

On the rise of neoliberalism, see, for example, David Harvey, *A Brief History of Neoliberalism* (Oxford, UK: Oxford University Press, 2005); Lisa Duggan, *The Twilight of Equality? Neoliberalism, Cultural Politics, and the Attack on Democracy* (Boston: Beacon Press, 2003); Mike Davis and Daniel Bertrand Monk, *Evil Paradises: Dreamworlds of Neoliberalism* (New York: New Press, 2007); and Naomi Klein, *The Shock Doctrine: The Rise of Disaster Capitalism* (New York: Metropolitan Books/Henry Holt, 2007).

3. Paula Ioanide, "'Oprah, Obama, and Cosby Say Blacks Should Just Work Harder, Isn't That Right?' The Myth of Meritocracy," in *Getting Real About Race: Hoodies, Mascots, Model Minorities, and Other Conversations*, ed. Stephanie M. McClure and Cherise A. Harris (Thousand Oaks, CA: SAGE, 2014), 67–78.

4. For comprehensive studies that disprove the popular belief that we live in a color-blind society with an equal opportunity structure, see George Lipsitz, *How Racism Takes Place* (Philadelphia: Temple University Press, 2011); Melvin Oliver and Thomas M. Shapiro, *Black Wealth/White Wealth: A New Perspective on Racial Inequality* (New York: Routledge, 1995); George Lipsitz, *The Possessive Investment in Whiteness: How White People Profit from Identity Politics*, rev. ed. (Philadelphia: Temple University Press, 2006); Douglas Massey and Nancy Denton, *American Apartheid: Segregation and the Making of the Underclass* (Cambridge, MA: Harvard University Press, 1993); and Williams, *Constraint of Race*.

5. Eduardo Bonilla-Silva, *Racism Without Racists: Color-Blind Racism and the Persistence of Racial Inequality in the United States*, 2nd ed. (Lanham, MD: Rowman & Littlefield, 2006); Eduardo Bonilla-Silva, *White Supremacy and Racism in the Post–Civil Rights Era* (Boulder, CO: L. Rienner, 2001).

6. Charles W. Mills, "White Ignorance," in *Race and Epistemologies of Ignorance*, ed. Shannon Sullivan and Nancy Tuana (Albany: State University of New York Press, 2007), 11–38.

7. Michael T. Taussig, *Defacement: Public Secrecy and the Labor of the Negative* (Stanford, CA: Stanford University Press, 1999), 2.

8. Mills, "White Ignorance," 22.

9. See, for example, research and tests on implicit bias developed by Tony Greenwald, Mahzarin Banaji, and Brian Nosek, available through the nonprofit organization Project Implicit. "Project Implicit," www.projectimplicit.net/index.html (accessed November 16, 2014).

10. David M. Amodio and Saaid Mendoza, "Implicit Intergroup Bias: Cognitive, Affective, and Motivational Underpinnings," in *Handbook of Implicit Social Cognition: Measurement, Theory, and Applications*, ed. Bertram Gawronski and B. Keith Payne (New York: Guilford Press, 2010), 355.

11. Amodio and Mendoza, "Implicit Intergroup Bias," 355.

12. Amodio and Mendoza, "Implicit Intergroup Bias," 357.

13. Amodio and Mendoza, "Implicit Intergroup Bias," 357.

14. Amodio and Mendoza, "Implicit Intergroup Bias," 357.

15. Jennifer Eberhardt, "Imaging Race," *American Psychologist* 60, no. 2 (February 2005): 182.

16. Eberhardt, "Imaging Race," 182.

17. Eberhardt, "Imaging Race," 182.

18. Eberhardt, "Imaging Race," 187.

19. The idea that affective or emotional responses to racial images, signs, or stereotypes are prediscursive or preconscious was theorized but not empirically demonstrated by Frantz Fanon, *Black Skin, White Masks*, trans. Charles Lam Markmann (New York: Grove Press, 1967). For contemporary studies on preconscious racism or implicit racial bias, see Eberhardt, "Imaging Race"; Jennifer L. Eberhardt, P. A. Goff, V. J. Purdie, and P. G. Davies, "Seeing Black: Race, Crime, and Visual Processing," *Journal of Personality and Social Psychology* 87, no. 6 (2004): 876–93; Jennifer Eberhardt, "Believing Is Seeing: The Effects of Racial Labels and Implicit Beliefs on Face Perception," *Personality and Social Psychology Bulletin* 29, no. 3 (2003): 360–70; David M. Amodio, "Stereotyping and Evaluation in Implicit Race Bias: Evidence for Independent Constructs and Unique Effects on Behavior," *Journal of Personality and Social Psychology* 91, no. 4 (2006): 652–61; David M. Amodio and Patricia G. Devine, "Interpersonal Relations and Group Processes: Stereotyping and Evaluation in Implicit Race Bias—Evidence for Independent Constructs and Unique Effects on Behavior," *Journal of Personality and Social Psychology* 91, no. 4 (2006): 652–61; Amodio and Mendoza, "Implicit Intergroup Bias"; David M. Amodio, "Intergroup Anxiety Effects on the Control of Racial Stereotypes: A Psychoneuroendocrine Analysis," *Journal of Experimental Social Psychology* 45, no. 1 (2009): 60–67; Saaid Mendoza, "Reducing the Expression of Implicit Stereotypes: Reflexive Control Through Implementation Intentions," *Personality and Social Psychology Bulletin* 36, no. 4 (2010): 512–23; and John F. Dovidio, Peter Samuel Glick, and Laurie A. Rudman, *On the Nature of Prejudice: Fifty Years After Allport* (Malden, MA: Blackwell, 2005).

20. Fanon, *Black Skin, White Masks*, 155.

21. On the construction of U.S. racial stereotypes, myths, and fallacies about Black people and their social effects, see, for example, Marlon T. Riggs, dir., *Ethnic Notions* (San Francisco: California Newsreel, 2004 [1986]); Herman Gray, *Watching Race: Television and the Struggle for "Blackness"* (Minneapolis: University of Minnesota Press, 1995); Donald Bogle, *Toms, Coons, Mulattoes, Mammies, and Bucks: An Interpretive History of Blacks in American Films*, 4th ed. (New York: Continuum, 2001); Patricia Hill Collins, *Black Sexual Politics: African Americans, Gender, and the New Racism* (New York: Routledge, 2005); and Eric Avila, *Popular Culture in the Age of White Flight: Fear and Fantasy in Suburban Los Angeles* (Berkeley: University of California Press, 2004).

On the construction of U.S. racial stereotypes, myths, and fallacies about Latino/as and their effects, see, for example, Arlene M. Dávila, *Latinos, Inc.: The Marketing and Making of a People* (Berkeley: University of California Press, 2001); Rosa Linda Fregoso, *MeXicana Encounters* (Berkeley: University of California Press, 2003); and Natalia Molina, *Fit to Be Citizens? Public Health and Race in Los Angeles, 1879–1939* (Berkeley: University of California Press, 2006).

On stereotypical constructions and myths about Arabs and Muslims in U.S. imaginaries, see Edward W. Said, *Orientalism* (New York: Vintage Books, 1978); Edward W. Said, *Culture and Imperialism* (New York: Vintage Books, 1994); Melani McAlister, *Epic Encounters: Culture, Media, and U.S. Interests in the Middle East, 1945–2000* (Berkeley: University of California Press, 2001); and Amy Kaplan and Donald E. Pease, *Cultures of United States Imperialism* (Durham, NC: Duke University Press, 1993).

22. Fanon, *Black Skin, White Masks*, 116, 155.

23. Ahmed, "Affective Economies," 120.

24. Ahmed, "Affective Economies," 120.

25. Žižek further claims that what generally appears to be political cynicism and lack of faith in governmental authorities and institutions actually makes the reproduction of the status quo even more efficient. Allowing cynicism and disidentification with state governments gives everyday people an affective sense of agency and freedom that is crucial to preserving the overarching ideologies that undergird a political regime. In essence, the affective feeling of political disidentification tends to function as a substitute for *actionable* political dissent. Having done their duty to *feel* oppositional using methods that liberal capitalist regimes permit and predict (Facebook complaints, petitions, etc.), people generally continue to revert back to passive complicity with the injustices they know their regimes perpetuate. Žižek's argument is therefore that ideology functions best when it presents itself as nonideological or as sensible truths that appear apolitical and timeless. However, if public disidentification is allowed to accumulate to the point that people begin to challenge a political regime's fundamental structure and meta-narratives (e.g., capitalism and/or white supremacy), state violence or mass dissidence may erupt. This indicates that the ideological efficacy of a political regime's reproduction mechanism is crumbling; to successfully preserve its authority, that regime must find a way to resignify political discontent. For example, the mass freedom movements of the post–World War II era created substantive crises in overtly white supremacist U.S. political regimes. This necessitated America's reconfiguration of white supremacist ideologies into color-blind ones and the resignification of antiracist political dissent simultaneously as revered moral goods (in the case of watered-down versions of Martin Luther King Jr.'s philosophies and practices) or criminalized deviance (e.g., the Black Panther Party's right to armed self-defense). See Slavoj Žižek, *The Sublime Object of Ideology* (London: Verso, 1989). For a great introduction to Žižek's philosophy, see Matthew Sharpe, "Slavoj Žižek," in *From Agamben to Žižek: Contemporary Critical Theorists*, ed. Jon Simons (Edinburgh: Edinburgh University Press, 2010), 243–58.

26. Jean Laplanche and J. B. Pontalis, "Fantasy and the Origins of Sexuality," *International Journal of Psychoanalysis* 49, no. 1 (1968): 1–18.

27. Teresa de Lauretis, "On the Subject of Fantasy," in *Feminisms in the Cinema*, ed. Laura Pietropaolo and Ada Testaferri (Bloomington: Indiana University Press, 1995), 64.

28. Jacqueline Rose, *States of Fantasy* (Oxford, UK: Clarendon Press and Oxford University Press, 1996), 3.

29. Sharpe, "Slavoj Žižek," 251.

30. Slavoj Žižek, *Tarrying with the Negative: Kant, Hegel, and the Critique of Ideology* (Durham, NC: Duke University Press, 1993), 200–38.

31. Cedric J. Robinson, *Forgeries of Memory and Meaning: Blacks and the Regimes of Race in American Theater and Film Before World War II* (Chapel Hill: University of North Carolina Press, 2007), xii.

32. Harding, quoted in Robinson, *Forgeries*, xiii.

33. Cedric Robinson, *Black Marxism: The Making of the Black Radical Tradition* (Chapel Hill: University of North Carolina Press, 2000).

34. Gloria Anzaldúa, *Borderlands/La Frontera: The New Mestiza*, 3rd ed. (San Francisco: Aunt Lute Books, 2007).

35. Edward W. Said and Jean Mohr, *After the Last Sky: Palestinian Lives* (New York: Pantheon, 1986).

36. James Baldwin, *No Name in the Street* (New York: Vintage, 2007); James Baldwin, *Collected Essays* (New York: Library of America, 1998).

37. W. E. B. Du Bois, *Black Reconstruction in America* (New York: Free Press, 1998).

38. Miriam Pawel, *The Union of Their Dreams: Power, Hope, and Struggle in Cesar Chavez's Farm Worker Movement* (New York: Bloomsbury Press, 2009); Susan Ferriss and Ricardo Sandoval, *The Fight in the Fields: Cesar Chavez and the Farmworkers Movement*, ed. Diana Hembree (New York: Harcourt Brace, 1997).

39. Harriet A. Jacobs, *Incidents in the Life of a Slave Girl: Written by Herself*, ed. Lydia Maria Child and Jean Fagan Yellin (Cambridge, MA: Harvard University Press, 1987); Ida B. Wells-Barnett, *On Lynchings* (Amherst, NY: Humanity Books, 2002).

40. W. E. B. Du Bois, *John Brown*, ed. David R. Roediger (New York: Modern Library, 2001); Lipsitz, *Possessive Investment in Whiteness*, vii–xx.

PART I

1. For a discussion of the entanglements of coercion and consent and of the ways that slave law permitted the legal recognition of Black humanity only when enslaved people committed a crime, see Saidiya V. Hartman, *Scenes of Subjection: Terror, Slavery, and Self-Making in Nineteenth-Century America* (Oxford, UK: Oxford University Press, 1997).

2. Michael Paul Rogin, *Fathers and Children: Andrew Jackson and the Subjugation of the American Indian* (New Brunswick, NJ: Transaction, 1991); Luana Ross, *Inventing the Savage: The Social Construction of Native American Criminality* (Austin: University of Texas Press, 1998).

3. For extensive analyses of fantasy constructions of Black hyperviolence, predatory hypersexuality, and criminalization in relation to the extralegal practices of lynching, see Grace Elizabeth Hale, *Making Whiteness: The Culture of Segregation in the South, 1890–1940* (New York: Vintage, 1999); William D. Carrigan and Clive Webb, *Forgotten Dead: Mob Violence Against Mexicans in the United States, 1848–1928* (New York: Oxford University Press, 2013); Philip Dray, *At the Hands of Persons Unknown: The Lynching of Black America* (New York: Random House, 2002); Robyn Wiegman, *American Anatomies: Theorizing Race and Gender* (Durham, NC: Duke University Press, 1995); and Calvin C. Hernton, *Sex and Racism in America* (New York: Anchor, 1992).

4. For the histories of fantasy constructions about Mexican American and Latino/a criminality tied to nativism, gender, sexuality, and citizenship and their tangible consequences, see Natalia Molina, *Fit to Be Citizens? Public Health and Race in Los Angeles, 1879–1939* (Berkeley: University of California Press, 2006); Mae Ngai, *Impossible Subjects: Illegal Aliens and the Making of Modern America* (Princeton, NJ: Princeton University Press, 2004); Tomás Almaguer, *Racial Fault Lines: The Historical Origins of White Supremacy in California* (Berkeley: University of California Press, 1994); Manfred Berg, *Popular Justice: A History of Lynching in America* (New York: Ivan R. Dee, 2011); Ken Gonzales-Day, *Lynching in the West: 1850–1935* (Durham, NC: Duke University Press, 2006); Rosa Linda Fregoso,

MeXicana Encounters: The Making of Social Identities on the Borderlands (Berkeley: University of California Press, 2003); and PBS Home Video, WGBH, and Alice McGrath, *The American Experience: Zoot Suit Riots* (Boston, MA: WGBH Educational Foundation; PBS Home Video, 2002).

5. For constructions of Asian and Asian American criminality, disease contamination, threats of miscegenation, empire subversion, and yellow perils, see Nayan Shah, *Contagious Divides: Epidemics and Race in San Francisco's Chinatown* (Berkeley: University of California Press, 2001); Robert G. Lee, *Orientals: Asian Americans in Popular Culture* (Philadelphia: Temple University Press, 1999); Gina Marchetti, *Romance and the "Yellow Peril?: Race, Sex, and Discursive Strategies in Hollywood Fiction* (Berkeley: University of California Press, 1994); Molina, *Fit to Be Citizens*; and Ngai, *Impossible Subjects*.

6. For the histories of such constructions of Arab and Muslims, see Melani McAlister, *Epic Encounters: Culture, Media, and U.S. Interests in the Middle East Since 1945*, 2nd ed. (Berkeley: University of California Press, 2005); Edward W. Said, *Covering Islam: How the Media and the Experts Determine How We See the Rest of the World*, rev. ed. (New York: Vintage, 1997); Douglas Little, *American Orientalism: The United States and the Middle East Since 1945*, 3rd ed. (Chapel Hill: University of North Carolina Press, 2008); Edward W. Said, *Culture and Imperialism* (New York: Vintage, 1994); and Edward Said, *Orientalism*, 25th Anniversary ed. (New York: Vintage Books, 2003).

7. Vesla Weaver, "Frontlash: Race and the Development of Punitive Crime Policy," *Studies in American Political Development* 21, no. 2 (2007): 247.

8. Weaver, "Frontlash," 248.

9. Weaver, "Frontlash," 230.

10. For an example of the extent to which the state went to undertake such criminalization, see Kathleen Cleaver and George N. Katsiaficas, *Liberation, Imagination, and the Black Panther Party: A New Look at the Panthers and Their Legacy* (New York: Routledge, 2001).

11. Julia Sudbury, "Celling Black Bodies: Black Women in the Global Prison Industrial Complex," *Feminist Review* 70 (2002): 61.

12. In his June 4, 1965, commencement address at Howard University, Johnson stated, "You do not wipe away the scars of centuries by saying: 'Now, you are free to go where you want, do as you desire, and choose the leaders you please.' You do not take a man who for years has been hobbled by chains, liberate him, bring him to the starting line of a race, saying, 'You are free to compete with all the others,' and still justly believe you have been completely fair. . . . This is the next and more profound stage of the battle for civil rights. We seek not just freedom but opportunity—not just legal equity but human ability—not just equality as a right and a theory, but equality as a fact and as a result." Lyndon B. Johnson, "Commencement Address at Howard University: 'To Fulfill These Rights,'" Washington, DC, June 4, 1965, www.lbjlib.utexas.edu/johnson/archives.hom/speeches.hom/650604.asp (accessed June 13, 2012).

13. For critiques of these transformations, see Kimberly Springer, *Living for the Revolution: Black Feminist Organizations, 1968–1980* (Durham, NC: Duke University Press, 2005); and Jimmie L. Reeves, "Re-Covering Racism: Crack Mothers, Reaganism, and the Network News," in *Living Color: Race and Television in the United States*, ed. Sasha Torres (Durham, NC: Duke University Press, 1998), 101.

14. Weaver, "Frontlash," 245.

15. Seth Freed Wessler, "Bills Modeled After Arizona's SB 1070 Spread Through States," Colorlines, March 2, 2011, colorlines.com/archives/2011/03/sb_1070_copycat_bills.html.

16. Gretchen Gavett, "Map: The U.S. Immigration Detention Boom—Lost in Detention," Frontline, October 18, 2011, www.pbs.org/wgbh/pages/frontline/race-multicultural/lost-in-detention/map-the-u-s-immigration-detention-boom/ (accessed June 24, 2014).

17. Alejandra Marchevsky and Beth Baker, "Why Has President Obama Deported More Immigrants Than Any President in U.S. History?" The Nation, March 31, 2014, www.thenation.com/article/179099/why-has-president-obama-deported-more-immigrants-any-president-us-history (accessed June 25, 2014).

18. Reeves, "Re-Covering Racism," 103.

19. Lee, Orientals, 145–79.

20. Tricia Rose, Black Noise: Rap Music and Black Culture in Contemporary America (Hanover, NH: Wesleyan University Press, 1994); Herman Gray, Watching Race: Television and the Struggle for "Blackness" (Minneapolis: University of Minnesota Press, 1995).

21. Swati Rana, "The Majority-Identified Minority," paper presented at the meeting "Antiracism Inc./Works: The Anti-Conference," American Cultures and Global Contexts Center, University of California, Santa Barbara, May 16–17, 2014.

22. The term underclass has been debated in numerous scholarly and public debates in response to William J. Wilson, The Truly Disadvantaged: The Inner City, the Underclass, and Public Policy (Chicago: University of Chicago Press, 1987).

23. Abby Goodnough, "Harvard Professor Jailed; Officer Is Accused of Bias," New York Times, July 21, 2009, www.nytimes.com/2009/07/21/us/21gates.html (accessed June 25, 2014).

24. Ruth Wilson Gilmore, "Globalisation and U.S. Prison Growth: From Military Keynesianism to Post-Keynesian Militarism," Race and Class 40, no. 2/3 (1999): 172.

25. John Schmitt, Kris Warner, and Sarika Gupta, The High Budgetary Cost of Incarceration (Washington, DC: Center for Economic and Policy Research, June 2010), 1. Schmitt and colleagues also state, "If incarceration rates had tracked violent crime rates, for example, the incarceration rate would have peaked at 317 per 100,000 in 1992, and fallen to 227 per 100,000 by 2008—less than one third of the actual 2008 level and about the same level as in 1980" (1).

26. Schmitt et al., High Budgetary Cost, 10.

27. Lisa Marie Cacho, Social Death: Racialized Rightlessness and the Criminalization of the Unprotected (New York: NYU Press, 2012), 8; emphasis in original.

28. Cle Shaheed Sloan, dir., Bastards of the Party, documentary (Fuqua Films, 2005); Mike Davis, City of Quartz: Excavating the Future in Los Angeles, new ed. (London: Verso, 2006).

29. Mike Davis, "A Prison Industrial Complex: Hell Factories in the Fields," The Nation, February 20, 1995.

30. Ruth Wilson Gilmore, Golden Gulag: Prisons, Surplus, Crisis, and Opposition in Globalizing California (Berkeley: University of California Press, 2007); Christian Parenti, Lockdown America: Police and Prisons in the Age of Crisis (New York: Verso, 1999); Marc Mauer and The Sentencing Project, Race to Incarcerate (New York: New Press, 1999); Davis, City of Quartz; Juanita Díaz-Cotto, Chicana Lives and Criminal Justice: Voices from El Barrio (Austin: University of Texas Press, 2006); Julia Sudbury, ed., Global Lockdown:

Race, Gender, and the Prison-Industrial Complex (New York: Routledge, 2005); Michelle Alexander, *The New Jim Crow: Mass Incarceration in the Age of Colorblindness* (New York: New Press, 2010).

31. Donna Selman and Paul Leighton, *Punishment for Sale: Private Prisons, Big Business, and the Incarceration Binge* (Lanham, MD: Rowman & Littlefield, 2010); Brigette Sarabi and Edwin Bender, *The Prison Payoff: The Role of Politics and Private Prisons in the Incarceration Boom* (Portland, OR: Western States Center and Western Prison Project, 2000); Anne Larason Schneider, "Public-Private Partnerships in the U.S. Prison System," *American Behavioral Scientist* 43, no. 1 (1999): 192–208.

32. Sarah Lawrence and Jeremy Travis, *The New Landscape of Imprisonment: Mapping America's Prison Expansion* (Washington, DC: Urban Institute, Justice Policy Center, April 2004), 9. Lawrence and Travis show in this research report that the growth in prison building did not occur evenly across the 50 states. Of the total growth in the number of prisons in the last quarter of the twentieth century, 63 percent occurred in the states of Texas, Florida, California, New York, Michigan, Georgia, Illinois, Ohio, Colorado, and Missouri. As a group, these 10 states had three times as many prisons in 2000 as in 1979—increasing from 195 facilities to 604 facilities.

33. James J. Stephan, "Census of State and Federal Correctional Facilities, 2005," National Prisoner Statistics Program, Bureau of Justice Statistics, October 2008, 1, bjs.ojp.usdoj .gov/index.cfm?ty=pbdetail&iid=530 (accessed March 4, 2012).

34. Gilmore, "Globalisation," 172.

35. Gilmore, "Globalisation," 172.

36. For an extensive study on the mutually reinforcing aspects of new drug laws, policing, sentencing, and incarceration, particularly those that pertain to the war on drugs, see Alexander, *New Jim Crow*.

37. According to Marc Mauer, director of the Sentencing Project, "If current trends continue, 1 of every 3 African American males born today can expect to go to prison in his lifetime, as can 1 of every 6 Latino males, compared to 1 in 17 White males. For women, the overall figures are considerably lower, but the racial/ethnic disparities are similar: 1 of every 18 African American females, 1 of every 45 Hispanic females, and 1 of every 111 White females can expect to spend time in prison." See Marc Mauer, "Addressing Racial Disparities in Incarceration," *Prison Journal* 91, no. 3 (2011): 88S, www.sentencingproject.org/detail/ publication.cfm?publication_id=373&id=120 (accessed February 28, 2012).

38. For extensive examinations of these shifts, see, for example, Deepa Fernandes, *Targeted: Homeland Security and the Business of Immigration* (New York: Seven Stories Press, 2007); Mark Dow, *American Gulag: Inside U.S. Immigration Prisons* (Berkeley: University of California Press, 2004); Elaine Hagopian, *Civil Rights in Peril: The Targeting of Arabs and Muslims* (Chicago: Haymarket Books; and London: Pluto Press, 2004); and Tram Nguyen, *We Are All Suspects Now: Untold Stories from Immigrant Communities After 9/11* (Boston: Beacon Press, 2005).

39. Fernandes, *Targeted*, 37.

40. Department of Homeland Security, *FY 2012 Budget in Brief* (Washington, DC: Department of Homeland Security, 2012), 75, www.dhs.gov/xlibrary/assets/budget-bib-fy2012 .pdf (accessed June 7, 2012).

41. "Throwing Good Money After Bad: Immigration Enforcement," Immigration Policy Center, May 26, 2010, www.immigrationpolicy.org/just-facts/throwing-good-money-after -bad-immigration-enforcement#_edn3 (accessed June 7, 2012).

42. Eithne Luibheid, *Entry Denied: Controlling Sexuality at the Border* (Minneapolis: University of Minnesota Press, 2002), 103–36.

43. Justin Akers Chacón and Mike Davis, *No One Is Illegal: Fighting Violence and State Repression on the U.S.-Mexico Border* (Chicago: Haymarket Books, 2006), 223.

44. Fernandes, *Targeted*, 191–96; Akers Chacón and Davis, *No One Is Illegal*, 215–25.

45. Fernandes, *Targeted*, 169–85.

46. Marc Mauer, "The Changing Racial Dynamics of the War on Drugs," The Sentencing Project, April 2009, www.sentencingproject.org/doc/dp_raceanddrugs.pdf (accessed December 5, 2014).

47. Vijay Prashad, *Everybody Was Kung Fu Fighting: Afro-Asian Connections and the Myth of Cultural Purity* (Boston: Beacon Press, 2001); Vijay Prashad, *The Darker Nations: A People's History of the Third World* (New York: New Press, 2008).

48. Gilmore, "Globalisation," 176.

49. For a discussion of such anticommunist domestic operations, see Lee, *Orientals*, 145–79.

50. Gilmore, "Globalisation," 176.

51. Donald Pease, *The New American Exceptionalism* (Minneapolis: University of Minnesota Press, 2009), 7.

52. Pease, *New American Exceptionalism*, 12.

53. Pease, *New American Exceptionalism*, 14.

54. Slavoj Žižek has written extensively on the psychoanalytical dimensions of transgressing the law and the illicit pleasure it evokes. See, for example, Slavoj Žižek, *The Parallax View* (Boston: MIT Press, 2006), 89–90.

55. Pease, *New American Exceptionalism*, 14–21.

56. For a brief historical overview of the rise of anti-Muslim sentiment in early Christianity (eighth and ninth centuries) and early modern Europe, see Tomaz Mastnak, "Western Hostility Toward Muslims: A History of the Present," in *Islamophobia/Islamophilia: Beyond the Politics of Enemy and Friend*, ed. Andrew Shryock (Bloomington: Indiana University Press, 2010), 29–52.

57. Said, *Orientalism*, 301.

58. Said, *Orientalism*, 286.

59. Said, *Culture and Imperialism*, 294.

60. Said, *Orientalism*, 311.

61. Said, *Orientalism*, 311–12.

62. Said, *Orientalism*, 311.

63. See, for example, Chandra Mohanty, "Under Western Eyes: Feminist Scholarship and Colonial Discourses," *Feminist Review* 30 (1988): 61–88; and Chandra Talpade Mohanty, *Feminism Without Borders: Decolonizing Theory, Practicing Solidarity* (Durham, NC: Duke University Press, 2003).

64. Andrew Shryock, ed., *Islamophobia/Islamophilia: Beyond the Politics of Enemy and Friend* (Bloomington: Indiana University Press, 2010), 7.

65. George W. Bush, "'Islam Is Peace' Says President," Remarks by the President at the

Islamic Center of Washington, DC, September 17, 2001, georgewbush-whitehouse.archives
.gov/news/releases/2001/09/20010917-11.html (accessed December 5, 2014).

66. Shryock, *Islamophobia/Islamophilia*, 9–10.

67. Shryock, *Islamophobia/Islamophilia*, 10.

68. Ghassan Hage, *White Nation: Fantasies of White Supremacy in a Multicultural Society* (New York: Routledge, 2000), 67.

69. For a detailed discussion of specific proxy wars, see Mahmood Mamdani, *Good Muslim, Bad Muslim: America, the Cold War, and the Roots of Terror* (New York: Pantheon Books, 2004), 63–109. For an in-depth analysis of U.S. involvement in Afghanistan against the Soviet Union leading to the formation of the Taliban, see pages 119–63 in Mamdani's book. For an extensive analysis of U.S. support of Saddam Hussein's regime in Iraq against Iran and the shift to aerial warfare and open aggression in Iraq, see pages 178–228 in Mamdani's book.

70. Hage, *White Nation*, 69.

71. Said, *Culture and Imperialism*, 291.

72. See Jack G. Shaheen, *Arab and Muslim Stereotyping in American Popular Culture* (Washington, DC: Center for Muslim-Christian Understanding, History, and International Affairs, Edmund A. Walsh School of Foreign Service, Georgetown University, 1997); and Jack G. Shaheen, *Reel Bad Arabs: How Hollywood Vilifies a People* (New York: Olive Branch Press, 2001).

73. McAlister, *Epic Encounters*, 199.

74. McAlister, *Epic Encounters*, 199.

75. McAlister, *Epic Encounters*, 211.

76. McAlister, *Epic Encounters*, 225.

77. McAlister, *Epic Encounters*, 233.

78. Michael Rogin, "'Make My Day!' Spectacle as Amnesia in Imperial Politics," in *Cultures of United States Imperialism*, ed. Amy Kaplan and Donald E. Pease (Durham, NC: Duke University Press, 1993), 506.

79. Mamdani, *Good Muslim, Bad Muslim*, 97.

80. Mamdani, *Good Muslim, Bad Muslim*, 97.

81. McAlister, *Epic Encounters*, 253.

82. Laicie Olson Heeley, "Growth in U.S. Defense Spending Since 2001," Center for Arms Control and Non-Proliferation, March 11, 2010, http://armscontrolcenter.org/issues/securityspending/articles/fy11_growth_since_2001/ (accessed March 12, 2012).

83. Laicie Olson Heeley, "Estimated Iraq and Afghanistan War Funding FY2001–FY2012," Center for Arms Control and Non-Proliferation, March 12, 2011, http://armscontrolcenter .org/issues/securityspending/articles/2001_2012_War_Funding/ (accessed March 12, 2012).

CHAPTER I

Portions of this chapter were originally published in the *Journal of Haitian Studies* 13, no. 1 (2007): 4–26, under the title "The Story of Abner Louima: Cultural Fantasies, Gendered Racial Violence, and the Ethical Witness." Reprinted with permission.

1. Michel S. Laguerre, *Diasporic Citizenship: Haitian Americans in Transnational America* (New York: St. Martin's Press, 1998), 130.

2. During President Aristide's 1993 exile in Washington, D.C., the station was central to

relaying broadcasts from Port-au-Prince and from rebel and underground radio throughout the United States. Laguerre, *Diasporic Citizenship*, 133.

3. Joan Dayan, "'A Receptacle for That Race of Men': Blood, Boundaries, and Mutations of Theory," *American Literature* 67, no. 4 (1995): 801–13.

4. Dayan, "Receptacle," 809.

5. Dayan, "Receptacle," 809.

6. Dayan, "Receptacle," 809.

7. Elizabeth A. McAlister, *Rara! Vodou, Power, and Performance in Haiti and Its Diaspora* (Berkeley: University of California Press, 2002), 3.

8. McAlister, *Rara*, 186.

9. McAlister, *Rara*, 184.

10. Neil Smith, "Giuliani Time: The Revanchist 1990s," *Social Text* 16, no. 4 (1998): 2.

11. Smith, "Giuliani Time," 3.

12. Smith, "Giuliani Time," 3.

13. Smith, "Giuliani Time," 4.

14. Allen Feldman, "Philoctetes Revisited: White Public Space and the Political Geography of Public Safety," *Social Text* 19, no. 3 (2001): 68.

15. Feldman, "Philoctetes Revisited," 68.

16. Smith, "Giuliani Time," 7–8.

17. Feldman, "Philoctetes Revisited," 70–71.

18. Feldman, "Philoctetes Revisited," 73.

19. Sherri-Ann P. Butterfield, "'We're Just Black': The Racial and Ethnic Identities of Second-Generation West Indians in New York," in *Becoming New Yorkers: Ethnographies of the New Second Generation*, ed. Philip Kasinitz, John H. Mollenkopf, and Mary C. Waters (New York: Russell Sage, 2004), 305.

20. Louima would later recant his assertion that Volpe and the other officer said this, claiming that he had been encouraged by a family member to politicize his story in this way. We might assume that it was necessary to recant the statement given Giuliani's political support for Louima. But the political implications of the statement were already in play, regardless of its truth value.

21. Much of the description that follows, unless otherwise noted, is outlined in the Memorandum and Order of *United States of America v. Justin Volpe*. It is important to note that several details of what happened are portrayed differently by various persons. As such, my retelling of this story does not attempt to be accurate but rather weaves together the sometimes contradictory narratives of different voices. For the full Memorandum and Order, see "78 F. Supp. 2d 76: United States v. Volpe," *Justia US Law*, December 13, 1999, law.justia.com/cases/federal/district-courts/FSupp2/78/76/2568994/ (accessed July 16, 2014).

22. Robert Draper, "Say a Prayer for Justin Volpe," *GQ*, February 2005, 5, www.gq.com/news-politics/newsmakers/200506/justin-volpe-sodomy-abner-louima-brooklyn-police (accessed May 30, 2014).

23. "King Kino: Fighting the 'Cowboys' from Haiti to Brooklyn," *Revolutionary Worker* 924 (September 21, 1997).

24. Draper, "Say a Prayer," 5.

25. Draper, "Say a Prayer."

26. Miguel Garcilazo, "A Bid at 70th for Christian Mercy?" *New York Daily News*, August 22, 1997, www.nydailynews.com/archives/news/bid-70th-christian-mercy-article-1.775390 (accessed May 30, 2014).

27. Mike McAlary, "Victim and City Deeply Scarred," *New York Daily News*, August 14, 1997, www.nydailynews.com/news/crime/victim-city-deeply-scarred-article-1.235522 (accessed May 20, 2014).

28. The identity of the second officer was suspected to be Thomas Schwarz, but this could not be confirmed by either Louima or the court testimonials.

29. McAlary, "Victim and City."

30. McAlary, "Victim and City."

31. Bill Farrell, Miguel Garcilazo, and Joel Siegel, "A Justice Plea as Heads Roll; Officers Must Pay, Victim Sez," *New York Daily News*, August 15, 1997, www.nydailynews.com/archives/news/justice-plea-heads-roll-officers-pay-victim-sez-article-1.772264 (accessed May 20, 2014).

32. Dan Barry, "Officers' Silence Still Thwarting Torture Inquiry," *New York Times*, September 5, 1997, www.nytimes.com/1997/09/05/nyregion/officers-silence-still-thwarting-torture-inquiry.html (accessed May 20, 2014).

33. Memorandum and Order of *United States of America v. Justin Volpe*.

34. Garcilazo, "Bid at 70th."

35. John Kifner, "Investigators Looking at New Allegations in Brutality Case," *New York Times*, August 21, 1997, www.nytimes.com/1997/08/21/nyregion/investigators-looking-at-new-allegations-in-brutality-case.html (accessed May 15, 2015).

36. Garry Pierre-Pierre, "In Hospital, Immigrant Gives Views On Brutality," *New York Times*, August 22, 1997, www.nytimes.com/1997/08/22/nyregion/in-hospital-immigrant-gives-views-on-brutality.html (accessed May 16, 2014).

37. Saidiya V. Hartman, *Scenes of Subjection: Terror, Slavery, and Self-Making in Nineteenth-Century America* (Oxford, UK: Oxford University Press, 1997), 3.

38. Hartman, *Scenes of Subjection*, 3–4.

39. Marie Brenner, "Incident in the 70th Precinct," *Vanity Fair*, December 1, 1997, www.vanityfair.com/magazine/archive/1997/12/louima199712 (accessed May 16, 2014).

40. For detailed accounts of the historical processes involved in converting ethnic Europeans into white Americans, see David R. Roediger, *The Wages of Whiteness: Race and the Making of the American Working Class* (New York: Verso, 1991); and David Roediger, *Working Toward Whiteness: How America's Immigrants Became White—The Strange Journey from Ellis Island to the Suburbs* (New York: Basic Books, 2005).

41. For a definitive study on this topic, see C. L. R. James, *The Black Jacobins: Toussaint L'Ouverture and the San Domingo Revolution* (New York: Vintage Books, 1963).

42. Stan Weir and George Lipsitz, *Singlejack Solidarity* (Minneapolis: University of Minnesota Press, 2004), 195.

43. George Lipsitz points out that Haiti's constitution posited flexible racial categories after Haiti's successful slave revolt by making all Haitians legally Black, regardless of their skin color. Meanwhile, those who had opposed freedom, including dark-skinned Haitians, came to be considered white. George Lipsitz, "Breaking the Silence: The Fugees and 'The Score,'" *Journal of Haitian Studies* 12, no. 1 (2006): 15. For an excellent discussion of the complexity of color representation in Haiti, see also Michel-Rolph Trouillot, "Culture, Color,

and Politics in Haiti," in *Race*, ed. Steven Gregory and Roger Sanjek (New Brunswick, NJ: Rutgers University Press, 1994), 146–74.

44. Jeb Sprague, *Paramilitarism and the Assault on Democracy in Haiti* (New York: Monthly Review Press, 2012).

45. Cedric Robinson, *Black Marxism: The Making of the Black Radical Tradition* (Chapel Hill: University of North Carolina Press, 2000).

46. Peter Linebaugh and Marcus Rediker, *The Many-Headed Hydra: Sailors, Slaves, Commoners, and the Hidden History of the Revolutionary Atlantic* (Boston: Beacon Press, 2000), 176.

47. Ida B. Wells-Barnett, *On Lynchings* (Amherst, NY: Humanity Books, 2002).

48. W. E. Burghardt DuBois, *Black Reconstruction in America, 186–1880* (New York: Free Press, 1998), 700.

49. David Marriott, *On Black Men* (New York: Columbia University Press, 2000), 8–9.

50. Robyn Wiegman, *American Anatomies: Theorizing Race and Gender* (Durham, NC: Duke University Press, 1995), 90.

51. Grace Elizabeth Hale, *Making Whiteness: The Culture of Segregation in the South, 1890–1940* (New York: Pantheon Books, 1998).

52. Wiegman, *American Anatomies*, 98.

53. For an in-depth analysis of the psychosocial dimensions of sexualized racial violence in lynching scenes, see Marriott, *On Black Men*, 1–22.

54. Wiegman, *American Anatomies*, 99.

55. Marriott, *On Black Men*, 123.

56. Susan chose not to give her last name in the interview with Mike McAlary to protect her family. Because of this, I refer to her by her first name. All quotes in this section are taken from Mike McAlary, "Gal Pal: He Couldn't Do It," *New York Daily News*, August 10, 2007, www.nydailynews.com/news/crime/gal-pal-couldn-article-1.235580 (accessed July 15, 2014).

57. Hartman, *Scenes of Subjection*, 79–114.

58. Danielle L. McGuire, "'It Was Like All of Us Had Been Raped': Sexual Violence, Community Mobilization, and the African American Freedom Struggle," *Journal of American History* 91, no. 3 (2004): 906–31.

59. Jonathan P. Hicks, "Protest Call: 'Something Has to Be Done,'" *New York Times*, August 14, 1997, www.nytimes.com/1997/08/14/nyregion/protest-call-something-has-to-be-done.html (accessed May 30, 2014).

60. Zenon Zawada, Miguel Garcilazo, Anne E. Kornblut, and Michele Mcphee, "Abuse Not New in This Nabe, Haitians Say," *New York Daily News*, August 15, 1997, www.nydailynews.com/archives/news/abuse-new-nabe-haitians-article-1.773482 (accessed May 20, 2014).

61. Zawada et al., "Abuse Not New."

62. Marjorie Valbrun, "Haitians in New York," Alicia Patterson Foundation, August 19, 2011, aliciapatterson.org/stories/haitians-new-york (accessed May 20, 2014).

63. Allen Feldman, "Political Terror and the Technologies of Memory: Excuse, Sacrifice, Commodification, and Actuarial Moralities," *Radical History Review* 85, no. 1 (2003): 62.

64. Feldman, "Political Terror," 62.

65. Kifner, "Investigators Looking at New Allegations."

66. Zawada et al., "Abuse Not New."

67. Garry Pierre-Pierre, "Haitians Expect Thousands to March Against Brutality,"

New York Times, August 28, 1997, www.nytimes.com/1997/08/28/nyregion/haitians-expect
-thousands-to-march-against-brutality.html (accessed May 20, 2014).

68. John Kifner, "Thousands Call on City Hall to Confront Police Brutality," *New York Times*, August 30, 1997, www.nytimes.com/1997/08/30/nyregion/thousands-call-on
-city-hall-to-confront-police-brutality.html (accessed May 20, 2014).

69. Kifner, "Thousands Call on City Hall."

70. William J. Bratton, "New York's Police Should Not Retreat," *New York Times*, August 19, 1997, www.nytimes.com/1997/08/19/opinion/new-york-s-police-should-not-retreat
.html (accessed May 20, 2014).

71. "Deflecting Blame: Dissenting Report of Mayor Giuliani's Task Force on Police-Community Relations (1998)," New York Civil Rights Coalition, 1998, 2, nycivilrights.org/
wp-content/themes/civilrights/pdf/Report5.pdf (accessed May 20, 2014).

72. Bob Herbert, "Connect the Dots," *New York Times*, August 24, 1997, www.nytimes
.com/1997/08/24/opinion/connect-the-dots.html (accessed May 20, 2014).

73. Herbert, "Connect the Dots."

74. Herbert, "Connect the Dots."

75. See Tom McEwen, "National Data Collection on Police Use of Force," Bureau of Justice Statistics and National Institute for Justice, April 1996, www.ojp.usdoj.gov/bjs/pub/
pdf/ndcopuof.pdf (accessed May 20, 2014).

76. Fresh in the memory of New York communities of color were numerous arbitrary deaths and beatings: Kevin Cedeno, 16, Black, fatally shot in the lower back at close range by Officer Anthony Pellegrini on April 4, 1997; Charles Campbell, 37, Black, fatally shot three times by Officer Richard Diguglielmo on October 4, 1996, over a parking space; Nathaniel Gaines, 26, Black Navy veteran fatally shot in the back by Officer Paolo Colecchia on July 4, 1996; Lebert Folkes, Jamaican immigrant, shot in the face by an undercover officer while being pulled out of his sister's car on February 11, 1996; Yong Xin Huang, 16, Chinese youth shot in the back by police officers after having his face smashed into a glass door on March 24, 1995; Anibal Carasquillo, 21, Puerto Rican, unarmed, fatally shot in the chest on January 22, 1995, by Marco Calderon; Anthony Baez, 29, Puerto Rican, choked to death by Officer Francis Livoti for accidentally hitting a police patrol car with a football on December 22, 1994. Stolen Lives Project, *Stolen Lives: Killed by Law Enforcement* (New York: National Lawyers Guild, Anthony Baez Foundation, and October 22nd Coalition to Stop Police Brutality, Repression, and the Criminalization of a Generation, 1999), 232–63.

77. "Deflecting Blame," 2.

78. For a detailed account of multiple cases in which police officers accused of brutality or unjustifiable shootings were exonerated, see Amnesty International, *Police Brutality and Excessive Force in the New York City Police Department*, June 1996 (AI Index: 52/36/96).

79. Robert Gooding-Williams, ed., *Reading Rodney King, Reading Urban Uprising* (New York: Routledge, 1993).

80. "King Kino."

81. "New York City Since Amadou Diallo," Stolen Lives Project, www.stolenlives.org/
Updates.html (accessed July 16, 2014).

82. Wiese and Bruder's convictions of 60 months in prison were overturned on appeal. See *United States v. Schwarz*, 283 f.3D 76 (NY Ct. App. 2d Cir. 2002).

83. "Convictions Against NY Police Reversed," BBC News, February 28, 2002, web. archive.org/web/20140102193617/http://news.bbc.co.uk/2/hi/americas/1847280.stm (accessed January 2, 2014).

CHAPTER 2

1. Melissa Cirillo and Sherry Ricchiardi, "Abu Ghraib Time Line," *American Journalism Review*, June–July 2004, www.ajr.org/article.asp?id=3730 (accessed July 19, 2014).

2. Suzanne Goldenberg, "Abu Ghraib Leaked Report Reveals Full Extent of Abuse," *The Guardian*, February 16, 2006, www.guardian.co.uk/world/2006/feb/17/iraq.suzanne-goldenberg (accessed July 19, 2014).

3. Seymour M. Hersh, "Torture at Abu Ghraib," *The New Yorker*, May 10, 2004, www .newyorker.com/archive/2004/05/10/040510fa_fact (accessed July 19, 2014); Seymour M. Hersh, *Chain of Command: The Road from 9/11 to Abu Ghraib* (New York: Harper Collins, 2004); Mark Danner, *Torture and Truth: America, Abu Ghraib, and the War on Terror* (New York: New York Review Books, 2004).

4. Donald Pease, *The New American Exceptionalism* (Minneapolis: University of Minnesota Press, 2009).

5. Scott Lindlaw, "Bush Gathers His Team for a Show of Solidarity," *Star-Ledger* (Newark, NJ), May 11, 2004; "Refusing to Face Facts," editorial, *St. Louis Post-Dispatch*, May 11, 2004 (accessed through LexisNexis, May 12, 2007).

6. "I'm Sorry But . . . ," editorial, *St. Louis Post-Dispatch*, May 9, 2004.

7. James Schlesinger, "The Truth About Our Soldiers," *Wall Street Journal*, September 9, 2004; "Voice of the Times," editorial, *Anchorage Daily News*, May 17, 2005 (accessed through LexisNexis, May 12, 2007).

8. Josh White and Scott Higham, "Army Calls Abuses 'Aberrations,'" *Washington Post*, July 23, 2004.

9. The infrastructural shifts in state, legal, and military policies and acts after September 11 have been extensively outlined by several scholars, including Lila Rajiva, *The Language of Empire: Abu Ghraib and the American Media* (New York: Monthly Review Press, 2005); Jana Evans Braziel, "Haiti, Guantánamo, and the 'One Indispensable Nation,'" *Cultural Critique* 64 (fall 2006): 127–60; Nadine Naber, "The Rules of Forced Engagement: Gendered Inscriptions of Terrorism on Arab and Muslim Bodies in the U.S.," paper presented at the Center for Cultural Studies, University of California, Santa Cruz, May 13, 2005; and Henry Giroux, "What Might Education Mean After Abu Ghraib: Revisiting Adorno's Politics of Education," *Comparative Studies of South Asia, Africa, and the Middle East* 24, no. 1 (2004): 3–22.

10. Giroux, "What Might Education Mean," 6.

11. "Washington Wire," *Wall Street Journal Abstracts*, July 2, 2004 (accessed through LexisNexis, October 1, 2006). For a detailed account of the ways in which the interrogation tactics at Abu Ghraib were sanctioned by the state and military personnel in the highest offices, see Hersh, *Chain of Command*, 1–72.

12. Samar Farah, "Cultural Lens: Judging You, Judging Me," *Christian Science Monitor*, March 14, 2002.

13. Emram Qureshi, "Misreading 'The Arab Mind,' the Dubious Guidebook to Middle East Culture That's on the Pentagon's Reading List," *Boston Globe*, May 30, 2004.

14. Hersh, "Torture at Abu Ghraib."

15. "The mother may attempt to prepare her son gradually for the circumcision operation by caressing his organ and playfully endeavoring to separate the foreskin from the glans. . . . This motherly caressing of the boy's penis may well go on at an age from which the boy retains distinct memories throughout his adult life. While this particular custom may be a local development, the association of the mother, and hence women in general, with erotic pleasure is something that Arab male infants in general experience and that predisposes them to accept the stereotype of the woman as primarily a sexual object and a creature who cannot resist sexual temptation." Raphael Patai, *The Arab Mind* (New York: Scribner's Sons, 1983), 33.

16. Jasbir K. Puar and Amit Rai, "Monster, Terrorist, Fag: The War on Terrorism and the Production of Docile Patriots," *Social Text* 20, no. 3 (2002): 122.

17. Jamie Glazov, "The Sexual Rage Behind Islamic Terror," Front Page Magazine, October 4, 2001, archive.frontpagemag.com/readArticle.aspx?ARTID=25196 (accessed July 20, 2014).

18. Glazov, "Sexual Rage."

19. "The sexuality of the male is seldom discussed expressly, but the tacitly assumed Arab male self-image is that of a man who will inevitably take advantage of any woman who strikes his fancy whenever circumstances enable him to do so. Consequently, he must be prevented by the same strict code of sexual conduct from ever being exposed to erotic temptation." Patai, *Arab Mind*, 33.

20. "Arab sexual mores assume that wherever and whenever a man and a woman of suitable ages happen to find themselves alone, they will be irresistibly driven to having sexual union even if they had never before seen each other, and even if the consequences could be most disastrous." Patai, *Arab Mind*, 33.

21. "The children are disciplined, if necessary severely, in order to make them accept, and acquiesce in, paternal rule. As a result of Arab child-rearing practices, the children learn to subordinate their own personal interests to those of the family as represented by the father or grandfather." Patai, *Arab Mind*, 27.

22. Patai, *Arab Mind*, 34.

23. "All these factors may make the Arab population more susceptible to illogical and magical thinking, including overt delusional thinking." *ShrinkWrapped*, November 1, 2006, shrinkwrapped.blogs.com/blog/2006/11/arab_culture_de.html (accessed February 20, 2007).

24. "All they knew was aggression, channeled outward, and they naturally did what they do best. It is highly doubtful that these young men can ever be engaged in the political process. Unfortunately, it increasingly appears that there are enough of them to completely derail any attempt to establish a civil society in Iraq." *ShrinkWrapped*, November 1, 2006.

25. "The only possible path to success is to use a total war strategy of 'defeat and destruction.' . . . The remaining options are either to sit back and await our own eventual subjugation or elimination *or* total annihilation of the enemy, as in genocide." *ShrinkWrapped*, comment posted by Grimmy, November 4, 2006, at 6:05 p.m. (accessed February 20, 2007).

26. D. C. McClelland, John W. Atkinson, Russell A. Clark, and Edgar L. Lowell, *The Achievement Motive* (New York: Appleton-Century-Crofts, 1953).

27. Quoted in Patai, *Arab Mind*, 37.

28. Patai, *Arab Mind*, 38.

29. Patai, *Arab Mind*, 39.

30. Patai, *Arab Mind*, 32.

31. Patai, *Arab Mind*, 28.

32. Nira Yuval-Davis shows how these two characteristics are common in gendered readings of women in nationalist contexts. See Nira Yuval-Davis, *Gender and Nation* (Thousand Oaks, CA: Sage, 1997). For contemporary discussions of the associations between submission and the veil (or *hijab*), see Rabab Ibrahim Abdulhadi, "Tread Lightly: Teaching Gender and Sexuality in the Time of War," *Journal of Women's History* 17, no. 4 (2005): 154–58; and Kevin J. Ayotte and Mary E. Husain, "Securing Afghan Women: Neocolonialism, Epistemic Violence, and the Rhetoric of the Veil," *NWSA Journal* 17, no. 3 (2005): 112–33.

33. Patai, *Arab Mind*, 126.

34. Patai, *Arab Mind*, 122.

35. Quoted in Patai, *Arab Mind*, 126.

36. "The self-image of the woman is practically identical with [the view that a woman's lust is greater than that of a man]. She is brought up to believe that once she found herself alone with a man, she would be unable to resist his advances; therefore, she must never allow herself to be found in such a situation." Patai, *Arab Mind*, 139.

37. Patai, *Arab Mind*, 141–42.

38. See Malek Alloula, *The Colonial Harem*, trans. Myrna Godzich and Wald Godzich (Minneapolis: University of Minnesota Press, 1986); and Fadwa El Guindi, *Veil: Modesty, Privacy, and Resistance* (New York: Berg, 1999).

39. For a deeper reflection on the rhetoric of saving Arab women, see Lila Abu-Lughod, "Do Muslim Women Really Need Saving? Anthropological Reflections on Cultural Relativism and Its Others," *American Anthropologist* 104, no. 3 (2002): 783–90.

40. Gayatri Spivak, *A Critique of Postcolonial Reason* (Cambridge, MA: Harvard University Press, 1999), 286.

41. Ayotte and Husain, "Securing Afghan Women."

42. John Otis, "First Lady Slams 'Gender Apartheid,'" *Houston Chronicle*, November 18, 2001.

43. "Unveiled," *60 Minutes II*, October 10, 2001, CBS.

44. Sora Song, "Headgear 101," *Time*, November 12, 2001, content.time.com/time/magazine/article/0,9171,1001197,00.html (accessed October 7, 2014).

45. Spivak, *Critique of Postcolonial Reason*, 287–88.

46. Riverbend, *Baghdad Burning II: More Girl Blog from Iraq* (New York: Feminist Press, 2006), 58.

47. Riverbend, *Baghdad Burning II*, 304.

48. Riverbend, *Baghdad Burning: Girl Blog from Iraq* (New York: Feminist Press, 2005), 259.

49. Riverbend, *Baghdad Burning*, 260.

50. Riverbend, *Baghdad Burning*, 261.

51. "I hope they are made to suffer . . . somehow I know they won't be punished. They'll be discharged from the army, at best, and made to go back home and join their families and cronies who will drink to the pictures and the way 'America's finest' treated those 'Dumb I-raki terrorists.' . . . I want something done about it and I want it done publicly. . . . I want their children and their children's children to carry on the story of what was done for

a long time—as long as those prisoners will carry along with them the humiliation and pain of what was done and as long as the memory of those pictures remains in Iraqi hearts and minds." Riverbend, *Baghdad Burning*, 261.

52. Riverbend, *Baghdad Burning*, 263.

53. Riverbend, *Baghdad Burning*, 263.

54. Ben Fishel, "Severin on Abused Prisoners at Abu Ghraib: '[W]e Treated Them Essentially to a Week in Las Vegas,'" Media Matters for America, June 1, 2006, mediamatters .org/video/2006/06/01/severin-on-abused-prisoners-at-abu-ghraib-we-tr/135851 (accessed July 21, 2014).

55. Fishel, "Severin on Abused Prisoners."

56. Fishel, "Severin on Abused Prisoners."

57. Andrew Seifter and Gabe Wildau, "Limbaugh on Torture of Iraqis: U.S. Guards Were 'Having a Good Time,' 'Blow[ing] Some Steam off,'" Media Matters for America, May 5, 2004, mediamatters.org/research/2004/05/05/limbaugh-on-torture-of-iraqis-us-guards -were-ha/131111 (accessed July 21, 2014).

58. "Abu Ghraib: Fraternity 'Hazing', a.k.a. 'Not as Bad as Saddam,'" Sourcewatch, Center for Media and Democracy, May 21, 2008, www.sourcewatch.org/index.php?title=Abu_ Ghraib:_Fraternity_%27Hazing%27,_a.k.a._%27Not_as_Bad_as_Saddam%27 (accessed October 5, 2012).

59. Nicole Casta, "Hannity Debated Rosie O'Donnell on Abu Ghraib Abuse: No Torture or Rape, Just 'Underwear on the Head of One' Prisoner," Media Matters for America, June 8, 2005, mediamatters.org/press/release/2005/06/08/hannity-debated-rosie-odonnell -on-abu-ghraib-ab/133313 (accessed July 21, 2014).

60. Comments in response to "Torture Test," posted by Greyhawk. Comments by Imperial Crusader posted on January 7, 2005, 04:46 p.m. See mudvillegazette.com/cgi-bin/mt/ mt-comments.cgi?entry_id=1989 (accessed January 18, 2007).

61. Fishel, "Severin on Abused Prisoners."

62. Neferti Tadiar, "Imperialism Without End?" keynote address, Great Lakes Association of American Studies Association (GLASA) Conference, Indianapolis, Indiana, March 19, 2005.

63. For examples of these liberal critiques, see Anne-Marie Cusac, "Abu Ghraib, USA," AlterNet, August 6, 2004, www.alternet.org/story/19479/abu_ghraib%2C_usa (accessed July 21, 2014); Deborah Pearlstein, "Promoting Abu Ghraib," AlterNet, October 26, 2004, www .alternet.org/story/20298/promoting_abu_ghraib (accessed July 21, 2014); Jesse Walker, "Abu Ghraib: More," Reason.com, May 1, 2004, reason.com/blog/2004/05/01/abu-ghraib -more (accessed October 2, 2012); and Lakshmi Chaudhry, "Seymour Hersh: Man On Fire," AlterNet, October 26, 2004, www.alternet.org/story/20309/seymour_hersh%3A_man_on_ fire (accessed July 21, 2014).

64. See, for example, Gregory Hooks and Clayton Mosher, "Outrages Against Personal Dignity: Rationalizing Abuses and Torture in the War on Terror," *Social Forces* 83, no. 4 (2005): 1632–35; and "U.S. Abuse of Iraqi Detainees at Abu Ghraib Prison," *American Journal of International Law* 98, no. 3 (2004): 591–96.

65. "Murtha Takes Aim at Abu Ghraib, Guantanamo," Think Progress, January 9, 2007, thinkprogress.org/2007/01/09/murtha-takes-aim-at-abu-ghraib-guantanamo (accessed January 18, 2007).

66. Patricia J. Williams, *Seeing a Color-Blind Future: The Paradox of Race* (New York: Noonday Press, 1997), 11.

67. For examples of scholarly works that have demonstrated connections between the infrastructures set up by the prison-industrial complex in the United States, Abu Ghraib, Guantánamo Bay, and the war on terror, see Jana Evans Braziel, "Haiti"; Michelle Brown, "'Setting the Conditions' for Abu Ghraib: The Prison Nation Abroad," *American Quarterly* 57, no. 3 (2005): 973–97; Allen Feldman, "Abu Ghraib: Ceremonies of Nostalgia," *Open Democracy*, October 18, 2004; Giroux, "What Might Education Mean"; Avery F. Gordon, "Abu Ghraib: Imprisonment and the War on Terror," *Race and Class* 48, no. 1 (2006): 42–59; Lila Rajiva, "Prometheus: The Emergence of the Police State in America," *CR: The New Centennial Review* 6, no. 1 (2006): 133–69; and Benjamin Whitmer, "'Torture Chambers and Rape Rooms': What Abu Ghraib Can Tell Us About the American Carceral System," *CR: The New Centennial Review* 6, no. 1 (2006): 171–94.

68. Cusac, "Abu Ghraib, USA"; Matthew Briggs, "From Abu Ghraib to Your Local Prison," AlterNet, July 1, 2004, www.alternet.org/story/19096/from_abu_ghraib_to_your_local_prison (accessed July 21, 2014).

69. Walter Benjamin, *Illuminations*, ed. Hannah Arendt; trans. Harry Zohn (New York: Schocken, 1969), 257; emphasis in original.

70. Response to Fishel, "Severin on Abused Prisoners," comment posted by rstybeach266, June 2, 2006, 4:39:24 p.m. (accessed October 1, 2012).

71. Comments in response to "'The Bottom Line' Abu Ghraib Video," WFMU's Beware of the Blog, February 20, 2006, blog.wfmu.org/freeform/2006/02/the_bottom_line .html (accessed July 21, 2014).

72. I thank Dr. Felice Blake for introducing me to the phrase "feeling good for feeling bad" to capture this dynamic.

73. Edward W. Said, *Culture and Imperialism* (New York: Vintage, 1994), 300.

74. Walter Benjamin, "The Work of Art in the Age of Mechanical Reproduction," in *Illuminations*, ed. Hannah Arendt; trans. Harry Zohn (New York: Schocken, 1969), 242.

75. "The horrible features of imperialistic warfare are attributable to the discrepancy between the tremendous means of production and their inadequate utilization in the process of production—in other words, to unemployment and the lack of markets." Benjamin, *Illuminations*, 242.

76. Jane Mayer, "The Politics of '24,'" *The New Yorker*, February 19, 2007, www.new yorker.com/magazine/2007/02/19/whatever-it-takes (accessed November 29, 2014).

77. Mayer, "Politics of '24.'"

78. Jonathan Beller, "Military-Industrial Complex," in *Shock and Awe: War on Words*, ed. Bregje van Eekelen, Jennifer González, Bettina Stötzer, and Anna Tsing (Berkeley, CA: North Atlantic Books, 2007), 97–99; emphasis in original.

79. Fishel, "Severin on Abused Prisoners."

80. Neferti Tadiar, *Fantasy-Productions* (Hong Kong: Hong Kong University Press, 2004), 264.

81. Tadiar, *Fantasy-Productions*, 264.

82. Tadiar, *Fantasy-Productions*, 267–68.

83. Richard Goldstein, "Stuff Happens! Don't Call It Torture. It's Just a Broomstick

up the Butt," *The Village Voice*, April 27, 2004, www.villagevoice.com/2004-04-27/news/
stuff-happens/ (accessed July 21, 2014).

84. "Feminists Yanar Mohammed of Iraq and Dr. Sima Samar of Afghanistan on the
Dire Situation for Women Under U.S. Occupation and Rising Fundamentalism," Democ-
racy Now, May 14, 2007, www.democracynow.org/article.pl?sid=07/05/14/1426259 (accessed
August 9, 2007).

85. "Feminists Yanar Mohammed and Dr. Sima Samar."

86. Iris Marion Young, *Responsibility for Justice* (New York: Oxford University Press,
2013), 95–122.

87. Iris Marion Young, "Political Responsibility and Structural Injustice," paper presented at the Lindley Lecture, Philosophy Department, University of Kansas, May 5, 2003, 17.

88. Tricia Rose, "Intimate Justice: Black Women's Sexuality and the Future of Black
Social Movements," unpublished paper, 10.

PART II

1. Matt Taibbi, *The Divide: American Injustice in the Age of the Wealth Gap* (New York:
Spiegel & Grau, 2014); Matt Taibbi, *Griftopia: A Story of Bankers, Politicians, and the Most
Audacious Power Grab in American History* (New York: Spiegel & Grau, 2011).

2. George Lipsitz, *How Racism Takes Place* (Philadelphia: Temple University Press, 2011), 13.

3. Lipsitz, *How Racism Takes Place*, 13.

4. George Lipsitz, *American Studies in a Moment of Danger* (Minneapolis: University
of Minnesota Press, 2001); David R. Roediger, *The Wages of Whiteness: Race and the Making
of the American Working Class* (New York: Verso, 1991).

5. In *Killing the Black Body: Race, Reproduction, and the Meaning of Liberty* (New York:
Vintage Books, 1999), Dorothy Roberts argues that what most people refer to as welfare
programs (needs-based assistance such as food stamps, health insurance for children, the
elderly, and people with disabilities through Medicaid, Temporary Assistance for Needy
Families, and public housing or Section 8 vouchers) originated from policy shifts during
the Progressive Era that sought to afford base levels of economic security to spouseless white
women with children. These policies assumed patriarchal households and marriage as normative ideals by which all other family formations were measured. Women and children
were considered the dependents of husbands, who were the sole breadwinners responsible
for obtaining a family wage, that is, enough money to support an entire household. Female-
headed households with children were therefore exceptions to this ideal, and white women
who ended up husbandless out of no fault of their own were considered deserving victims
that the state would step in to aid. As Roberts argues, "The resulting maternalist welfare
policy provided government aid so that the female victims of misfortune and male irre-
sponsibility would not have to relinquish their maternal duties in the home in order to join
the work force" (203). From their inception, needs-based welfare policies were linked with
moral, gendered, and racial assumptions and goals. Poor immigrant families who sought
aid had to demonstrate conformity with the aforementioned American patriarchal family
standards. "Aid generally was conditioned on compliance with moral provisions and was
often administered by juvenile court judges who specialized in punitive and rehabilitative
judgments" (204). Meanwhile, Black mothers were simply excluded. The New Deal policy

reforms that emerged in the 1930s relegated mothers' aid to programs separate from programs for men. Although social insurance programs such as Social Security and unemployment insurance provided fixed amounts predominantly to white male wage earners, recipients of Aid to Families with Dependent Children had to face regular surveillance from government bureaucrats who had the discretion to determine whether they were eligible and how much they received. Eligibility depended not only on meeting certain means standards but also on tests that probed into whether clients had "proper" sexual behavior and "suitable homes" (203–205). For a full analysis see Roberts, *Killing the Black Body*, 203–208; and Linda Gordon, *Pitied but Not Entitled: Single Mothers and the History of Welfare, 1890–1935* (New York: Free Press, 1994).

6. Roberts, *Killing the Black Body*, 207.

7. For a full analysis on the positive impact of the Great Society programs on Black economic positioning, see Linda Faye Williams, "An Assault on White Privilege: Civil Rights and the Great Society," in Linda F. Williams, *The Constraint of Race: Legacies of White Skin Privilege in America* (University Park: Pennsylvania State University Press, 2003), 107–66. For the backlash against these programs and the shift to retrenchment beginning with the Nixon administration through the Reagan-Bush era, see Linda Faye Williams, "The Path Bends: Retrenchment from Nixon Through Reagan-Bush," in *Constraint of Race*, 167–218.

8. Clarence Y. H. Lo, *Small Property Versus Big Government: The Social Origins of the Property Tax Revolt* (Berkeley: University of California Press, 1990), 5.

9. Lo, *Small Property*, 5.

10. Lo, *Small Property*, 5.

11. Daniel Patrick Moynihan and U.S. Department of Labor, Office of Policy Planning and Research, *The Negro Family, the Case for National Action* (Washington, DC: U.S. Government Printing Office, 1965).

12. Roberts, *Killing the Black Body*; Angela Y. Davis, *Women, Race, and Class* (New York: Random House, 1981); Patricia Hill Collins, *Black Sexual Politics: African Americans, Gender, and the New Racism* (New York: Routledge, 2005); Kimberly Springer, *Living for the Revolution: Black Feminist Organizations, 1968–1980* (Durham, NC: Duke University Press, 2005).

13. Springer, *Living for the Revolution*, 38.

14. Springer, *Living for the Revolution*, 39.

15. Elena Gutiérrez, *Fertile Matters: The Politics of Mexican-Origin Women's Reproduction* (Austin: University of Texas Press, 2008), 14.

16. Gutiérrez, *Fertile Matters*, 21.

17. Gutiérrez, *Fertile Matters*, 29.

18. Gutiérrez, *Fertile Matters*, 27.

19. Gutiérrez, *Fertile Matters*, 27.

20. Gutiérrez, *Fertile Matters*, 34.

21. For a great summary of policy shifts toward neoliberalism during the Reagan era, see David Harvey, *A Brief History of Neoliberalism* (Oxford, UK: Oxford University Press, 2005).

22. Thomas Shapiro, quoted in Lipsitz, *How Racism Takes Place*, 4.

23. Jimmie Reeves, *Cracked Coverage: Television News, the Anti-Cocaine Crusade, and the Reagan Legacy* (Durham, NC: Duke University Press, 1994), 97.

24. Gutiérrez, *Fertile Matters*, 24.

25. For full analysis, see Reeves, *Cracked Coverage*, 73–104.

26. Herman Gray, *Watching Race: Television and the Struggle for "Blackness"* (Minneapolis: University of Minnesota Press, 1995), 20.

27. See Hill Collins, *Black Sexual Politics*, 119–48.

28. U.S. Department of Defense, *Demographics 2010: Profile of the Military Community* (Washington, DC: Office of the Deputy Under Secretary of Defense for Military Community and Family Policy, n.d.), 17–18, www.militaryonesource.mil/12038/MOS/Reports/2010_Demographics_Report.pdf (accessed June 4, 2014).

29. William A. Darity and Samuel L. Myers, "Impacts of Violent Crime on Black Family Structure," *Contemporary Economic Policy* 8, no. 4 (1990): 15–29.

30. William A. Darity and Samuel L. Myers, "Family Structure and the Marginalization of Black Men: Policy Implications," in *The Decline in Marriage Among African Americans: Causes, Consequences, and Policy Implications*, ed. M. Belinda Tucker and Claudia Mitchell-Kernan (New York: Russell Sage Foundation, 1995), 263.

31. Darity and Myers, "Family Structure," 264; William A. Darity and Samuel L. Myers, "Does Welfare Dependency Cause Female Headship? The Case of the Black Family," *Journal of Marriage and the Family* 46, no. 4 (1984): 765.

32. Jill Quadagno, *The Color of Welfare: How Racism Undermined the War on Poverty* (Oxford, UK: Oxford University Press, 1994), 175.

33. For an extensive analysis of Johnson's War on Poverty policies, see Williams, "Assault on White Privilege," 106–65; see also Quadagno, *Color of Welfare*, 176.

34. Williams, "The Path Bends," 192–93.

35. Kenneth Neubeck and Noel A. Cazenave, *Welfare Racism: Playing the Race Card Against America's Poor* (New York: Routledge, 2001), 132.

36. For an in-depth examination of punitive policies tied to drug dependency and reproduction, see Dorothy Roberts, "Making Reproduction a Crime," in Roberts, *Killing the Black Body*, 150–201.

37. Neubeck and Cazenave, *Welfare Racism*, 132.

38. Study by the Committee on Ways and Means, quoted in Williams, "The Path Bends," 194.

39. For an extensive analysis of welfare reform during the Clinton years, see Linda Faye Williams, "Racially Charged Policy Making: Crime and Welfare Reform in the Clinton Years," in Williams, *Constraint of Race*, 248–77; see also Kenneth Neubeck and Noel A. Cazenave, "After AFDC and the Return of States' Rights Era Welfare Racism," in Neubeck and Cazenave, *Welfare Racism*, 177–214.

40. Ezra Klein, "Aid to Needy Families on the Decline," *Washington Post*, April 9, 2012, www.washingtonpost.com/business/economy/2012/04/09/gIQApXT06S_graphic.html (accessed July 2, 2014).

41. Neubeck and Cazenave, *Welfare Racism*, 148.

42. Evelyn Nakano Glenn, "Race, Gender, and Unequal Citizenship in the United States," in *The Changing Terrain of Race and Ethnicity*, ed. Maria Krysan and Amanda E. Lewis (New York: Russell Sage Foundation, 2004), 187–202.

43. Mae Ngai, *Impossible Subjects: Illegal Aliens and the Making of Modern America*

(Princeton, NJ: Princeton University Press, 2004), 3; emphasis in original. For extensive analyses of the convergences between immigration policies and the reproduction of racial hierarchies, see David Roediger, *Working Toward Whiteness: How America's Immigrants Became White—The Strange Journey from Ellis Island to the Suburbs* (New York: Basic Books, 2005); Nayan Shah, *Contagious Divides: Epidemics and Race in San Francisco's Chinatown* (Berkeley: University of California Press, 2001); Natalia Molina, *Fit to Be Citizens? Public Health and Race in Los Angeles, 1879–1939* (Berkeley: University of California Press, 2006); Ngai, *Impossible Subjects*; Robert G. Lee, *Orientals: Asian Americans in Popular Culture* (Philadelphia: Temple University Press, 1999); Laura Briggs, *Reproducing Empire: Race, Sex, Science, and U.S. Imperialism in Puerto Rico* (Berkeley: University of California Press, 2002); Krysan and Lewis, *Changing Terrain*; Douglas S. Massey, Jorge Durand, and Nolan J. Malone, *Beyond Smoke and Mirrors: Mexican Immigration in an Era of Economic Integration* (New York: Russell Sage Foundation, 2003); and Thomas Muller, "Nativism in the Mid-1990s: Why Now?" in *Immigrants Out! The New Nativism and the Anti-Immigrant Impulse in the United States*, ed. Juan F. Perea (New York: New York University Press, 1997), 105–18.

44. For a discussion of the specificity of post–civil rights nativism, see George J. Sanchez, "Face the Nation: Race, Immigration, and the Rise of Nativism in Late Twentieth Century America," *International Migration Review* 31, no. 4 (1997): 1009–30.

45. Ghassan Hage, *White Nation: Fantasies of White Supremacy in a Multicultural Society* (New York: Routledge, 2000); Sara Ahmed, *The Cultural Politics of Emotion* (New York: Routledge, 2004), 42–61.

46. For a more extensive discussion of the rise of nativism in the 1970s, see Gutiérrez, *Fertile Matters*, 14–34; and Leo R. Chavez, *Covering Immigration: Popular Images and the Politics of the Nation* (Berkeley: University of California Press, 2001), 19–21.

47. Chavez, *Covering Immigration*, 7.

48. Carol Morello and Ted Mellnik, "Census: Minority Babies Are Now Majority in United States," *Washington Post*, May 17, 2012, www.washingtonpost.com/local/census-minority-babies-are-now-majority-in-united-states/2012/05/16/gIQA1WY8UU_story.html (accessed July 2, 2014).

49. Chavez, *Covering Immigration*, 6–7.

50. "Federation for American Immigration Reform," Southern Poverty Law Center, n.d., www.splcenter.org/get-informed/intelligence-files/groups/federation-for-american-immigration-reform-fair (accessed September 8, 2012); Heidi Beirich, "Federation for American Immigration Reform's Hate Filled Track Record," *Intelligence Report* 128 (winter 2007), www.splcenter.org/get-informed/intelligence-report/browse-all-issues/2007/winter/the-teflon-nativists (accessed July 2, 2014); "Immigration Protesters Joined by Neo-Nazis in California," Southern Poverty Law Center, August 4, 2005, www.splcenter.org/get-informed/news/immigration-protesters-joined-by-neo-nazis-in-california (accessed July 2, 2014); "John Tanton Is the Mastermind Behind the Organized Anti-Immigration Movement," *Intelligence Report* 106 (summer 2002), www.splcenter.org/get-informed/intelligence-report/browse-all-issues/2002/summer/the-puppeteer?page=0,2 (accessed July 2, 2014); "John Tanton's Network," *Intelligence Report* 106 (summer 2002), www.splcenter.org/get-informed/intelligence-report/browse-all-issues/2002/summer/the-puppeteer/john-tantons-network (accessed July 2,

2014); "Profiles of 20 Nativist Leaders," *Intelligence Report* 129 (spring 2008), www.splcenter.
org/get-informed/intelligence-report/browse-all-issues/2008/spring/the-nativists?page=0,16
(accessed July 2, 2014); "The Man: A Biography of Kris Kobach," Southern Poverty Law
Center, January 2011, www.splcenter.org/get-informed/publications/when-mr-kobach-comes
-to-town/the-man-a-biography-of-kris-kobach (accessed August 18, 2012); Suy Buchanan and
Tom Kim, "The Nativists," *Intelligence Report* 120 (winter 2005), www.splcenter.org/get-in
formed/intelligence-report/browse-all-issues/2005/winter/the-nativists-0 (accessed November
29, 2014); Leah Nelson, Evelyn Schlatter, and Heidi Beirich, "When Mr. Kobach Comes to
Town: Nativist Laws and the Communities They Damage," January 2011, www.splcenter
.org/get-informed/publications/when-mr-kobach-comes-to-town (accessed July 3, 2014);
"Immigrants Targeted: Extremist Rhetoric Moves into the Mainstream," Anti-Defamation
League, 2007, www.adl.org/civil_rights/anti_immigrant/dont_speak_for_me.asp (accessed
August 26, 2012); Jean Stefancic, "Funding the Nativist Agenda," in Perea, *Immigrants Out*,
119–35; Deepa Fernandes, *Targeted: Homeland Security and the Business of Immigration* (New
York: Seven Stories Press, 2007), 201–38.

51. Buchanan and Kim, "The Nativists"; Nelson et al., "When Mr. Kobach Comes to
Town"; "The Man: A Biography of Kris Kobach."

52. For a great documentary on this struggle, see Ari Luis Palos, dir., *Precious Knowledge*
(Dos Vatos Productions, 2011).

53. Vijay Prashad, *The Poorer Nations: A Possible History of the Global South* (London:
Verso, 2014).

54. Chavez, *Covering Immigration*, 90–93.

55. Chavez, *Covering Immigration*, 215–62.

56. See Otto Santa Ana, *Brown Tide Rising: Metaphors of Latinos in Contemporary American Public Discourse* (Austin: University of Texas Press, 2002), 69, 83 (Tables 3.1 and 3.2).

57. Santa Ana, *Brown Tide Rising*, 101–102; emphasis in the original.

58. Daniel HoSang, *Racial Propositions: Ballot Initiatives and the Making of Postwar
California* (Berkeley: University of California Press, 2010), 182–91.

59. According to Justice Department statistics, noncitizen prisoners account for
only 5.9 percent of the combined federal and state prisoners, some of which may be
documented. Similarly, the incarceration rate for native-born men between 18 and 39
who commit the majority of crimes is five times higher than for foreign-born men. Paul
Waldman, Elbert Ventura, Robert Savillo, Susan Lin, and Greg Lewis, *Fear and Loath-
ing in Prime Time: Immigration Myths and Cable News* (Washington, DC: Media Matters
Action Network, 2008).

60. For an extensive discussion of Mexican-origin and African American women's sterilization at LACMC, see Gutiérrez, *Fertile Matters*, 35–54.

61. Neubeck and Cazenave, *Welfare Racism*, 148.

62. Roberts, *Killing the Black Body*, 104–201.

63. Juanita Díaz-Cotto, *Chicana Lives and Criminal Justice: Voices from El Barrio* (Austin: University of Texas Press, 2006), 1–30.

64. Jael Silliman, Anannya Bhattacharjee, and Angela Yvonne Davis, *Policing the National Body: Sex, Race, and Criminalization* (Cambridge, MA: South End Press, 2002); Jael
Silliman, Ynestra King, and the Committee on Women, Population, and the Environment,

Dangerous Intersections: Feminist Perspectives on Population, Environment, and Development (Cambridge MA: South End Press, 1999); Julia Sudbury, ed., *Global Lockdown: Race, Gender, and the Prison-Industrial Complex* (New York: Routledge, 2005).

65. See, for example, Gloria Feldt, *The War on Choice: The Right-Wing Attack on Women's Rights and How to Fight Back* (New York: Bantam Dell, 2004); and Cristina Page, *How the Pro-Choice Movement Saved America: Freedom, Politics, and the War on Sex* (New York: Basic Books, 2006).

CHAPTER 3

1. Clyde Adrian Woods, "Katrina's World: Blues, Bourbon, and the Return to the Source," *American Quarterly* 61, no. 3 (2009): 445.

2. I borrow the phrases *hostile privatism* and *defensive localism* from George Lipsitz to refer to people's affective and materialist investments in hoarding property and neighborhood advantages derived from cumulative histories of racial discrimination in housing solely for individual gain or community aggrandizement. Through municipal ordinances, zoning laws, taxation, and homeowners' associations, people invested in defensive localism aim to keep advantages in school funding, municipal services, and amenities in their neighborhoods while dissociating from the surrounding citywide or statewide collective goods. Likewise, unearned advantages that favor homeowners through taxation, zoning, federal, and state policies encourage the hostile privatism of individual property holders who seek to accrue wealth individually while increasingly disinvesting from communally sustainable resources and goods. George Lipsitz, *How Racism Takes Place* (Philadelphia: Temple University Press, 2011), 13.

3. Woods, "Katrina's World," 436.

4. Clyde Adrian Woods, *Development Arrested: The Blues and Plantation Power in the Mississippi Delta* (London: Verso, 1998), 29.

5. I borrow the term *emotional ecosystems* from Mindy Fullilove, who argues that the social bonds and relationships that hold neighborhoods together, particularly among folks who are asset poor, are critical to their psychological and physical sustenance and well-being. When neighborhoods are destroyed by policies such as urban renewal, these network-rich webs are radically uprooted, disrupting not merely people's homes but also the psychic and physiological ecosystems that give them support. Mindy Fullilove, *Root Shock: How Tearing Up City Neighborhoods Hurts America and What We Can Do About It* (New York: One World/Ballantine, 2004), 11.

6. "HUD Outlines Aggressive Plan to Bring Families Back to New Orleans' Public Housing," news release, June 14, 2006, archives.hud.gov/news/2006/pro6-066.cfm (accessed July 7, 2012).

7. U.S. Congress, House Committee on Financial Services, *Federal Housing Response to Hurricane Katrina: Hearing Before the Committee on Financial Services, U.S. House of Representatives*, 110th Cong., 1st sess., February 6, 2007 (Washington, DC: U.S. Government Printing Office, 2007), 273.

8. U.S. Congress, House Committee on Financial Services, *Federal Housing Response to Hurricane Katrina*, 317.

9. Lisa K. Bates and Rebekah A. Green, "Housing Recovery in the Ninth Ward," in

Race, Place, and Environmental Justice After Hurricane Katrina: Struggles to Reclaim, Rebuild, and Revitalize New Orleans and the Gulf Coast, ed. Robert D. Bullard and Beverly Wright (Boulder, CO: Westview Press, 2009), 234–35.

10. Legislation to compensate homeowners for housing reconstruction was approved 10 months after Hurricane Katrina had passed. The company responsible for administering the Road Home Program recorded only 50,000 out of 184,000 applications two years after Katrina; they cited funding shortfalls for the inaction. See Chris Kromm and Sue Sturgis, *Hurricane Katrina and the Guiding Principles on Internal Displacement: A Global Human Rights Perspective on a National Disaster* (Durham, NC: Institute for Southern Studies, January 2008), 23–24.

11. U.S. Congress, House Committee on Financial Services, *Federal Housing Response to Hurricane Katrina*, 275.

12. William P. Quigley, "Obstacle to Opportunity: Housing That Working and Poor People Can Afford in New Orleans Since Katrina," *Wake Forest Law Review* 42, no. 2 (2007): 402.

13. "The Battle to Save New Orleans Public Housing," Democracy Now, December 20, 2007, www.democracynow.org/2007/12/20/the_battle_to_save_new_orleans (accessed July 6, 2012).

14. Jane M. Henrici, Allison Suppan Helmuth, and Rhea Fernandes, "Mounting Losses: Women and Public Housing After Hurricane Katrina," Institute for Women's Policy Research, August 2010, 1, www.iwpr.org/publications/pubs/mounting-losses-women-and-public-housing-after-hurricane-katrina (accessed July 7, 2012).

15. Quigley, "Obstacle to Opportunity," 405; Kromm and Sturgis, *Hurricane Katrina*, 23.

16. Quoted in Consent Order, *Greater New Orleans Fair Housing Action Center and Wallace Rodrigue v. St. Bernard Parish and St. Bernard Parish Council*, Civil Action 2:06-CV-07185-HGB-SS, Document 104, February 20, 2008, 2, www.lawyerscommittee.org/admin/fair_housing/documents/files/0025.pdf (accessed October 8, 2014).

17. U.S. Congress, House Committee on Financial Services, *Federal Housing Response to Hurricane Katrina*, 92.

18. U.S. Congress, House Committee on Financial Services, *Federal Housing Response to Hurricane Katrina*, 92.

19. Stephanie Caruso, "Homeowner Dreads Rentals," *Times-Picayune*, March 31, 2009, sec. Metro-Editorial, 6.

20. Chris Holmes, "St. Bernard Homeowners Won't Give Up Fight," *Times-Picayune*, July 12, 2008, sec. Metro-Editorial, 6.

21. Julie Landry, "A Stable, Affordable Parish," *Times-Picayune*, October 6, 2006, sec. Metro-Editorial, 6.

22. Landry, "Stable, Affordable Parish," 6.

23. Donna Kathmann, "St. Bernard Protecting Lifestyle," *Times-Picayune*, October 8, 2006, sec. Metro-Editorial, 6.

24. Randy Bourdreaux, "Working vs. Nonworking Poor," *Times-Picayune*, October 28, 2006, sec. Metro-Editorial, 6; Jean P. Smith, "Vouchers Push Rents Sky-High," *Times-Picayune*, October 17, 2006, sec. Metro-Editorial, 4.

25. Chris Vogler, "Section 8 Is a Threat to Stability," *Times-Picayune*, November 2, 2006, sec. Metro-Editorial, 6.

26. Chris Roberts, "Poverty Is not a Crime; Clustering It Should Be," *Times-Picayune*, February 27, 2007, sec. Metro-Editorial, 4.

27. Quoted in George Lipsitz, "Learning from New Orleans: The Social Warrant of Hostile Privatism and Competitive Consumer Citizenship," *Cultural Anthropology* 21, no. 3 (2006): 453.

28. Mark Waller, "LaBruzzo Considering Plan to Pay Poor Women $1,000 to Have Tubes Tied," *Times-Picayune*, September 23, 2008, www.nola.com/news/index.ssf/2008/09/labruzzo_sterilization_plan_fi.html (accessed July 25, 2012).

29. Waller, "LaBruzzo Considering Plan."

30. "WHJI and NOWHC Respond to LaBruzzo," A Katrina Reader, n.d., katrinareader.org/whji-and-nowhc-respons-labruzzo (accessed July 27, 2012).

31. Clyde Adrian Woods, "Les Misérables of New Orleans: Trap Economics and the Asset Stripping Blues, Part 1," *American Quarterly* 61, no. 3 (2009): 771.

32. Douglas Massey and Nancy Denton, *American Apartheid: Segregation and the Making of the Underclass* (Cambridge, MA: Harvard University Press, 1993).

33. For detailed statistics on these indicators of well-being, see Woods, "Les Misérables of New Orleans," 773.

34. George Lipsitz, *The Possessive Investment in Whiteness: How White People Profit from Identity Politics*, rev. ed. (Philadelphia: Temple University Press, 2006); Lipsitz, *How Racism Takes Place*; Robert D. Bullard and Beverly Wright, *Race, Place, and Environmental Justice After Hurricane Katrina: Struggles to Reclaim, Rebuild, and Revitalize New Orleans and the Gulf Coast* (Boulder, CO: Westview Press, 2009); Thomas Shapiro, *The Hidden Cost of Being African American: How Wealth Perpetuates Inequality* (New York: Oxford University Press, 2004); Melvin Oliver and Thomas M. Shapiro, *Black Wealth/White Wealth: A New Perspective on Racial Inequality* (New York: Routledge, 1995).

35. Daphne Spain, "Race Relations and Residential Segregation in New Orleans: Two Centuries of Paradox," *Annals of the American Academy of Political and Social Science* 441 (January 1, 1979): 83.

36. Spain, "Race Relations," 89.

37. Martha Mahoney, "Law and Racial Geography: Public Housing and the Economy in New Orleans," *Stanford Law Review* 42, no. 5 (1990): 1275.

38. Spain, "Race Relations," 90.

39. Spain, "Race Relations," 90.

40. Spain, "Race Relations," 91. As Spain points out, voter registration of Black adults may not actually present a full picture of actual Black population concentration in these wards, because historically Black people have had lower rates of voter registration in areas that are economically marginalized. But the 1977 election of the first Black mayor of New Orleans may have correlated with higher Black voter registration and generally supports the view the Black residential concentration was increasing by the late 1970s.

41. For an analysis of federal, state, and private forces involved in housing discrimination tied to New Orleans public housing, see Mahoney, "Law and Racial Geography," 1257–60; Margaret C. Gonzalez-Perez, "A House Divided: Public Housing Policy in New Orleans," *Louisiana History* 44, no. 4 (2003): 443–61; Lipsitz, *Possessive Investment in Whiteness*; Lipsitz, *How Racism Takes Place*; and David Roediger, *Working Toward Whiteness: How*

America's Immigrants Became White—The Strange Journey from Ellis Island to the Suburbs (New York: Basic Books, 2005).

42. George Lipsitz, "The Racialization of Space and the Spatialization of Race Theorizing the Hidden Architecture of Landscape," *Landscape Journal* 26, no. 1 (2007): 10–23; Shapiro, *Hidden Cost of Being African American*; Oliver and Shapiro, *Black Wealth/White Wealth*.

43. Mahoney, "Law and Racial Geography," 1260.

44. Woods, "Les Misérables of New Orleans," 773.

45. Adam Fairclough, quoted in Woods, "Les Misérables of New Orleans," 773.

46. Kelly Knapp, "The Salience of Race in the Context of Katrina," Working Paper, University of Southern California, May 15, 2006, 17.

47. Spain, "Race Relations," 92.

48. Woods, "Les Misérables of New Orleans," 772.

49. Woods, "Katrina's World."

50. The Defend New Orleans Public Housing website, www.defendneworleanspublic housing.org (accessed December 21, 2007), which is now defunct, listed 60 organizations that endorsed the following demands: "(1) No Demolition until 1:1 replacement is guaranteed; (2) Resident participation in any redevelopment planning." These organizations included: Advocates for Environmental Human Rights; Agenda for Children African American Leadership Project; American-Arab Anti-Discrimination Committee of New Orleans; Amnesty International USA; Anti Racism Working Group; Ashe Cultural Arts Center; Baptist Peace Fellowship of North America; Black Love Movement; Center for Empowered Decision Making; Central City Partnership; Christian Unity Baptist Church; Churches Supporting Churches; Common Ground Health Clinic; Craige Cultural Center; Critical Resistance New Orleans; C3/Hands Off Iberville; Ebenezer Baptist Church; European Dissent; Faith in Action Evangelistic Team; Faith Temple Church of God the Holy Ghost Center, New Orleans First United Baptist Church; FYRE Youth Squad; Gert Town Revival Initiative Inc.; Greater New Orleans Fair Housing Action Center; Hope House; INCITE! New Orleans; Institute of Women and Ethnic Studies; Left Turn Magazine; Louisiana Justice Institute; Louisiana Unity Coalition on Black Civic Participation; Malcolm X Grassroots Movement; Mennonite Central Committee, New Orleans; Mennonite Disaster Service; Millions More Movement; Moving Forward Gulf Coast Inc.; NAACP Legal Defense and Educational Fund Inc.; National Association for the Advancement of Colored People (NAACP); National Coalition on Black Civic Participation; National Hip-Hop Political Convention; National Trust for Historic Preservation; New Orleans Interfaith Worker Justice; New Orleans International Human Rights Film Festival; New Orleans Women's Health and Justice Initiative; New Orleans Women's Health Clinic; New Orleans Workers' Center for Racial Justice; Nothin' but Fire Records; Pax Christi, New Orleans; People's Hurricane Relief Fund; People's Institute for Survival and Beyond; Praxis Project; Renaissance Project; Restaurant Opportunities Center, New Orleans; Safe Streets, Strong Communities; Situations: Project for the Radical Imagination; Southern Christian Leadership Conference; Total Community Action Faith Collaborative; Twomey Center for Peace Through Justice; United Teachers of New Orleans; Welfare Rights Organization; Youth Inspirational Connection Inc.; and Youth Media Council.

51. Rachel E. Luft, "Beyond Disaster Exceptionalism: Social Movement Developments in New Orleans After Hurricane Katrina," *American Quarterly* 61, no. 3 (2009): 516. For a longer discussion on the use of a human rights framework to stage the struggle for the right of return, see Luft's discussion on pages 516–24.

52. *Yolanda Anderson et al. v. Alphonso Jackson, Secretary of the United States Department of Housing and Urban Development, et al.*, U.S. District Court for the Eastern District of Louisiana 2007, Civil Action No. 06-3298, sec. B(5), E.D.La. 9-11-2007.

53. "Thousands of New Orleans Public Housing Units to Be Destroyed as 200,000+ Low-Income Residents Remain Displaced," Democracy Now, June 20, 2006, www.democracynow.org/2006/6/20/thousands_of_new_orleans_public_housing (accessed July 25, 2012); "Battle to Save New Orleans Public Housing"; "HUD Poised to Tear Down New Orleans Public Housing Developments," Democracy Now, December 12, 2007, www.democracynow.org/2007/12/12/hud_poised_to_tear_down_new (accessed July 25, 2012); "As Police Arrest Public Housing Activists in New Orleans, Federal Officials Try to Silence Leading Attorney for Low-Income Residents," Democracy Now, January 31, 2007, www.democracynow.org/2007/1/31/as_police_arrest_public_housing_activists (accessed July 25, 2012); "Community and Resistance After Katrina: Jordan Flaherty and Tracie Washington on the Fight to Save New Orleans," Democracy Now, August 30, 2010, www.democracynow.org/2010/8/30/community_resistance_after_katrina_jordan_flaherty (accessed July 25, 2012); "Fight to Reopen New Orleans Public Housing 'Horrible Slow and Tragic,'" Democracy Now, September 4, 2007, www.democracynow.org/2007/9/4/fight_to_reopen_new_orleans_public (accessed July 25, 2012).

54. "Fight to Reopen New Orleans Public Housing."

55. U.S. Congress, House Committee on Financial Services, *Solving the Affordable Housing Crisis in the Gulf Coast Region Post Katrina, Part I: Statement of Tracie L. Washington, Director, NAACP Gulf Coast Advocacy Center*, 110th Cong., 1st sess., February 22, 2007.

56. Henrici et al., "Mounting Losses," 1–2.

57. Bill Walsh, "Feds Oppose Full Replacement of N.O. Public Housing Units," *Times-Picayune*, September 26, 2007, www.nola.com/timespic/stories/index.ssf?/base/news-2/1190786785155740.xml&coll=1 (accessed July 25, 2012).

58. Mark Alan Zelden, "Taxpayers Abused Long Enough," *Times-Picayune*, February 14, 2007, sec. Metro-Editorial, 6.

59. Erica Williams, Olga Sorokina, Avis Jones-DeWeever, and Heidi Hartmann, *The Women of New Orleans and the Gulf Coast: Multiple Disadvantages and Key Assets for Recovery. Part II. Gender, Race, and Class in the Labor Market* (Washington, DC: Institute for Women's Policy Research, July 2006). As Williams and colleagues argue, because of substandard wages and persistent underemployment and/or unemployment, "Many of the poor do in fact work, but are unable to make ends meet. Nationally, 45.3 percent of the population 16 and older living below the poverty line worked in 2004 (51.3 percent of poor men and 41.4 percent of poor women). In New Orleans city, the rate was slightly higher for women than nationally (45.4 percent vs. 41.4 percent), and substantially lower for men (39.1 percent vs. 51.3 percent). . . . Such high rates of employment among the poor indicate that many jobs simply do not provide enough hours of work or dollars per hour to enable families to escape poverty despite their considerable efforts" (11).

60. For examples of these narratives and fantasy constructions throughout U.S. history, see Patricia Hill Collins, *Black Sexual Politics: African Americans, Gender, and the New Racism* (New York: Routledge, 2005); Marlon T. Riggs, dir., *Ethnic Notions*, documentary (San Francisco: California Newsreel, 2004); Cedric J. Robinson, *Forgeries of Memory and Meaning: Blacks and the Regimes of Race in American Theater and Film Before World War II* (Chapel Hill: University of North Carolina Press, 2007); and Ida B. Wells-Barnett, *On Lynchings* (Amherst, NY: Humanity Books, 2002).

61. Aside from the well-documented mismanagement, complete chaos, dysfunction, and corruption of FEMA, New Orleans reconstruction has also been severely affected by the infrastructural dysfunction of the Housing Authority of New Orleans (HANO). As a result of corruption, negligence, and leadership turnover, HANO has been in partial receivership by the U.S. Department of Housing and Urban Development (HUD) since 1979 and in full administrative receivership since 2002. HANO operated 7,000 public housing units in New Orleans, 5,100 of which were occupied by low-income households. Under the U.S. Housing Act of 1937, as amended in 1998, HUD has two years to restore a troubled agency to functional status. Because this has not been accomplished, HANO has essentially been run by HUD, with decisions about public housing being made by HUD authorities. This merger does not allow review processes between local housing authorities and HUD, creating significant conflicts of interest, because HUD is technically the entity meant to supervise and review HANO. As an example of what HUD's failure to restore HANO has produced, Louisiana senator Mary Landrieu's letter to HUD secretary Alphonso Jackson indicates that HANO's current administrative receiver does not even live in New Orleans and that the chairman of the HANO board is a HUD official in Fort Worth, Texas. See Sheila Crowley's statement in U.S. Congress, House Committee on Financial Services, *Federal Housing Response to Hurricane Katrina*, 86, 267. In addition, HUD secretary Alphonso Jackson was under investigation for awarding HUD contracts to friends of President Bush (Elisabeth Williamson, "Probe Finds Jackson Urged Favoritism in HUD Contracts," *Washington Post*, September 22, 2006). Jackson was also suspected of withdrawing federal funding from the Philadelphia Housing Authority as a result of PHA director Carl Greene's refusal to give valuable public land to a friend of Jackson's ("Philadelphia Story: HUD Secretary Alphonso Jackson Faces Familiar Allegations from the City's Housing Authority," *Washington Post*, February 11, 2008). According to "Philadelphia Story," "No fewer than four [housing] authorities are investigating Housing and Urban Development Secretary Alphonso Jackson for his alleged role in helping award lucrative contracts to friends at housing agencies in New Orleans and the Virgin Islands."

62. For much more detailed analyses of housing discrimination along racial lines in the private housing market, see Jeannie Haubert Weil, "Discrimination, Segregation, and the Racialized Search for Housing Post-Katrina," in *Through the Eye of Katrina: Social Justice in the United States*, ed. Kristin Ann Bates and Richelle S. Swan (Durham, NC: Carolina Academic Press, 2007), 221–38; National Fair Housing Alliance, *No Home for the Holidays: Report on Housing Discrimination Against Hurricane Katrina Survivors* (Washington, DC: National Fair Housing Alliance, December 20, 2005); and National Fair Housing Alliance, *Still No Home for the Holidays: Report on Housing and Housing Discrimination in the Gulf Coast Region* (Washington, DC: National Fair Housing Alliance, December 22, 2006).

63. Manuel Pastor, Robert D. Bullard, James K. Boyce, Alice Fothergill, Rachel Morello-Frosch, and Beverly Wright, *In the Wake of the Storm: Environment, Disaster, and Race After Katrina* (New York: Russell Sage Foundation, 2006).

64. See Kristen L. Buras, "Benign Neglect? Drowning Yellow Buses, Racism, and Disinvestment in the City That Bush Forgot," in *Schooling and the Politics of Disaster*, ed. Kenneth J. Saltman (New York: Routledge, 2007), 103–22.

65. Kenneth Brad Ott, "The Closure of New Orleans' Charity Hospital After Hurricane Katrina: A Case of Disaster Capitalism," Master's thesis, University of New Orleans, 2012, scholarworks.uno.edu/td/1472 (accessed July 16, 2012); Woods, "Les Misérables of New Orleans," 784–87.

66. Bates and Green, "Housing Recovery."

67. For a detailed account of these interrelated housing issues, see Sheila Crowley, "Where Is Home? Housing for Low Income People After the 2005 Hurricanes," in *There Is No Such Thing as Natural Disaster*, ed. Chester Hartman and Gregory D. Squires (New York: Routledge, 2006), 121–66.

68. Lipsitz, *Possessive Investment in Whiteness*, 106.

69. Lipsitz, *How Racism Takes Place*, 3.

70. Amy Liu and Allison Plyer, *The New Orleans Index: Tracking the Recovery of New Orleans and the Metro Area* (Washington, DC: Brookings Institution Metropolitan Policy Program; and New Orleans: Greater New Orleans Community Data Center, August 2009), 17–23. For detailed neighborhood data based on the 2010 census, the American Community Survey of 2006–2010, and the 2010 Local Employment Dynamics data, see the Greater New Orleans Community Data Center website, www.datacenterresearch.org/data-resources/neighborhood-data/ (accessed November 28, 2014).

71. Martin Savidge, "What's Next for Public Housing in New Orleans?" MSNBC.com, February 21, 2006, www.msnbc.msn.com/id/11485681/ns/nbcnightlynews/t/whats-next-public-housing-new-orleans/ (accessed July 25, 2012).

72. Williams et al., *Women of New Orleans*, 26–29.

73. *Anderson et al. v. Jackson et al.*

74. "Police Arrest Public Housing Activists."

75. "All Out to Defend New Orleans Public Housing Activist Sharon Jasper," C3/Hands Off Iberville, July 11, 2010, c3handsoffiberville.blogspot.com/2010/07/all-out-to-defend-new-orleans-public.html (accessed July 25, 2012).

76. "New Orleans Police Attack Peaceful March at St. Bernard," December 16, 2007, www.youtube.com/watch?v=9GPjNhVUzqk&feature=youtube_gdata_player (accessed July 25, 2012).

77. "New Orleans City Hall Protest, December 20, 2007, Video 1," December 20, 2007, www.youtube.com/watch?v=5jvhp4iZFdo&feature=youtube_gdata_player (accessed July 25, 2012); "New Orleans City Hall Protest, December 20, 2007, Video 2," December 20, 2007, www.youtube.com/watch?v=1b6zGunXBas&feature=youtube_gdata_player (accessed July 25, 2012); "New Orleans City Hall Protest, December 20, 2007, Video 3," December 20, 2007, www.youtube.com/watch?v=W4ksBmZqTRk&feature=youtube_gdata_player (accessed July 25, 2012); "New Orleans City Council Shuts Down Public Housing Debate," December 21, 2007, www.youtube.com/watch?v=cMBWAXfGsc4&fea

ture=youtube_gdata_player (accessed July 25, 2012); "New Orleans: Man-Made Disaster," Big Noise Films, n.d., www.bignoisefilms.com/videowire/38-latest/80-new-orleans-man -made-disaster (accessed July 25, 2012).

78. "New Orleans Police Taser, Pepper Spray Residents Seeking to Block Public Housing Demolition," Democracy Now, December 21, 2007, www.democracynow.org/2007/12/21/ new_orleans_police_taser_pepper_spray (accessed July 25, 2012).

79. "New Orleans Police Taser."

80. Indeed, HUD seemed to be the primary agent advocating for the demolitions, because the New Orleans City Council endorsed these federal decisions through the absence of opposition and dissent. Two months after they unanimously voted to go ahead with the demolitions, the City Council stated that if they had decided to keep the public housing units, New Orleans would have "los[t] federal funding for future redevelopment and assistance for displaced residents wanting to return home." "Response to United Nations Statement Regarding Public Housing Demolition in New Orleans," New Orleans City Council, February 28, 2008, www.nocitycouncil.com/newsfiles/2008/2008Feb28NewOrleansCity CouncilStatement.pdf (accessed March 7, 2008).

81. "New Orleans Police Taser, Pepper Spray Residents."

82. Jessica Pardee and Kevin Gotham, "HOPE VI, Section 8, and the Contradictions of Low-Income Housing Policy," *Journal of Poverty* 9, no. 2 (2005): 2.

83. Pardee and Gotham, "HOPE VI," 2.

84. Brittany Libson, "River Garden: New Orleans' Model for Mixed-Income Housing," *Social Policy* 37, no. 3 (2007): 104.

85. Libson, "River Garden," 103.

86. Libson, "River Garden," 104.

87. Libson, "River Garden," 105.

88. U.S. Congress, House Committee on Financial Services, *Federal Housing Response to Hurricane Katrina*, 359.

89. Libson, "River Garden," 100.

90. National Fair Housing Alliance, *Still No Home for the Holidays*, 15.

91. James Fraser, "The Promise of Mixed-Income Housing for Poverty Amelioration," n.d., 2–3, www.law.unc.edu/documents/poverty/publications/jimfraserpolicybrief.pdf (accessed March 13, 2008).

92. Akeem the Dream, *No Surrender No Retreat* (New Orleans, LA: Nothin' But Fire Records, 2007), December 31, 2007, www.youtube.com/watch?v=j8eTlD2VExE&feature= youtube_gdata_player (accessed July 26, 2012).

93. Sue Hilderbrand, Scott Crow, and Lisa Fithian, "Common Ground Relief," in *What Lies Beneath: Katrina, Race, and the State of the Nation*, ed. South End Press Collective (Cambridge, MA: South End Press, 2007). See also katrinareader.org/common-ground -collective (accessed July 27, 2012).

94. Malik Rahim, "This Is Criminal," in South End Press Collective, ed., *What Lies Beneath* 65–68; "'This Is Criminal': Malik Rahim Reports from New Orleans," A Katrina Reader, n.d., katrinareader.org/criminal-malik-rahim-reports-new-orleans (accessed July 27, 2012).

95. "Remembering Althea Francois, Beloved Louisiana Black Panther, Prison Abo-

litionist, 'Pillar in Our Struggle,'" *San Francisco Bay View*, March 12, 2010, sfbayview
.com/2010/remembering-althea-francois-beloved-louisiana-black-panther-prison-abolitionist
-%E2%80%98pillar-in-our-struggle%E2%80%99/ (accessed July 27, 2012).

96. For extensive examination of the significance of the Neville Brothers and their ties
to Mardi Gras Indians, see Lipsitz, *How Racism Takes Place*, 211–37; and George Lipsitz,
"Mardi Gras Indians: Carnival and Counter-Narrative in Black New Orleans," in *American
Studies: An Anthology*, ed. Janice A. Radway, Kevin K. Gaines, Barry Shank, and Penny Von
Eschen (Malden, MA: Wiley-Blackwell, 2009), 290–98.

97. Mark Guarino, "The Big Easy Bounces Back with Its Own Hip-Hop Beat," *Christian Science Monitor*, July 22, 2010, www.csmonitor.com/The-Culture/Music/2010/0722/
The-Big-Easy-bounces-back-with-its-own-hip-hop-beat/ (accessed July 27, 2012).

98. For extensive discussions on the significance of the Mardi Gras Indians to grassroots
organizing, resistance, and cultural traditions rooted in the Blues epistemology, see Lipsitz,
Possessive Investment in Whiteness, 237–48; and Lipsitz, *How Racism Takes Place*, 211–37.

99. Joanna Dubinsky, "An Unfragmented Movement: Interview with Shana Griffin,"
February 6, 2006, www.incite-national.org/media/docs/1037_unfragmented.pdf (accessed
May 22, 2008).

100. For a longer articulation of the key intersections between reproductive violence,
disaster, and public asset stripping, see Shana Griffin and Clyde Adrian Woods, "The Politics of Reproductive Violence: An Interview with Shana Griffin by Clyde Woods, March
12, 2009," *American Quarterly* 61, no. 3 (2009): 583–91.

101. Charmaine Neville, "How We Survived the Flood," in South End Press Collective,
ed., *What Lies Beneath*, 28–30.

102. Janelle White, quoted in Alisa Bierria, Mayaba Liebenthal, and INCITE! Women
of Color Against Violence, "To Render Ourselves Visible: Women of Color Organizing and
Hurricane Katrina," in South End Press Collective, ed., *What Lies Beneath*, 34.

103. Bierria et al., "To Render Ourselves Visible," 39; emphasis mine.

104. Bierria et al., "To Render Ourselves Visible," 44.

105. INCITE! Women of Color Against Violence website, www.incite-national.
org//?s=46&m=21 (accessed May 19, 2008).

106. Patterson, Sunni, "We Made It," February 13, 2008, www.youtube.com/watch?v=
gvruVHVPOZE&feature=youtube_gdata_player (accessed July 27, 2012). Reprinted with
permission.

107. "'The Resilience of the People Is What Carries This City Forward': Poet Sunni
Patterson and Hip-Hop Artist Truth Universal Reflect on New Orleans Two Years After
Katrina," Democracy Now, August 31, 2007, www.democracynow.org/2007/8/31/the_resil
ience_of_the_people_is (accessed July 25, 2012).

CHAPTER 4

1. Brentin Mock, "Immigration Backlash: Violence Engulfs Latinos," *Intelligence Report*
128 (winter 2007), www.splcenter.org/get-informed/intelligence-report/browse-all-issues/2007/
winter/immigration-backlash (accessed November 29, 2014).

2. Two skinheads attacked Ritcheson at a house party in Houston, Texas, on April 22,
2006. David Henry Tuck and Keith Robert Turner knocked Ritcheson unconscious, burned

him with cigarettes, called him a spic and a wetback, attempted to carve a swastika on his chest, poured bleach on him, and finally anally raped him with a patio umbrella pole. Thirty surgeries later, Ritcheson returned to school and eventually testified in front of the U.S. House of Representatives Judiciary Committee, which was deliberating the strengthening of federal hate crime laws. Less than three months later, Ritcheson committed suicide. Mock, "Immigration Backlash."

3. "Border Vigilantes Get Death in Arizona Double Murder," *Intelligence Report* 142 (summer 2011), www.splcenter.org/get-informed/intelligence-report/browse-all-issues/2011/ summer/border-vigilantes-get-death-in-arizon (accessed July 25, 2014).

4. Ian Gordon and Tasneem Raja, "164 Anti-Immigration Laws Passed Since 2010? A MoJo Analysis," *Mother Jones*, March/April 2012, www.motherjones.com/politics/2012/03/ anti-immigration-law-database (accessed August 4, 2014).

5. Rigel C. Oliveri, "Between a Rock and a Hard Place: Landlords, Latinos, Anti-Illegal Immigrant Ordinances, and Housing Discrimination," *Vanderbilt Law Review* 62, no. 1 (2009): 56.

6. Jill Louise Esbenshade, *Division and Dislocation: Regulating Immigration Through Local Housing Ordinances* (Washington, DC: Immigration Policy Center, American Immigration Law Foundation, summer 2007), 9, www.immigrationpolicy.org/images/File/specialreport/ IPC%20Special%20Report%20PR.pdf (accessed August 4, 2014).

7. For a timeline on the various legal battles over Hazleton's ordinances, see Leah Nelson, Evelyn Schlatter, and Heidi Beirich, "When Mr. Kobach Comes to Town: Nativist Laws and the Communities They Damage," Southern Poverty Law Center, January 2011, 21, www.splcenter.org/get-informed/publications/when-mr-kobach-comes-to-town (accessed September 7, 2012).

8. For extensive discussions on John Tanton and FAIR, see Elena Gutiérrez, *Fertile Matters: The Politics of Mexican-Origin Women's Reproduction* (Austin: University of Texas Press, 2008), 73–93; "Federation for American Immigration Reform," Southern Poverty Law Center, n.d., www.splcenter.org/get-informed/intelligence-files/groups/federation-for-american -immigration-reform-fair (accessed September 8, 2012); and Heidi Beirich, "Federation for American Immigration Reform's Hate Filled Track Record," *Intelligence Report* 128 (winter 2007), www.splcenter.org/get-informed/intelligence-report/browse-all-issues/2007/winter/ the-teflon-nativists (accessed September 8, 2012).

9. David A. Fahrenthold, "Self-Deportation Proponents Kris Kobach, Michael Hethmon Facing Time of Trial," *Washington Post*, April 24, 2012, www.washingtonpost.com/politics/ time-of-trial-for-proponents-of-self-deportation/2012/04/24/gIQAe6lheT_story.html (accessed August 18, 2012); "The Man: A Biography of Kris Kobach," Southern Poverty Law Center, January 2011, www.splcenter.org/get-informed/publications/when-mr-kobach-comes -to-town/the-man-a-biography-of-kris-kobach (accessed August 18, 2012).

10. Marisa Bono, "Don't You Be My Neighbor: Restrictive Housing Ordinances as the New Jim Crow," *Modern American* 3, no. 2 (2007): 31–34.

11. Nelson et al., "When Mr. Kobach Comes to Town," 9; Fahrenthold, "Self-Deportation Proponents."

12. Nelson et al., "When Mr. Kobach Comes to Town," 16.

13. Adam Liptak, "Blocking Parts of Arizona Law, Justices Allow Its Centerpiece," *New*

York Times, June 25, 2012, www.nytimes.com/2012/06/26/us/supreme-court-rejects-part-of
-arizona-immigration-law.html (accessed September 9, 2012).

14. Fahrenthold, "Self-Deportation Proponents."

15. Esbenshade, *Division and Dislocation,* 2.

16. Esbenshade, *Division and Dislocation,* 2.

17. Jennifer Moroz, "Immigrants Gone, but at What Cost? Riverside Deals with Law of
Unintended Consequences," *Philadelphia Inquirer,* January 21, 2007, articles.philly.com/2007
-01-21/news/25220694_1_brazilian-community-thousands-of-illegal-immigrants-immigrant
-community (accessed August 17, 2012); Esbenshade, *Division and Dislocation,* 12–13.

18. Jaime Longazel and Benjamin Fleury-Steiner, "Exploiting Borders: The Political
Economy of Local Backlash Against Undocumented Immigrants," *Chicana/o Latina/o Law
Review* 30, no. 43 (2011): 43–63.

19. "Escondido (City), California," U.S. Census Bureau, State and County Quick Facts,
July 8, 2014, quickfacts.census.gov/qfd/states/06/0622804.html (accessed August 24, 2012);
Arcela Núñez-Álvarez, Carolyn Kitzmann, and Ana M. Ardóon, *Mission Park Community
Survey: Escondido, California* (San Marcos: National Latino Research Center, California State
University, June 2006), 9–10, www.escondido.org/Data/Sites/1/media/pdfs/Neighborhood/
MissionParkCommunitySurvey.pdf (accessed November 29, 2014).

20. Booyeon Lee, "Escondido to Look at Housing Ordinance," *San Diego Union-
Tribune,* August 13, 2006.

21. "Targeting Landlords Who Rent to Illegal Immigrants," *All Things Considered,*
weekend ed., National Public Radio, October 21, 2006.

22. The ordinance read: "Because such individuals are not in this country lawfully,
there is an increased chance that they will reside in dwelling units without typical leasing,
payment and other tenancy arrangements that enable the civil and regulatory processes of
this City to be effective. The regulations of the City regarding housing and property maintenance often depend upon reporting by residents and neighbors as a means of bringing
unlawful conditions to the City's attention. Because illegal aliens do not wish to call attention to their presence, such individuals are less likely to report such conditions, and notify
authorities, or to participate in subsequent proceedings to remedy such conditions. This
creates an increased likelihood that housing and property maintenance violations will remain unreported, and, because such conditions are unreported, an increased chance that
such conditions will multiply in the future." "Escondido, Calif., Ordinance No. 2006-38
R," American Civil Liberties Union, October 18, 2006, www.aclu.org/immigrants-rights/
escondido-calif-ordinance-no-2006-38-r (accessed August 18, 2012).

23. Núñez-Álvarez et al., *Mission Park Community Survey,* 7.

24. Núñez-Álvarez et al., *Mission Park Community Survey,* 23–26.

25. "Escondido, Calif., Ordinance No. 2006-38 R," 2.

26. Oliveri, "Rock and a Hard Place," 65.

27. These violations included (1) violation of the supremacy clause; (2) violation of the
contracts clause; (3) violation of the First Amendment and Article I, Section 1 of the California Constitution; (4) violation of equal protection; (5) violation of procedural due process; (6) violation of 42 USC, Section 1981; (7) violation of the Federal Fair Housing Act;
(8) violation of the Fair Employment and Housing Act, Calif. Gov. Code, Section 12955, et

seq.; (9) violation of the Unruh Act, Calif. Civ. Code, Sections 51 and 52; (10) violation of legitimate police powers; and (11) state law preemption. See *Roy and Mary Garrett; Escondido Human Rights Committee; Jane Doe 1; Jane Doe 2 v. City of Escondido*, 465 F. Supp. 2d 1043, 2006 U.S. Dist. Lexis 93453 (S.D. Cal. 2006).

28. This recommendation was clearly made by the community survey conducted by the National Latino Research Center. Núñez-Álvarez et al., *Mission Park Community Survey*.

29. For extensive legal analyses of anti-immigrant housing ordinances, see Oliveri, "Rock and a Hard Place"; Daniel Eduardo Guzman, "'There Be No Shelter Here': Anti-Immigrant Housing Ordinances and Comprehensive Reform," *Cornell Journal of Law and Public Policy* 20 (2010): 399–439; Bono, "Don't You Be My Neighbor"; and Todd Donnelly Batson, "No Vacancy: Why Immigrant Housing Ordinances Violate FHA and Section 1981," *Brooklyn Law Review* 74 (fall 2008): 131–58.

30. "Escondido, Calif., Ordinance No. 2006-38 R."

31. Oliveri, "Rock and a Hard Place," 115 and footnote 245. See also "Garrett v. City of Escondido, California," American Civil Liberties Union, December 14, 2006, www.aclu .org /immigrants-rights/garrett-v-city-escondido-california-0 (accessed November 29, 2014).

32. Oliveri, "Rock and a Hard Place," 116.

33. Complaint, Rosner & Mansfield, LLP, ACLU Foundation of San Diego and Imperial, and MALDEF, *Garrett et al. v. City of Escondido*.

34. John A. Houston, in *Garrett et al. v. City of Escondido*, 15–18.

35. Paul Eakins and Noelle Ibrahim, "Hundreds Show Up to Protest or Support Escondido Law," *Union-Tribune San Diego*, October 5, 2006, web.utsandiego.com/news/2006/oct/05/hundreds-show-up-to-protest-or-support-escondido/ (accessed August 4, 2014).

36. "Reporters Discuss Escondido Housing Ordinance," KPBS Public Broadcasting, October 6, 2006, www.kpbs.org/news/2006/oct/06/reporters-discuss-escondido-housing -ordinance/ (accessed September 9, 2012).

37. Vicki Ruiz, "Nuestra América: Latino History as United States History," *Journal of American History* 93, no. 3 (2006): 662.

38. Ruiz, "Nuestra América," 656.

39. Ruiz, "Nuestra América," 660, 663, 666–67, 670.

40. Ruiz, "Nuestra América," 671.

41. Eakins and Ibrahim, "Hundreds Show Up to Protest."

42. David Fried, "More than 1,250 North County Students Protest Immigration Bill," *Union-Tribune San Diego*, March 28, 2006, www.utsandiego.com/news/2006/mar/28/more -than-1250-north-county-students-protest/ (accessed November 29, 2014).

43. Daniel Muñoz, "Escondido Hispanics Feeling Under Siege," *La Prensa San Diego*, September 24, 2010, laprensa-sandiego.org/featured/escondido-hispanics-feeling-under -siege/ (accessed August 4, 2014).

44. Fried, "1,250 North County Students Protest."

45. Kitty Calavita, "The New Politics of Immigration: 'Balanced-Budget Conservatism' and the Symbolism of Proposition 187," *Social Problems* 43, no. 3 (1996): 285.

46. "Protests Greet Tough City Immigration Law," *Hannity & Colmes*, Fox News Network, October 19, 2006, www.foxnews.com/on-air/hannity/transcript/2006/10/20/vote -prohibiting-landlords-renting-illegals-causes-riots (accessed October 22, 2014).

47. Paul Reyes, "'It's Just Not Right': The Failures of Alabama's Self-Deportation Experiment," *Mother Jones*, March/April 2012, www.motherjones.com/politics/2012/03/alabama-anti-immigration-law-self-deportation-movement (accessed August 4, 2014).

48. For a short summary of immigrants' contributions to the U.S. economy, see Justin Akers Chacón and Mike Davis, *No One Is Illegal: Fighting Violence and State Repression on the U.S.-Mexico Border* (Chicago: Haymarket Books, 2006), 155–70.

49. For an extensive study on how the property tax revolts in California influenced a decline in big business taxes, see Clarence Y. H. Lo, *Small Property Versus Big Government: The Social Origins of the Property Tax Revolt* (Berkeley: University of California Press, 1990).

50. For an extensive study of these issues, see Douglas S. Massey, Jorge Durand, and Nolan J. Malone, *Beyond Smoke and Mirrors: Mexican Immigration in an Era of Economic Integration* (New York: Russell Sage Foundation, 2003).

51. "Protests Greet Tough City Immigration Law."

52. "Protests Greet Tough City Immigration Law." Abed did not cite any specific source or authority for the fiscal burden statistics he cited or any study he used to support his contention that Escondido had gauged public support for the ordinance.

53. "A North County Times review of the e-mails sent to council members dating from July 1 [2006], shortly before the rental ban was first proposed, to Oct. 5—after the first vote on the ordinance was taken—indicates that the messages were about 72 percent in support of the ordinance to 28 percent against. Of the more than 240 e-mails, many were copies repeatedly sent to several council members at once. Some were from people who do not live in Escondido." Edward Sifuentes, "Math on Immigrant Population Doesn't Add Up, Experts Say," *North County Times*, November 4, 2006.

54. "Protests Greet Tough City Immigration Law."

55. "Protests Greet Tough City Immigration Law."

56. Jonathan Brindle, "Residential Parking Ordinance Alternatives," Staff Report, Escondido City Council, June 13, 2007, www.ci.escondido.ca.us/parking/June_13_Staff_Report.pdf (accessed September 9, 2012); Escondido City Council, City of Escondido Meeting Minutes for August 16, September 27, October 4, and October 18, 2006; Booyeon Lee, "Escondido to Pursue Housing Ordinance," *San Diego Union-Tribune*, August 17, 2006, www.utsandiego.com/uniontrib/20060817/news_7m17imm.html (accessed September 9, 2012).

57. "Escondido, Calif., Ordinance No. 2006-38 R."

58. J. Harry Jones and David E. Graham, "Escondido Council OKs Immigration Ordinance," *North County Times*, October 5, 2006.

59. Lee, "Escondido to Pursue Housing Ordinance."

60. Lee, "Escondido to Pursue Housing Ordinance."

61. David Roediger, *Working Toward Whiteness: How America's Immigrants Became White—The Strange Journey from Ellis Island to the Suburbs* (New York: Basic Books, 2005); David R. Roediger, *The Wages of Whiteness: Race and the Making of the American Working Class* (New York: Verso, 1991).

62. Escondido City Council, Meeting Minutes for August 16, September 27, October 4, and October 18, 2006.

63. Escondido City Council, Meeting Minutes for October 4, 2006, 250.

64. S. Mitra Kalita, "Dissonant Voices Inside the Border," *Washington Post*, May 11,

2006, www.washingtonpost.com/wp-dyn/content/article/2006/05/10/AR2006051002014
.html (accessed August 26, 2012).

65. Edward Sifuentes, "Claudia Spencer Is Part of Unconventional Anti-Illegal Immigrant Group," *North County Times*, October 22, 2006, www.nctimes.com/news/local/article_425e1161-8263-5f57-b286-e384945fdf7b.html (accessed August 26, 2012).

66. "Jones Joins American Hispanic Coalition to Support Immigration Enforcement Legislation," press release, July 18, 2006, jones.house.gov/press-release/jones-joins-american-hispanic-coalition-support-immigration-enforcement-legislation (accessed September 10, 2012).

67. "The Support Arizona/Boycott San Diego Coalition (SABSDC)," San Diego Citizen's Brigade, n.d., sandiegobrigade.webs.com/sabsdcoalition.htm (accessed August 4, 2014).

68. Kim Voss and Irene Bloemraad, eds., *Rallying for Immigrant Rights: The Fight for Inclusion in 21st Century America* (Berkeley: University of California Press, 2011), 3.

69. Library of Congress, "Bill Summary and Status, 109th Congress (2005–2006), H.R. 4437," n.d., thomas.loc.gov/cgi-bin/bdquery/z?d109:H.R.4437: (accessed November 29, 2014)).

70. "Immigrant Rights Groups Call for Massive Nationwide General Work Strike and Economic Boycott," Democracy Now, April 28, 2006, www.democracynow.org/2006/4/28/immigrant_rights_groups_call_for_massive (accessed August 5, 2014).

71. Amy Goodman and Juan Gonzalez, "The Meaning of the May Day Marches and the Future of the Immigrant Rights Movement," Democracy Now, May 2, 2006, www.democracynow.org/2006/5/2/the_meaning_of_the_may_day (accessed August 5, 2014).

72. Goodman and Gonzalez, "Meaning of the May Day Marches."

73. After a four-month investigation into U.S.-based anti-immigrant groups, the SPLC's 2002 *Intelligence Report* concluded "that the appearance of an array of groups with large membership bases is nothing more than a mirage. In fact, the vast majority of American anti-immigration groups—more than a dozen in all—were either formed, led, or in other ways made possible through Tanton's efforts." Southern Poverty Law Center, "John Tanton Is the Mastermind Behind the Organized Anti-Immigration Movement," *Intelligence Report* 106 (summer 2002), www.splcenter.org/get-informed/intelligence-report/browse-all-issues/2002/summer/the-puppeteer (accessed September 16, 2012).

74. Lee, "Escondido to Pursue Housing Ordinance."

75. Lee, "Escondido to Pursue Housing Ordinance."

76. Lee, "Escondido to Pursue Housing Ordinance."

77. Escondido City Council, Meeting Minutes for October 4, 2006, 4:00 p.m. Meeting Minutes, 249.

78. For an extensive analysis of such public health discourses, see Natalia Molina, *Fit to Be Citizens? Public Health and Race in Los Angeles, 1879–1939* (Berkeley: University of California Press, 2006).

79. Gutiérrez, *Fertile Matters*, 17–25.

80. Gutiérrez, *Fertile Matters*, 63.

81. Gutiérrez, *Fertile Matters*, 63.

82. Gutiérrez, *Fertile Matters*, 53.

83. Gutiérrez, *Fertile Matters*, 53.

84. "John Tanton Is the Mastermind"; "John Tanton's Network," *Intelligence Report* 106

(summer 2002), www.splcenter.org/get-informed/intelligence-report/browse-all-issues/2002/
summer/the-puppeteer/john-tantons-network (accessed September 15, 2012).

85. The websites for these four organizations are www.populationconnection.org/site/
PageServer for Population Connection, www.npg.org for Negative Population Growth, www
.balance.org for Population-Environment Balance, and www.capsweb.org for Californians
for Population Stabilization. All websites accessed September 15, 2012.

86. Daniel HoSang, *Racial Propositions: Ballot Initiatives and the Making of Postwar
California* (Berkeley: University of California Press, 2010), 130–200.

87. Chris Crass, "Controlling Gendered Immigrants and Racialized Populations:
Overpopulation, Immigration, and Environmental Sustainability," Alternative Media
Project, December 24, 2004, www.infoshop.org/texts/immigration.html (accessed No-
vember 7, 2006).

88. Lindsey Grant and Leon F. Bouvier, "Perspectives on Immigration: The Issue Is
Overpopulation," *Los Angeles Times*, August 10, 1994.

89. Grant and Bouvier, "Perspectives on Immigration."

90. H. Patricia Hynes, "Taking Population Out of the Equation: Reformulating $I =
PAT$," in *Dangerous Intersections: Feminist Perspectives on Population, Environment, and De-
velopment*, ed. Jael Silliman and Ynestra King (Cambridge, MA: South End Press, 1999),
39; emphasis in original.

91. Hynes, "Taking Population Out of the Equation," 44.

92. Lisa Cacho, "Disciplinary Fictions: The Sociality of Private Problems in Contemporary California," Ph.D. dissertation, University of California, San Diego, 68.

93. Esbenshade, "Division and Dislocation," 5.

94. Brindle, "Residential Parking Ordinance Alternatives," 10–11.

95. Eric Avila, *Popular Culture in the Age of White Flight: Fear and Fantasy in Suburban
Los Angeles* (Berkeley: University of California Press, 2004).

96. Goodman and Gonzalez, "Meaning of the May Day Marches."

97. Mike Davis, *City of Quartz*, new ed. (New York: Verso, 2006), xvii.

98. Davis, *City of Quartz*, xvii.

99. Davis, *City of Quartz*, xviii.

100. Yara Simon, "Singer Lupillo Rivera Spit on While Defending Buses Transferring
Undocumented Children to Murrieta, California," *Latin Post*, July 4, 2014, www.latinpost.
com/articles/16423/20140704/singer-lupillo-rivera-spit-defending-buses-transferring-undoc
umented-children-murrieta.htm (accessed August 6, 2014); "'Worst of the American Spirit':
Advocates Decry Anti-Immigrant Protests, Urge Asylum for Children," Democracy Now,
July 11, 2014, www.democracynow.org/2014/7/11/worst_of_the_american_spirit_advocates
(accessed August 6, 2014).

EPILOGUE

1. "For Trayvon Martin," July 17, 2013, www.youtube.com/watch?v=EG6RirUct3Y&
feature=youtube_gdata_player (accessed August 13, 2014).

2. Sophia Terazawa, "You Know Her," *Shawn Greenwood Working Group Newsletter*,
August 2013. Reprinted with permission.

3. Ben Kuebrich, "Anti-Drone Activist's One-Year Sentence Will Not Deter Movement,"

Truthout, July 31, 2014, www.truth-out.org/opinion/item/25297-anti-drone-activists-one
-year-sentence-will-not-deter-movement (accessed August 13, 2014).

4. "Tompkins County Legislature Shows Contempt for Public," Occupy Ithaca, March
6, 2014, occupyithaca.blogspot.com/2014/03/tompkins-county-legislature-shows.html (accessed August 15, 2014).

5. James Baldwin, *Collected Essays* (New York: Library of America, 1998), 293–94.

6. Audre Lorde, *Sister Outsider: Essays and Speeches* (Berkeley, CA: Crossing Press,
2007), 110–13.

INDEX

Abed, Sam (councilman, City of Escondido), 181, 187–89, 195

Abu Ghraib, 7, 81, 83, 91, 175; conservative responses to, 83, 94–98; liberal responses to, 83, 98–108; official responses to, 82; prison, 81–83, 92–93; public feelings about, 2, 97–99, 102–5, 107–8; resistance to tortures at, 26, 92–94, 108–12

Ade, Dubian, 209

Affect, 1–3, 4; negative types of, 13, 120, 122; *See also* Emotions

Affective: economies, 3, 6, 26, 38, 46, 127, 134, 223n1; enjoyment, 19–21, 37, 47, 51, 99, 135, 137; investments, 6–7, 45, 51, 128; pleasure, 3, 6, 19, 21, 37, 43, 51, 107–8, 158, 167, 231n54; receptivity, 15–16, 21, 23, 38, 147, 214; shame, 37, stigmatization, 2, 5, 115; valorization, 115; *See also* Emotional economies

Aid to Families with Dependent Children (AFDC), 117, 242n5

Akuno, Kali, 160

Alliance of Haitian Migrants, 73

American Border Patrol (ABP), 130, 175

Amodio, David, 13

Angola 3, 167

Anti–big government, 4–5, 117, 138

Anticapitalist movements, 42

Anti-immigrant: agendas, 133, 178–79; discrimination, 26, 176; municipal ordinances, 176–83; policies, 34, 40, 131, 137, 176, 198; sentiments, 97, 136, 138

Anti-imperialist movements, 42, 98

Antijail movements, 212–20

Anti-Latino/a: discrimination, 7, 189; violence, 175, 211; public feelings, 7, 131, 178, 185

Antipoverty programs, 33, 116, 125

Antiracist justice: movements, 30–33, 98, 150–54, 159–61, 165– 73, 184–86, 192–94, 203–5, 208–20; conceptualization of, 2, 15–16, 137; challenges related to, 11; emotional economies that encourage, 23–26

Antiwar movements, 98, 105, 211–12, 215

Antiwelfare: public feelings, 115–22, 136–38,

143–47, 154–58, 161–65; policies, 125–28, 136–38, 141–43

Antoine, Patrick, 62–64

Anzaldúa, Gloria, 25

The Arab Mind, 83–90, 96. *See also* Patai, Raphael

Arab Muslims: constructions of, 4, 10, 22, 30, 44, 132, 225n21; media representations of, 48–51, 94–98, 106–8; orientalist discourses about, 44–48, 83–91; policies affecting, 34, 40–41, 52–53; public feelings about, 14–15, 29, 37, 98, 103–5, 109

Aristide, Jean-Bertrand (president of Haiti), 57, 66

Arizona SB 1070, 34, 131, 178, 192

Austin Fertility Survey, 196

Baldwin, James, 25, 216–18

Barletta, Lou (mayor, City of Hazleton), 177

Beck, Glenn, 135

Behavioral deficiencies, 10, 32, 122, 219

Bell, Sean, 79, 209

Beller, Jonathan, 107

Benjamin, Walter, 26, 102–3, 105, 108

B.G. (Christopher Dorsey), 168

Black Panther Party for Self-Defense, 31, 67

Black Panther Party organizers, 67, 166

Blues agenda, 140–41, 150–54, 165–73

Blues epistemology, 141, 159, 173

Bonilla-Silva, Eduardo, 10–11, 16

Border Angels, 205

Bourbon agenda, 145, 150

Bourbon class, 140. *See also* Neo-Bourbon class

Bourbonism, 140–41, 147. *See also* Neo-Bourbonism

Bratton, William J. (police commissioner, New York City), 76

Brown, John, 26

Bruder, Thomas, 61–62, 65, 79

Bush, George W., 46, 52, 97, 103, 139

Bush, George H.W. administration, 57, 162

Bush, George W. administration, 52, 82, 98–100, 103, 111, 154

Bush, Gino, 219

Bus Riders Union, 205

Cacho, Lisa, 38, 200

Carcerality. *See* Incarceration

California Coalition for Immigration Reform (CCIR), 130, 198

Calliope, a.k.a. B.W. Cooper, public housing development (New Orleans), 142, 148, 153–54, 167, 168

Centers for Disease Control and Prevention (CDC), 57

Chev Off the Ave, 167

CIA, 21, 50, 52

Civilian Complaint Review Board (CCRB), 76

Clinton administration, 5, 40, 57, 126

Club Rendez-Vous, 55, 61–62, 65, 67, 78

C-Murder (Corey Miller), 167

Coalition to Stop the Demolitions, 152, 169

Coalition to Stop the Tompkins County Jail Expansion, 212–14, 219

Coe, Barbara, 130

Cold war, 42–43, 48, 51–52

Collins, Patricia Hill, 119

Colmes, Alan, 187–88

Color-blind discourses, 4–5, 11; related to Arab terrorism, 50; related to criminality, 31–32, 37, 42; related to nativism, 130–32, 176, 185, 189–92, 198, 202, 204; related to neoliberalism, 143–47, 156, 161–65; related to reproductive rights, 137–38

Color-blind racism, 9–17

Common Ground, 166

Community Development Block Grant (CDBG), 141

Conner, Roger, 130

Connerly, Ward, 35

Council for Inter-American Security, 130

Council of Conservative Citizens (CCC), 130

Council of Dominican Educators, 74

Cosby, Bill, 36
Cosby Show, 35, 123
Crime: associations, with immigrants, 131, 135, 180–81; associations, with people of color, 10, 22, 35, 78, 131, 135, 143–45; associations, with public housing, Section 8 residents, and renters, 143–45, 154, 162; as code for race, 36–37; as constructed threat, 4, 17, 23, 189; policies related to, 20, 31–34, 38–39; public feelings about, 2, 6, 36, 43, 189, 219; social problems tied to, 38–39, 147
Criminality: antiracist struggles associated with, 31–33; constructions of, 22, 38–39, 65, 122–23, 136, 145, 166, 214; emotional economies tied to, 4–6, 39–40, 113, 132, 166, 219; media representations of, 34–37, 39; social panics related to, 4–6, 14–15, 59, 101, 136; state practices related to, 75
Critical Resistance, 166
Cultural pathologies of poverty, 5, 32, 35, 117
Customs and Border Protection (CBP), 41

Danner, Mark, 81
Davis, Angela Y., 119, 219
Davis, Mike, 40, 60, 203–4
DeAtkine, Norvell, 83
Democracy Now!, 152, 203
Desert Storm Operation, Iraq, 51
Desire public housing project (New Orleans), 149, 166, 168, 171
Diallo, Amadou, 77, 209
Dinkins, David (mayor, New York City), 58, 61
Dobbs, Lou, 135
DuBois, W.E.B., 25, 68
Duvalier, François "Papa Doc" (president of Haiti), 55, 66, 74
Duvalier, Jean-Claude "Baby Doc" (president of Haiti), 55

Eberhardt, Jennifer, 13–14
Economic Recovery Tax Act (1981), 117
Ehrlich, Paul, 130, 195–96, 198–99

Emotional economies, 1–9, 12–15, 23–25; and American exceptionalism, 42–51, 94–98, 101–8; based on Blues epistemologies, 150–54, 159–61, 165–73; and carceral expansion, 4, 29–39; and criminality, 30–39, 58–61; of ethical witnessing, 24–26, 64–66, 108–12, 203–5; of Haitian resistance, 66–67, 73–75; and immigration, 128–38, 179–83; and military expansion, 4, 42–53; and nativism, 128–38, 178–79, 187–92, 195–203; and orientalism, 83–91, 94–98; of shame, 2, 12, 37, 92–93, 98–99, 103–4, 114–15, 118–20, 127, 132, 156, 217–19; and social wage retrenchment, 5, 113–15, 125–28; socially shared, 2, 15, 19, 44, 84, 120, 155; of stigma, 2, 5, 36, 47, 57, 115, 119, 127, 129, 132, 134, 138, 156, 165–66, 214, 219; and welfare assistance, 115, 117–22, 124–28, 143–47, 154–59, 161–65; unconscious dimensions of, 12–17
Emotional losses, 1–2, 9, 39, 53, 58, 98, 112, 121, 130, 137
Emotional rewards, 1–2, 9, 77, 112, 121, 124, 156, 162, 195
Emotions, 2–3, 6, 12, 15–16, 19–23
English First, 130
English-only movement, 198
Epistemologies, 11, 24; Blues, 140–41, 150, 159, 170, 173, 247n1, 255n98; of ethical witnessing, 24–26, 173; of the oppressed, 26, 108, 184; of white ignorance, 11–12, 15, 143
Escondido City Council, 179, 183, 190–91, 205
Establishing Penalties for the Harboring of Illegal Aliens in the City of Escondido (EPHIA) ordinance, 179–83, 185, 189, 195, 200
Ethical witnessing: epistemologies of, 23–26; to immigrants rights, 204–5; to oppression in New Orleans, 170–73; to police brutality of Abner Louima, 64–66, 73–75, 80; traditions and practices of, 26, 209, 219; to tortures at Abu Ghraib, 93, 108–12

Everad, Don, 163

Exceptionalism, U.S., 22, 28, 43–46, 46, 51–53, 81–84, 101, 104–8, 215. *See also* Ideological fantasy, of U.S. exceptionalism

Fair housing, 116, 178; advocacy, 163–64, 186; legal violations of, 155, 181–82

Fair Housing Act, Federal (1968), 116, 142

Fallon, Jeffrey, 62–63

Family Support Act, 125

Fanon, Frantz, 14–15, 23–24

Fantasy. *See* Ideological fantasy

FBI, 21, 34, 38, 50

Federation for American Immigration Reform (FAIR), 130, 177–78, 191, 194, 196, 198

Feelings: of outrage, 64, 73, 77, 94–95, 97–98, 102, 208; public, 1–4, 28, 125, 136, 138, 143, 151, 200; of shame, 2, 12, 77, 81, 83, 88, 92–93, 98–99, 103–4, 114–15, 118–19, 127–28, 132, 156, 217–19; of shock, 81, 93–94, 98–99, 102, 169

Feldman, Allen, 42, 60, 73

Fischer public housing development (New Orleans), 168

Food and Drug Administration (FDA), 57, 75

Francois, Althea, 166

Fraser, James, 164

Gallo, Ed (councilman, City of Escondido), 181, 195

Garvey, Marcus, 67

Gilmore, Craig, 219

Gilmore, Ruth Wilson, 42, 219

Giuliani, Rudolph (mayor, New York City), 58–61, 78

Goldstein, Richard, 109–10

Goldwater, Barry, 32–33

Goodman, Amy, 203

Gray, Herman, 123

Greater New Orleans Fair Housing Action Center (GNOFHAC), 163–64

Great Society programs, 125, 243n7

Greenwood, Shawn, 208–9

Gregory D (Greg Duvernay Jr.), 168

Griffin, Shana, 169–70

Guantánamo, 57, 98

Gulf War, 52. *See also*, Iraq War

Gutiérrez, Elena R., 120, 196

Hage, Ghassan, 47–48

Haitian American Alliance, 74

Haitian Enforcement Against Racism, 74

Haitian Revolution, 66

Hamer, Fannie Lou, 67

Hannity, Sean, 95, 187

Hannity & Colmes, 187

Hardin, Garrett, 130

Harding, Sandra, 24

Heritage Foundation, 131, 161

Hersh, Seymour, 81

Hethmon, Michael, 177–78

Hijab, 90–91

Homeland Security, Department of (DHS), 34, 41, 136, 139

HOPE VI redevelopments, 163, 166

Housing and Urban Development, Department of, (HUD), 141–42, 151–55, 158–59, 161–64, 166

Housing Authority of New Orleans (HANO), 141–42, 148, 150–53, 159, 161–64

Hurricane Katrina, 2, 139–40, 154, 157, 162

Hynes, H. Patricia, 199–200

Hyperfertility. *See* Immigration: associations, with hyperfertility

Iberville public housing development (New Orleans), 168–69

IDEAS (Improving Dreams, Equality, Access, and Success) chapters, 205

Ideological fantasy, 17–22; affective and emotional dimensions of, 19–22; of economic self-reliance 22, 114, 122–24, 127–30, 132–33, 138, 146, 154–57, 161; of law and order, 21–22, 28–31, 33, 37, 40, 53, 59, 65–67, 75; unconscious dimensions of, 18–19; of U.S. exceptionalism 21–22, 28, 43–44, 51, 53, 83, 91, 105

Ideology, unconscious dimensions of, 17–23, 226n25

Illegal aliens, 128; constructions of, 4, 36, 176, 191; as color-blind code for race, 10, 120; media representations of, 123, 133–35; municipal ordinances related to, 176–83; as taxpayer-burdens, 33, 114–15, 120–21, 180. *See also* Immigrants, undocumented

Illegal Immigration Reform and Immigrant Responsibility Act (IIRIRA), 40

Immigrants, undocumented: associations with crime, 37, 133–35; contributions to U.S. economy, 187–88; discrimination against, 5, 26, 176; divisions between documented immigrants and, 190–91; media representations of, 123, 133–35, 187–89; municipal ordinances against, 176–83; as persecutory enemies, 19–22, 33, 129; policies affecting, 34, 40–41, 125–27, 131, 137, 176, 193, 198; public feelings about, 5, 97, 131–33, 136, 138, 176, 179, 200–202; as taxpayer-burdens, 33, 114–15, 120–21, 129–30, 180–81. *See also* Illegal Aliens; Immigration, undocumented

Immigrants rights movements, 192–94

Immigration: associations, with crime, 131, 133–35; associations, with hyperfertility, 123, 127, 129, 133–38; associations, with illegality, 128, 133–35, 178; associations, with overpopulation, 123, 131, 133–35, 177, 195–200; associations, with taxpayer burdens, 120–21, 123, 131, 133–35, 187–92; as constructed threat, 5, 14–15, 22–23, 101, 133–35, 200–203; demographic shifts related to, 130, 179, 200; policies related to, 10, 41, 56, 128, 136–38, 176–83; public feelings about, 1–2, 6, 15, 48, 203, 205, 208, 215

Immigration, undocumented: associations with Latino/as and nonwhite immigrants, 14–15, 22, 120–21, 129–33; docu-mented immigrants against, 190–92; ideological fantasies related to, 22–23, 127, 129–30; media representations of, 133–35; municipal ordinances related to, 176–83; policy shifts related to, 40–41, 127, 131–132, 135, 136–38; public feelings about, 1–3, 5–6, 14–15, 101, 120–21, 132

Immigration and Naturalization Service (INS), 123, 136

Immigration Customs and Enforcement (ICE), 29, 34, 41, 204

Immigration-industrial complex, 41

Immigration Reform Law Institute (IRLI), 177

Imperialism, U.S., 1–3, 7, 9–11 15–16, 24–26, 82–83; emotional economies of, 42–44; exceptionalism and, 42–44, 46, 50–51, 82–83, 84, 91, 101–7; governmental poli-cies related to, 51–53; media representa-tions that help justify, 48–51, 90–91, 94–98; orientalist discourses that help sustain, 44–48, 83–91; resistance to, 92–94, 108–12

Implicit racial bias, 13–16, 225n19

Incarceration: discourses that legitimate, 34–40; expansion of, 28, 33–34, 206; emo-tional economies tied to, 29, 109; as form of justice, 79–80, 100–101, 107–8, 110; policies related to, 40–41, 136–37; resistance to, 166, 170, 208, 211–14, 218–20

INCITE! Women of Color Against Violence, 169–70

Iraq War, 7, 52, 98–99, 104

Iran-Contra deal, 52

Iran hostage crisis, 49

Iran-Iraq war, 52

Islamophilia, 44–48

Islamophobia, 44–48

Jackson, Alphonso (secretary of HUD), 154, 158, 252n61

Jacobs, Harriet, 25

James, Devon, 209

Jay Electronica (Timothy Elpadaro Thed-
ford), 168
Johnson, Lyndon B., 32–33, 116, 125, 228n12
Jouissance, 19–21
Justice for Janitors campaign, 205
Juvenile (Terius Gray), 167–68

Katey Red (Katey Red Kenyon Carter), 168
King Kino, 61, 78. *See also* Phantoms
King, Martin Luther, Jr., 29, 111, 171
King, Robert Hillary, 167
King, Rodney, 77
Kobach, Kris, 130, 177–78

Labor/Community Strategy Center, 205
Laffite public housing development (New
Orleans), 142, 153, 167–68
Lavalas movement, 66
Laurel Foundation, 131
Law and order: discourses about, 30–34, 129,
195; as ideological fantasy, 20–22, 28–31,
33, 37, 40, 53, 59, 65–67, 75; media rep-
resentations of, 34–37; policies related
to, 40–41, 58–61, 75–77; public emo-
tional investments in, 6, 27, 37, 42, 51;
resistance to, 65–68, 77–80
Lipsitz, George, 115, 143, 149, 157
Lo, Clarence, 117
Lorde, Audre, 218
Louima, Abner, 7, 55, 61–80
Luxembourg, Rosa, 105

Magnolia, a.k.a. C.J. Peete, public housing
development (New Orleans), 148, 167–68
Magnolia Shorty (Renetta Yemika Lowe-
Bridgewater), 167
Majority-identified minorities, 36–38
Malcolm X (El-Hajj Malik El-Shabazz), 29,
171
Mamdani, Mahmood, 51
Mannie Fresh (Byron O. Thomas), 168
Mardi Gras Indians, 167, 255n98
Martin, Trayvon, 208–11
Master P (Percy Robert Miller), 167

McAlary, Mike, 65, 70–73
McAlister, Melani, 49–50, 52
Means-based assistance, 126
Melpomene, a.k.a. Guste Apartments, public
housing development (New Orleans),
148, 168
Mexican-American/La Raza Studies Program
(Tucson Unified School District), 131
Mikolashek, Paul T. (Lt. Gen.), 82
Military-carceral expansion, 1–6, 29–53, 113,
211
Military-industrial complex, 107, 112
Mills, Charles W., 11–12
Minuteman American Defense, 175
Minuteman Project, 175, 191
Minutemen, 18–19, 192, 194
Minutemen, San Diego, 180, 183, 195
Mississippi Delta, 139–40, 150
Mixed-income developments, 151, 153, 161–65
Mohammed, Yanar, 110–11
Montana, Allison "Tootie," 167
Mollen Commission, 76–77
Moore, Bill, 26
Moynihan, Daniel Patrick, 117
Moynihan Report, 117–18

NAFTA (North American Free Trade Agreement), 135, 188
Nagin, Ray (mayor, New Orleans), 152, 158
National Welfare Rights Organization, 116
Nativism, 1–3, 7, 9–11, 15–16, 24–26; color-
blind discourses related to, 129, 131–32,
176, 185, 189–92; emotional economies
of, 128–133, 135; environmental debates
related to, 198–200; governmental policies related to, 127–28, 136–38; media
representations that support, 133–35,
187–92; municipal ordinances related to,
176–83, 185–92, 200–202; overpopulation discourses that support, 120–22, 131,
133–34, 177, 195–201; resistance to, 183–
86, 192–94, 203–5; spatial and aesthetic
ideals based on, 200–203; violence related to, 175–76

Needs-based assistance, 121, 242n5. *See also* Means-based assistance

Neo-Bourbon agenda, 157–58, 159

Neo-Bourbon class, 158–59, 161, 165

Neo-Bourbonism, 145–46, 154, 159, 170

Neoliberal restructuring: and incarceration, 35–36; national, 2–6, 24; and public housing, 154–58; resistance to, 159–61, 165–73; and social welfare goods, 112–15, 119–25, 129–30, 132–33, 138

Neo-Nazi nativist groups, 131

Neville Brothers, 167

Neville, Charmaine, 169

New York Police Department (NYPD), 55, 58–59, 61, 73–78

Newman, Ron (councilman, City of Escondido), 181, 195

New Orleans City Council, 142, 152, 157, 159, 162–63

New Orleans Women's Health Clinic (NOWHC), 146, 170

Nicholas, Jay, 61–62

Nixon, Richard, 33

Nuestra América, 183–86

Numbers USA, 130, 194, 198

Obama, Barack, 34, 159

One-to-one replacement housing, 151, 153, 159

Ontology, 24, 26, 107

O'Reilly Factor, 135

Orientalism, 44–48, 88–91, 228n6

Orientalist discourses, 44–48, 83–91

Organization for Women's Freedom in Iraq, 110

Overpopulation. *See* Nativism, overpopulation discourses that support

Patai, Raphael, 83–89, 96, 106

Patterson, Sunni, 170–73

Pease, Donald, 43

People's Hurricane Relief Fund, 151, 160

Perry, James, 142, 163

Persecutory enemies, 19–23; constructions of, related to economic self-sufficiency, 115–

122; constructions of, related to law and order, 30–42; constructions of, related to U.S. exceptionalism, 44–51, 84, 107

Personal Responsibility and Work Opportunity Reconciliation Act (PRWORA), 126–27, 136

Pfeiler, Lori Hold (mayor of City of Escondido), 181, 195

Phantoms, 61

Pioneer Fund, 131

Police brutality, 26, 31, 55, 58, 76–77, 79, 81, 83, 159–61, 216; resistance to, 73–75, 78. *See also* Police violence

Police violence, 7, 31, 41, 58–64, 68–72, 76–77, 159–61, 166; resistance to, 26, 58, 65–68, 73–75, 78–80, 159–61, 166–67, 216. *See also* Police brutality; Policing

Policing: emotions tied to, 4, 39, 101, 178; expansion of, 28, 39–40, 162–63; resistance to, 204, 208, 211–20; tactics, 17, 33–34, 58–61, 150, 165, 169, 182

Population Connection. *See* Zero Population Growth (ZPG)

Post–civil rights era: hegemonic public feelings during, 5, 22, 25, 38, 121, 128–29; ideological fantasies during, 28–29, 31–42, 43–48, 114–122, 127, 155; immigrant exclusion during, 136, 176, 187–92, 202; social inequalities during, 1–5, 122, 127; social panics during, 14, 22

Powell, Colin, 35, 52

Pratt, Lawrence, 130

Prison abolition, 219

Prison-industrial complex, 38, 40–41, 124

Prisons. *See* Incarceration.

Pro-immigration advocacy, 132, 192–94, 203–5

Proposition 187, California, 127, 131, 134, 136

Public feelings. *See* Feelings, public

Public housing: demolition of, 141–42, 161–65; divestment from, 7, 125, 153; New Orleans campaign to stop demolition of, 151–54, 159–61, 166–69; restrictive policies tied to, 136, 148–50; stigmatization of, 2, 6–7, 143–47, 154–58, 161–65

Publics, dominant U.S. or American, 5–6,
    8–10, 28, 30–31, 92, 176

Quigley, Bill, 152

Racial justice. *See* Antiracist justice
Rahim, Malik, 166
Rara bands, 57–58, 66
Racism, 3, 15–16, 30–36; color-blind, 9–11, 16,
    137; anti-Arab, 50–51, 102–5 (*see also* ori-
    entalism); gendered, 2–3, 9–11, 15–16,
    24–26, 109, 146, 158, 189, 208–9, 218; re-
    lated to property interests, 142–150, 154–
    58, 161–65; unintentional or unconscious
    dimensions of, 11–16, 17–23
Rebel Diaz, 218
Reagan administration, 52, 125
Reagan, Ronald, 33–35, 49, 52, 119, 125–26
Reaganism, 33, 125
Reeves, Jimmie, 35
Rejouis, John, 62, 65
Reproductive practices: and Black women,
    123, 136, 145; and Mexican-origin and/or
    Latina women, 120, 136, 195–98
Reproductive rights, 137
Rice, Condoleezza, 35
Riverbend, 91–94
Ritcheson, David, 175
Roberts, Dorothy, 119
Roberts, Glenda "Goldie," 167
Robinson, Cedric, 24–25
Rose, Jacqueline, 18
Rose, Tricia, 118
Ruda Real (Kairuba Brown), 167–68
Rumsfeld, Donald, 82

Safe Streets/Strong Communities, 166
Said, Edward, 25, 44–45, 48, 84, 88, 105
Save Our State (SOS), 130, 176
Schlesinger, James R., 82
Schwarz, Charles, 61–62, 65, 78
Self-deportation movement, 177–78
Senate Armed Services Committee, 82
Senate Bill 1070 (Arizona), 34, 131, 178, 192

Sess 4–5, 160, 166
Shapiro, Thomas, 121, 157
Sharpton, Al, 79
Shawn Greenwood Working Group
    (SGWG), 208–20
Shryock, Andrew, 46–47
Sierra Club, 198–99
Social wage retrenchment, 3–6, 116, 223n2;
    neoliberal discourses justifying, 113–16;
    emotional economies that legitimate, 115–
    22, 128, 133, 143–47, 154–58; policies re-
    lated to, 125–27, 136–38, 141–43. *See also*
    Social welfare goods, Welfare
Social welfare goods, 1, 4, 114–16, 212; divest-
    ment from, 125–28, 136–38; emotional
    stigmas tied to, 5, 115–25, 129–33. *See also*
    Social wage retrenchment
Soulja Slim (James Adarryl Tapp, Jr.), 167
Southern Poverty Law Center (SPLC), 175
Spencer, Claudia, 191
Spencer, Glenn, 130
Spivak, Gayatri, 90
Springer, Kimberly, 119
St. Bernard public housing development
    (New Orleans), 142, 148, 153–54, 159, 167
Stein, Dan, 130, 177
Sterilization, coercive, 136
Stolen Lives Project, 77
Stop-and-frisk policing tactics, 17. *See also*
    Policing, tactics
Strom, Cordia, 130
St. Thomas (renamed River Garden HOPE
    VI Redevelopment) public housing de-
    velopment (New Orleans), 163–64, 168
Sudbury, Julia, 32
Surnow, Joel, 106
Systematic Alien Verification for Entitle-
    ments (SAVE), 183

Tadiar, Neferti, 108–9
Tanton, John, 130–31, 134, 177, 196, 198
Taussig, Michael, 11
Temporary Assistance for Needy Families
    (TANF), 126

Terazawa, Sophia, 209–11

Terrorism: associations with Arabs and/or Muslims, 44–48, 85; ideological fantasies related to, 21–23, 28, 44, 215; media representations of, 48–51, 94–98, 106–8; policy shifts related to, 34, 40–41, 135; public feelings about, 1–6, 14–15, 29, 94, 109, 113

Thomas, Clarence, 35

Till, Emmett, 67, 172

Till, Mamie, 67

Tompkins County (New York), 212–15, 219

Tough-on-crime policies, 20, 33, 39

Turetzky, Eric, 61

Turk (Tab Virgil, Jr.), 167

Turner, Joseph, 130, 176

Upstate Coalition to Ground the Drones and End the Wars, 211

Undocumented and Unafraid movement, 205

Undocumented immigrants. See Immigrants, undocumented

USA PATRIOT Act, 40

U.S. English, 198. See also English-only movement

Vietnam War, 42, 51–52

Voices of Citizens Together (VCT), 130

Volpe, Justin, 61–72, 75, 78–79, 233n21

Waldron, Marie (councilwoman, City of Escondido), 179–81, 185, 195

War on drugs, 34–36, 51, 123, 126, 137

War on Poverty, 116, 125

War on terror, 7, 51–52, 81, 83, 96–99, 106

Washington, Tracie L., 152–53

Weaver, Vesla, 31

Welfare dependence: discourses about, 113–18, 143–47, 154–58; social panics about, 14, 22, 136; emotional economies about, 1, 5–6, 15, 22, 120–25, 127, 132, 138, 143–47, 150, 154–58, 166. See also Public housing

Welfare queen, 10, 32, 119, 122–23

Welfare reform policies, 5, 126. See also Social wage retrenchment; Social welfare goods

Wells, Ida B., 25, 67

Wiegman, Robyn, 67

Wiese, Thomas, 61–62, 65, 79

Williams, Linda Faye, 125

Williams, Patricia J., 100

Wilson, Pete (governor), 33, 134

Women's Health and Justice Initiative (WHJI), 146

Workfare requirements, 59, 125

Young, Iris Marion, 111

Young, Mia (pseud. Mia X), 167

Zero Population Growth (ZPG), 130, 198

Zero tolerance policing, 58–61

Žižek, Slavoj, 17–20, 226n25

Beneath the Surface of White Supremacy: Denaturalizing U.S. Racisms
Past and Present
Moon-Kie Jung
2015

Race on the Move: Brazilian Migrants and the Global Reconstruction of Race
Tiffany D. Joseph
2015

The Ethnic Project: Transforming Racial Fiction into Racial Factions
Vilna Bashi Treitler
2013

On Making Sense: Queer Race Narratives of Intelligibility
Ernesto Javier Martínez
2012

The authorized representative in the EU for product safety and compliance is:
Mare Nostrum Group
B.V Doelen 72
4831 GR Breda
The Netherlands

www.ingramcontent.com/pod-product-compliance
Lightning Source LLC
Chambersburg PA
CBHW020842270326
41928CB00006B/514